BORDERS, CULTURE, AND GLOBALIZATION

BORDERS, CULTURE, AND GLOBALIZATION
A CANADIAN PERSPECTIVE

Edited by Victor Konrad and Melissa Kelly

University of Ottawa Press
2021

University of Ottawa **Press**
Les **Presses** de l'Université d'Ottawa

The University of Ottawa Press (UOP) is proud to be the oldest of the Francophone university presses in Canada as well as the oldest bilingual university publisher in North America. Since 1936, UOP has been enriching intellectual and cultural discourse by producing peer-reviewed and award-winning books in the humanities and social sciences, in French and in English.

www.press.uOttawa.ca

Library and Archives Canada Cataloguing in Publication

Title: Borders, culture, and globalization: a Canadian perspective / editors: Victor Konrad and Melissa Kelly.
Names: Konrad, Victor A., editor. | Kelly, Melissa, 1981- editor.
Description: Includes bibliographical references and index.
Identifiers: Canadiana (print) 20200351109 | Canadiana (ebook) 20200351370 | ISBN 9780776636733 (softcover) | ISBN 9780776636740 (hardcover) | ISBN 9780776636757 (PDF) | ISBN 9780776636764 (EPUB) | ISBN 9780776636771 (Kindle)
Subjects: LCSH: Canadian-American Border Region—Social life and customs. | LCSH: Canadian-American Border Region—Social conditions. | LCSH: Borderlands—Social aspects—Canada. | LCSH: Globalization—Social aspects—Canada.
Classification: LCC FC95.5 .B67 2021 | DDC 306.0971—dc23

Legal Deposit: Second Quarter 2021
Library and Archives Canada

Production Team

Copy editing	James Warren
Proofreading	Robbie McCaw
Index	Édiscript enr.
Typesetting	John van der Woude, JVDW Designs
Cover design	Édiscript enr.

Cover Image

Beyond Borders by Aili Kurtis

The authors have made every effort to contact rights holders to request permission to use their images, but in case of omission, the publisher will gladly make amendments and updates to the publication at the earliest possible opportunity.

© University of Ottawa Press 2021
All rights reserved.

No part of this publication may be reproduced or transmitted in any form or by any means, or stored in a database and retrieval system, without the prior permission.

In the case of photocopying or any other reprographic copying, please secure licenses from:

Access Copyright
www.accesscopyright.ca
1-800-893-5777

For foreign rights and permissions:
www.iprlicense.com

The University of Ottawa Press gratefully acknowledges the support extended to its publishing list by the Government of Canada, the Canada Council for the Arts, the Ontario Arts Council, the Social Sciences and Humanities Research Council and the Canadian Federation for the Humanities and Social Sciences through the Awards to Scholarly Publications Program, and by the University of Ottawa.

 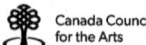 

Table of Contents

List of Figures vii
List of Tables ix

Foreword 1
Acknowledgements 3

Introduction
Culture, Globalization, and Canada's Borders
Victor Konrad and Melissa Kelly 7

Viewing Border Culture

1. Sight and Site on the Line: The Cultural Imaginary of Borderlands in North America
   Lee Rodney 39

2. Imagining Nighttime Detroit
   Michael Darroch 61

3. Bordering Things: Objects and Subjugated Struggle at the Border
   Anelynda Mielke and Nadya Pohran 85

4. *Border Cultures*: A Retrospective
   Part 1. A Context for *Border Cultures* and Conversations with the Curator
   Victor Konrad 107

   Part 2. *Border Cultures*: The Exhibitions
   Srimoyee Mitra 115

Borders and Culture in Motion

5. The Snowbirds: A Cultural Movement across Borders
   Melissa Kelly 131

6. Passing Through or Living Here: Body and Self In-Between and On Edge in the Borderland Region of Stanstead, Quebec, and Derby Line, Vermont
   Sandra Vandervalk 163

7. North American Cyber New Regionalism in Canada: Online Cultural Borderlands and Change through New Media
   Alexander Rudolph 187

8. #Welcome Refugees: A Canadian Phenomenon That Illustrates the Temporal Dimension of Border Constructs
   Renata Grudzien 215

Placing and Replacing Border Culture: Indigenous Perspectives

9. Across Borders and Cultures: Thomas King's Artistic Activism
   Evelyn P. Mayer 233

10. In the Space between Aboriginal Sovereignty and National Security: Re-engaging Border Security and Mohawk Culture at Akwesasne
    Laetitia Rouvière 255

11. Sport, Globalization, and the Bordering Process: The Iroquois Nationals Lacrosse Team and the Issue of Contested National Identities
    Heidi Weigand and Colin Howell 277

12. A Biocultural Planning Approach for Managing Transborder Cultural Heritage Landscapes
    Scott Cafarella, Joel Konrad, and Rebecca Sciarra 293

Conclusion

Borders, Culture, and Globalization: Some Conclusions, More Uncertainties, and Many Challenges
Melissa Kelly and Victor Konrad 319

Contributors 337
Index 343

List of Figures

FIGURE 1.1.	The Border Bookmobile, Ambassador Park, Windsor, Ontario, 2011	45
FIGURE 1.2.	The Border Bookmobile, Belle Isle, Detroit, 2011	45
FIGURE 1.3.	Political Equator 3: June 3–4, 2011	49
FIGURE 1.4.	Re/Thinking Paul Bunyan (Maine and Quebec), Coborn Gore border crossing, 2012	51
FIGURE 1.5.	Buoyant Cartographies workshop, September 1, 2018	53
FIGURE 2.1.	Neighbours	62
FIGURE 2.2.	Detroit Light Tower	67
FIGURE 2.3.	Detroit, MI, Campus Martius and Opera House	68
FIGURE 2.4.	Locations of Street Lights. Map of the City of Detroit, Michigan	69
FIGURE 2.5.	Campus Martius at night, Detroit, Michigan	70
FIGURE 2.6.	Night Scene, Windsor, Ontario, Canada. Detroit in the Distance, ca. 1930	72
FIGURE 2.7.	Skyline at Night from Windsor, Canada	72
FIGURE 2.8.	The Heart of Detroit at Night	73
FIGURE 2.9.	The Heart of Detroit by Moonlight	73
FIGURE 2.10.	View of Ambassador Bridge at Night, Sandwich, near Windsor, Canada, ca. 1930s	74
FIGURE 2.11.	Ambassador Bridge at Night, between Detroit, Michigan, and Windsor, Ontario, ca. 1930s	74
FIGURE 2.12.	Cross-Border Communication, 2009	80
FIGURE 2.13.	Shaping Our City, January 3, 2014	80
FIGURE 5.1.	Participants by age group	143
FIGURE 10.1.	Map of the border in Akwesasne	260
FIGURE 12.1.	Conceptual illustration of a biocultural planning system	296

FIGURE 12.2. Niagara Escarpment Biosphere Reserve designations.. 299
FIGURE 12.3. Study area boundaries and policy context map......... 309
FIGURE 12.4. Biocultural planning zones within the study area.... 311

List of Tables

TABLE 5.1. Travel by Canadians to the United States in 2014...... 137
TABLE 5.2. Maximum amount of time permitted abroad (to maintain healthcare benefits).................................. 139
TABLE 10.1. Sources of authority in Akwesasne 260
TABLE 12.1. Feature layers used in GIS bioregional planning analysis of the study area 306

Foreword

Emmanuel Brunet-Jailly, Borders in Globalization (BIG) Program Lead

Borders in Globalization is a multidisciplinary and international research program funded through a SSHRC Partnership Grant and the European Union's Jean Monnet Program. From 2012 to 2020, collaborators from across Canada and fifteen other countries collected data on borders. Our core research focus was to challenge the well-established conception of borders as primarily sovereign territorial boundaries that have emerged out of international treaties. The research program thus addressed fundamental *how*, *why*, and *what* questions about borders, a very important contribution to knowledge in a globalizing world where movement is increasingly scrutinized everywhere, not just at the sovereign boundary lines of states, and at a time when goods seem to travel more easily than humans. Indeed, the regulation of human flows across borders is fraught and highly contentious, and even today people in the thousands die crossing borders yearly.

Our team studied border history and culture, mobility and security, environmental sustainability, and governance. As illustrated by this book, and the University of Ottawa Press series Borders in Globalization, our research program initially approached those questions from the perspective of territories, regions, and states, collecting evidence that there were multiple challenges to the "territorial trap" assumption.

In this edited collection, Victor Konrad and Melissa Kelly, along with members of their research team, document and explore the relationship between Westphalia's international boundary lines and culture. Their research focuses on the bordering effects of international boundaries on culture; scale, spatiality, and the motions of culture(s) straddling boundary lines; and de-bordering borderlands.

Their findings point to (1) the multifaceted and scalar multiplicity of culture, and (2) the essential understanding that borders and cultures are "in motion." Culture encompasses multitudes of individuals, de-bordering and re-bordering individuals' agency, as well as spaces and territories, even extending beyond territories, in the a-territorial social production of cultures. The construction and reconstruction of cultures weave individual identities together above and beyond any Westphalian international boundary line.

More generally in our Borders in Globalization research, we found that, more than ever before, states' border policies straddled their sovereign boundary lines—that is, that networked policies overlapped many different jurisdictional scales, including but not exclusively that of the sovereign territories of other states. Our second hypothesis, that contemporary borders in globalization were the result of processes that in many instances were fundamentally "a-territorial," was also confirmed when we found that bordering processes were not uniquely territorial but rather fundamentally linked to movements across the world. We discovered that bordering policies increasingly *disregarded* the territorial limits of states, sometimes implementing borders thousands of kilometres away from their international boundary line.

Our findings suggest that the borders of globalization are not always contiguous or territorial. The primary reason for this paradigmatic transformation is that states that had the policy capacity to do so were implementing border crossings *at the source* of movement. These new local and global border "markers" appear in regulatory systems and production chains organizing the mobility of trade flows and humans. For instance, states and private sector actors are implementing data collection policies allowing for the pre-clearance of global trade flows and migration movements; individuals and objects are cleared by authorities of their place of destination prior to leaving their place of origin. Contrary to traditional states' territorial bordering, *a-territorial bordering obeys a fundamentally different logic*—a logic primarily concerned with functional belonging and driven by the development of mechanisms based on trust. This finding points toward new, yet understudied, phenomena that are continuing to transform borders in the twenty-first century.

All our works are available on https://biglobalization.org.

Acknowledgements

The contributions to this book connect border culture research and practice in Canada to further an advanced understanding of how culture is integral to viewing and engaging with borders, bordering and borderlands. As one of the six core thematic volumes in the Borders in Globalization series, this edited book provides a comprehensive examination of border culture in Canada, yet the volume also focuses on themes of viewing border culture, borders and culture in motion, and placing and replacing border culture. This Canadian perspective on borders, culture, and globalization engages substantially with Canada's regional expression of border culture and inevitably with the differentiation, linkage and integration of culture across the border with the United States. The book conveys a unique and extensive perspective on current research and understanding of border culture by providing insights from scholars and practitioners in the fields of border culture policy implementation, heritage management and artistic representation. The chapters included in the volume engage with and develop current border culture thinking and theory, and border issues that are timely and significant to our understanding and management of borders, culture and globalization.

An overview and critical assessment of border culture requires the contributions of experts in various disciplines and fields. We have been fortunate to draw on the expertise and insights of graduate students, post-doctoral fellows, and faculty at universities across Canada. Furthermore, we have engaged the participation of contributors in curatorial, culture policy, and heritage management fields. All of the chapters convey significant and engaging studies in their own right, and, when assembled in this book, the chapters combine to form a fresh and timely perspective on border culture. To each and every contributor to this volume, we say thank you for your commitment to this project, and your efforts to work with us to publish the book.

This book is published as a volume in the Borders in Globalization (BIG) series. Publication is supported in part by the Social Sciences and Humanities Research Council of Canada through its Partnership Grant Program (Grant 895-2012-1022). The lead on the grant is Dr. Emmanuel Brunet-Jailly, University of Victoria. We would like to acknowledge the leadership and direction of Professor Brunet-Jailly in this project. It has been a pleasure and a privilege to work with Emmanuel and his colleagues at the University of Victoria. We are pleased to acknowledge the special efforts and commitment of Nicole Bates-Eamer, the BIG project manager. Also, we wish to take this opportunity to thank the faculty, administrators and students at Carleton University who played a part in the development and delivery of BIG project components. Special thanks are due to the support of the BIG project over eight years by the chairs and the faculty, staff and students of the Department of Geography and Environmental Studies. Several DGES students and others from across Carleton University were BIG project participants. Some are contributors to this book. Also, among the contributors are faculty and graduate students from BIG partner institutions and agencies across Canada. There are numerous colleagues in the BIG project—leads, faculty colleagues, students, staff—who have had some role in facilitating, supporting, and contributing to the work of the "culture" component of the BIG project. We are grateful for their interest and commitment to exploring border culture in Canada.

In any project of this scope and duration, the commitment of a few people to the project stands out and makes all of the difference in the outcome. In addition to the contributors to the book, we would like to acknowledge the special interest and support of Anne-Laure Amilhat Szary (Grenoble), Darlene Gilson (Carleton), Gillian Roberts and David Stirrup (Culture and the Canada-US Border Project), and Ron Williamson (Archaeological Services Inc.).

A very special thank you goes to Aili Kurtis for allowing us to use the image of her painting "New Directions at the Border" for the cover of this book.

Finally, we would like to thank the University of Ottawa Press for direction and support in preparing the book for publication. The entire team at UOP has been exceptional in their efforts to publish this volume in the Borders in Globalization series. The acquisitions editor, Caroline Boudreau, has worked with us since the start of the book project and offered constant encouragement, advice and support. The production team, headed by Maryse Cloutier, has offered discerning and exemplary direction to prepare the manuscript for publication. Also, we would like to acknowledge the valuable comments and excellent suggestions of the anonymous reviewers who read the original manuscript. It has been our privilege to work with the University of Ottawa Press to publish *Borders, Culture, and Globalization: A Canadian Perspective*.

Victor Konrad, Westport, Ontario, Canada
Melissa Kelly, Ottawa, Ontario, Canada
December 15, 2020

INTRODUCTION

Culture, Globalization, and Canada's Borders

Victor Konrad and Melissa Kelly

It is November 2020. The prevailing story remains the COVID-19 pandemic, and all other stories are now intertwined with it. Since March, the border has been closed between Canada and the United States for all but essential travel, and it will remain closed until the end of 2020 if not longer. Essential travel is for medical, work, emergency response, cross-border trade, and official government and military activities. At the border in Blaine, Washington, and White Rock, British Columbia, personal vehicle crossings in April dropped from 10,000 to 2,000 per day. In the Pacific coast communities near the border, the economic impact of the closure is substantial as nondiscretionary travel for shopping and tourism, among other personal interaction across the border, has halted (BPRI 2020). Laurie Trautman, director of the Border Policy Research Institute, estimates that the public health concern may continue to reduce travel once the border reopens (McCarthy 2020, 4). The previous significant drop in cross-border traffic, after the events of 9/11 in 2001, resulted in border crossing reductions that persisted until 2010, when the Vancouver Olympics and a stronger Canadian dollar led to annual border entries rising to 11.9 million, finally exceeding the 9 million entries a decade earlier in 2000 (BPRI 2020). The impact of the COVID-19 pandemic, just as the impact of 9/11, certainly has devastating economic and social consequences for the local and regional economies along the

Pacific coast, but these consequences also alter and disrupt the underlying border culture—the reflection and repository of human engagement at a boundary—that has formed and reformed in the integrated cross-border region (Konrad 2010).

This border culture, like the border itself, is socially constructed, mainly by people who reside close to the border and live with its effects of coincident separation and linkage, the constant change and motion surrounding the line, the meshed or delineated identities that emerge, and the innovative and exemplary production and expression of imagination and creativity focused on the border. For example, Jim Lynch sets *Border Songs* (2010) in the borderlands of Washington and British Columbia. It is the story of Brandon Vanderkool, a six-foot-eight, tongue-tied, dyslexic, and awkward US Border Patrol agent who guards thirty miles of largely invisible boundary. This book is a rich portrait of humour, tenderness, and charm of life at the border. *Border Songs* reveals the idea of borders between places, people, natural and human worlds, and past and future ways of life, as the book creates a perceptive awareness and sense of place of this piece of the Canada-US border. According to a review in *The New York Times*, this is "where next-door neighbours can live in different countries—both spiritually and legally" (Meyer 2009). This vibrant and challenging life on and at the edge nourishes border culture.

We begin with a story of borders and culture from the Pacific coastal region because, among the border regions of Canada and the United States, the Pacific coast stands out with distinctive and demonstrative expressions of border culture. Often described as Cascadia (Alper 1996; Ricou 2002; Sparke 2000, 2002), and more recently as the Salish Sea (Tucker and Rose-Redwood 2015), this cross-border, yet transborder and seemingly international, region is an ideal place to begin a book on culture and Canada's borders in globalization. Here, the international boundary was established only late in the nineteenth century. Indigenous peoples along the coast sustain and affirm cross-border identities (Marker 2015). Immigrant cultures, among them the Dutch and South Asian, express vibrant and distinctive language, religion, and material culture in enclaves on both sides of the boundary, and often use the border, or "work the line," to their social and economic advantage (Konrad 2010; Konrad and Everitt 2013). Cannabis culture prevails on both sides of and despite the border (Magnus et al. 2019). Here the "Northwest Sound" emerged as a music tradition nurtured and extended throughout the cross-border region

(Gill 1993). And all of these facets of culture and cultural expression were enabled by the idea of a cultural and natural region of Cascadia, a transnational region conveniently distanced and beyond the mountains from eastern heartlands of the United States and Canada.

Substantial attention and research was focused on Pacific Northwest border culture in the Borders in Globalization project (an extensive, multidisciplinary project focused on Canada's borders in the context of globalization; see http://www.biglobalization.org). Recently, a large component of this scholarship was published in a special issue of the *Journal of Borderlands Studies* (Hallgrímsdóttir and Bates-Eamer 2020). Indeed, the literature of border culture focused on the Pacific coast is so extensive that our aim in this volume is to focus on other Canada-US borderland regions and balance the coverage. It is important to acknowledge that border culture is evident and significant in all cross-border regional contexts, and that the Borders in Globalization project is publishing regional books and special issues of journals to address border culture as well as other aspects of borders in the North, the western interior, Atlantic Canada, Quebec, and, of course, the Pacific region. This book references and acknowledges border culture all across Canada, but chapters draw on case studies focused primarily in central Canada and written by authors who have shared perspectives, ideas, and research in several ways to collaborate on an integrated volume.

Introducing Border Culture

In an integrated yet divided world, the interplay of cultures and borders needs to be disaggregated, scaled, and differentiated in order to ascertain and frame the key processes in bordering culture. Consistent with current directions in border research (Ptak et al. 2020), a focus on these processes, then, may enable a more comprehensive understanding of border culture and its relationship with globalization. Prominent among these processes, with regard to border culture, are cultural integration and disintegration, the shift beyond Indigeneity, and the extension of cultural continuity. In order to approach these processes, and the manifestations of borders in globalization that develop from them, we focus initially on viewing border culture. How do we see the border? How do we imagine border spaces and places? What images of the border emerge and prevail? Then we acknowledge that, and try to articulate how, borders and culture operate in motion. How do we recognize border constructs? How are cultural movements formed and sustained across borders? How do people transition across borders? What new cultures and spaces are formed? Finally, we focus on placing and replacing border culture. Borders, after all, are part of continua just as they signify demarcation, and the placement of border culture in space and time is fundamental to understanding how borders in globalization work. Where do border and culture intersect? What aspects of border and culture create identity? How does cross-border culture work? How do we manage transborder cultural heritage?

This volume aims to explore all of these questions in order to widen and integrate the dialogue about borders and culture in globalization. Currently, debates about identity, cultural production, and cultural dynamism in borderlands are often discrete. The goal is to collect and relate the discourse about borders and culture and to focus this undertaking in the context of Canada's borders in globalization. In order to achieve this goal, the volume draws extensively on the current research on borders and culture related to Canada's border regions. Scholars and practitioners, all participants in some way in the Borders in Globalization project funded by the Social Sciences and Humanities Research Council of Canada (SSHRC), contribute their insights and perspectives on border culture. Many of the contributors are students or postdoctoral fellows affiliated with the Borders in Globalization project. Their works, and the contributions of established scholars and experienced consultants and cultural heritage specialists, together provide a body of research about the role and significance of border culture in a rapidly evolving border regime engaging Canada with its neighbours and the rest of the world. Consistent with the goals of the Borders in Globalization project, and international consensus on the importance of the scholar-practitioner interface in boundary studies (Pratt 2010), the research on border culture has engaged practitioners in government and the private sector as well as university scholars to assess how culture and borders intersect, work, and impact our lives.

Why do we focus on border culture when security, trade, migration, sustainability, and governance issues at the border and in the borderlands appear to be more pressing, and perhaps more significant? Our response is that border culture is actually intertwined with all of these other concerns, and that the post-9/11, twenty-first-century differentiation between the United States and Canada is inherently a clash of cultures. The border between the United States and Canada has become a unicultural border (Konrad 2020), where US bordering prevails with a narrower definition of admissibility. At the border, Canadian multiculturalism is at odds with American identity and exceptionalism (Lipset 1996), despite the fact that the United States is just as multicultural in practice as Canada, but without an official policy (Palmer 1976). The border, ostensibly less important as a barrier to movements of goods and trusted travellers, actually gains credence and effect as a sorting mechanism for culture that is either prohibited by American law or deemed un-American by opinion in the United States. Consequently, cultural diversity complicates and slows border work, and a unicultural border emerges in Canadian deference to US authority and hegemony.

Our suggestion is that border specialists in both academic and nonacademic realms need to reimagine the Canada-US border through a lens of border culture. It is imperative to acknowledge the power of culture at the border and of the border. Imaginaries position and code a complex, varied, and plural bordering between peoples, and these imaginaries and their manifestations must be understood in order to comprehend the complexity of the Canada-US border that is found increasingly everywhere between the countries, in expanding and diverse borderlands. To comprehend this new border requires a new paradigm to encompass border culture as well as other border universals.

Contextualizing Border Culture

The culture that humans produce emerges from specific geographical spaces but also transcends them, meeting and crossing borders. Yet in an ostensibly borderless world, where currents of thought, human migrants, built forms, and messages criss-cross the globe, the cultural landscapes produced at or near borders may engage, merge, and conflict, and these landscapes may also become matters for nation-based preservation. Culture can be something to preserve or cling onto in the face of expanding flows of ideas, people, goods, and capital; thus, teasing out this interplay of border and culture, how culture alters borders and how borders alter culture must be central to any investigation of borders and globalization.

Border studies acknowledge the importance of exploring and understanding the role of culture in bordering people and states.

Formative border studies, among them works by Peter Sahlins (1989) and Oscar Martinez (1994) in history; Fredrik Barth (1969), Anthony P. Cohen (1986), and Hastings Donnan and Thomas Wilson (1994) in anthropology; and Michael Kearney (1991) in sociology, all address the relationship between borders and culture. In geography, the sub-field of political geography dominated border studies, and early appraisals by Julian Minghi (1963) and J. R. Victor Prescott (1987) focused on political dimensions of borders and saw culture as implicit if not peripheral. With the advent of globalization and the cultural turn, geographical studies of borders and bordering acknowledged the role of culture and focused on aspects of landscape and identity (Rumley and Minghi 1991; Paasi 1995). Similarly, in political science, this acknowledgement of the role of culture and rethinking borders beyond the state developed as the field addressed globalization (Walters 2006). Border studies in literature developed momentum in the 1980s and 1990s (Lecker 1991) and saw considerable attention in recent decades as scholars assessed the literary culture of borders in globalization (Johnson and Michaelsen 1997; Jay 1998; Sadowski-Smith 2002; Limon 2008). Paul Jay (2014) reviews this transnational turn in literary studies, and collections express its vitality worldwide.

The scholarship increasingly crosses disciplines (Schimanski and Wolfe 2017; Schimanski and Nyman 2021). In a Canada-US context, the collections offered by David Stirrup and Gillian Roberts (2010), Roberts and Stirrup (2013), and Roberts (2018) are exemplary. In the twenty-first century, border studies have moved steadily toward an interdisciplinary dialogue (Newman 2006), and border culture has been a consistent, although, initially, not widely acknowledged, component of the interdisciplinary approach to border studies. During the last decade, in response to reviews of progress in the field (Newman 2006; Kolossov 2005; Brunet-Jailly 2005; Parker, Vaughan-Williams, et al. 2009), border culture has seen substantial attention in border studies research consortia around the world, including EUBORDERSCAPES in Europe (http://www.euborderscapes.eu), ABORNE in Africa (http://www.aborne.net), and Culture and the Canada-US Border (CCUSB; https://www.kent.ac.uk) and Borders in Globalization (BIG; http://www.biglobalization.org), both centred in or on Canada. The overall impact has been a substantial proliferation of border culture case studies worldwide, as well as several assessments of what we have accomplished in border culture studies. This literature is addressed in the next section on theorizing border culture.

At this point in the contextualization of border culture, we focus on the Canada-United States borderlands in order to set the stage for this volume. Roberts and Stirrup (2013, 1) articulate the prismatic quality of the Canada-US border "through which and at which broader questions of political, economic, and cultural relations within the Americas come into focus." They go on to review the cultural implications of the border and the "parallel encounters"—a protective barrier against Americanization: "[A] site of policing bodies and identities marked by racialization, gender, and sexuality; a threat to Indigenous sovereignties; a dividing line between a welfare state and the epitome of capitalism; a zone where state-funded culture meant to be 'good for us' stands guard against imported popular culture; a contact zone where reading and viewing practices might be inflected with national significance; and what appears to be a sharp contrast to the militarized US-Mexico border, even while agreements such as NAFTA locate Canada increasingly in relation to Mexico in particular and the Americas more generally" (Roberts and Stirrup 2013, 1–2). "Opening up the Canada-US border as discursive terrain to examine its function in and in relation to cultural texts," Roberts and Stirrup (2013, 3) assert, is timely and necessary. Roberts (2015) sustains the momentum of the CCUSB initiative in her text *Discrepant Parallels: Cultural Implications of the Canada-US Border*, which is heralded as a "succinct mapping of the central role of the 49th parallel in giving form to a distinctly Canadian identity, as well as a powerful display of how Border Studies and notions of the hemispheric are reshaping (North) American Studies" (Weier 2017, 1–2). In *Reading between the Borderlines* (2018), Gillian Roberts offers a collection of border studies on cultural production and consumption that explores literature, film, music, and other cultural media draws on the continued research of many of the contributors to Roberts and Stirrup's *Parallel Encounters* (2013), and edges the "ideals and realities of transnational cultural work" beyond the border (Roberts 2018). Today, in 2020, with a pandemic and a US president both raging, and the border locked in and locked down, it is indeed again both timely and necessary to examine border culture, not only at the line but into the borderlands of Canada and the United States, and North American interaction more broadly (Correa-Cabrera and Konrad 2020).

This continued assessment of border culture in a Canada-US context is enabled by a firm base of research. Early studies demonstrated a cross-disciplinary commitment from historians, anthropologists, sociologists, political scientists, geographers, and specialists in English and French literature and cultural studies in the Borderlands Project (McKinsey and Konrad 1989; Lecker 1991; Daoust et al. 1991). From this initial integration of disciplines in exploring Canada-US border culture, the fields have often followed their own approaches, paths, and pedagogies, with many excellent contributions too numerous to cite (extensive reviews of the literature are found in Konrad and Nicol 2008, 2011; Roberts and Stirrup 2013; Roberts 2015). With the special issue of the *American Review of Canadian Studies* edited by Stirrup and Roberts (2010) and such events as the symposium on Borders/Borderlands: Culture and the Canada-US International Boundary, hosted by the US Library of Congress (https://www.loc.gov/folklife/Symposia/borders/index.html), a multidisciplinary approach was re-engaged and celebrated. This plural, integrative, and dynamic collaboration has been a hallmark of both the CCUSB and BIG, as the two projects have generated a wealth of case studies as well as integrated, cross-disciplinary assessments of what Canada-US border culture, and border culture more widely, actually is and what it does. Yet the target keeps moving and evolving. The border is actually borders, and the metonym of the Canada-US border as Canada in Canadian culture has diffused as a meme through the Internet. We have moved from rediscovering and reimagining the border to encountering borders beyond the line and, now, to evaluating the perseverance of border culture in the face of overwhelming challenges from pandemics and populist/neo-nationalist intransigencies. Paradoxically, this is what enlivens and rejuvenates border culture; it needs to be in motion, ever-changing, on a live edge.

The dynamic relationships between borders and culture are what create and sustain "cultural islands" that are spatially distinct. Put another way, we cannot speak of distinct cultures without reference to borders. But this relationship at the same time is always in motion, and in borderlands, we see, simultaneously, cultural continuity and discontinuity. Furthermore, the zone of borderland transition is increasingly extended. Yet, despite this fluidity, this dynamism, specific cultural representation clearly is highly resonant, often stridently so, among individuals and communities, and can at times provide expressions of resistance or antagonism. The interplay between border and culture is what forms a sense of identity among those who claim Indigeneity but also among those excluded from that identity. The contradictions are multiple, however, as border and culture both push toward a singular sense of belonging—pressing toward homogeneity in cultural identity—and plural expressions of identity. At the same time, which cultural products and practices manage to and do not manage to cross borders suggests an underexplored selectivity in these processes. And the array of cultural expressions, of course, often plays differently at or near the border, and at different scales.

Theorizing Border Culture

Before we introduce the contributions to this volume, and discuss the three approaches—viewing border culture, borders and culture in motion, placing and replacing border culture—we offer a brief and, hopefully, accessible discussion of border culture theory. An extensive literature has emerged on border culture and culture at the border. Thought about border culture draws extensively from disciplines in the humanities and the social sciences and originates in nineteenth-century formative discussions and debates about culture and borders in anthropology, history, and geography. Since then, the formation, extension, dynamics, expression, materialization, and impact of border culture have garnered substantial inquiry in most fields where human interaction with boundaries is considered. The following brief discussion cannot address all of the advances in understanding the intersection of borders and culture. More comprehensive and detailed recent assessments are found in works by Victor Konrad and Heather Nicol (2011), Chiara Brambilla (2015), Johan Schimanski and Stephen Wolfe (2017), Roberts and Stirrup (2013) Roberts (2015, 2018), Lee Rodney (2017), and Schimanski and Jopi Nyman (2021).

Border culture emerges through the intersection and engagement of imagination, affinity, and identity. This production of culture usually is most evident and materialized in the borderlands (Konrad 2012). Border culture is evident wherever boundaries separate or sort people and their goods, ideas, or other belongings. This is because different realization, knowing, and civility meet and negotiate at these edges, whether they are formal nation-state limits to territory or lines between ethnicities, classes, or genders where "othering" is practiced. In these contexts, border culture is created, reinforced, challenged, removed, reinvented, enacted, and displayed in many forms.

In order to understand what border culture is, it is useful to first explore the interplay of borders and culture. Borders and culture do not intuitively occupy the same space. In fact, the anthropologist Franz Boas considered culture as integrative of space, whereas borders were viewed as the limits of territory and edges of space (Boas 1932, 612). Social scientists of the time generally viewed borders as containers of the nation-state and lines that separated people who could be differentiated by language and a set of other characteristics related to nationality. In their view, a distinctive culture either ended or changed at borders or it ought to do so. These were strong and resilient ideas that permeated modern thought. Fredrik Barth and colleagues challenged this notion in their efforts to draw attention to the boundaries of ethnic groups, and in so doing sought to examine interdependencies and symbiosis across boundaries, to evaluate persistence of cultural rather than national borders, to explore differentiation, dichotomization, and integration across boundaries, and to assess identity maintenance across borders (Barth 1969). Today, our ideas of culture and of borders have both evolved. Culture is viewed as imagined, produced, and refined constantly, and it is conceptualized as evolving knowledge, civility, and aesthetics shared by groups of people who may or may not be spatially proximate (Jensen and Richardson 2007).

Culture is also a repository of consciousness and a "common sense," which is to say that culture is hegemonic (Gramsci 1985). The power of this cultural hegemony lies in its invisibility and latency; culture does not seem political, but it is because it is pervasive (Adamson 1980; Crehan 2002; Mitchell 2000). Borders are seen as socially constructed, multiscalar, and variable in durability and permeability (Newman and Paasi 1998; Donnan and Wilson 1999; Laine 2016). Both culture and borders are human social constructs, and both are interacting more extensively and constantly in globalization. The interplay of a broadened, more malleable, more elaborately scaled, more demonstrative, and more accessible array of cultural ideas, with a more extensive and intensive display of borders, prevails around the globe (Konrad and Nicol 2011). This heightened interaction of borders and culture calls for more attention to the imagination and materialization of culture across boundaries (Roberts 2015, 2018) to provide not only insights into how borders work but also how people deal with boundaries and how humans create and reconstruct borderlands.

But what is border culture? Border culture emerges at the intersection of cultural meaning. Human beings build themselves into the world by creating meaning. Meaning pervades what we say and do.

Culture gives meaning to action by situating underlying states in an interpretive system (Saleebey 1994). Part of this cultural meaning relates to and activates the boundaries of being (Shweder 1984). Border culture is that part of meaning, and border culture, viewed through the lenses of critical geography and anthropology, is situated in political cultural geography (Mitchell 2000), and, as anticipated if not articulated by Gramsci (Forgacs 2000), border culture is found most explicitly in landscapes of domination, power relations, identity, and politics of difference. Borders and culture are in motion, assembling in edge places and spaces of prominence, where they become locations for resistance and ritualized culture at the border.

Yet our theories of culture and border culture are grounded in the essentialist view of culture and caught in the "territorial trap" (Agnew 1994). Culture remains viewed as a bounded system contained in a defined territory. Culture is expected to be homogeneous (Lugo 1997). Culture is shared by members of society. "This territory-oriented rhetoric of culture, cultural border and boundary faces a great challenge in a multicultural society because intense contacts between various cultural carriers blur the clarity of the demarcation lines" (Chang 1999). So, border culture is no longer culture at the margins but rather culture at the heart of geopolitics, flows, and experience of the transnational world. Border culture may be situated away from the border: in world cities, at airports, in detention centres and immigrant enclaves. Border culture may be at once a manifestation and imaginary. Border culture is an integral component of borders in motion. Border culture is experienced by more people in more circumstances than ever before.

Distinct approaches have evolved to visualize, empathize, understand, and explain border culture in the social sciences and the humanities. In the social sciences, "articulative" explanation has prevailed. Studies have focused on how culture inhabits borders, constituting and reinventing borderlands. Recently, social scientists have focused on the creation of "borderscapes" and transnational regions (Rajaram and Grundy-Warr 2008; Brambilla 2015). Overall, there is a growing interest in the transformation of the meaning of border, and this has resulted in extensive mapping and analysis of the terrain of border studies. In the humanities, there is a decided focus on the appreciation of culture at the border. Parallel encounters are visualized and articulated to express the mobility of cultural forms and cultural stereotypes, and the circulation and relationality of cultural products (Roberts and Stirrup 2013). Some studies explore the heavier presence of borders in traumas, dislocations, diaspora, and other border-entwined experiences (Schimanski and Wolfe 2017). Overall, the humanistic approach is appreciation of the terrain of border studies (Roberts and Stirrup 2013).

We view border culture theory and theorizing in four contexts: confluence, differentiation, beyond binaries, and with shifting interfaces. In a sense, these contexts document the evolution of border culture thinking and relate the insights of border culture to the broader advances in border studies theory. These contexts are not "periods" of border culture theory building, nor are they necessarily distinct or exclusive. Rather, the contexts provide convenient groupings of theoretical insight to help assemble the incremental understanding of border culture. Also, rather than linked with any specific discipline, these contexts accommodate insights from across the humanities and social sciences to advance a cross-disciplinary framework for theorizing border culture.

Confluence establishes the basic understanding that border culture entails relating international forces operating between nations to transnational forces produced by the presence of one nation within another (Fein 2003). There are multiple planes of border culture that emerge within nations, between nations, across and at borders. These planes are found at different scales and may be multiscalar (Laine 2016). Yet these planes connect more than they differentiate border culture because confluence is the prevailing incentive and force, and this confluence seeks to link, align, and even integrate culture at the multiple borderlines with the agency of borderlands. To know border culture, then, is to capture both the "essential" and the "imagined" qualities of hybridization and differentiation at borders and in the borderlands (Shimoni 2006). So, the planes of border culture are not simply evident because they are realized; they are also apparent because they are imagined. Border culture in confluence may be incipient and only partially imagined or realized. Often it is "creolized" through a manipulation of social identities and affiliations, and border culture becomes negotiated culture, one type of the fluid, syncretic cultures that appear in bordered areas (Cusick 2000). Understanding border culture means acknowledging the partiality and incompleteness of cultural shells that continue to prevail in the nation-state and predominate in its territory. Whereas confluence alters and erodes these cultural shells, often at the fringes of national territory, the shells remain evident and often sufficiently hardened to resist forces of engagement, hybridization, sharing, and integration. To comprehend border culture arising through confluence, we must go beyond rationalizations to daydream about allowances, thick margins, receptors, and interfaces, which are both possible and plausible where nations meet and cultures intersect anywhere around the globe. Also, confluence is not easily and effectively reversible. Liminal and "third spaces" do not revert into previous forms (Gupta and Ferguson 1997). Consequently, to believe that a "wall" will overcome confluence and reassert a previous state of distinction, or of differentiation, has no foundation.

Yet theories of border culture are also rooted in a more extensive comprehension of *differentiation*. This is not simply the demarcated difference of nation-states at the boundary but a more deeply incised difference constructed with the power of cumulative discourse (Foucault 1971). The construction of difference may have its roots in nationalisms, but it is conveyed in the differentiation at the line, a differentiation asserted and supported by border culture that can be both nationalistic and fiercely "borderlands" in its nature. Borderlands convey the dialectic of cultural continuity and discontinuity. Pressures toward homogeneity in cultural identity vie with more extensive forces of heterogeneity to diffuse and complicate identities at and near borders. This may give rise to differentiation as competition to establish who has the right to inhabit the borderland, who is a "belonger" (Konrad and Everitt 2013). Also, this imperative toward differentiation has led to the practice of "teichopolitics": the building of walls and barriers at borders (Rosière and Jones 2012). In globalization, border culture is geopolitically coded into popular representations to border a world that is increasingly difficult to grasp for people who navigate this world more rapidly and extensively (Konrad and Nicol 2011).

Theorizing border culture also requires that we think about borders *beyond binaries* (Mayer 2014). This is very difficult to do because the binaries are so ingrained in our thinking about borders. Yet, if we do think beyond binaries, the idea of border culture moves forward and is advanced to another level of knowing borders and culture. In this sense, identity separation and polarization (Villa 2000; Vila 2003) engage with notions of hybridity (Anzaldúa 1987, Rosaldo 1993). The debate between advocates of hybridity and those forwarding identity separation and polarization in border culture has, according to

Heyman (2012), distracted us from the complexity of the intertwined processes of blending and separating, which, in reality, characterize borderlands. "One-state-one-territory" and "one-society-one-culture" conceptualizations are challenged and displaced in the articulation of border culture, at least in theory (Rosaldo 1993; Heyman 2012). In the real world, borders and culture are in motion constantly (Konrad 2015), and border culture may prevail for a while and then diffuse, and it may be more evident in the borderlands than elsewhere. Consequently, borderlands have become a privileged locus of hope, a space of crossroads, new ground for securing relation, and a place for celebrating difference (Michaelsen and Johnson 1997). Yet border culture is as much about contestation and trauma as it is about newfound commonalities and celebration of difference.

Theorizing border culture in globalization is then about *shifting interfaces*. Border culture is sometimes about positive engagement and other times about contestation. Multiple levels of cross-border culture are linked with socially constructed and reconstructed identities (Konrad and Nicol 2008, 2011). We need to accommodate these shifting interfaces by scaling border culture theory within the emerging multiscalar and relational motion framework of border theory (Ptak et al. 2020). According to Rodney (2017), border culture is conveyed through shifting and impermanent representational constructs, which are porous and permeable interfaces that offer the possibility of political change and negotiation. This requires *Looking Beyond Borderlines* (Rodney 2017) and "seeing like a border" (Rumford 2011). Also, Chad Richardson and Michael Pisani (2012, 2017) show how "structural bias" (incumbency bonus, false balance) often overwhelms borderlands and presents issues as even-sided despite disproportionate amounts of evidence of asymmetries and shifts.

Border culture is evident and performed in the borders and controls constructed more emphatically after the events of 9/11 (Balibar 2002) and in the "frisk society" that has evolved (Urry 2007). According to Jacques Rancière (2010), border culture is materializing as "dissensus" rather than consensus. This border culture is expressed as "borderities," wherein contemporary mobile borders relate to sovereignty, territory, and spatial politics (Amilhat Szary and Giraut 2015). Accordingly, the "borderscapes" are more diverse, complex, political, and traumatic in globalization (Rajaram and Grundy-Warr 2008; Brambilla 2015). Also, the border, and in this case the Canada-US border, has become more personalized and disaggregated in the minds of borderlanders at Niagara (Helleiner 2016). In fact, some localities, Stanstead, Quebec, and Derby Line, Vermont, for example, have emerged as places with distinctive border culture, where "line dancing" is practiced and residents employ a border "game" to establish ownership of borderlands increasingly controlled by agencies outside the cross-border community (Vandervalk 2017). If we acknowledge that culture gives meaning to action through interpretive systems, what is the meaning of culture at the border?

A theory of border culture must address and contain several components now recognized as fundamental to understanding how culture impacts on borders and how borders affect culture. These are fundamentals of border imaginaries, cultural production, and cultural identities at the border. Border culture is conveyed in imaginaries and productions that are linked to identities constructed in the borderlands, and these identities underlie the enforcement of control and resistance to power that also comprise border cultures. Understanding border culture is a key component in comprehending borders in motion in an increasingly transnational world. In the Borders in Globalization project, we explore the interplay of borders and culture, identify the fundamental currents of border culture in motion, and establish an approach to understanding how border culture is placed and replaced in globalization.

Viewing Border Culture

Border imaginaries link with the cultural meaning of landscape, aesthetics, identities, belonging, settlement, community, migration, work, play, stories, and other forms of border experience. Some of these imaginaries are life securing. They are the perceptions of the necessities for survival in the borderlands and they include views on whom to align with, where to cross the border, how to behave in border crossing, and, generally, how to compromise in between. These are not necessarily the imaginaries of the state but rather grass-roots, borderlands approaches. Some imaginaries may be deemed life sustaining for they are aligned with everyday facilitation of life in the borderlands. Other imaginaries are life enriching and reflect the mutual engagement and linkage of creative people and agencies across borders. Cultural production emerges from all of these types of imaginaries. Culture is on the move and cultural productions of bordering are everywhere and particularly concentrated in borderlands. And, as established in recent theoretical and empirical studies, interactions among cultural components are complex and multidimensional rather than binary (Mayer 2014; Rodney 2017). In a sense, culture is being decolonized with expanding transnationalism, but when this happens border culture may produce both predictable representations of hybridity and more unpredictable forms derived from contestation. It appears that borders undergoing decolonization and other significant changes encourage more cultural production than more stable borders. Consequently, it is probable that extensive cultural production at borders conveys expanded cultural meaning in transnationalism and globalization.

The first part of this volume explores the ways in which people imagine and objectify the border. As in the following two sections of the volume, our goal in this section is to offer several academic explorations and a policy-relevant illustration of how border culture works and is applied, relates to life in the borderlands, and is employed as a concept in artistic representation, border navigation, and cultural heritage preservation and management. The first chapter in the section "Viewing Border Culture" introduces the cultural imaginary of borderlands through the role of art and media projects in resuscitating borderlands in North America. In recent decades, the promise and celebration of the borderlands in the 1990s was replaced by the era of the borderline. As borders have become more relational and mobile virtual interfaces, these borders have become actualized through embodied behaviours and concrete objects. Lee Rodney, in "Sight and Site on the Line: The Cultural Imaginary of Borderlands in North America," illustrates how bodily metaphors of the border as wound and the boundary as a cultural skin materialize as abjected sites in cultural imagination. These are sites of "dissensus," as opposed to consensus (Rancière 2015), and they make us question authority and the exclusionary paradigms of Western aesthetics. The sites are at once relational, conditional, and diverse, and they make us want to see the border even more. Accordingly, Rodney shows us, in the contexts of both the Mexico-US border and the Canada-US border at Detroit-Windsor, projects of crossing, mapping, reimagining, performing, and documenting the line that offer alternative imaginaries and understanding of space and identity along new "social trails" across the border.

Michael Darroch's chapter is also located at the Windsor-Detroit interface. Darroch explores the imagining of nighttime Detroit in a richly illustrated essay about how, in illumination and in darkness, iconic features in Detroit's skyline produce moods and atmospheres that affect Windsor. As Darroch indicates, cultural experiences of night and day are not typically theorized in borderlands, and so this chapter offers a unique insight and contribution to this volume. Nighttime cultural life is expressed as an intense local experience that rounds out the rhythms of the border city as they are imagined and practiced. Although Detroit glows over Windsor to both enchant and revile across the border, the boundary and/as the river enables Windsor to be an "intimate onlooker," perceiving, imagining, and participating in nighttime Detroit. The border between darkness and light is diffused and recast as Detroit's electrified images cross the border and are processed in Windsor. Symbolic objects of cultural significance, the "beaming" Penobscot Building for example, become central in this cross-border engagement. Darroch illustrates how the Penobscot Building, and other iconic structures in nighttime Detroit, are vividly imaginable but perhaps always just beyond reach.

Similarly, symbolic objects are central in the chapter by Anelynda Mielke and Nadya Pohran about border struggles and the importance of symbolism in imagining and negotiating borders. Using several examples, and particularly one man's fight in Montréal to escape imprisonment in a church and attain the right to remain in his adoptive country, Mielke and Pohran draw on the work of theorists Rancière (1999), Guha (1983), and Latour (2004) to convey how physical objects play a central role in a marginal entity's struggle against oppressive state practices in Canada and elsewhere. Objects or physical things are central at the border as instrumental and pivotal in struggles to formulate and assert legitimacy and to claim asylum, as well as in border interactions more generally. Borders exist within remotely located symbolic objects, as well as within the nonmaterial consciousness of individuals who imagine crossing or otherwise interacting with borderlines. Reproduction and representation of these objects, and the imaginaries that imbue the objects with meaning, create a fluid making of the border. Swirling about these lively borders, even those removed from borderlines, is border struggle, and this struggle generates a politics of materiality, producing spectacles of suffering and spaces of sanctuary. This chapter explores this dynamic and expanding "borderworld" and the cultures that emerge from and inhabit it.

The final chapter in this section of the volume is a retrospective on the *Border Cultures* series at the Art Gallery of Windsor, 2013–2015.

The chapter includes a synopsis of the exhibitions drawn from the published catalogue *Border Cultures* (Mitra 2015) and a "conversation" between the curator, Srimoyee Mitra, and other authors in this volume—Lee Rodney, Michael Darroch, and Victor Konrad—about the exhibitions, and Mitra's assessment of the meaning and impact of the works. Konrad offers a contextual frame for border art related to the Canada-US border, first to introduce the artistic imaginary of the border and then to situate the chapter within this section of the volume. Launched in 2013, the *Border Cultures* series of exhibitions were developed to deepen our understanding of what it means to be a border city in the twenty-first century. "This three-part exhibition was conceptualized as a research platform, bringing together regional, national and international artists to examine the complex and shifting notions of national boundaries" (Mitra 2015). The works of the artists offered in the exhibitions collectively and consecutively mark a sparking of imaginaries and the production of culture at and about the border.

Capturing Borders and Culture in Motion

The mobility of borders has been recognized as an expanding, complex phenomenon in globalization (Amilhat Szary and Giraut 2015). Borders are simply, constantly, and even elaborately in motion at and beyond the line (Konrad 2015). This mobile characteristic of borders renders them more difficult to pin down and to understand than the stable and static lines once believed to situate and establish boundaries in space and time. New paradigms incorporating motion are required to establish where and how borders are situated, scaled, related, and linked. Also, to understand borders in motion, it is necessary to coincidentally measure and describe the role and influence of the border at the boundary, in the borderlands, and beyond. This requires depicting and assessing borders in motion on a wider canvas and definitely beyond binary constructs. It requires evaluating the movements across and around borders as processes related to each other in multidimensional spatial and temporal interaction. Yet all this fluidity has guideposts and produces signatures that may help us to understand the nature of borders in motion.

Cultural movements have always crossed boundaries. With this realization we can begin to address border culture as part of this "relational motion" (Ptak et al. 2020) universal of borders and visualize border culture as, at once, a flow, an embodiment, and a cybernetic construct. Chapters in "Borders and Culture in Motion" address all of these conditions. In chapter 5, Melissa Kelly evaluates the cultural movement of snowbirds across the border between Canada and the United States and explores the sociocultural impacts of borders encountered by the Canadian seasonal migrants as they settle for the winter in Florida. Snowbirds are beyond classification as tourists or residents in the US. They are "in-between" and they represent a new form of continental integration in globalization, with implications for citizenship, belonging, and people's participation in society. With the intensification of social relations and consciousness across world-time and world-space (Steger and James 2013), globalization has changed the scale and the scope of international migration (Sheller and Urry 2004), and new migration patterns have emerged. One pattern displays increasing belonging through a sense of community beyond nation-states and their borders. Kelly's research, based on interviews with snowbirds in Florida, identifies integrated border spaces in the communities of American and Canadian seasonal migrants. Within these communities are found shifting modes of belonging to a community wherein respondents report more friends than ever and a winter-to-winter schedule that allows and enhances the sense of belonging. Yet snowbirds are definitively Canadian, and while in Florida they discover new meanings of being Canadian, which they express in acts of patriotism and efforts to remain Canadian and to reap the healthcare and other benefits of their citizenship.

From communities beyond the border, the section moves to a community on the border. A community's culture changes as security tightens (Burnett 2019). Sandra Vandervalk considers the in-between way of being that is unique to living on the edge and in the middle place of Stanstead, Quebec, and Derby Line, Vermont. Using conceptual frameworks of liminality (Turner 1969) and phenomenology (Merleau-Ponty 1962), Vandervalk explores the contradiction between inside and outside in a threshold place. This way of being, states Vandervalk, troubles the non-borderlander's assumption of the border as a line that divides and separates, because residents of Stanstead-Derby Line have made their own sense of the bewildering liminal zone of the border. Their actions embody liminality into a style of existence and an identity in the in-between place. In this place, borderlanders comfortably inhabit both sides of the line, where they perform national identity yet live daily lives with an in-between way of being in the world.

The next chapter moves us back to the North American scale. Alexander Rudolph makes the case for a North American cyber new regionalism, which results in an online cultural demarcation or re-bordering. He asks, how will lack of domestic control of the Internet contribute to Canadian culture and what are the implications of any possible changes in Canadian culture? This is, first of all, a study of the immense process of North American regionalization and integration with the Internet. Rudolph employs cultural-semantic modelling to show the physical reality of the cyberspace and the "new" regionalism of active integration and convergence in North America, and particularly between the US and Canada. Will anticipated future integration and convergence leave *la Francophonie* and other minorities behind, and will Canadian-content funding be sufficient to combat homogenization? Rudolph suggests that, instead, new media are a form of cultural and linguistic preservation, wherein through video-sharing platforms, innovation and preservation of cultural heritage becomes more expedient and content more accessible. Border culture in the realm of new media is multidimensional and multiscalar.

Chapter 8, the final chapter in "Borders and Culture in Motion," discusses the recent Canadian government program designed to transfer and resettle Syrian refugees into Canada from their war-torn homeland. In "#WelcomeRefugees: A Canadian Phenomenon That Illustrates the Temporal Dimension of Border Constructs," Renata Grudzien introduces and analyzes the Canadian program to fast-track refugee resettlement during a critical period of political anticipation in Canada when the newly elected Liberal government devised a highly visible process of refugee settlement to showcase its new policies. The new dimension of Canada's border construct was indeed time, and this time emerged as the new territory to traverse in the process of crossing the border. Grudzien articulates five phases of border crossing, which are actually five stages and five borders: identification of Syrian refugees for resettlement in the refugee camps, processing of the refugees overseas, transport to Canada, welcome at the Canadian border, and, finally, settlement and community integration. Visualizing the border in process and motion in these five steps further challenges the territorial hegemony of border constructs and allows us to evaluate each border phase, to recognize the efficiencies in expanding the border construct, and, essentially, to view the border as a living, mobile organism.

Placing and Replacing Border Culture:
Focus on Indigenous Borders

Evolving border culture is more than the parallel alignment of bordering and re-bordering and culture change. When and where the processes of cultural change and bordering intertwine, the placement, and replacement, of border and culture are at first distinct and then merge and result in something new. Perhaps this is analogous to the alloy of copper and tin forming bronze, but more likely it is a complex meshing whereby more or less of culture change or replacement links with multiscalar bordering dynamics. This overall process is sufficiently complex and multifaceted that researchers have preferred to view it as a black box and explore the inputs and the outcomes. If there are constants, however—a place, or a cultural presence—the processes of placing and replacing border culture may provide clearer insights. The section "Placing and Replacing Border Culture: Indigenous Perspectives" takes this approach and features three studies focusing on aspects of Indigenous border culture. These works engage with and expand on a growing literature of Indigenous encounters with borders, more specifically, Canada's borders (Roberts 2015, 2018). The final chapter, on planning and managing transborder cultural heritage landscapes, expands the focus and provides a public policy approach to placing and replacing border culture.

Chapter 9 offers a literary perspective "across borders and culture." Evelyn P. Mayer approaches Thomas King's artistic activism by examining Indigenous voices in figurative borderlands settings of diverse cultural expressions, border representations, and identity negotiations. Drawing mainly on King's recent books *The Inconvenient Indian* and *The Back of the Turtle*, Mayer explores dimensions of motion and fluidity and practices of artistic activism, subversion, resistance and survival, and liminality. She elaborates a space of opportunity, oscillating between complexity and multiplicity, on the one hand, and identity and belonging, on the other. In this context, geopolitical boundaries are invariably pitted against the Native presence. Yet it is beyond reserves that the "art/s of 'survivance'" show more promise of utopian borders related to culture, community, and Canada.

Laetitia Rouvière articulates the space between Aboriginal sovereignty and national security at Akwesasne. This chapter, originally published in French in *The Canadian Geographer/Le Géographe canadien* (Rouvière 2019), is here translated and revised for publication in

English. Akwesasne is situated at the intersection of multiple borders between communities, provincial and state jurisdictions, and national territories. The Mohawk reserves of Saint Regis and Akwesasne are nestled between Ontario, Quebec, and New York State, the United States and Canada, and Cornwall and Massena. Whereas Mohawk culture prevails across this intersection of multiscalar jurisdictions, the borders continue to impact the movement, activities, and, ultimately, the identity of the Indigenous population on the reserves. This chapter explores the multiscalar bordering of Akwesasne and the community interactions and engagements with "state" jurisdictions. Other divisions—religion, clan, politics, settlement—are apparent at the community scale. All of this bordering dissects and separates space, place, and habitation on the reserves in numerous ways, particularly in the recent phase of increased border security. Yet Mohawk community adjustment strategies to multiscalar imperatives, and the overall cultural empowerment among the Mohawk through effective "working of the border," are strengthening rather than weakening Mohawk identity and management of their territory.

Heidi Weigand and Colin Howell, in their chapter on sport and bordering, continue the focus on Indigenous peoples, the Iroquois (Haudenosaunee) people specifically. The chapter highlights the contested nature of existing borders and illustrates the restricted agency of the Iroquois National Lacrosse Team in its efforts to attend the 2010 World Lacrosse Championship in the United Kingdom. The team was denied the use of Haudenosaunee passports to enter the UK, although the passports allowed border crossing between Canada and the US. This situation exposes the modern colonial power relationships involving Canada, the UK, and the US, with the Haudenosaunee caught in a complex web of increasing national security concerns, international and nation-state conflicts, and engagement of political voices raised through new media to support the athletes. Furthermore, the chapter shows, through the prism of sport, the intersectional dimensions of national identity and contested borderland communities, and it illustrates how sport is an integral part of the bordering process and a place for staging disputes involving national identity and sovereignty.

In the final chapter, Scott Cafarella, Joel Konrad, and Rebecca Sciarra—all cultural and natural heritage specialists working for government agencies and private consulting firms in Ontario—offer a practitioners' view on a "Biocultural Planning Approach for Managing

Trans-Border Cultural Heritage Landscapes." Rather than focus on Indigenous heritage exclusively, this study promotes an "associative" cultural landscape assessment and management model, in which Indigenous heritage is an integral component in a holistic approach to comprehensive natural environment and cultural landscape preservation in a bordered context. This perspective is consistent with recent efforts to engage Indigenous participation and direct involvement in heritage work. Archaeological Services Incorporated (ASI), a firm with which all of the authors of this chapter have been affiliated, is a leading proponent of this work in Ontario. On June 17, 2020, Grand Chief Konrad Sioui of the Huron Wendat Nation proclaimed, "The Huron-Wendat Nation places the preservation, protection and promotion of its patrimonial, ancestral, and cultural rights and interests at the heart of its activities in South Wendake (central Southern Ontario)." "To help achieve this objective," Chief Sioui continued, "ASI has embraced the opportunity to transfer archaeological expertise and knowledge to the Huron-Wendat Nation. This partnership aims at reconciliation and supports an innovative corporate ethic sought by Indigenous peoples in a contemporary world" (Sioui 2020, 1).

The chapter also epitomizes the partnerships forged between government, the private sector, and academe in the Borders in Globalization project supported by SSHRC. The study notes the lack of legislation and policy that effectively integrates conservation of significant cultural and natural resources in a holistic manner, as well as the difficulty of using current planning tools to scale-up the conservation of cultural resources that transcend political boundaries. "How can cross-jurisdictional biocultural landscapes be assessed, evaluated and managed to ensure that cultural heritage is accessible, sustainable, and contributes to overall quality of life?" The authors show how biocultural planning proceeds from theory to practice, and how this illustrates the transfer of cultural practices and knowledge along borders to create new regional identities, thereby affirming the importance of regions and sense of place in a globalizing world. In essence, the border becomes part of the integrated resources (Sohn 2014). By employing a case study of the northeastern corner of the Niagara Peninsula, bordered by natural and human boundaries, the authors provide a richly detailed assessment of the cross-jurisdictional landscape and illustrate how the biocultural planning zones confirm the border as resource through the interplay of heritage, the politics of difference, and national identity.

Engaging Border Culture at the Canada-US Border

Too often, in the course of reacting and responding to the changes at the border brought about by the events of 9/11 and the aftermath of security primacy advocated by both the US and Canada, Canadians and Americans have railed against the changes at the border but not held off to consider the fundamental alterations and continuities in border culture underlying the changes. Both Americans and Canadians have expressed concerns, complained about wait times, and showed alarm at interdictions and assaults on civil and human rights, among other stories of bordering excesses. These accumulating stories, and the imaginaries fed by them, have stoked incendiary interactions of border cultures that question, at least, and confront, at most, the cross-border accumulation and integration of borderlands culture long established between Canada and the United States. Yet these imaginaries and representations of resistance and confrontation are also evidence of an active and vibrant border culture that engages with the border and numerous facets of bordering to accommodate the relationship between Americans and Canadians, even though the administrations in Washington, DC, and Ottawa may not be in concert. Border culture, then, is the vessel of engagement between the countries—assuming many forms, exuding a variety of expressions, and changing shapes—but border culture does not disappear once it is developed. It is, in a way, a constant in the processes of bordering, re-bordering, and de-bordering. Accordingly, as a constant, border culture may be visualized as a thread that runs throughout the process of globalization, particularly as globalization relates to borders. It follows that we need to understand border culture in order to comprehend globalization. Also, in times of shock and upheaval, such as during a globe-gripping pandemic, the need to explore and try to understand the culture that works to separate and join at borders is even more immediate.

References

Adamson, Walter L. 1980. *Hegemony and Revolution: A Study of Antonio Gramsci's Political and Cultural Theory*. Berkeley: University of California Press.

Agnew, John. 1994. "The Territorial Trap: The Geographical Assumptions of International Relations Theory." *Review of International Political Economy*, no. 1 (Spring): 53–80.

Alper, Donald K. 1996. "The Idea of Cascadia: Emergent Transborder Regionalisms in Pacific Northwest-Western Canada." *Journal of Borderlands Studies* 11 (2): 1–22.

Amilhat Szary, Anne-Laure, and Frédéric Giraut, eds. 2015. *Borderities: The Politics of Contemporary Mobile Borders.* New York: Springer.

Anzaldúa, Gloria. 1987. *Borderlands/La Frontera: The New Mestiza.* San Francisco: Aunt Lute.

Balibar, Étienne. 2002. *Politics and the Other Scene.* New York: Verso.

Barth, Fredrik. 1969. *Ethnic Groups and Boundaries.* Oslo: Universitetsforlaget.

Boas, Franz. 1932. *Anthropology and Modern Life.* New York: Norton.

BPRI (Border Policy Research Institute). 2020. "COVID-19 and the US-Canada Border: Retail Shopping Destinations for Canadians in Whatcom County." *Border Research Institute Publications* 119. https://cedar.wwu.edu/bpri_publications/119.

Brambilla, Chiara. 2015. "Exploring the Critical Potential of the Borderscapes Concept." *Geopolitics* 20 (1): 14–34.

Brunet-Jailly, Emmanuel. 2005. "Theorizing Borders: An Interdisciplinary Perspective." *Geopolitics* 10 (4): 633–649.

Burnett, John. 2019. "US-Canada Border Community's Culture Changes as Security Tightens." National Public Radio (NPR). November 21, 2019. https://www.npr.org/2019/11/21/781138076/u-s-canada-border-communitys-culture-changes-as-security-tightens.

Chang, Heewon. 1999. "Re-examining the Rhetoric of the Cultural Border." Critical Multicultural Pavilion. Accessed September 23, 2020. http://www.edchange.org/multicultural/papers/heewon.html.

Cohen, Anthony P. 1986. *Symbolizing Boundaries: Identity and Diversity in British Cultures.* Manchester: Manchester University Press.

Correa-Cabrera, Guadalupe, and Victor Konrad, eds. 2020. *North American Borders in Comparative Perspective.* Tucson: University of Arizona Press.

Crehan, Kate. 2002. *Gramsci, Culture and Anthropology.* Berkeley: University of California Press.

Cusick, James G. 2000. "Creolization and the Borderlands." *Historical Archaeology* 34 (3): 46–55.

Daoust, Marie-José, Lauren McKinsey, Jean Papineau, and Laurent-Michel Vacher, eds. 1991. *Une frontière dans la tête : culture, institutions et imaginaires canadiens.* Montréal: Liber.

Donnan, Hastings, and Thomas M. Wilson, eds. 1999. *Borders: Frontiers of Identity, Nation and State.* Oxford: Berg.

———. 1994. *Border Approaches: Anthropological Perspectives on Frontiers.* Lanham, MD: University Press of America.

Fein, Seth. 2003. "Culture across Borders in the Americas." *History Compass* 1 (1): 1–6. https://doi.org/10.1111/1478-0542.025.

Forgacs, David. 2000. *The Gramsci Reader, Selected Writings 1916–1935.* New York: New York University Press.

Foucault, Michel. 1971. *The Order of Things.* New York: Vintage.

Gill, Warren. 1993. "Region, Agency, and Popular Music: The Northwest Sound, 1958–1966." *The Canadian Geographer/Le Géographe canadien* 37 (2): 120–131.

Gramsci, Antonio. 1985. *Selections from Cultural Writings.* Edited by David Forgacs and Geoffrey Newell-Smith. Cambridge, MA: Harvard University Press.

Guha, Ranajit, ed. 1983. *Subaltern Studies: Writings on South Asian History and Society.* Delhi: Oxford University Press.

Gupta, Akhil, and James Ferguson, eds. 1997. *Culture, Power, Place: Explorations in Critical Anthropology.* Durham, NC: Duke University Press.

Hallgrímsdóttir, Helga K., and Nicole Bates-Eamer. 2020. "BIG (Borders in Globalization): Borders and Bordering Processes in the Pacific Northwest." In "British Columbia's Borders in Globalization." Special issue, *Journal of Borderlands Studies* 35 (4): 497–503. https://doi.org/10.1080/08865655.2020.1768886.

Helleiner, Jane. 2016. *Borderline Canadianness.* Toronto: University of Toronto Press.

Heyman, Josiah McC. 2012. "Culture Theory and the US-Mexico Border." In *A Companion to Border Studies,* edited by Thomas M. Wilson and Hastings Donnan, 48–65. Oxford: Blackwell.

Jay, Paul. 2014. *Global Matters: The Transnational Turn in Literary Studies.* Ithaca, NY: Cornell University Press.

———. 1998. "The Myth of America and the Politics of Location: Modernity, Border Studies, and the Literature of the Americas." *Arizona Quarterly: A Journal of American Literature, Culture and Theory* 54 (2): 165–192.

Jensen, Anne, and Tim Richardson. 2007. "New Region, New Story: Imagining Mobile Subjects in Transnational Space." *Space and Polity* 11 (2): 137–150.

Johnson, David E., and Scott Michaelsen, eds. 1997. *Border Theory.* Minneapolis: University of Minnesota Press.

Kearney, Michael. 1991. "Borders and Boundaries of State and Self at the End of Empire." *Journal of Historical Sociology* 4 (1): 52–74.

Kolossov, Vladimir. 2005. "Border Studies: Changing Perspectives and Theoretical Approaches." *Geopolitics* 10 (4): 606–632.

Konrad, Victor. 2020. "Re-imagining the Border between Canada and the United States." In *North American Borders in Comparative Perspective,* edited by Guadalupe Correa-Cabrera and Victor Konrad, 72–97. Tucson: University of Arizona Press.

———. 2015. "Toward a Theory of Borders in Motion." *Journal of Borderlands Studies* 30 (1): 1–17.

———. 2012. "Conflating Imagination, Identity and Affinity in the Social Construction of Borderlands Culture between Canada and the United States." *American Review of Canadian Studies* 42 (4): 530–548.

———. 2010. "'Breaking Points' but No 'Broken Border': Stakeholders Evaluate Border Issues in the Pacific Northwest Region." *Border Policy Research Institute Publications* 79. https://cedar.wwu.edu/bpri_publications/79.

Konrad, Victor, and John C. Everitt. 2013. "Borders and 'Belongers': Transnational Identities, Border Security, and Cross-Border Socio-economic Integration in the United States Borderlands with Canada and the British Virgin Islands." *Comparative American Studies* 9 (4): 288–308.

Konrad, Victor, and Heather Nicol. 2011. "Border Culture, the Boundary between Canada and the United States of America, and the Advancement of Borderlands Theory." *Geopolitics* 16 (1): 70–90.

———. 2008. *Beyond Walls: Re-inventing the Canada-United States Borderlands.* Aldershot, UK: Ashgate.

Laine, Jussi P. 2016. "The Multiscalar Production of Borders." *Geopolitics* 21 (3): 465–482.

Latour, Bruno. 2004. *Politics of Nature.* Cambridge, MA: Harvard University Press.

Lecker, Robert. 1991. *Borderlands: Essays in Canadian-American Relations.* Toronto: ECW Press.

Limon, J. E. 2008. "Border Literary Histories, Globalization, and Critical Regionalism." *American Literary History* 20 (1–2): 160–182.

Lipset, Seymour M. 1996. *American Exceptionalism: A Double-Edged Sword.* New York: Norton.

Lynch, Jim. 2010. *Border Songs.* New York: Penguin Random House.

Lugo, Alejandro. 1997. "Reflections on Border Theory, Culture and the Nation." In *Border Theory*, edited by D. E. Johnson and S. Michaelsen, 43–67. Minneapolis: University of Minnesota Press.

Magnus, Samantha, Helga K. Hallgrímsdóttir, Nicole Bates-Eamer, and Victor Konrad. 2019. "Overgrowing the Border? An Examination of Cascadian Culture and Cannabis Legalization." *Journal of Borderlands Studies* 34 (4): 505–526. https://doi.org/10.1080/08865655.2019.1619474.

Marker, Michael. 2015. "Geographies of Indigenous Leaders: Landscapes and Mindscapes in the Pacific Northwest." *Harvard Educational Review* 85 (2): 229–253.

Martinez, Oscar. 1994. *Border People: Life and Society in the US-Mexico Borderlands.* Tucson: University of Arizona Press.

Mayer, Evelyn P. 2014. *Narrating North American Borderlands: Thomas King, Howard F. Mosher, and Jim Lynch.* Frankfurt: Peter Lang.

McCarthy, Grace. 2020. "Impacts from Border Restrictions Could Linger." *The Northern Light*, May 21, 2020. https://www.thenorthernlight.com/stories/impacts-from-border-restrictions-could-linger,10530.

McKinsey, Lauren, and Victor Konrad. 1989. *Borderlands Reflections: The United States and Canada.* Orono: University of Maine Press.

Merleau-Ponty, Maurice. 1962. *Phenomonology of Perception.* New York: Routledge and Kegan Paul.

Meyer, Philipp. 2009. "'Outlaws' Paradise." *New York Times,* August 30, 2009. https://www.nytimes.com/2009/08/30/books/review/Meyer-t.html.

Michaelsen, Scott, and David E. Johnson. 1997. "Border Secrets: An Introduction." In *Border Theory,* edited by D. E. Johnson and S. Michaelsen, 1–41. Minneapolis: University of Minnesota Press.

Minghi, Julian. 1963. "Boundary Studies in Political Geography." *Annals, Association of American Geographers* 53 (3): 407–428.

Mitchell, Don. 2000. *Cultural Geography.* Oxford: Blackwell.

Mitra, Srimoyee. 2015. *Border Cultures.* London: Black Dog Publishing.

Newman, David. 2006. "Borders and Bordering: Towards an Interdisciplinary Dialogue." *European Journal of Social Theory* 9 (2): 171–186.

Newman, David, and Anssi Paasi. 1998. "Fences and Neighbours in the Post-Modern World: Boundary Narratives in Political Geography." *Progress in Human Geography* 22 (2): 186–207.

Paasi, Anssi. 1995. *Territories, Boundaries and Consciousness: The Changing Geographies of the Finnish-Russian Border.* New York: Wiley.

Palmer, Howard. 1976. "Mosaic versus Melting Pot? Immigration and Ethnicity in Canada and the United States." *International Journal* 31 (3): 488–528.

Parker, Noel, and Nick Vaughan-Williams et al. 2009. "Lines in the Sand? Towards an Agenda for Critical Border Studies." *Geopolitics* 14 (3): 582–587.

Pratt, Martin. 2010. "The Scholar-Practitioner Interface in Boundary Studies." *Eurasia Border Review* 1 (1): 29–36.

Prescott, J. R. Victor. 1987. *Political Frontiers and Boundaries.* London: Allen and Unwin.

Ptak, Thomas, Jussi P. Laine, Zhiding Hu, Yuli Liu, Victor Konrad, and Martin van der Velde. 2020. "Understanding Borders as Dynamic Processes: Capturing Relational Motion from Southwestern China's Radiation Center." *Territory, Politics, Governance.* https://doi.org/10.1080/21622671.2020.1764861.

Rajaram, Prem Kumar, and Carl Grundy-Warr, eds. 2008. *Borderscapes: Hidden Geographies and Politics at Territory's Edge.* Minneapolis: University of Minnesota Press.

Rancière, Jacques. 2015. *Dissensus: On Politics and Aesthetics.* New York: Bloomsbury.

———. 2010. *Chronicles of Consensual Times.* New York: Continuum.

———. 1999. *Disagreement: Politics and Philosophy.* Minneapolis: University of Minnesota Press.

Richardson, Chad, and Michael J. Pisani. 2017. *Batos, Bolillos, Pochos, Pelados: Class and Culture on the South Texas Border.* Austin: University of Texas Press.

———. 2012. *The Informal Underground Economy of the South Texas Border*. Austin: University of Texas Press.

Ricou, Laurie. 2002. *The Arbutus/Madrone Files: Reading the Pacific Northwest*. Corvallis: Oregon State University Press.

Roberts, Gillian, ed. 2018. *Reading Between the Borderlines: Cultural Production and Consumption Across the 49th Parallel*. Montréal and Kingston: McGill-Queen's University Press.

———. 2015. *Discrepant Parallels: Cultural Implications of the Canada-US Border*. Montréal and Kingston: McGill-Queen's University Press.

Roberts, Gillian, and David Stirrup, eds. 2013. *Parallel Encounters: Culture at the Canada-US Border*. Waterloo, ON: Wilfrid Laurier University.

Rodney, Lee. 2017. *Looking Beyond Borderlines: North America's Frontier Imagination*. New York: Routledge.

Rosaldo, Renato. 1993. *Culture and Truth: The Remaking of Social Analysis*. Boston: Beacon.

Rosière, Stéphane, and Reece Jones. 2012. "Teichopolitics: Re-Considering Globalization through the Role of Walls and Fences. " *Geopolitics* 17 (1): 217–234.

Rouvière, Laetitia. 2019. "Entre souveraineté indigène et sécurité nationale: négocier la sécurité frontalière et la culture Mohawk à Akwesasne." *The Canadian Geographer/Le Géographe canadien* 63 (1): 57–68.

Rumford, Chris. 2011. "Seeing Like a Border." *Political Geography* 30 (2): 67–68.

Rumley, Dennis, and Julian V. Minghi, eds. 1991. *The Geography of Border Landscapes*. New York: Routledge.

Sadowski-Smith, Claudia, ed. 2002. *Globalization on the Line: Culture, Capital, and Citizenship at U.S. Borders*. New York: Palgrave Macmillan.

Sahlins, Peter. 1989. *Boundaries: The Making of France and Spain in the Pyrenees*. Berkeley: University of California Press.

Saleebey, Dennis. 1994. "Culture, Theory and Narrative." *Social Work* 39 (4): 351–359.

Schimanski, Johan, and Jopi Nyman, eds. 2021. *Border Images, Border Narratives: The Political Aesthetics of Boundaries and Crossings*. Manchester: Manchester University Press.

Schimanski, Johan, and Stephen F. Wolfe, eds. 2017. *Border Aesthetics: Concepts and Intersections*. Oxford: Berghahn.

Sheller, Mimi, and John Urry. 2004. *Tourism Mobilities: Places to Play, Places in Play*. New York: Routledge.

Shimoni, Baruch. 2006. "Cultural Borders, Hybridization, and a Sense of Boundaries in Thailand, Mexico and Israel." *Journal of Anthropological Research* 62 (2): 217–234.

Shweder, Richard A. 1984. *Culture Theory: Essays on Mind, Self and Emotion*. Cambridge: Cambridge University Press.

Sioui, Konrad. 2020. "Notice to Our Collaborators: Strategic Partnership between the Huron-Wendat Nation and Archaeological Services Inc. (ASI)." Huron-Wendat Nation, Wendake, June 17, 2020.

Sohn, Christophe. 2014. "Modelling Cross-Border Integration: The Role of Borders as a Resource." *Geopolitics* 19 (3): 587–608.

Sparke, Matthew. 2002. "Not a State, but More than a State of Mind: Cascading Cascadias and the Geoeconomics of Cross-Border Regionalism." In *Globalization, Regionalization and Cross-Border Regions*, edited by Markus Perkmann and Ngai-Ling Sum, 212–238. London: Palgrave Macmillan.

———. 2000. "Excavating the Future in Cascadia: Geoeconomics and the Imagined Geographies of a Cross-Border Region." *BC Studies: The British Columbia Quarterly*, no. 127 (Autumn): 5–44.

Steger, Manfred B., and Paul James. 2013. "Levels of Subjective Globalization: Ideologies, Imaginaries, Ontologies." *Perspectives on Global Development and Technology* 12 (1–2): 17–40.

Stirrup, David, and Gillian Roberts. 2010. "Introduction to the ARCS Special Issue on Culture and the Canada-US Border." *American Review of Canadian Studies* 40 (3): 321–325.

Tucker, Brian, and Reuben Rose-Redwood. 2015. "Decolonizing the Map? Toponymic Politics and the Rescaling of the Salish Sea." *The Canadian Geographer/Le Géographe canadien* 59 (2): 194–206.

Turner, Victor. 1969. *The Ritual Process: Structure and Anti-structure*. Chicago: Aldine.

Urry, John. 2007. *Mobilities*. London: Polity.

Vandervalk, Sandra. 2017. "Line Dancing." Master's thesis, Carleton University.

Vila, Pablo. 2003. *Ethnography at the Border*. Minneapolis: University of Minnesota Press.

Villa, Raul H. 2000. *Barrio-Logos: Space and Place in Urban Chicano Literature and Culture*. Austin: University of Texas Press.

Walters, William. 2006. "Rethinking Borders Beyond the State." *Comparative European Politics* 4 (2–3): 141–159.

Weier, Sebastien. 2017. Review of *Discrepant Parallels: Cultural Implications of the Canada-US Border*, by Gillian Roberts. *European Journal of American Studies*, reviews 2017-1, document 10. http://journals.openedition.org/ejas/11971.

VIEWING BORDER CULTURE

CHAPTER 1

Sight and Site on the Line
The Cultural Imaginary of Borderlands in North America

Lee Rodney

Resuscitating Borderlands in the Era of the Borderline

This chapter considers contemporary art and media projects located in North American border regions in the last decade and their role as critical practices and forms of translocal resistance against the tide of separation and securitization that has governed borders since 2001. I aim to contextualize two collaborative transborder "research-creation" projects that I have been involved with since 2010 and the questions they raise in relation to cultural borderlands between Canada and the United States. I am interested in comparative borderlands perspectives and the role that borderlands can have as heterogeneous regions that offer the possibility for navigating political change through activating an understanding of place outside of national settler cultures or histories. In mapping the "affective economies" (Ahmed 2004) of borders, many recent art and media practices locate how borderlands produce forms of alterity while also revealing new struggles, patterns of belonging, or "communities of sense" that stand apart from national concerns. The recognition and localization of Indigenous histories and territorial rights plays an important role in challenging the power of national borders by activating a spatial imagination that is not bound by a geographic line. In the US-Mexico borderlands, the role of Indigeneity in counteracting the power of the borderline has long been recognized (Anzaldúa 1987); yet a widespread understanding of cultural borderlands that traverse the Canada-US boundary remains partial and contingent in comparison. This is particularly the case when one considers how Indigeneity or cultural hybridity traverses, overrides, or occludes the Canada-US boundary line as a form of spatial knowledge. Arguably, this is changing as Indigenous artists and activists question the legitimacy of the Canada-US boundary line in vital ways (Miner 2014; Devine 2015).

I begin with the premise that borders are first understood through images, as maps are powerful pictures drawn by borderlines. Borders are maintained culturally as both virtual or imagined places *and* as embodied experiences in concrete locations. They are also archival formations produced through social and political crises over time (Young 2019). Although borders form the periphery of the nation-state, they are often imagined from the centre or they are sensed in ways that are not easily quantified. In the twenty-first century, images continue to have a significant hold on the national imagination of borders as intensively mediated sites that have become representational motifs of globalization's failures and fractures, intensifying a nationalist politics of fear over the last two decades (Konrad and Nicol 2011; Rodney 2017). This is not to discount the effect that borders have on the places they traverse or the people that move through them, but to acknowledge the cultural imagination of the border and its meaning in national and global contexts.

In North America, borders have worked to shape national consciousness since their formation in the eighteenth and nineteenth centuries, shifting in their cultural meaning and relative political importance over time. In the twenty-first century, it is often noted that North Americans are just as likely to cross borders in airports as through land ports of entry, and new forms of extraterritorial borders have engendered significant commentary as technologies of US border control (Correa-Cabrera and Saudt 2014; Roberts and Stirrup 2013). Yet the persistent image of the Mexico-US land border and, since 2017, the Canada-US border as sites of apparent crisis has kept the idea of the land border at the forefront of mainstream media and political debates. There has been a pervasive media focus on the borderline itself as a site of invasion, produced by media spectacle of various kinds, from crime dramas such as *The Border* (CBC) or *Narcos* (Netflix) to the coverage of the 2018 "migrant caravan" on social media and mainstream networks. The recurring message is that borders are inherently dangerous places or zones of vice, and no amount of border security is ever enough. While borders are maintained as securitized administrative sites, they are also maintained politically as both virtual or imagined places. This view of the border has influenced the ways in which political debates on immigration are unfolding in the US, Canada, and Mexico.

What has become lost in the noise of crisis media and entertainment television of the last decade is the sense of optimism that had once accompanied the promise of the borderless world in the 1990s, the celebration of hybridity that could be found in the Mexico-US borderlands as a region that spanned the line both historically and as an ideal for the future. So too has the idea of the borderland as a zone of historic migration routes that connect Indigenous peoples of the Americas withered in recent political consciousness. The Chicano/a mantra "We didn't cross the border, the border crossed us," so frequently reiterated from the 1970s through the 1990s, has rarely been noted in recent years. The borderline and its enforcement have overtaken our understanding of cross-boundary regions, and transverse migration routes that do not correspond to international borders in North America have been moved off the map. Yet these older narratives point to national borders as colonial artifacts and are out of step with the trend toward greater border enforcement, contradicting nationalist ideals of the border as they have been emerging in the last two decades.

In this way, border regions have served as sites for a number of activists, artists, and writers to question the ways that contemporary bordering practices condition our thinking about territory, power, and belonging through tracing how communities that span or cross the border have been disconnected as border security has increased since 2001. Given the centrality of borders as key geopolitical sites within globalization, one might ask what role art might play in understanding their operations. Or to put it another way, how might we understand borders in terms of their "affective economies" (Ahmed 2004)? One way of beginning to answer this question is to say that borders are sensed. They do not have the permanence that we tend to attribute to them. They are also maintained culturally as both virtual or imagined places *and* as embodied experiences in concrete locations.

In recent years, scholars have articulated how borders have become "relational" and "mobile" (Amilhat Szary and Giraut 2015) as borderscapes that fold both inward and outward and as "practices, performances and discourses" (Brown 2010; Rajaram 2007). This departs from an earlier descriptive trend toward describing borders viscerally: Rob Shields (2006, 226) writes that borders are virtual interfaces that are actualized through "embodied behaviours and concrete objects." He describes the habitual routines and the soft operational culture of the border (from quotidian crossings to policing, patrolling, defining, refining, and redefining) as the "real meat" of this subject rather than the border's hard "exoskeleton of gates, fences, signage or border posts." Their enforcement is performative and embodied (Shields 2006). Shields is not alone in describing borders in terms of the body politic of the nation-state: the Chicana poet Gloria Anzaldúa very famously referenced the US-Mexico border as an open wound on the Americas, "una herida abierta" that never heals, "the lifeblood of two worlds merging to form a third country—a border culture" (Anzaldúa 1987). In a very different context in the nineteenth century, the German geographer Friedrich Ratzel described nation-state borders as "a skin of the living state" (Henrikson 2011, 86). I am compelled to think about how powerful these diverse bodily metaphors are in activating our imagination around borders: in Anzaldúa's case as a continental wound, in Ratzel's, conversely, as a kind of ethnic skin.

Borders are activated by the differential cultures they produce. This is the case whether one considers the US-Mexico border, where there is no distance between the two nations, or the gaping maritime border between North Africa and Europe, where the Mediterranean serves as the zone of separation between two worlds. These two locations have become emblematic of global border crises in which Europe and North America strive to maintain a distinction between the Global North and the Global South as a cultural schism. In this vein, it is often thought that the Canada-US border does not have a differential "culture" in the same way that these highly securitized and mediatized borders have. Until recently, border studies in Canada tended to shy away from comparative contexts under the presumption that the nationalized Anglo-settler histories in Canada and the US are similar enough to treat the border as an abstraction of political economy, or as fodder for jokes. When I first began researching cultural expressions of borders in a comparative North American context, I often ran up against the presumption that the Canada-US border does not have a "culture." Variations on the idea that the Canada-US border has no culture emerge through a kind of geographic determinism whereby borderlands are also seen to be cultural wastelands that lack legitimacy within mainstream national consciousness.

Over the course of the twentieth century, border regions in North America have stood as abjected sites in the cultural imagination: as sites of criminality (from Prohibition to the so-called war on drugs that began over thirty years ago) or the environmental degradation and destruction wrought by transnational industry since the 1960s. More recently, borderlands spaces have been again cast as sites of "migrant invasions." We are familiar with these locations from the reports from Roxham Road, in Canada, on the New York-Quebec border, that started in 2017 and the so-called migrant caravan that dominated headlines in the last six months of 2018.

Border regions and borderlands are not celebrated or articulated in the same way that national cultures are. In this, they fit Raymond Williams's distinction between capital "C" Culture and a plurality of small "c" cultures that often escape notice (Williams 1998). Borderlands and border cultures are relational, conditional, and diverse. On the subject of the Canada-US border, one has to be an astute observer. We tend to read borders in terms of a play between visibility and invisibility—almost as though we want to be able to see the border marked in space in the same way that we see it on a map. And, within globalization's recent history, we tend to want to "see" the border more than ever. Border building in the form of walls and security fences has increased since 1989 rather than abated (Vallet 2016).

My research considers borderlands as "sites of dissensus" activated to question both the authority of the nation-state and the exclusionary paradigms of Western aesthetics (Rodney 2017). My conceptual thinking around the role of the senses in bordering practices has been informed by Jacques Rancière's distinction between the "aesthetics of politics" and the "politics of aesthetics," which provides a theoretical basis to consider both the historical development of national borders in North America and more recent restructuring exercises of the last two decades (Rancière 2010b). Following Rancière, governmental practices of bordering are visual strategies that have created North American borders as a specific, naturalized "distribution of the sensible" that frames a common idea of security policy. This is the case whether one considers the built environment of a border wall or a media report of migrant apprehensions near the borderline. Rancière's idea of consensus is rather atypical. For him, consensus is not something that is arrived at democratically but rather through the "visibility of the common" that is framed by objectifying situations so that they are no longer open for discussion (Rancière 2010a). However, as a "distribution of the sensible" the border is also subject to disruption through forms of "dissensus" that reorder our perception of the space, however temporarily, to consider it otherwise.

The Border Bookmobile: Mapping Affect on the Canada-US Border

Border regions are difficult places to research and characterize in terms of history and culture as national narratives are materially embedded in capital cities in museums and archives. The historical archives of the Canada-US border are mostly held in Ottawa or Washington, DC, and writing about borderlands culture is complicated by the schism between local knowledge and political history, which tends to be written along national lines. In response to this schism, I developed a transborder travelling archive, the Border Bookmobile, a project that served as a means to contextualize the border cities of Windsor and Detroit within the shifting narratives of border regions in North America and other parts of the world in the aftermath of 9/11 and the 2008 economic crisis (figure 1.1). Housed in a 1993 Chrysler minivan, the collection also served as an impromptu meeting place where visitors would share impressions of the "other side" or stories of significant border crossings.

The project ran between 2009 and 2013 and visited twelve public sites in Windsor, Detroit, and Toronto. Its collection grew as the project did, and eventually it was exhibited in the form of a public reading room and archive at the Art Gallery of Windsor during the 2013 *Border Cultures* exhibition (curated by Srimoyee Mitra, see chapter 4, this volume). As part of *Border Cultures*, it additionally served as the site for public workshops and talks that took up ideas around borders within and between cities as well as the production of space within borderlands in more heterogeneous and contested parts of the world. Workshops and seminars focused on narratives of migration across borders in the Americas as well as the local impact of new passport regulations on low-income populations in downtown Windsor and Detroit since 2009.

In pulling together a collection of local history (books, maps, photographs, and ephemera) for the bookmobile, I became aware that Windsor's history only tangentially references Detroit and that Detroit's history is entirely free of any reference to Windsor. This was the case in looking at local libraries and archives, where collections reflected national histories. Official history stops at the border, but

TOP: **FIGURE 1.1.** The Border Bookmobile, Ambassador Park, Windsor, Ontario, 2011. *Source:* Photo, Lee Rodney. BOTTOM: **FIGURE 1.2.** The Border Bookmobile, Belle Isle, Detroit, 2011. *Source:* Photo, Lee Rodney.

long-time residents of both cities will suggest a very different interpretation of place, one that is often narrated by a sense that the two cities were, in the past, continuous and uninterrupted and that Windsor was one of many Detroit neighbourhoods rather than a border town of another country (see also Darroch, chapter 2, this volume). I made a series of short videos, a collage of impressions about these border cities as told by residents on either side: Windsorites talked about Detroit and Detroiters recalled their time spent in Windsor. Many people relayed the difficulty of crossing after 2009, when passport regulations became more stringent (Rodney 2014).

If the Canada-US border was known for many years as the world's longest undefended boundary during the Cold War, it was also forming in the late 1960s as a formidable cultural barrier between Canada and its southern neighbour. Canada's post-1967 story posited a cultural mosaic as a more enlightened answer to America's melting pot, neither metaphor working particularly well to describe the historic subtexts of race and class in either country. Implicit in the idea of the mosaic was a more suspicious rewriting of history, whereby Canada understood itself on moral high ground in relation to its American neighbour, with its long public history of slavery and systemic racism. Between Windsor and Detroit, the Canada-US border absorbs these national narratives in a partial and contingent fashion. The Windsor-Detroit region, like many other border regions in North America, has been marked by cultural, environmental, and economic turmoil. In 1967, as Windsor celebrated Canada's Centennial with ceremonial brass, Detroit was in the throes of its Great Rebellion, the city on lockdown after the national guard was sent in during five intense days of civil disturbance in response to growing racial segregation and profiling in the city (McMahon and Hoffmann 2014). Again in 2017, Canada's 150th anniversary coincided with the 50th anniversary of the Detroit Rebellion. The collision of these two narratives, one of national pride and the other national shame, has tended to frame Windsor's view of its American neighbour. The site of the Canada-US border here has also become a significant racial barrier between Windsor's predominantly suburban, White working class and Detroit's predominantly black, urban population.

The Border Bookmobile served to mitigate the divergent perspectives of Windsor and Detroit as border cities and to make sense of why so much of the urban region felt emptied out. When looking at historical photographs of both cities, the visual record of the local suggested the optimism of the past and the possibilities for an international city that spanned the Canada-US border: crowded streets and pictures of multiple ferries that ran across the river almost constantly until the 1950s. Plans for the "Americanada Teleferry," a gondola that was proposed to link Detroit's Cobo Center to Windsor's waterfront in the 1960s, accompanied Detroit's bid for the Olympics in 1964.

The project emerged in response to a series of crises in North America that manifested quite squarely in Windsor and Detroit. The most apparent of these was the crisis of mobility after 9/11. But the economic recession as well as the long, slow decline of urban culture that began in the middle of the twentieth century also played a part in the post-urban malaise that had set in. The Border Bookmobile sought to research some of these complex problems by pulling together an archive of books and ephemera to serve as a historical and comparative resource where conventional public resources were slim or dispersed across national lines. While this archive could never be complete or perhaps even that useful to form lasting connections across the border, it provided a means to remap the region in terms of the multiple borders that have emerged here, particularly since the 1950s.

The bookmobile's archive came together as a collection to serve not only as a historical repository of material about these cities, but also, and more importantly, as a form of experimental research, pedagogy, and urban exchange. As a community archive, it worked to reconcile the multiple and conflicting histories about the region and to think beyond the immediate crisis of the border that had hit Windsor so squarely in 2008. The bookmobile's collection was housed in a 1993 Chrysler minivan, itself a product of local history as the Windsor Assembly Plant was the first to manufacture the iconic vehicle. The van and its collection served to solicit oral history as visitors shared memories and experiences of living in this border region. In talking to people about their everyday experiences of the border as well as their relationship to the other side, the project aimed to draw out the type of affect that the border produces as a series of micro-political views that locates the region's history within larger narratives of globalization. For three years, the Border Bookmobile travelled throughout locations in Windsor and Detroit as a social platform that aimed to animate and activate discussion on the history and future of the two cities as well as the impact of changes in border policies that were taking place at the time. The bookmobile's archive chronicled the changing relationship between the two largest cities on the Canada-US border as a microcosm of the shifting status of the international boundary between the two countries. The archive also highlighted the variety of ways that borders have been imagined, represented, and constructed in North America since their formation in the nineteenth century: first as colonial and nationalizing instruments, then tourist attractions in the twentieth century, and most recently as part of a larger security and surveillance complex.

Crossing, Walking, and Counter-Mapping: Reimagining the Border Otherwise

The Border Bookmobile emerged as a form of social practice to activate conversations about the shifting nature of the Canada-US border. Social, locative, and relational practices in the arts have become increasingly important forms of collaborative artistic practice in the last decade. Arts collectives and creative collaborative networks worldwide have emerged in response to the fractious political pressures around migration that have become manifest within contested borderlands sites. In the last decade, many artists, activists, and creative researchers have responded to the oversimplified political rhetoric about border regions by a variety of walking and participatory counter-mapping events and projects. These often explore questions of belonging, movement, and displacement in and around national boundaries in global contexts.

"Border art," as it was characterized in the 1990s, took place as performative or public acts on the physical site of the border. The genre has developed and shifted as the physical space of the border has expanded and border surveillance practices have multiplied beyond the site of the borderline itself. Where the emphasis of borderlands discourse tended to be performative and literary in the 1990s, relational art and architecture, social practices, and tactical and locative media approaches have all worked to make visible the complex and interrelated problems that manifest at the border, even though they may originate elsewhere. At the same time, the long-standing relationship between aesthetics and politics as mutually exclusive domains has been challenged from a number of perspectives, through questioning the limits of the domain of each sphere and the degree to which they are understood as separate modes of thinking and sensing. The relationship between the political and the aesthetic has been reoriented through new configurations described in terms like "migratory aesthetics," "relational aesthetics," or "decolonial aesthetics," or through mediatic configurations such as "tactical media" and "electronic disturbance." The Electronic Disturbance Theatre refers to its collaborative practice as "artivism" rather than activism in discussing the impact of their Transborder Immigrant Tool, a well-known locative media project that distributed a GPS cell phone application to migrants to help navigate the hostile cross-border territory of the Sonoran Desert in 2007 (Electronic Disturbance Theatre, n.d.). This shift between the domains of politics and aesthetics is notable in a number of practices that blur the lines between the two.

Since the Transborder Immigrant Tool was devised in 2007, locative media practices have provided alternative forms of navigating, mapping, and comprehending the conceptual and physical territory of borderland spaces in North America. Practices of walking are critical to understanding borderlands in terms of the social flows (both contemporary and historical) that are embedded in these spaces. The Political Equator conference, organized by Estudio Teddy Cruz and the NGO Alta Terra and held in the San Ysidro-Tijuana borderlands in 2011, organized an "irregular crossing" for participants. The

FIGURE 1.3. Political Equator 3: June 3–4, 2011. *Source:* Photo, Lee Rodney.

peripatetic conference began in San Ysidro, moving to the Tijuana Estuary on the second day through a drainage culvert under the newly constructed border wall that afternoon. This atypical crossing from the US into Mexico was staged as a participatory event for the conference, challenging the ideas of legal and illegal flows by reversing the logic of clandestine migration through tunnels and other unofficial points of entry to circumvent the architecture of the border wall. Nearly a hundred conference participants waited in a drainage culvert to enter Mexico from the US, where an impromptu checkpoint was established with Mexican border agents who performed their normal duties stamping passports for day tourists to Tijuana (Cruz 2011).

In a similar vein, three years later, across the continent on the Canada-US border, the Tug Collective staged Re/Thinking Paul Bunyan, a group crossing as a parade at the Maine-Quebec border featuring a large-scale puppet, an effigy of the legendary figure of Paul Bunyan. A careful reading of the Paul Bunyan story from 1929 revealed his origin story as a turn-of-the-twentieth-century migrant worker who left Quebec and became the legendary patron saint of the lumber industry and westward expansion in the US. The transborder crossing parade from the US into Canada sought to symbolically return Mr. Bunyan to his "native" Québécois "homeland." This carnivalesque transborder walk took place in 2014 at Coborn Gore, a rural crossing between northern Maine and Quebec. Gaelyn and Gustavo Aguilar have worked as the Tug Collective for many years, organizing workshops and collaborative projects that activate social issues in contested spaces. Their work engages mapping as a central metaphor, producing "contingent, unpredictable and open-system maps," as a form of Deleuzian cartography that is capable of "unearthing" alternative understanding of space and identity. They have frequently worked in the US-Mexico borderlands, and their practice is informed by a borderlands ethos, emphasizing the importance of holding open multiple and heterogeneous sources of knowledge and practice "without the antagonistic imperative to choose sides" (Aguilar and Aguilar 2012).

These forms of collaborative resistance against the borderline as a partition can be found in both the 2011 Political Equator conference (US-Mexico) and the 2014 Re/Thinking Paul Bunyan crossing (US-Canada). As transborder, peripatetic events, participants walk along or through spaces that are increasingly reserved for

FIGURE 1.4. Re/Thinking Paul Bunyan (Maine and Quebec), Coborn Gore border crossing, 2012. *Source:* Photo, Gaelyn Aguilar.

automobiles and trucks. The projects thus activate lines of desire that form "social trails" activated through performative walks (Aguilar and Aguilar 2012). While the circumstances for each crossing are remarkably varied, the border has served in these cases as a theatre of the mind, activating an alternative imagination of its intended purposes with border authorities serving as key actors in these performative crossings. In both instances, the port of entry is activated as a site study: from its security infrastructure to its economic and environmental impacts.

While North American borders worked as instruments of colonization in the nineteenth century, we are less inclined to think of them this way in the twenty-first century. However, some of the most strident critical openings of the border have come from a decolonial perspective. The artist collective Postcommodity has worked along the US-Mexico border to contest the militarization of Indigenous territory: the construction of the border fence and increasing surveillance throughout the region. Their large-scale project, Repellent Fence (Postcommodity 2015), was a temporary transborder line stretching two miles from Douglas, Arizona, to Agua Prieta, Sonora, across the US-Mexico border through traditional Tohono O'odham lands. The

Repellent Fence was formed through a series of "scare eye" balloons creating a line that ran perpendicular to the US-Mexico boundary. The balloons were enlarged versions of commercial agricultural balloons used to repel birds from crops. Postcommodity's series of giant balloons across the US-Mexico border worked to "suture" communities that are divided by the fence and to symbolically connect Indigenous peoples of the Americas hemispherically. Their work positions Indigenous struggles within the context of contemporary immigration crises by correlating migration routes with Indigenous trade routes, thereby calling attention to the border as a colonial instrument of control. As a series of dots connecting American and Mexican territory with Indigenous ancestral land, the Repellent Fence asks us to sense an erasure that the US-Mexico border fence has systematically enacted in all of its guises, from a surveyed line in the nineteenth century to a highly militarized zone in the twenty-first. In traversing the border across Tohono O'odham lands, the Repellent Fence serves as a tactic to open out this nationalized and highly securitized territory to a decolonial perspective that is silenced in the current political moment.

Buoyant Cartographies:
Alternative Mapping Practices of the Detroit River

Inspired by borderlands art projects like Postcommodity's Repellent Fence, I organized a mobile research-creation workshop in September 2018 (with Justin Langlois, Michael Darroch, Talysha Abu-Bujold, Taien Ng-Chan, Donna Akrey, and Holly Schmidt). This group of artists, historians, and geographers guided investigations of the space of the Detroit River as a migratory route to bring the histories of the Great Lakes into a wider transboundary understanding of migration in the Americas. We intentionally positioned the river as a point of connection or thoroughfare rather than as a dividing line that the international boundary line runs through. We thus focused our attention on specific shoreline locations on or at the river's edge. Our group included Indigenous and non-Indigenous collaborators as well as local and visiting participants. At the southernmost tip of the Great Lakes system, the Detroit River connects Lake St. Clair with Lake Erie, and it presently divides the nation-states of Canada and the United States, and the cities of Windsor, Ontario, and Detroit, Michigan. Focusing our attention on this river border as a material site and geopolitical space enabled us to investigate alternate possibilities for sensing and envisioning the layered and conjoined histories of this fluid space. The Ojibwe name for this location is *waawiiatanongziibi*, or where the river bends, suggesting a radically different spatial imaginary than the divided space that has been established through colonial and national histories (Nahdee 2016). Experimental cartographies can thus help to develop alternate ways of experiencing such sites, an initial step toward decolonizing the spatial imaginary through a project of delinking. Our Buoyant Cartographies workshop focused on performative and intermedial investigations into spatial meanings and their construction through walking workshops conducted on the Detroit and Windsor shorelines, as well as on Peche Island, which sits in the middle of the Detroit River.

Buoyant Cartographies took place on the Detroit River, with presentations on histories of migration that took place prior to the twentieth century. The workshop began with the premise that Great Lakes waterways can be understood as active sites for tracing alternative, decolonial histories that move beyond modern nation-state dichotomies. While the Great Lakes currently form a water border that separates Canada from the United States, the workshop began with the Detroit River as a historic point of connection rather than division. As the Canada-US border becomes increasingly regulated, thinking about social and cultural relationships that traverse these

FIGURE 1.5. Buoyant Cartographies workshop, September 1, 2018. *Source*: Photo, Lee Rodney.

borders becomes difficult and negatively impacts how decolonization unfolds as a political project. Tracing a transborder cultural geography of the Great Lakes (one that is neither American nor Canadian) is an important step toward counteracting the limited understanding of borderlands as sites that become visible through the media, mainly through crises of trade or global migration.

The workshop explored the historical and cultural relationships between water, practices of transit, and histories of migration before the border was established in this region as a decolonial approach to thinking beyond the nationalized spaces of the Canada-US borderlands. In combining the mapping practices of the three collaborative research groups (the IN/TERMINUS Research Group, the Hamilton Perambulatory Unit, and Float School, from Windsor, Hamilton, and Vancouver respectively), our conversations elicited an understanding of the creation of the Great Lakes borderlands through a significantly longer historical perspective, one motivated by ecological and decolonial issues rather than current national maps. Our interests coalesced around the Great Lakes waterways as an alternative spatial imaginary, a space of connection rather than division. As the Canada-US border runs through the centre of Lakes Superior, Huron, Erie, and Ontario, the Great Lakes have been subject to competing national priorities and environmental standards as well as border surveillance exercises. These twenty-first-century political pressures to interpret borderlines as hard limits or boundaries tend to erase forms of vernacular knowledge and cross-border cooperation.

Like the Political Equator conference that took place on the US-Mexico border in 2011, our Buoyant Cartographies workshop served as a peripatetic discussion and "stratigraphic walk" that traced the strata observed by workshop participants. During our three shoreline tours, we presented public walks that emphasized different forms of transborder history and migration across the river and traced the ways in which Indigenous history and Black history have been occluded in the public spaces that flank the official Windsor and Detroit Riverwalks. We also spent time on the Detroit River observing the migration of industrial and environmental particulate, as well as the return of migratory species to Belle Island (US) and Peche Island (Canada).

"The Water Communication" was a descriptive phrase used in the 1783 Treaty of Paris to describe the Great Lakes as a central conduit between American and British territorial possessions (Bellfy 2013). This colonial description of the international boundary between

Canada and the US, one that runs through Great Lakes, suggests a more open and fluid interpretation of settler territory than is currently permitted through our twenty-first-century national-security complex that has emerged on the Great Lakes. As water has traditionally posed problems for geographic surveys and boundary demarcation, we focused on mapping the ways in which water has facilitated (and continues to facilitate) the movement of people, animals, and plants across the Detroit River and the surrounding region. This region is near the centre of the Great Lakes Basin and is one of the oldest continuously settled regions in North America. It is home to the Three Fires Confederacy of the Ojibwe, Odawa, Potawatomi, and Huron-Wendat Peoples. The historian Phil Bellfy (Chippewa) describes the fraught history of the border in this region—especially in the upper Great Lakes, where successive colonial-era treaties describe only a loose boundary following the flow of Lakes Superior and Huron through the St. Mary's River—as a "water communication" that granted sovereign rights to Indigenous peoples residing at *Bawating*, the "gathering place" of the Chippewa and Ojibwe, who are now divided by the present-day Canada-US border (Bellfy 2013, 206). Extending Bellfy's historical research on Indigeneity in the upper Great Lakes, Dylan Miner (Wiisaakodewinini/Métis) refers to the entire Great Lakes watershed—a cultural region that "we should properly call *Anishinaabewaki*"—as an *axis mundus*, a cosmic axis (Miner 2014, 2).

The French colonial outpost Le D'Etroit was situated at the "narrows" of the Detroit River at the site of present-day Detroit, Michigan, and Windsor, Ontario. The site has been described by American historians as a "frontier metropolis" (Dunnigan 2001). Recent historical accounts have woven together a more complex understanding of the nature of trade and slavery within this region. In her book *The Dawn of Detroit*, historian Tiya Miles describes the Detroit River in the seventeenth, eighteenth, and nineteenth centuries as the "straits of slavery," pulling together histories of the French fur trade and the American slave trade into a continuous and overlapping narrative in the middle of the continent (Miles 2017). Miles weaves together Indigenous and Black history into a transboundary account. Historical projects like this are essential to understanding the Detroit River and the Great Lakes region more generally as a significant geographic passage that has enabled many forms of "trade" and migration, casting new light on the legacy of the underground railroad and histories of slavery that extend into Upper and Lower Canada.

One of the main goals of the Buoyant Cartographies workshop was to research, visit, and map a particularly contested site on the Detroit River: the bend in the Detroit River that is currently the proposed site of the Gordie Howe International Bridge between Sandwich, Ontario, and Delray, Michigan. This heavily trafficked and politically contested site is situated where the River Rouge runs into the Detroit River at Springwells, Michigan, and where the Sandwich Mineral Springs and Lagoon entered the settlement of Sandwich, Ontario, until the early part of the twentieth century. This area forms an axis across the river that is conjoined geologically; it is a rich location in the Aboriginal histories of the Potawatomi, the Ojibwe, and the Odowa (Ferris 2009), as well as the Wyandot of Anderdon (Walsh 2017). However, these histories are difficult to sense as the industrial landscape and the growing border complexes on the Canadian and American shores dominate the landscape and limit access. Currently, salt mines run underneath the Detroit River and the international border cuts down its centre; the river here has become a barrier rather than a point of connection or contact. As such, this mapping workshop served to ask significant questions around the relationships between landscape, territory, and conventionally held notions of power, such as which national narratives and spaces are celebrated and prized and what histories are occluded or hidden from view (Ng-Chan 2020)? The maps produced in the workshop represent layers of information from diverse contributors and offer new perspectives to the shoreline-river relationship in ways that complicate our understanding of the Detroit River as an environmental wasteland or international dividing line.

This ongoing research-creation project aims to complicate the role of the Great Lakes in forming part of the Canada-US border. In mapping translocal knowledge and enabling collaborative forms of public history, our workshop located and marked critical insertion points in the mainstream narratives that mark public spaces along the Windsor and Detroit shorelines in official ways. In future projects, we aim to print self-guided walking tours that emphasize where transborder histories and environmental and Indigenous knowledge should be recognized, and in what ways these histories are occluded through the present-day spatial order dominated by the urban landscapes and the disorienting infrastructure of the border patrol complexes on either side. As a form of "research creation," Buoyant Cartographies took its lead from the spatial turn in the arts, through which new articulations of "communities of sense" have been established to describe a fundamental shift in the way that we understand aesthetics and politics as mutually informing one another rather than as separated domains (Hinderliter et al. 2011).

Conclusion

"Communities of sense," however tangential or temporary they might be, are vital to understanding border culture and borderlands. The projects discussed here, whether on the US-Mexico or Canada-US border, share a view to the borderlands that is informed by temporary and relational events. These events create communities of sense that work against the spatial partitioning of the border and the colonial and national histories embedded in the spatial duality imposed through the borderline. Recognizing and mapping what can be traced or sensed within the borderlands does not come at the expense of political activism; rather, it deepens our awareness of the multiple and diachronic social trails that persist in spite of the tightly controlled spaces of the border. The projects discussed here create counter-cartographies that use mapping processes to visualize forms of historical erasure as well as the complexities of conflict that are not apparent in geographic convention. Counter-cartography holds a kind of metaphorical power in tracing histories of oppression: writing on the history of slavery in early Detroit for example, Tiya Miles encourages us to "flip our maps" to forget what we know about the city in the middle of the American "mid-West" (2017, 3). The inverted or subjective map calls into question ingrained ideas about the division between the Global South and Global North, tying into subjective forms of cartography that visualize conflictual or ambiguous relationships that are often produced in borderlands spaces.

The projects discussed in this chapter follow a growing interest around "borderscapes" that seek to account for the role of aesthetics in comprehending contemporary bordering practices. The concept of the "borderscape" extends the insights of borderlands discourse by considering its complexity and relationality as a cultural, political, and technological formation (Rajaram and Warr 2007; Dell'Agnese and Amilhat Szary 2015; Schimanski 2019). However, the projects here are also specific to a North American context, and thus seek to draw attention to the settler-colonial conditions shared at both the northern and southern borders of the US. Thus, the way that the projects focus on the embodied experience of being at the border call attention, once again, to the borderlands as undivided and continuous. As such, they work with and against the overriding imaginary produced by the borderscape. Walking in environments designed for automobile traffic calls attention to the counter-cartographies we can employ to understand the ways in which borders become naturalized and invisible through territorial narratives and the spatial partitioning of the built environment. Each project draws out the transborder flows, diasporas, and migrations that enable a richer understanding of political and social space in some of the multiple borderlands in North America, suggesting how we might imagine other lines and points of connection that contest the singularity of the borderline.

Acknowledgements

The author would like to thank the Social Sciences and Humanities Research Council of Canada for a Connection Grant to support the 2018 Buoyant Cartographies workshop, as well as the artists Donna Akrey and Taien Ng-Chan of the Hamilton Perambulatory Unit (Hamilton, Ontario); Michael Darroch (York University), co-director of the IN/TERMINUS Research Group; and Justin Langlois and Holly Schmidt of Float School (Vancouver).

References

Ahmed, Sara. 2004. "Affective Economies." *Social Text* 22 (2): 117–139.

Aguilar, Gaelyn, and Gustavo Aguilar. 2014. "Re/Thinking Paul Bunyan at the Maine-Quebec Border." Tug Collective. https://www.tugcollective.org/paul-bunyan.

———. 2012. "Fuzzy Frontiers: A Performative Materialization of Intentionality." *Critical Studies in Improvisation/Études critiques en improvisation* 8 (2). https://doi.org/10.21083/csieci.v8i2.2121.

Amilhat Szary, Anne-Laure, and Frédéric Giraut. 2015. *Borderities: The Politics of Contemporary Mobile Borders.* New York: Springer.

Anzaldúa, Gloria. 1987. *Borderlands/La Frontera: The New Mestiza.* San Francisco: Aunt Lute Books.

Bellfy, Phil. 2013. "Indigenous People Look at the Canada-U.S. Border." In *Beyond the Border: Tensions across the Forty-Ninth Parallel in the Great Plains and Prairies,* edited by Kyle Conway and Timothy Pasch 199–222. Montréal and Kingston: McGill-Queen's University Press.

Brown, Wendy. 2010. *Walled States, Waning Sovereignty*. Cambridge, MA: MIT Press.

Correa-Cabrera, Guadalupe, and Kathleen Staudt. 2014. "An Introduction to the Multiple US-Mexico Borders." *Journal of Borderlands Studies* 29 (4): 385–390. https://doi.org/10.1080/08865655.2014.982473.

Cruz, Teddy. 2011. "Political Equator 3: Reimagining the Border." *Domus for Design*, June 24, 2011. https://www.domusweb.it/en/architecture/2011/06/24/political-equator-3-reimagining-the-border.html.

Dell'Agnese, Elana, and Anne-Laure Amilhat Szary. 2015. "Borderscapes: From Border Landscapes to Border Aesthetics." *Geopolitics* 20 (1): 4–13.

Devine, Bonnie. 2015. *Battle for the Woodlands*. Acrylic paint, graphite, paper, felt, and beads, 5.5 m × 2.4 m. Art Gallery of Ontario.

Dunnigan, Brian. 2001. *Frontier Metropolis: Picturing Early Detroit, 1701–1838*, Detroit: Wayne State University Press.

Electronic Disturbance Theatre. n.d. *Transborder Immigrant Tool*. Accessed September 24, 2020. https://anthology.rhizome.org/transborder-immigrant-tool.

Ferris, Neal. 2009. *The Archeology of Native Lived Colonialism*, Tucson: University of Arizona Press.

Henrikson, Alan K. 2011. "Border Regions as Neighbourhoods." In *The Ashgate Companion to Border Studies*, edited by Doris Wastl-Walter, 85–102. Farnham, UK: Ashgate.

Hinderliter, Beth, William Kaizen, Vered Maimon, Jaleh Mansoor, and Seth McCormick. 2011. *Communities of Sense: Rethinking Aesthetics and Politics*. Durham, NC: Duke University Press.

Konrad, Victor, and Heather N. Nicol. 2011. "Border Culture: The Border between the United States and Canada and the Advancement of Borderlands Theory." *Geopolitics* 16, no. 1 (January): 70–90.

McMahon, Marian, and Phil Hoffmann. 2014. *Racing Home*. Montréal: Adventures in Research Coalition. http://racinghome.ca/.

Miles, Tiya. 2017. *The Dawn of Detroit*. New York: New Press.

Miner, Dylan. 2014. *Lake-Effect: Rurality and Ecology in the Great Lakes*. East Lansing, MI: Metrospace Gallery.

Mitra, Srimoyee. 2015. *Border Cultures*. London: Black Dog Publishers.

Nahdee, Russell. 2016. "Notes on Indigenous History in Windsor-Essex." Unpublished document. Turtle Island Aboriginal Education Centre, University of Windsor.

Ng-Chan, Taien. 2020. "Strata-Mapping the Detroit River Border with the Hamilton Perambulatory Unit." *Intermédialités*, no. 34. https://doi.org/10.7202/1070880ar.

Postcommodity. 2015. Repellent Fence (website). http://postcommodity.com/Repellent_Fence_English.html.

Rajaram, Prem Kumar, and Carl Grundy-Warr. 2007. *Borderscapes: Hidden Geographies and Politics at Territory's Edge.* Minneapolis: University of Minnesota Press.

Rancière, Jacques. 2010a. *Chronicles of Consensual Times.* Translated from French by Steven Corcoran. London: Continuum Press.

———. 2010b. *Dissensus: On Politics and Aesthetics.* Translated from French by Steven Corcoran. London: Continuum Press.

Roberts, Gillian, and David Stirrup. 2013. *Parallel Encounters: Culture at the Canada-US Border.* Waterloo, ON: Wilfrid Laurier University Press.

Rodney, Lee. 2017. *Looking Beyond Borderlines: North America's Frontier Imagination.* New York: Routledge.

———. 2014. Frontier Files (documentation of the Border Bookmobile Project and Archive). Accessed September 24, 2020. http://frontierfiles.org.

Schimanski, Johan. 2019. "Border Aesthetics." *International Lexicon of Aesthetics,* Autumn 2019. https://lexicon.mimesisjournals.com/archive/2019/autumn/BorderAesthetics.pdf.

Shields, Rob. 2006. "Boundary Thinking in Theories of the Present: The Virtuality of Reflexive Modernization." *European Journal of Social Theory* 9 (2): 223–237.

Vallet, Elisabeth. 2016. *Borders, Fences and Walls: State of Insecurity?* New York: Routledge.

Walsh, Martin. 2017. "Revenge Against the Idol: Competing Magical Systems on the Detroit River, 1670." *Michigan Historical Review* 43 (2): 55–63.

Williams, Raymond. 1998. "The Analysis of Culture." In *Cultural Theory and Popular Culture: A Reader,* edited by John Storey, 2nd ed. Athens: University of Georgia Press.

Young, Julie. 2019. "The Border as Archive: Reframing the Crisis Mode of Governance at the Canada-US Border." Paper presented at the annual meeting of the American Association of Geographers, Washington, DC, April 2019.

CHAPTER 2

Imagining Nighttime Detroit

Michael Darroch

Cultural experiences of night and day are not typically theorized in terms of borderlands or transnational cultures. Nighttime cultural life is typically identified with the intensity of urban environments and viewed through the lens of local experience rather than at the level of transnational encounters. For this reason, urban border environments offer a peculiar opportunity to consider the intense local experience of nighttime culture combined with the social and political dynamics of transnational borderlands. Border cities invite us to consider the rhythms of the city on, at, and through border culture, whether they are understood as fluid and integrated urban spaces divided by international borderlines beyond their immediate control or as the historical development of separate city enclaves abutting the same border. In this paper, I reflect upon the border cities of Detroit, Michigan, and Windsor, Ontario, which lend themselves to studying urban nighttime as both practiced and imagined across the US-Canada border. Border environments that are porous for some and impermeable for others, such as Windsor-Detroit, are productive zones for stimulating multifocal habits of vision that help us to understand the imprint made by nighttime culture on the region as a whole.

A city's nighttime is part of its signature, tied to our capacity to imagine the scale of activity or stasis that it fosters. Detroit's position on the Canadian border affords us an opportunity to examine the visual culture of its nighttime through the asymmetrical relationship

FIGURE 2.1. Neighbours. These images of Detroit at night appeared in the first issue of The Ambassador yearbook. *Source*: Assumption College High School 1939. Courtesy of the Southwestern Ontario Digital Archive, Leddy Library, University of Windsor.

between Detroit's dominant place-image and Windsor's more ambivalent sense of itself. As Detroit has emerged from bankruptcy proceedings since 2013, competing images of urban illumination and darkness have been resurrected in debates about the city's possible futures. Nostalgia for its history as a city of technical innovation—one of the first North American cities to be illuminated by electric light—has been set into relief by representations of shifting daytime and nighttime activities and city spaces plunged into darkness as its finances and infrastructure collapsed. These shifting atmospheres of illumination have evoked a range of emotional and sensual reflections on the ways in which Detroit's night is imagined and experienced, augmented through the perspectives offered by the borderline.

I first experienced Detroit at dusk, from a different country. I had arrived by train at the terminal station of Windsor, Ontario, which struck me as a kind of outpost or lookout, a small Canadian border city perched on the southeast bank of the Detroit River, opposite the dominantly lit skyline of downtown Detroit. Its peculiar location on the edge of the southwest Ontarian peninsula, tucked into the middle of Great Lakes—a point that is both terminal within

Ontario and central within the American Midwest—left me with a feeling of simultaneous connection and dislocation. Invited for a job interview at the University of Windsor the next day, I sat in my "full riverfront view" hotel room, peering out over the panorama of Detroit's nighttime skyline. This first encounter with nighttime Detroit deeply engraved itself into my subsequent appreciation of both cities.

The experience of urban nighttime has come under increasing scrutiny in cultural and historical analysis (Blum 2003; Edensor 2012). I am concerned in this essay with the ways in which perceptions and understandings of nighttime in Windsor and Detroit are wrapped up with the cities' divisions, with the borderline condition of this urban region, brought to light (as it were) most recently by the renewed debate in Detroit regarding urban illumination. To consider this, I must in part rely on my own experiences of these cities, as a resident of Windsor for nearly a decade and a frequent visitor to Detroit. (As a Caucasian, dual Canadian-US citizen, I have had the opportunity to cross this border.) The borderline condition of Windsor-Detroit encompasses a series of cultural disjunctions that only become apparent when one has been immersed in these environments and their histories.

From the vantage point of Windsor, Detroit's downtown feels as if you could reach out and touch it, yet it remains perpetually removed from Windsor's urban imagination. As Victor Konrad and Melissa Kelly note in their introduction to this volume, the "border between the United States and Canada has become a unicultural border," a point that compels us to, "reimagine the Canada-US border through a lens of border culture" (introduction). My goal in this paper is to explore how this urban structure, Detroit's presence beside and in Windsor, feels in the everyday lives of citizens in Windsor. (As my colleague Karen Engle, who co-edited the original version of this essay, once expressed, Detroit will always be Windsor's Lacanian *objet petit a*.) The research for this paper is also inspired by the writings of my colleague Lee Rodney (2017), who asks in her contribution to this volume, "How might we understand borders in terms of their 'affective economies'"? She argues: "One way of beginning to answer this question is to say that borders are sensed. They do not have the permanence that we tend to attribute to them. They are also maintained culturally as both virtual or imagined places *and* as embodied experiences in concrete locations" (chapter 1; see also Darroch, Engle, and

Rodney 2019). Drawing upon historical visual documents and contemporary media texts, I consider how Detroit's nighttime feels in, and with, Windsor—a nighttime rife with the tension between sociable activities (such as its renowned music scenes) and its depiction as a crime-ridden murder capital. One part of my argument is that the fullness of Detroit's self-concept as a nighttime city is deeply involved with how Detroit is seen from Windsor, even if today Detroiters largely ignore the city's status as a border city. Countless glossy coffee-table compendiums of Detroit images, "ruin porn," popular cultural histories of the city, as well as proposals for Detroit's urban reinvention have been published in recent years, in which Windsor is hardly mentioned as a footnote (see Gallagher 2013; LeDuff 2013). Yet Detroit's visual self-understanding has always relied upon the possibility of being seen from the outside, from across the river.

We may all be able to imagine nighttime in a city such as Detroit, but our capacity to imagine Detroit is heightened on location in Windsor where we both see and imagine the city simultaneously (I can see part of Detroit's skyline from my kitchen window through the leafy back yards of Windsor's Walkerville district). As Detroit's population grew rapidly in the 1930s and 1940s through domestic and international migration, Windsor must have felt a world apart, an outpost of the British Empire jutting into the centre of the Midwest. Detroit's population reached more than two million residents, the fourth-largest city in the United States. Yet the period of US Prohibition ending in 1933 had helped to shape Windsor's character by nourishing cross-border postwar networks of smuggling and prostitution, influencing Windsor's image as Canada's "Sin City" (Carey and Marak 2011; Karibo, 2015). At that time, the US-Canada border, of course, symbolized different colonial and national histories, but the borderlands in Windsor-Detroit remained porous, built upon and across the traditional land routes and waterways of the Wyandot and the Three Fires Confederacy of First Nations, comprised of the Ojibway, the Odawa, and the Potawatomi peoples. For early French settlers, the Detroit narrows represented a strategic location providing access and protection. Citizens from both cities have long crossed the river border in search of consumption, entertainment, vice, and fantasy—or to seek asylum from political struggles, originally by ferry, but later via the Ambassador Bridge and the Windsor-Detroit Tunnel (built in 1929 and 1930 respectively). Drawing on her archival research and ethnographic studies of local history, Rodney recalls in her essay for this volume that long-time residents of both cities acknowledge a nostalgia for a pre-9/11 border culture, one "that is often narrated by a sense that the two cities were, in the past, continuous and uninterrupted and that Windsor was one of many Detroit neighbourhoods rather than a border town of another country" (chapter 1). Windsor's economy tends to thrive or suffer depending on the free circulation of cross-border traffic, shifting patterns of industrial prosperity, shifting currency relations, and passport regulations. In so many ways, Windsor today remains organized around the magnetism of the border. On Windsor's current skyline, one of the few notable features is the urban screen on Caesar's Casino, facing Detroit. Citizens of both cities converge on their respective riverfronts for recreational activities, summer music festivals, carnivals, and other fairs. But the view is nonetheless asymmetrical: Detroit's entrancing skyline beckons to Windsor to participate in an imaginary urban sphere, in a big-city good life that, within Windsor, is only available in limited forms. Yet the skyline itself simultaneously masks Detroit's internal divisions, its histories of segregation and racism, deeply tied to the impoverished and distressed state of vast areas and neighbourhoods in contrast with its resurging downtown and midtown districts. These tensions are equally tied up with the shift from day to night in Detroit, an atmosphere that is palpable to the population across the river.

With thickening border regulations since 9/11 and Detroit's recent emergence from bankruptcy, downtown activities and nightlife in each city have taken a turn away from vice and toward planned cultural entertainment. If nocturnal illumination captures our desire for nighttime economies of consumption, entertainment, fantasy, or transgression, then Windsorites have continually been taunted into wondering what kinds of cultural scenes are welcoming and accessible, or obscured and hostile, on the other side. Since the early 2000s, Detroit has capitalized on its identification with techno and electronica music scenes by staging a range of music festivals in the riverfront Hart Plaza, including Movement Electronic Music Festival, an annual electronic music festival on Memorial Day weekend that now draws over one hundred thousand visitors. Just as downtown Windsor experiences the glow of downtown Detroit's electric illumination, Windsor neighbourhoods near the riverfront are immersed in the sounds of electronic music and accompanying crowds. In 2001, during the second year of the original Detroit Electronic Music Festival, a Windsor city councillor lodged a complaint regarding cross-border noise. An editorial in the *Windsor Star* (2001) lamented Windsor's attitude toward festival cultures and riverfront events in general, arguing that a bit of noise from Detroit only serves to demonstrate the added value in downtown festivals that draw tourists and families. Detroit's recently established *nuit blanche* festival DLECTRICITY, alongside the Movement festival, is suggestive of both the city's history of innovation and the desire to provide safe sociability through illumination and sound. Mega-events such as these absorb the expressive energies of clandestine parties and raves in Detroit's abandoned spaces, recirculating a feeling of transgressive behaviour to populations for whom these activities may be otherwise inaccessible. For Windsorites who experienced the rise of Detroit rave culture, the sensation of vibrations emanating from Movement is powerfully evocative. The thicker border has also allowed Windsor to challenge its own dominant place-image as a nighttime playground for escaping Detroiters—a hub for underage Americans to frequent bars, nightclubs, and strip clubs—and reimagine itself instead as a safe downtown cultural and university campus district.

Illumination

The capacity to observe one city from another in an environment such as Windsor-Detroit invites us to reconsider the relationship between illumination, darkness, and visualization in North American cities. Vision has long dominated collective representations of urban nighttime—our capacity to see through the darkness (Zardini 2005). We experience and remember nighttime in the city predominantly through imagistic and cinematic aesthetic forms. Artificial street lighting has extended the day and provided a sense of safety, yet one now accompanied by the possibility of increased observation. Cities worldwide have increasingly sought to transform nighttime into planned cultural environments and economies, encouraging activities of night and day to interpenetrate in the twenty-four-hour city (Straw 2014). Yet even in cities where nighttime is saturated with amenities, the night also evokes an aura of violence, danger, or unruliness (Schivelbusch 1995; Blum 2003). Tensions between our sense of the nocturnal city as a space-time that is sometimes hospitable and comforting and our sense that it is sometimes hostile or distressing pervade representations of Detroit and are magnified from the vantage point of Windsor. Detroit stands for both a celebration of urban illumination and a history of obscurity and negligence—a desire to look away.

It is remarkable that in Detroit, among the first cities to experiment with tower street lighting (Nye 2015), as much as 40 percent of the city's street lights were defunct in 2013. A city that celebrated the dawn of urban electrification in the late nineteenth and early twentieth centuries—street lights and electric trolleys—was in 2017 celebrating a massive LED overhaul of its municipal lighting system and the launch of a new downtown tram route. In his 1888 review *Municipal Lighting*, Fred H. Whipple (2017) noted: "Detroit is the only large city in the world lighted wholly by the tower system. The city limits comprise about 21 square miles, the whole of which is thus lighted. There are 122 towers of 153 feet each" (157). With a population of some 230,000, Detroit's one-square-mile business centre boasted twenty light towers, about a thousand feet apart, with towers in adjacent residential neighbourhoods and suburbs spreading out to two and three thousand feet apart (see figures 2.2 and 2.3). Gesturing to its reputation as a Paris of the West, Whipple (2017) remarks that the "press of the country has uniformly conceded the city to be the best lighted of any in the world. All its streets, yards, alleys, back yards and grounds are illuminated as effectually as by the full moon at the zenith. The blending of light from the mass of towers serves to prevent dense shadows" (157).

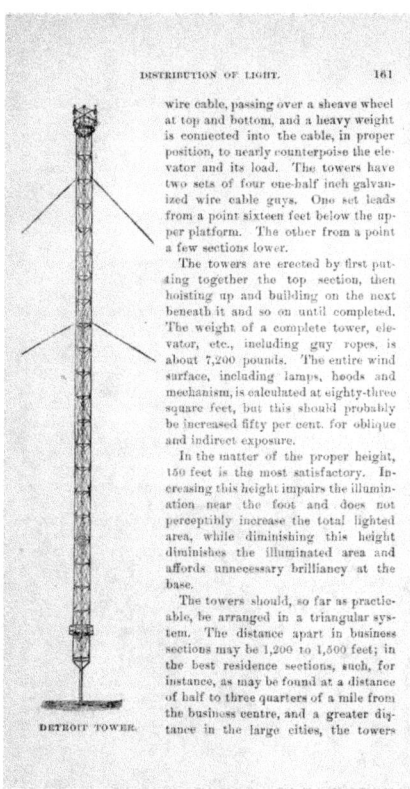

FIGURE 2.2. Detroit Light Tower. A Detroit light tower depicted in Fred H. Whipple's *Municipal Lighting*. Whipple was president of the Detroit-based electric compilers and publishers Fred H. Whipple Co. and secretary of a special committee convened by the Common Council to determine "the feasibility of the city owning and operating its own electric lighting plant." *Source:* Whipple 1888.

In nearby Flint, Michigan, the city council argued that "in rendering our streets safe to all who traverse them at night; in largely preventing crime of every kind; in aiding us to attain that degree of peace and quiet which commends itself to every order-loving citizen, the benefits of this system of light can hardly be estimated" (Whipple 2017, 163). Detroit's mayor, H. S. Pingree,

FIGURE 2.3. Detroit, MI, Campus Martius and Opera House. A Detroit light tower can be seen on Detroit's Campus Martius. *Source:* Glover, L.S. and Detroit Publishing Company, between 1900 and 1910. Library of Congress, Prints & Photographs Division, Detroit Publishing Company Photograph Collection.

stated in his message to the Common Council of January 14, 1890, that "lighting the streets is as much a public matter as street paving and cleaning, sewer building, maintaining and improving the parks and boulevards, supplying water or providing protection against fire" (Detroit 1896, 10). A map of Detroit's street lights in 1897 depicts the widespread distribution of light towers and poles (figure 2.4). Street lights were lit "every night from one half hour after sunset to one hour before sunrise, the time being somewhat extended on very cloudy or stormy evenings and on dark mornings" (Detroit 1896, 35).

Urban electrification brought not only greater visibility but also increased mobility within and between the cities. Electric trolleys were implemented in Detroit in 1892, as depicted in 1910 in figure 2.5.

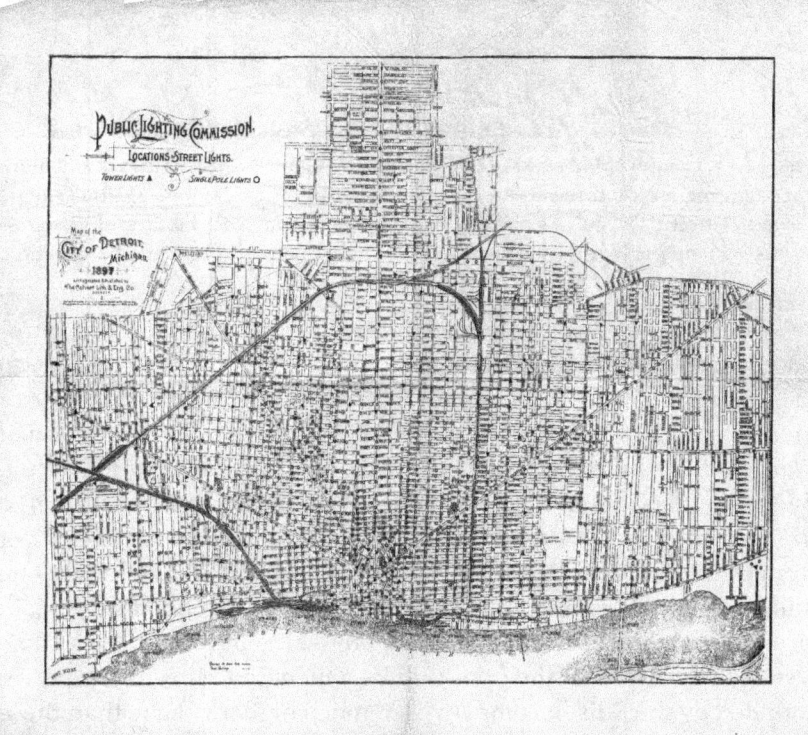

FIGURE 2.4. Locations of Street Lights. Map of the City of Detroit, Michigan. This 1897 map published by the Detroit Public Lighting Commission details the extent of public tower lights and single pole lights in Detroit. *Source:* Calvert Lith & Eng. Co. and the Public Lighting Commission, Detroit, 1897. Courtesy of the Detroit Historical Society.

FIGURE 2.5. Campus Martius at night, Detroit, Michigan. Electric Railways and nighttime lighting are captured in this 1910 image of Detroit's Campus Martius square. *Source:* Detroit Publishing Company, between 1910 and 1920. Library of Congress, Prints & Photographs Division, Detroit Publishing Company Photograph Collection.

Across the river in Windsor, electric streetcars had been introduced in 1886 (often claimed to be among the first in North America) to bring residents from Sandwich Town through downtown Windsor to the foot of Devonshire Road, in what was then the separate town of Walkerville, where they could catch the Walkerville ferry to Detroit. By 1913, a plan was in place to connect Windsor's electrical system to the Detroit Edison Company. Cables would cross the Detroit River from Detroit's Delray district to Sandwich Town, at the time a separate municipality adjacent to Windsor, and would be extended east to join Walkerville's Power and Light Company—although local councillors were concerned that "the lines will be a menace to life, as the power supplied by the Edison company is of much higher voltage than those of the local company" (*Windsor Evening Record* 1913, para. 1).

The visual culture of the border cities since the early 1900s has been asymmetrical, a century-long infatuation with the ways in which Detroit appears to Windsor. During the years of Detroit River ferry traffic, the cities' hectic ports and ferry docks were vibrant spheres of economic and cultural interpenetration. Billboards and painted commercial signs on buildings communicated across the river as passengers trundled over on the fifteen-minute ferry ride. Nancy W. Barr, writing for the Detroit Institute of Arts' recent exhibition *Detroit After Dark*, notes that "electrification helped accentuate grand and dramatic views of the city at night," in reference to a photograph of the "impressive Detroit skyline at night as seen from Windsor" (Barr 2016, 8–9). Detroit's skyline is historically implanted in Windsor's visual identity (a University of Windsor student once offered me the comment that Windsor "owns" the Detroit skyline). Detroit tour guides almost universally display the skyline as an entry into understanding the city, suggesting the only way to gain perspective of Detroit as a whole is from Windsor (Rodney 2014). This was also the scene when Kevin Orr, Detroit's emergency financial manager, appointed in 2013, held a press conference regarding the city's bankruptcy filing in front of a podium labelled "Reinventing Detroit" and depicting a view of the Detroit skyline from Windsor (Darroch 2014). Postcards from the first part of the twentieth century depict Detroit's nighttime luminosity as seen from downtown Windsor. Other images offer a snapshot of one city's lit-up downtown, with the other cross-border city in the shadows.

In figures 2.6 and 2.7, the beams of Detroit's Penobscot Building reach across the river to inundate neighbouring Windsor. Each of these images gestures to Detroit as an immersive atmosphere for Windsorites. There is a sense of enchantment in figure 2.6, where an interiority to Windsor's cozy streetscapes is accentuated by the grandiosity and phantasmagorical character of Detroit's electrification. In figure 2.7, Detroit is pictured in an oneiric state, the shapes of buildings illusory and undefined. Tim Edensor offers an apt description of such illuminated landscapes, arguing that "distances are difficult to fathom, illuminated buildings appear to float, areas of darkness are impregnable to sense making, and scale and proportion may be illusory, factors which combine to produce the oneiric dimensions of illuminated, nocturnal space, particularly in the city" (Edensor 2012, 1107). In other images from the 1920s and 1930s depicting the "Heart of Detroit," represented from a position above Detroit's brightly lit Campus Martius Square, part of Windsor's built environment is visible in the background as integrated city space. In figure 2.8, nighttime lighting seems to merge Detroit and Windsor, erasing the river/

border—a rendering taken from a photograph of a Graf Zeppelin visit to Detroit in 1929 in which the dots of lights of Windsor in the distance are in fact less visible. In figure 2.9, Windsor is clearly a separate

TOP: **FIGURE 2.6.** Night Scene, Windsor, Ontario, Canada. Detroit in the Distance, ca. 1930. Detroit's Penobscot Building glows over Windsor in this postcard. *Source:* Post Card & Greeting Co Ltd. University of Windsor, Leddy Library, Mike Skreptak Collection; Black Binder 3. Courtesy of the Southwestern Ontario Digital Archive, Leddy Library, University of Windsor. BOTTOM: **FIGURE 2.7.** Skyline at Night from Windsor, Canada. The same view acknowledges the viewpoint from Windsor but omits the city. *Source:* Published by United News Co., Detroit, Michigan. Courtesy of the Burton Historical Collection, Detroit Public Library.

city space on the other side of the river, shrouded in darkness, illuminated only by moonlight just as thunderclouds threaten to obscure the moon.

TOP: **FIGURE 2.8.** The Heart of Detroit at Night. This postcard rendering is based on a 1929 photograph of the Graf Zeppelin's visit to Detroit, in which the string of lights on the Windsor side are less dominant than in the postcard. *Source:* Published by United News Co., Detroit, MI. Courtesy of the Burton Historical Collection, Detroit Public Library. BOTTOM: **FIGURE 2.9.** The Heart of Detroit by Moonlight. Windsor is visible as an unlit urban environment in the background. *Source:* Metrocraft, Everett, MA. Courtesy of the Burton Historical Collection, Detroit Public Library.

These postcards capture again the atmospheric and at times oneiric quality of Windsor's relationship to Detroit, cities at once connected and separated, a tension that permeates the emotive tone of Windsor. In keeping with the long history of nighttime visualization,

TOP: **FIGURE 2.10.** View of Ambassador Bridge at Night, Sandwich, near Windsor, Canada, ca. 1930s. This postcard features a common iconic view of the Ambassador Bridge from the vantage point of Sandwich Town, in Windsor, a desirable image for cross-border tourists and travellers. *Source:* Frontier Files Collection, Windsor, Canada. Courtesy of Lee Rodney. BOTTOM: **FIGURE 2.11.** Ambassador Bridge at Night, between Detroit, Michigan, and Windsor, Ontario, ca. 1930s. The clear majority of postcard views of the Ambassador Bridge depict it from the vantage point of Sandwich Town or Windsor. Many, such as in this case, feature a low-flying airplane from which, one can imagine, the view of the Detroit skyline would be spectacular. *Source:* Frontier Files Collection, Windsor, Canada. Courtesy of Lee Rodney.

illumination and darkness have also been key features in imagining these cities' connection or separation. Ferry services eventually fully halted in 1942, more than a decade after the addition of both the Ambassador Bridge and the Windsor-Detroit tunnel in the years 1929–1930 (Roach 1988). As befits the asymmetrical relationship between the cities, the majority of nighttime images of the bridge—an iconic feature relating the cities' ambivalent relationship and offering a brilliant view of Detroit's nighttime skyline—depict it from the perspective of Windsor, looking across to Detroit.

The bridge tower sign was installed at the outset of construction, but only in 1981 did the Detroit International Bridge Company agree with both cities to add a "necklace of lights" to the suspension cables (Mason 1987, 214–215). The lighting of the bridge at dusk brings an intriguing distinctiveness to the bridge, while the electrification of downtown and the city's skyline become less distinct during the transformation from day to night. Writing in 1960 of the potential of complex lighting for urban environments, the designer György Kepes (1961) captured the mood of Windsor's view of Detroit: "Few people would deny that it is a rewarding esthetic experience to perceive the first stages of transformation at dusk. In this first phase, the major forms and spaces of the cityscape are still clearly indicated, but a new system of space is superimposed on this form world through the change of the dark window holes into bright sparks of electric light. Streets once marked by the boundaries of buildings receive their new outlines in street lights" (159). While the bridge's brightly lit cables have been a staple of nighttime imagery since the 1980s, the tunnel has been less frequently depicted in the visual culture of the cities. It seems ironic that the bridge currently deposits a traveller either directly onto a freeway leaving Detroit's city centre or in dilapidated southwest city neighbourhoods, while the tunnel from Windsor propels the traveller into the city's glowing downtown.

Darkness

Tim Edensor has written compellingly about the ways in which nocturnal illumination and darkness shape affective atmospheres of experience. The term "atmosphere," he contends, exemplifies a blurring between "discrete emotional and affective geographies" (Edensor 2012, 1105). Windsor's borderlands are suffused with the atmospheric moods emanating from Detroit, whether through illumination and darkness, through weather systems that can be seen approaching from southeast Michigan, or through human activity—Windsor's shoreline is inundated with the rhythms and sounds of car traffic, the Detroit People Mover—a monorail that makes an occasional riverfront pass—and downtown festivals and events. These environmental conditions and cultural energies lend themselves to the mood of Windsor's urban space, at times shaping warm atmospheres of proximity, integration, and neighbourliness, and at other times cooling off to generate feelings of anxiety, disconnection, and even fear. The need to imagine nighttime Detroit thus penetrates deep into Windsor's emotional state of mind, particularly in the imagination of its youth and artistic communities, which have long participated in Detroit's nocturnal music and art scenes. Marcel O'Gorman (2007) recounts his experience of growing up in Windsor: "When I was a kid, growing up in Windsor, my parents forbade me from going to Detroit. It was the dark continent, a place to be repressed. Watching Detroit (d)evolve from across the river was like watching a slow-motion Hurricane Katrina. The waves kept rolling in, but there were no rescue 'copters in sight—not even police choppers." But kids did cross over, most famously techno artist Richie Hawtin, aka Plastikman, who penetrated the Detroit rave scene in the 1980s to become one of Detroit techno's best-known representatives. Nevertheless, for many Windsorites, the physical distance across the Detroit River and the security and surveillance that now engulf border politics preclude a full investment in identifying with Detroit, generating a sense of angst and anxiety that may be on the rise with the changing dynamics of border control. At night, the border beckons to the possibility of transgressing social boundaries, a possibility that finds little cultural expression in Windsor's more conservative urban spheres but equally forbids such participation.

Even more dominant themes in popular cultural media representations, and in everyday dialogue, are the overladen relationships between race, racialized spaces, and the affective atmospheres of darkness in North American cities (Talbot 2007). Discussions of vice and crime all too often converge euphemistically with racial prejudice and the ways in which people gesture to the history of racialized space in a city such as Detroit (Bunge 2011; Sugrue 2014). Before Detroit's bankruptcy in 2013, the proportion of street lighting that required replacing evoked such broad narratives of Detroit's steady, decades-long decline. In 2014, the State of Michigan established a new

City of Detroit Public Lighting Authority to embark on an ambitious course of replacing inoperative street lighting, some 40 percent of the city's street lighting infrastructure. By the end of 2016, sixty-five thousand new energy-efficient LED lights had been installed across the city, allowing Mayor Mike Duggan to brag that Detroit is now the largest US city to install all LED street lights (Reindl 2016). The need to provide nighttime lighting (so at odds with its early reputation as a "Paris of the West") invites us to consider the relationship of light technology to our experiences of and emotional responses to specific places and times and a pervasive impression that nighttime danger is generated by the incapacity to see. Detroit's encounter with a lack of illumination resurrected long-held understandings of our emotional response to such technologies in the city. In an interview, Public Lighting Authority chair Maureen Stapleton equates new LED technology with safety, suggesting that people may fear the loss of older light poles, but "we will light this city and people will begin to feel safe again" (Reindl 2013). As J. C. Reindl (2013) wrote in the *Detroit Free Press*: "Across the city's 139 square miles, tens of thousands of other people are still living in the dark and with all the problems that brings—more crime and traffic accidents and a heightened sense of vulnerability that forces many to plan their lives around the setting sun for fear of getting mugged on their own streets."

Nighttime in Detroit has thus also long been depicted as menacing, and crime-ridden, troubled, or distressed neighbourhoods become synonymous with the city, a site of endemic crime and arson. Frequent references to the pre-Halloween "Devil's Night" and the city's counter initiative "Angels' Night," launched in the 1990s, are euphemistic for the city's long-troubled race relations. While Detroit's downtown is experiencing rapid post-bankruptcy gentrification, the portrayal of Detroit as danger city or murder capital circulates widely in media reports and is perpetuated through the circulation of "ruin porn" photography, urban explorer blogging, and amateur videos. (Googling "Detroit night" in December 2017 delivered countless videos with adjectives such as "shocking," "haunting," "eerie," and "terrifying," and titles including "Detroit's Deep Dark Hoods at Night," largely portraying a windscreen cam filming a car cruising through various Detroit thoroughfares and neighbourhood streets, peering at local citizens [CharlieBo313 2016].) For its part, Windsor has also garnered conflicting reputations, on the one hand, as a Canadian sin city, beginning with Prohibition-era smuggling and postwar illicit economies tied to a cross-border circulatory landscape of goods and people (Karibo 2012), and, on the other hand, as a cleaner and safer urban environment than its border-city neighbour (recall Michael Moore's claim that Canadians do not lock their doors in *Bowling for Columbine*). Indeed, in 2012, the *Windsor Star* reported that "Windsor remains one of the least homicidal communities in the country," while "Detroit continues to earn its dubious title of the most dangerous city in the U.S." (Chen 2012).

Detroit and Windsor thus each provide an opportunity to consider shifting attitudes toward morality, crime, and nighttime sociability and consumption and associated attempts to revitalize downtown spaces and foster positive nighttime cultural activities. Indeed, the acclaimed *Border Cultures* exhibitions at the Art Gallery of Windsor curated by Srimoyee Mitra, as described in this volume, invite viewers to grapple with the US-Canada border as a historically racialized line. Detroit's 1967 Great Rebellion brought the city to a standstill, closing the border during Canada's centenary celebrations. It is arguable that in the collective cultural imagination, Windsor has remained a largely White enclave opposite a largely Black Detroit, despite immigration and growth in both city spheres (for example, the many Arabic cross-border communities between Windsor and Dearborn). As Mitra notes in this volume: "In contrast to the homogeneous visual regimes of mass media that emphasize the fixity of the border, the exhibitions repeatedly staged it as an uneven, transformative, and luminal space for the articulation of agency, pain, fear, desire, and social justice" (chapter 4). It is here, I think, that we may usefully draw upon Raymond Williams's notion of a structure of feeling. Windsor's location accentuates and reifies the ways in which Detroit is enmeshed in much larger discourses of US inner cities. In keeping with Williams and Orrom's (1954) claim that "it is in art, primarily, that the effect of the totality, the dominant structure of feeling, is expressed and embodied" (21), it is instructive to consider instances of creative expression that have engaged with Detroit's nighttime condition. As the Detroit Institute of Arts' 2016 exhibition *Detroit After Dark* made clear, the history of nighttime Detroit photography has accompanied mid-twentieth-century interest in the changing architecture, after-hours cultures, and crime of modern city life. Unlike night photography in other major cities that has remained aesthetically bound up with the experience of walking, however, nighttime Detroit images are often taken from difficult-to-reach vantage points, emphasizing the need to navigate nighttime Detroit by car and the failing state of public services. Scott Hocking's sweeping nocturnal landscapes of industrial sites and decaying buildings lay bare the discrepancy between geographies of corporate infrastructure and the increasing reliance in Detroit (before its LED revolution) on single and unpredictable sources of light from private spaces. This is a theme taken up by numerous photographers, including Jon Deboer and Dave Jordano, as well as in a recent exhibition by architect and artist Catie Newell at the University of Michigan Museum of Art (2016). Newell's *Overnight* consists of both an installation and photographs from her ongoing series *Nightly* that emphasize the materiality of light and dark as they intersect with and activate the broader architectural environment. The project recalls Kepes's call to reconsider the emotional context of our use of illuminative technologies: "A focused source of light, such as a candle, a lamp, or a fireplace, generates a focused attention, almost a feeling of warmth or nesting. Our interests are so function-centred that such emotional use of light is rarely given thought" (Kepes 1961, 160). Newell's Nightly series avoids clichéd ruined landscapes and focuses instead on the city's transformation from day to night and the feeling of nighttime urban spaces in which darkness outweighs illumination, largely in the neighbourhoods around East Grand Boulevard and the Grand Belt. Overnight consists of photographs from *Nightly* as an environment for the installation of aluminum and copper wiring, referencing the changing technologies of street lighting currently underway in the city (Lawrence 2016).

If artists engaging with the nuances of nighttime Detroit have largely ignored its relationship to Windsor, artists and creative collectives in Windsor have embraced the border condition of this strange urban environment. The Broken City Lab, led by Justin Langlois and students at the University of Windsor and active in Windsor from 2009 to 2015, proposed a series of social practice urban interventions, workshops, and brainstorming sessions to provide spaces to record our emotional and collective responses to the urban condition in these cities.

Cross-Border Communication (figure 2.12) was produced in 2009, at the height of the Great Recession, drawing on what the group termed "the desperate need to communicate with Detroit, Michigan, from Windsor, Ontario" (Broken City Lab 2009). Cross-Border Communication projected messages, including "We're in This

Together" and "Windsor + Detroit = BFF?" onto buildings facing Detroit at the riverside intersection of Windsor's main street, Ouellette Avenue. The team worked with local high-school students to design and implement the projection, calculating the size of the letters to make them visible from Detroit. By reframing the Windsor skyline as a spectacle, the project worked as a commentary on the phantasmagorical character of Detroit's skyline and encapsulated a desire to reverse

TOP: FIGURE 2.12. Cross-Border Communication, 2009. The Broken City Lab's Cross-Border Communication project, during the Great Recession of 2009. *Source:* Photograph by Cristina Naccarato. Courtesy of Justin Langlois and Broken City Lab. BOTTOM: FIGURE 2.13. Shaping Our City, January 3, 2014. During its key period of activity from 2009 to 2015, the Broken City Lab hosted numerous brainstorming workshops to consider creative perspectives on the scale of dynamic change in the border cities. *Source:* Photograph by Walter Petrichyn. Courtesy of Justin Langlois and Broken City Lab.

the asymmetrical relationship between the cities—a desire to remind Detroiters that Windsorites were equally implicated in the emotional anxiety of Great Recession political turbulence.

Conclusion

I have tried to suggest that Windsor is in a privileged position—as what I have elsewhere called an "intimate onlooker" (Darroch 2014)—to apprehend the affective atmospheres that emanate from Detroit. My goal has been to explore the long-term technological histories but also recent histories of the cities in order to apprehend ways in which Detroit creates and shifts moods that extend spatially and virtually to Windsor in specific forms and contexts. Detroit and Windsor, one of the first urban regions in North America to embrace electricity and technologies of illumination, have long been cities that pride themselves on technological innovation. This history evokes deeply rooted nostalgic reactions among residents, highlighted by recent histories of Detroit's failing municipal lighting systems, the city's bankruptcy, and powerful commonplace associations between urban decline, darkness, race, and crime. Yet despite these associations and fears, the visual power of Detroit's skyline has always retained its phantasmagorical character, a sense of enchantment and wonder that forever beckons across the border. If Windsorites frequently broadcast their own urban anxieties against the backdrop of their larger US neighbour, then Detroit's nighttime skyline equally works as an illuminated screen that broadcasts and reflects the exhilaration of urban nightlife—vividly imaginable but perhaps always just beyond view or reach (Darroch and Nelson 2009). Deeply embedded in the structure of this peculiar cross-border urban environment, illumination and darkness shape the atmospheres through which Windsorites perceive, imagine, and participate in nighttime Detroit.

Acknowledgments

A version of this paper was originally published as "Imagining Nighttime Detroit" in Karen Engle and Yoke-Sum Wong, eds., *Feelings of Structure: Explorations in Affect*, 29–47 (Montréal and Kingston: McGill-Queen's University Press, 2018). Initial research for this essay was supported by a Social Sciences and Humanities Research Council of Canada Insight Development Grant, "The Urban Night as

Interdisciplinary Object" (2012–2015), on which the author was a co-applicant. The author wishes to thank the project's director, Will Straw, for his comments on the essay. He would also like to acknowledge the University of Windsor, particularly the Faculty of Arts, Humanities, and Social Sciences, for continuing to support the IN/TERMINUS Creative Research Collective that he co-directs with Lee Rodney, whose insights and advice have been invaluable to this essay.

References

Ambassador (The). 1939. Assumption College High School Yearbook, 2–3. Windsor: University of Windsor Publications.

Barr, Nancy B. 2016. *Detroit After Dark: Photographs from the Collection of the Detroit Institute of Arts*. Detroit: Detroit Institute of Arts.

Blum, Alan. 2003. "Nighttime." In *The Imaginative Structure of the City*, 141–163. Montréal and Kingston: McGill-Queen's University Press.

Broken City Lab. 2009. "Cross-Border Communication: Want to be Friends? (and Other Things We Needed to Say)." November 19, 2009. http://www.brokencitylab.org/tags/cross-border-communication/.

Bunge, William. 2011. *Fitzgerald: Geographies of a Revolution*. Athens: University of Georgia Press, 2007.

Carey, Elaine, and Andrae M. Marak. 2011. *Smugglers, Brothels, and Twine: Historical Perspectives on Contraband and Vice in North America's Borderlands*. Tucson: University of Arizona Press.

CharlieBo313. 2016. "Detroit's Deep Dark Hoods at Night." April 21, 2016. YouTube video, 5:39. https://www.youtube.com/watch?v=66DO3794Kw8.

Chen, Dalson. 2012. "A Tale of Two Cities: Windsor and Detroit Murder Rates Show Stark Contrast." *Windsor Star*, December 4, 2012. http://windsorstar.com/news/local-news/a-tale-of-two-cities-windsor-and-detroit-murder-rates-show-stark-contrast.

Darroch, Michael. 2014. "Border Scenes: Detroit ± Windsor." *Cultural Studies* 29 (3): 298–325.

Darroch, Michael, Karen Engle, and Lee Rodney, eds. 2019. "Ressentir (les frontières)/Sensing (Borders)." Special issue, *Intermédialités*, no. 34.

Darroch, Michael, and Kim Nelson. 2009. "Windsoria: Border/Screen/Environment." *Public* 40:56–65.

Detroit (Michigan). 1896. *Annual Report of the Public Lighting Commission of the City of Detroit, Michigan*. Detroit: The Commission.

Edensor, Tim. 2012. "Illuminated Atmospheres: Anticipating and Reproducing the Flow of Affective Experience in Blackpool." *Environment and Planning D: Society and Space* 30 (6): 1103–1122.

Gallagher, John. 2013. *Revolution Detroit: Strategies for Urban Reinvention*. Detroit: Wayne State University Press.

Karibo, Holly. 2012. "Ambassadors of Pleasure: Illicit Economies in the Detroit-Windsor Borderland, 1945–1960." PhD diss., University of Toronto.

Kepes, György. 1961. "Notes on Expression and Communication in the Cityscape." *The MIT Press* 90 (1): 147–165.

Lawrence, Dave. 2016. "U-M Photography Exhibition Explores a Dark Detroit." University of Michigan, Office of the Vice President for Communications, Arts and Culture (website). May 25, 2016. http://arts.umich.edu/news-features/u-m-photography-exhibition-explores-a-dark-detroit/.

LeDuff, Charlie. 2013. *Detroit: An American Autopsy*. New York: Penguin.

Mason, Philip P. 1987. *The Ambassador Bridge: A Monument to Progress*. Detroit: Wayne State University Press.

Nye, David. 2015. "The Transformation of American Urban Space. Early Electrical Lighting, 1875–1915." In *Urban Lighting, Light Pollution and Society*, edited by Josiane Meier, Ute Hasenöhrl, Katharina Krause, and Merle Pottharst, 30–34. London: Routledge.

O'Gorman, Marcel. 2007. "Detroit Digital: On Tourists in the Apocalypse." *CTheory*. https://journals.uvic.ca/index.php/ctheory/article/view/14516/5376.

Reindl, J. C. 2016. "Detroit Streetlights Go from Tragedy to Bragging Point." *Detroit Free Press*, December 15, 2016. http://www.freep.com/story/news/local/michigan/2016/12/15/detroit-streetlights-go-tragedy-bragging-point/95483846/.

———. 2013. "Why Detroit's Lights Went Out." *Detroit Free Press*, November 17, 2013. http://www.usatoday.com/story/news/nation/2013/11/17/detroit-finances-dark-streetlights/3622205/.

Roach, Al. 1988. "Walkerville's Last Passenger Ferry." *Walkerville Times*. http://www.walkervilletimes.com/lastferry.htm.

Rodney, Lee. 2017. *Looking Beyond Borderlines: North America's Frontier Imagination*. New York: Routledge.

———. 2014. "Art and the Post-Urban Condition." In *Cartographies of Place*, edited by Michael Darroch and Janine Marchessault, 253–269. Montréal and Kingston: McGill-Queen's University Press.

Schivelbusch, Wolfgang. 1995. *Disenchanted Night: The Industrialization of Light in the Nineteenth Century*. Berkeley: University of California Press.

Straw, Will. 2014. "Urban Night." In *Cartographies of Place*, edited by Michael Darroch and Janine Marchessault, 188–197. Montréal and Kingston: McGill-Queens University Press.

Sugrue, Thomas J. 2014. *The Origins of the Urban Crisis: Race and Inequality in Postwar Detroit*. First Princeton classics edition. Princeton: Princeton University Press.

Talbot, Deborah. 2007. *Regulating the Night: Race, Culture and Exclusion in the Making of the Night-time Economy*. London: Routledge.

Whipple, Fred H. (1888) 2017. *Municipal Lighting*. Germany: Hansebooks.
Williams, Raymond, and Michael Orrom. 1954. *Preface to Film*. London: Film Drama.
Windsor Evening Record. 1913. "Walkerville Councillors Served with Injunction." December 9, 1913.
Windsor Star. 2001. "Decibels and Curfews." Editorial. May 30, 2001.
Zardini, Mirko. 2005. "Toward a Sensorial Urbanism." In *Sense of the City: An Alternate Approach to Urbanism*, edited by Mirko Zardini, 17–27. Montréal: Canadian Centre for Architecture.

CHAPTER 3

Bordering Things

Objects and Subjugated Struggle at the Border

Anelynda Mielke and Nadya Pohran

This chapter outlines the centrality of objects, or physical *things*, at the border as instrumental and pivotal in struggles to formulate and assert legitimacy and to claim asylum, as well as in border interactions more generally. Our crucial argument is that borders are not limited to their geographically located borderlines; rather, borders also exist within remotely located symbolic objects as well as within the nonmaterial consciousness of individuals who seek, or desire, to cross (or to not), or otherwise interact with borderlines. The complications with borderlines are well understood, especially where borders are "'too lively' to be pinned down," as in the stretch of border between Serbia and Bosnia and Herzegovina defined by the Drina River, as discussed by Čarna Brković and Stef Jansen (2018). This is also true where physical human bodies inhabit ambiguously bordered spaces, as in the border between Stanstead, Quebec, and Derby Line, Vermont, examined in this volume by Sandra Vandervalk (chapter 6, this volume). The case we discuss here is one of sanctuary, and it occurs geographically far from the border that demarcates the political struggle the case concerns. We examine, then, not the geographical cohabitation or conflict along a physical border, as in the cases of the Drina River or the Vermont-Quebec border, but a struggle that, though it is geographically removed from the borderline, is crucially and inarguably a border struggle.

As a means of creating a theory-driven foundation on which our own argument will stand, in the first half of this chapter we look to compatible and complementary theories that, in the context of the politics of materiality, argue that seemingly external objects are central to understanding the phenomenon at hand. We draw on Ranajit Guha (1983) and subaltern theories of what constitute politics, and on Jacques Rancière (1999) and also on Bruno Latour (2004) to establish this centrality of objects. Our purpose in engaging with these theorists and their theories in our discussion of borderlines and borders is to use their insights to contextualize, undergird, and strengthen our own argument: borders also exist in bordering *things*. The notion of spectacle, as understood by such "politics of visibility" scholars as Lilie Chouliaraki (2006), Luc Boltanski (1999), Susan Sontag (1977), Sharon Sliwinski (2011), Thomas Keenan (2002), and others, similarly informs our analysis. Spectacle in this sense refers to an image (or set of images) observed by an audience, remotely or in person. The scholarship on spectacle focuses especially on the spectacle of suffering, which invites empathy and recognition in advance of tangible political action.

In the second half of this chapter, we shift our attention from these theoretical frameworks to a lived experience that highlights how these theories are enacted and lived out in the world, focusing on the case of a Montréal asylum seeker by the name of Abdelkader Belaouni—a blind, diabetic migrant who took refuge in a Catholic church in order to stay in Canada. The lived experience of Belaouni illuminates the importance of physical objects, *things*, and the church as a place of refuge from the controlling and policing efforts of the official border, as well as the significance of spectacle, as defined above. The case of Belaouni supports our theoretical argument that borders are not, in fact, limited to physical borderlines. Moreover, his case points toward a new era of representation in which image capture and spectacle are central. The reproduction and representation of objects further augments their significance at borders (already places of heightened spectacle, observation, and representation). Our emphasis on things and spectacle draws from and contributes to a growing body of scholarship on materiality (Demetriou 2019; Dimova and Demetriou 2019), making a case for the significance of materiality and objects to border studies.

Through the combination of theory and a case study of the experiences of asylum seekers such as Belaouni, we posit that the border is becoming less defined as a boundary between two ideologically and geographically separate lands. Instead, we should expand our notion of "border" to encompass a series of experiences and interactions that spill over predetermined bounds and render them less and less significant. It is in this vein that we write of bordering *things*. While the word "things" is often criticized for its innate ambiguity, it is precisely its ambiguity and vagueness that renders it such a fitting description for the phenomena we seek to describe: bordering *things* encapsulate both the series of interactions that occur at borderlines but also, crucially, the physical objects in, around, and related to borders. This innate ambiguity that we are arguing for shares some features with the work of Sarah Green, who suggests that any discussion of borders must, to borrow Dimova and Demetriou's summary of Green, "leave much room for doubt and speculation" (2019, xii). In this chapter, we analogously place a spotlight onto the bordering *things that may* appear marginal. We do this not in the manner of proclaiming that bordering *things* are, in a concrete sense, the border—as if the border could be so neatly defined! Rather, we suggest that they need to be seriously considered when discussing the border because they act as crucial "points" and thus become "a series of points" (both used in Green's sense of the terms) which are a part of the border. Indeed, as Green argues, the border should not be thought of as a neat and tidy line—at least not one that is static (Green 2019). We instead argue that physical objects—*things*—can be thought of as political objects that are fundamentally responsible for the over spilling of borders. As *things* are politicized, they facilitate a series of transgressive interactions in which borders' alleged limits and boundary lines are profusely extended (if not obliterated).[1] In this sense, the argument we are putting forth has deep resonances with the work of Olga Demetriou, who argues that any alleged line thought to neatly demarcate a border "is a ruse" and that "the more we take this materiality as something obvious the more it begins to disappear" (2019, 16).

These physical objects, or *things*, are not located only at the borderlines dividing sovereign states. Indeed, because crossers interact with the border in many places and spaces aside from the borderlines

---

1   This type of mediated extension is becoming increasingly normalized through a series of spectacles that are less geographically constrained than ever before, thanks to the proliferation of media and the rapid and nearly immediate reproduction of imagery.

that delineate the edges of a country, it is crucial to recognize and highlight the ways in which bordering *things* can be (in the sense of physical locations) rather distant and far removed from borderlines. Regardless of their physical locations, these symbolic objects define border experiences and struggles, shaping crossers' identities (Mielke 2017). The border is represented beyond its physical limits by the badges, uniforms, decals, emblems, and other paraphernalia that signal its presence in border authorities and centres. The border is a collection of objects at the line that traditionally demarcates it; bordering *things* include CCTV cameras, barbed wire, fingerprinting apparatuses, as well as the small booklets of paper that determine whether one can traverse a physical borderline or not. The border is a collection of objects at its true margin, and it is a collection of objects, *things*, that overspills these bounds and frequently imprints upon the lives of those that cross it. The fact that these *things* are not consistently in the geographical location of traditional borderlines does not mean that they are not indelibly linked to the experience of borders; by retaining their crucial link to border-related power, they become, we argue, a fundamental and crucial part of the border itself. In other words, the border is a collection of objects, regardless of *where* these objects are. This definition of border, as existing beyond a geographical location, grounds our own arguments. Spectacles of suffering, as in the case of Belaouni, provoke various audience responses depending on which perspective dominates the transmission and mediation (Boltanski 1999). In Belaouni's case, the spectacle was intended (and succeeded) in garnering support for this border crosser, amounting to a recognition of both the legitimacy of his plight as well as his claim to a right to remain in Canada. We note that Lee Rodney, also in this volume (chapter 1, this volume), argues that "borders are first understood through images." Rodney's chapter focuses first on maps as the image of the border, but we argue that spectacles, such as that of Belaouni, also belong to the category of border imagery; border images are not always images *of* the geographical border.

Expanded Politics

There are clear examples within political theory of how politics can be conceived of as far more than one might originally anticipate. For Ranajit Guha and the subalternists, "politics" is more than what Gandhi and Nehru and the political elites did in a system the British left behind in the Indian subcontinent. Guha asserts that the "backward"—at least as conceived by Eric Hobsbawm (1978), for instance—violence of peasants, their rebellions and uprisings, count as "politics." To deny such an expansion of the political is to write an elitist history (Guha 1983; Chakrabarty 2000). We must see the politics in peasant uprisings, in rallies, and in street protests. In other words, we must see even those marginal elements—which, on account of their marginality, may appear as if they are different than, or perhaps extraneous to, the *real* matter at hand—as part and parcel of the matter itself. As we shall see, this applies just as much to borderlines as it does to politics, and the context of politics is particularly illuminating for our discussion here.

For subalternists, the difference in Eastern versus Western capitalism lies in the contributions of the bourgeoisie. Guha "saw the Western bourgeoisie as having achieved a consensual liberal culture by speaking for 'the masses,' whereas the universalization of capital failed outside the West because the bourgeoisie did not consensually exploit the subaltern classes, could not represent the people's will" (Mielke 2017, 4; see also Chibber 2013). Much of what Guha writes dovetails nicely with the notion of "everyday resistance" put forward by James C. Scott (1987). Just like elections, amendments, and closed-door meetings, acts of everyday resistance are political activities. Much later work, including that of Gopika Solanki (2007) exploring "doorstep courts," build on these subalternist ideas about the expansion of what counts as political. Social movement theorist Andrew Barry (2001, 194) writes that an act is political if "it opens up new sites and objects of contestation." Subaltern studies have recently come in for some criticism, however. In *Postcolonial Theory and the Specter of Capital*, Vivek Chibber criticizes the subalternists' claim "that there is a deep fault line separating Western Capitalist notions from the postcolonial world" (2013, 53). Chibber writes that Guha in particular believed that capitalism failed outside the West because the upper classes did not have the consent of the lower classes to exploit them, something the bourgeoisie did effectively obtain in the Global North. Chibber (2013, 90–91) suggests that any advances in liberal political culture are the result of struggle against capitalism: "The English bourgeoisie and the French 'capitalists' were no more interested in building an encompassing political nation than the Birlas or Tatas in India." Resistance—overt and subversive—is responsible for any movement toward a more liberal political order. The determinants lie with the people, in other words, not with the elite. This is as true of the French as the Birlas and Tatas. Chibber's critique makes it even more important that we broaden what we mean by politics. Advancing liberal political culture depends on it, in Canada and abroad.

Resistance brings political change, advances liberal political culture, but in order to discuss resistance in any meaningful way, we must examine those power structures that are being resisted, and recognize that power itself is exercised in the interaction between those "in power" and those resisting them. Power exists within the shifting, changing process of politics itself; it is far from static. Politics "happens" as this resistance takes place, even and perhaps especially in an everyday context, as explored by J. Scott (1978), Barry (2001), and many others. Guha's contribution hinged on the in-depth study of everyday politics. Chakrabarty (2000, 23) writes that Guha "examined rebel practices to decipher the particular relationships—between elites and subalterns and between subalterns themselves—that are acted out in these practices, and then attempt[ed] to derive from these relationships the elementary structure...of the 'consciousness' inherent in those relationships."

Taking into account the work of Guha, we must recognize that politics does not take place exclusively within well-recognized and recognizable political structures; it also occurs within the consciousness of individuals who interact with political ideas and ideologies—even if and when they do so in places and manners that we may not have thought of as "political." Politics takes place when new spaces are opened for contestation (Barry 2001). We take this helpful insight and apply it to borders: there exists a *consciousness* within the many crossers and individuals who interact with the border. Consequently, the borders must be conceptualized as not just the physical location of a borderline but also as residing in collective and individual psyches and consciousnesses. We further extend this argument to bordering *things*—that is, to the objects that bear the border's significance, its mark, and its power. As crucial reference points to, and objects entangled with the power structures of, borderlines, bordering *things* in effect become part of the border itself. Demetriou argues that "materiality" and "immateriality" should not be understood as dichotomous; rather, they are fundamentally connected to each other (2019, 17). Building on Demetriou, we argue that the defining features of the borderline should not be understood as dichotomous relative to bordering *things*, which also point back to, and thus embody, the border. These *things*, in grounding and entering border struggles (regardless of where these take place), are political objects. These things participate in politics. Thus we theorize "border politics" as the assemblage of things and humans that are engaged in contestations concerning a border, regardless of where those contestations take place geographically. Border politics is no longer the purview of heads of state signing treaties or officials engaging in sanctioned diplomacy. Border politics takes place in the context of the everyday. Abdelkader Belaouni's sanctuary in a Montréal church exemplifies this everyday border politics in a location far from any national border. Everyday people and everyday objects constitute border politics.

We cannot talk about power without also discussing resistance; power and resistance are two sides of an endosymbiotic reality. Resistance is constantly taking place. Indeed, resistance in the everyday sense, J. Scott's (1987) sense, is ever-present. It takes place when subjugated bodies avoid law enforcement authorities, when parishioners or priests protect those being sought for deportation by the state. Both power and resistance are not just represented but actually embodied, made real, by the *things*—physical objects—at borders, both as geographical boundaries and in the physical spaces where the border remains present despite being geographically far removed. It can be helpful at this point to call to mind the influential work of Michel Foucault, who rejects the notion that power originates in, and subsequently emerges from, a singular governmental or other institutional structure (Foucault 1978, 93; 1986). He instead speaks of power as an "impersonal force that permeates a plurality of sites and which is neither unidirectional nor exclusively top-down. This power is present everywhere. Individuals, who simultaneously dominate others and are involved in their own domination by others, move along the threads of networks of both power and resistance—since resistance, too, is intertwined with power" (Pohran 2020, 179). One especially important point to take from this Foucauldian understanding of power is that the alleged binary (of ruler and ruled, or of powerful and powerless, or of oppressor and oppressed, etc.) is dissipated. This argument that neither power nor resistance can be singularly identified or located is crucial to our discussion here: bordering *things* play an important role in the ongoing establishing and re-establishing of the border.

The notion that bordering *things* play an unequivocal role in realizing (that is, comprehending) and real-izing (that is, making real) the border will become clearer in the discussion below of church sanctuary and the role of places of worship in protecting subjugated bodies from the gaze (and if not the gaze, then at least the physical reach) of the state. First, let us further examine the role that physical objects play in politics. Their role is one that is famously expressed and conducted in Bruno Latour's work. Objects are political, Latour (2004, 15) informs us:

> There might be no continuity, no coherence, in our opinions, but there is a hidden continuity and a hidden coherence in what we are attached to. Each object gathers around itself a different assembly of relevant parties....Each object may also offer new ways of achieving closure without having to agree on much else. In other words, objects—taken as so many issues—bind all of us in ways that map out a public space profoundly different from what is usually recognized under the label of "the political."

In this vein, Latour's ideas expand on and coalesce with the findings that the subalternists, in particular Guha, brought to our understanding of politics. Politics is bigger than what takes place in the annals of power, the "official" channels historically reserved for a privileged few and handed down from the Greeks; politics is about something bigger, and it takes place as a function of, embodied in and embellished by, physical objects and things.

Rancière has a fascinating example that captures well the power artifacts and objects associated with the border might have on the body of an undocumented migrant. He tells Herodotus's story of the slaves and the Scythian horsewhip. This narrative emphasizes the power of symbols in the lives of subaltern and subjugated people. Objects and things have power over all of us. The story goes like this: When the Scythians were off at battle far away, their slaves became more powerful and started to rebel to the point where they could take the place of their masters. They rebelled and were going to fight and overpower their masters when the latter returned home. And this would have been successful if the masters had not used the horsewhip: the symbol of subjugation that had so often been wielded to overpower the subaltern classes into their servitude. Although their rebellion was almost successful, the Scythian slaves' defeat was secured when the returning warriors (their former masters) took up horsewhips instead of spears and bows (Rancière 1999). The Scythian slaves perceived themselves as equal to the warriors as long as both sides held battle armaments. The key point to take from this example is that it was not actually might or physical force that made the Scythians the victors in their skirmish with their former slaves. Instead, their massive victory is owed to a "mere" symbol. The symbolic object—not through the brute force of its physical power but through its symbolic power—subjugated the Scythian slaves to their former masters, returning their bodies to a subaltern existence. Indeed, from this example we learn that *things* have immense power to effect change in the physical realm and in human power dynamics.

Symbols carrying the weight of the border similarly wield impressive power over border crossers. Along the Drina River, which demarcates a large part of the border between Serbia and Bosnia and Herzegovina, somewhat conflicting signs have been installed over time to stake out border claims (Brković and Jansen 2018). At numerous international borders, symbols ranging from uniforms on officers to flags to extensive signage directing traffic and bodies attempt to control human movement. And in cases of "illegitimate" subaltern crossers, state symbols amount to Scythian horsewhips, subduing the subaltern presence, relegating it to the margins of life, at or even beyond the border. In order to contest the superseding power of symbols over a subaltern, to successfully mount a resistance, the subaltern must develop a voice. The capacity to speak back and comprehend speech is imperative for political participation, according to Rancière (1999): "Once a subaltern class can understand and speak back to the existing police order, the existing order is disrupted because the subaltern's subalterity was contingent on its being voiceless" (as quoted in Mielke 2017, 6). Rancière agrees with Guha on the importance and centrality of physical objects to the struggle of subjugated groups and the nature of politics itself. Guha's examination of the subaltern and the expansion of what counts as politics began with symbolism. Regarding the peasant rebellions that so shaped his view of politics and the nature of political power itself, Guha (1983, 75) writes: "It was a political struggle in which the rebel appropriated and/or destroyed the insignia of his enemy's power and hoped thus to abolish the marks of his own subalterity" (see also Chakrabarty 2000).

Upon accepting that subjugation is a matter of symbols and their power over subjugated classes, peoples, or individuals, we need to explore how this impacts our understanding of borders. The border is mediated and represented by a series of powerful objects that subject crossers to its strength, and there is no shortage of bordering *things* that wield the symbolic power of the border. Consider, for example, the specific visual cues that transform an automobile into a police car; a police badge or the United States Immigration and Customs Enforcement (ICE) decal are extremely powerful cues, though few would put forth the argument that these *things* are powerful in and of themselves in a strictly material sense. Rather, they are powerful because the strength of the border resides within them, a strength that transcends and exceeds even the bodily, physical force practiced by the officials that wear these symbols. The guns and batons and other armaments border officials carry are equally powerful because of the symbolic power contained in, and expressed by, them. While we are not dismissing the concrete physical power that these armaments do contain, it is their symbolic power—and the immense amplification of it—that interests us here. The Scythian horsewhip remains active today in countless interactions and experiences of subjugated subaltern individuals with the border. Everyday border politics involves attempts to resist, to erase the marks of subalternity—we will see this in concrete terms in the Belaouni case.

Spectators and Spectacles

It is imperative to discuss the construction and implications of spectacle. The border is itself a spectacle, a place of hypervigilance. Even a totally "legitimate" crosser experiences several gazes that aim to scrutinize and assess their legitimacy. There is the rolling footage of many cameras, the photographing of a licence plate, the border official asking the crosser to roll down a window and open a trunk to expose the contents of the car, and so forth. The hypervigilance around immigration has merely increased the intensity of the spectacle focused on individuals crossing the border, especially when they fall into an "undocumented" category. The debate around full-body scanners rages on (Rygiel 2013, 170). This is a debate around precisely how *seen* crossers are allowed to be by border controllers without violating the crosser's privacy. At the border, we are examined, watched, and *seen* deeply—or, at least we are scrutinized for any and all signs of a threat. This is what Brighenti (2007) calls control visibility; it is a visibility that aims to restrict, to keep an account of, human movement. Control visibility conveys the sense of being evaluated, transforming "visibility into a strategic resource for regulation"

(Brighenti 2007, 339). There are many ways of being seen, however. In contrast, Brighenti discusses recognition (vis-à-vis evaluation) as the object of social visibility, which constitutes "a fundamentally enabling resource" (Brighenti 2007, 339). The scrutiny experienced by border crossers constitutes control visibility, but often the demands made by crossers can be read as demands for a change in *how* the state sees crossers—not just in terms of "legitimate" versus "illegitimate," but as subject to types of visibility that are "enabling" versus "controlling." A demand for recognition is a demand for a change in how one is made visible.

A "witnessing fever"—relying on a global public sphere—has gripped individuals and international organizations that devote themselves to creating transnational spaces for the mediation of far-off suffering (Kurasawa 2009, 93; see also Chouliaraki 2006). Knowledge of suffering in distant places provokes a range of responses from "publics"—who are themselves defined and constituted in their identity as targets of such messages (Keenan 2002). "Testimonial actors," or those who see it as their role to witness suffering and present it to distant audiences, fear incomprehension and indifference in response to their efforts (Kurasawa 2009).

Audience members doubt the honesty of media portrayals and correctly recognize that the difficulty of recognizing who the "true" victims are is rivalled only by the impossibility of identifying "true" humanitarians. Many postmodern theorists describe how media's participation in politics has generated a system where the distinction between "reality" and representation is obliterated. A new space is constructed through media and the use of narrative, fusing (or smashing together) the space of the suffering victim with the space of the "safe" spectator (Nayar 2009). Representation melts into reality as photographers' cameras are conflated with armaments in battle (Keenan 2002; see also Gregory 2004). The collapsing of the mediated space into that of the "real" makes action in the space of "reality" (non-mediated space) impossible (Keenan 2002; Boltanski 1999). Media overspills the precincts of a channel showing distant happenings and invites intervention on behalf of the unfortunates portrayed. Media becomes an omnipresent participant, at once representing and constituting distant realities. And these victims can easily take on varying levels of legitimacy, depending on how their suffering is made visible, how their victimhood is mediated. Judith Butler's exposition of frames that differentiate between "grievable" and disposable lives not only explains indifference, but also the support for destruction of some lives in the defence of others (or, indeed, other ways of life) (Butler 2010).

As a result, some mediated disasters have prompted unprecedented outpourings of support for victims (recent examples are found in coverage of Typhoon Haiyan in November 2013 and the Haitian earthquake of 2010). The Live 8 Concerts in 2005—led by Bob Geldof in an effort to mobilize support for the United Nations' Millennium Development Goals—responded to decades of visual reporting on poverty in Africa (Torchin 2012), while others have been met with more widespread skepticism, as when, in 2006, some political leaders of Australia and Canada expressed anger at their states' willingness to evacuate thousands of dual nationals from Lebanon during the thirty-four-day war between Hezbollah and Israel (Stasiulis 2013). It has long been argued that the policies adopted by some world powers (whether labelled Euro-American, Western, or the Global North) actively perpetuate or neglect suffering. Others existing in different sociocultural, economic, and/or citizenship categories (Gregory 2004; Chouliaraki 2006; Shohat and Stam 1994; see also Walters 2014). These others are unfortunate but unavoidable casualties when they are not entirely invisible, or, à la Butler, not "living" at all (Butler 2010).

Throughout this process, the people who suffer never (or almost never) represent or express themselves directly. Leshu Torchin (2012, 591) summarized this phenomenon in the following way: "[A]lthough contemporary visual-culture scholarship compels our recognition that media are not transparent delivery systems of information, the faith in exposure remains seductive." Hence, audiences continue to trust the visual image presented by global media, despite increasing evidence that casts doubt on the honesty and effectiveness of such portrayals. This apparent paradox underlines the importance and timeliness of a lot of study and attention to this topic. As we will see, Abdelkadar Belaouni's plight became a spectacle—televised extensively, represented in various media across space and time, accelerated by the endorsement of prominent politicians and others. Renata Grudzien's work, also in this volume (chapter 8, this volume), examines the Canadian movement to welcome refugees; in such efforts, countless spectacles and narratives similar to that of Belaouni's were expressed and leveraged to produce particular policies. In many of these cases, as in others (Sliwinski 2011; Boltanski 1999; Chouliaraki 2006), crossers do not remain at the centre of their own narrative or spectacle, in the sense of having the power to control or direct what is said or shown about them. Belaouni remained at the centre of his own spectacle and had some power to direct it. His hosting of radio broadcasts, for instance, empowered some of his authentic voice to be expressed. The degree to which his voice and personal expression directed the spectacle is somewhat unique and likely helped produce audience sentiment in favour of recognizing his legitimate status. The success of his efforts to legitimize his asylum claim relied on many others (the aforementioned politicians, as well as activists and others) contributing to the spectacle, inviting a broader audience to recognize his plight.

Having summarized and explored some of the key theoretical frameworks in which our own argument is grounded, we now return to the topic of borders and bordering *things*. The coalescing of the two concepts explored above—spectacle and the expansion of the political (à la Guha and others)—leads us to a new perspective on borders and crossers. The space of the political expands to encapsulate areas far beyond the geographical border, areas that are now thought to form a part of its margins. Undocumented migrants are often interacting with the border even while they are geographically far removed from it. The definition of border thus comes to include an amorphous series of tentacles, expanding in strength and growing out from the centre of power to capture crossers that might have evaded or "legitimately" traversed from another region months or years ago.

Case Study: Abdelkader Belaouni

At this point we can turn to a case study that we have thus far only hinted at and referred to in passing: that of the migrant activist and asylum seekers who remained in Canada by taking refuge in a Catholic church in Montréal. We offer this case study as a way of demonstrating that our main theoretical argument, that borders should be conceptualized not just as the physical location of borderlines but also as the bordering things which extend the reach of the border, can be seen in concrete ways in the experiences of migrants and asylum seekers. We first highlight the way that the church building, and its use as a place of refuge, enacts the symbolic power of reversing subjugation. We also examine the ways in which small material objects such as Popsicle sticks are crucially used in enacting activism.

Abdelkader Belaouni is a blind, diabetic migrant who spent nearly four years in a Catholic church in Pointe-Saint-Charles, Montréal, to avoid deportation by Canadian authorities. Belaouni is from Algeria but left his home country in 1996 for the US. He felt his position become more precarious and feared deportation following the events of September 11, 2001, and so came north to Canada, where he hoped his chances of remaining in the country would be more favourable. When he received notification that he was to be deported by Canadian immigration authorities, he sought refuge in St. Gabriel's Church in Montréal, starting January 1, 2006. With the cooperation of the church and the ongoing kindness of an ever-expanding community of friends, Belaouni was able to reside in the church permanently. He only left this temporary home in 2009, when the Canadian government granted him permanent resident status. The *Montreal Gazette* noted, "While at the church, Belaouni hosted radio broadcasts on McGill University's CKUT, learned to play the piano, guitar and flute, recorded two albums and wrote two books—a memoir and a volume on Algerian history" (as quoted in M. Scott 2015). His release followed the involvement of many community organizations and leaders in the Montréal area. This included a committee, thousands of signatures on petitions, and postcards mailed to immigration in support of his cause (Canadian Press 2009). When finally granted permission to stay in Canada, Belaouni poignantly declared, "I was not born here, but in my mind, this is my country....It is as if God has given me a newfound ability to see."[2] And, of the individuals who not only directly enabled him to last for those nearly four years in the church but who also were crucial in securing through their activism permission for him to stay, Belaouni declared: "To say 'thank you' is not strong enough. I do not have words....I cannot simply say 'thank you.' To them, I say: I love you with a strong love, I think of you day and night."[3] One cannot miss the emotion in his statement; Belaouni is immensely grateful to both the specific people who helped him along his journey but also to the church more broadly, for he had consistent cooperation and support from the church

---

2   Authors' translation. Quoted in Desroches 2015, para. 2–3. "'Je suis fier d'être canadien. Je ne suis pas né ici, mais dans mon cerveau, c'est mon pays, lance-t-il sans hésiter quand on lui demande ce qu'il a éprouvé quand il a obtenu sa citoyenneté au terme d'un long combat. 'C'est comme si Dieu m'avait donné mes yeux une autre fois.'"

3   Authors' translation. Quoted in Desroches 2015, para. 21. "'Merci, ce n'est pas assez fort. Je ne trouve pas de mots,' dit-il. Pendant quatre ans, des gens m'ont aidé. Je ne peux pas simplement dire merci. Je leur dis : je vous aime très fort, je pense à vous jour et nuit.'"

as an institution throughout his four years in refuge. Additional support, in the form of activist performance, further invited a reframe of the Belaouni spectacle, demanding recognition and empathy instead of control visibility. This activism employed banal everyday objects to create an additional spectacle, further illustrating our point that border struggles and border politics can occur in spaces far removed from geographical borderlines and can employ materiality, imagery, and symbolism that exceed that of the official border.

Objects of Protest: Reclaiming Spectacle for Border Activism?

What is interesting in light of these changes to regimes and administrations, which have such far-reaching and potentially deleterious consequences for border crossers and migrants, is the potential to refashion spectacle and leverage its power in defence of the crosser or the subaltern body facing forced deportation or other legal action. Reclaiming spectacle in the case of Abdelkader Belaouni and his stay in St. Gabriel's Church in the Montréal neighbourhood of Pointe-Saint-Charles took the form of Popsicle sticks on pavement.

Popsicle sticks are representative of summer, of childhood, even of kids making crafts in grade school. These are not symbols of imprisonment or of oppression. Two activists, Anita Schoepp and Ayeesha Hameed, used these little wooden sticks to represent Abdelkader Belaouni's entrapment in the church. For the activists, an artist and a researcher, Belaouni's situation amounted to imprisonment. Hameed (2011, 127) describes it as follows: "The day-to-day experience of living in a church forms another form of incarceration." So, to illustrate this reality, the two of them took Popsicle sticks and placed them on the pavement outside the Montréal passport office in Complexe Guy-Favreau. They placed four of the sticks vertically and laid another across the top, in a style reminiscent of lines etched on the walls of a prison to keep track of the days that passed by. This Popsicle stick display was to enumerate the days Belaouni had spent as a "prisoner" inside the church-prison: "We…took 902 sticks, each marked for a day he was incarcerated, and placed them on the ground: four in a row and one across, like a prisoner marking days on the wall of a cell" (Hameed 2011, 129). Importantly, the activists did not simply provide the passport offices with the relevant data concerning Belaouni: they demonstrated it, and in their demonstration, they made use of powerful symbols. Specifically, by first symbolically calling to mind the experiences of childhood freedom and enjoyment through the Popsicle sticks and then using these symbols to highlight the imprisoned subjugated body of the migrant Abdelkader Belaouni, Schoepp and Hameed refashioned activism into spectacle.

Latour (2004) examines the centrality of objects, and his analysis is pertinent here. The Popsicle sticks on pavement became symbols of the felt, lived, and experienced oppression faced by the subjugated subaltern body at the hands of the state. These objects formed a spectacle that counteracted the spectacle that the state forces on migrants like Belaouni—the roving eyes of the ever-present authorities seeking transgressive bodies. The spectacle put forward by the activists invited recognition, social visibility, in response to the control visibility that state actors visit on "illegitimate" crossers (Brighenti 2007). Schoepp and Hameed utilized Popsicle sticks and the power of symbolism to convey the subjugated experience in response to the symbols wielded by the subjugating force. In short:

> The identity and fate of this asylum seeker would be determined by a struggle that took place over the very concept spelled out by the Popsicle sticks. If their message was denied, as was being done by the Canadian state, then Belaouni remained a stateless person in the eyes of the law, and a prisoner in the eyes of his supporters. If their message were accepted, understood and acted upon by the Canadian government, as was eventually done, then Belaouni would receive permission to stay in Canada legitimately. (Mielke 2017)

Hameed and Schoepp wielded the power of spectacle, in the sense that their spectacle was experienced in a threatening way by those in power. They were photographed by security, which intrigued the protesters: "Toward the end…the security guards crossed the street and followed us off the property of the park, and in an effort to intimidate us began to take pictures of the sticks on the ground. Ironically, they also took pictures of a message written in chalk that described Kader's incarceration for their own records" (Hameed 2011, 129).

In this case, the activists responsible for the creation of the spectacle in the form of the Popsicle sticks on this particular (significant) square of pavement before the Montréal passport office, were themselves rewarded with the attention of the authorities' gaze on them. "The presence of physical objects provides a focal point for officials' attention, so that dispute is based around the presence of the object" (Mielke 2017, 18) rather than the actual ideology or debate surrounding the controversy in question. Schoepp and Hameed's representation of Belaouni's entrapment in the sanctuary of St. Gabriel's Catholic Church allowed the authorities to focus on the transgression of placing Popsicle sticks on the pavement in that particular square, for example. The spectacle the activists created highlighted, and perhaps temporarily and geographically overshadowed for a specific moment, the spectacle of Abdelkader Belaouni's experience itself.

We end this chapter by weaving together the multiple threads we have presented. Our central argument has been that the concept of a border should not be limited to the geographical spaces in which borderlines are physically located, or images and representations of those geographical borders. Rather, we need to widen and broaden our definition of what precisely constitutes a border: the seemingly ubiquitous prevalence of bordering *things*—that is, the physical (and, importantly, symbolic) objects that are themselves embedded with power—necessitate that we recognize that the border is not confined to its physical borderlines. Insights from politics of visibility literature, particularly that of spectacle, have enabled us to demonstrate how border spectacles and images can be situated far from the geographical border, as can border objects or *things*. Indeed, individuals—depending on where they stand in reference to the legal systems of immigration—either embody and exhort, or are confronted by, the power of the border even when they are physically far from it. The border can discipline bodies even when they are far from its traditional geographical locations.

We have noted a similar theory—of the centrality of objects and of the importance of highlighting that which may seem marginal to, or distinct from, the "real" matter at hand—in the works of Guha, Latour, and other subaltern theorists who advocate for a radical reconsideration of what counts as politics. Rancière further helps us understand this phenomenon, as well as the importance of symbolism to both the subjugation of subaltern classes and their resistance to that subjugation, a notion supported and explored by Guha as well. Picking up on this importance of symbolism and applying it to the study of borders, we have shown that bordering *things* contain a deeply embedded symbolic power. Physical objects and symbols participate in the politics of the border.

The case of Abdelkader Belaouni highlights how the border, and the power of the border, attain a very real presence in lived experience, despite the fact that a crosser's physical location may be relatively far from any borderlines. His experience gives us further reason to question the assumption that a border is defined by a geographical location between two distinct countries or cultures. On the contrary, Belaouni's case demonstrates that the border is real-ized (i.e., made real) through bordering *things*, regardless of their physical proximity to any borderlines. The contemporary spectacle around these objects that define and centre border struggles can be reclaimed and refashioned by activists seeking to express recognition of the struggles of subaltern bodies at the border. In effect, these activists seek to bring empathy and recognition (as social visibility) to the spectacle of the crosser, countering the control visibility with which the gaze of the state is imbued. In activists' efforts, physical objects—in this case, Popsicle sticks—ground the spectacle, inviting recognition. *Things* are therefore made political, and centre political spectacle, for both the activist and the crosser, which spurred on the activism in question. These contestations, interactions, acts of refuge, advocations, and the like are all "part of the process of the border" (Demetriou 2019, 32). The notion of a border that is "'too lively' to be pinned down," in Brković and Jansen's (2018) description, may also apply to this case, wherein border politics, spectacle, and materiality influence experiences far removed from geographical borderlines.

That borders and border theory are continuously being constructed, just as culture itself is, is something we bear in mind as we conclude this chapter. We hope that our contribution to the discussion, both theoretical and with regard to our case study, lends a broadened perspective to the definition and theorization of what borders and border culture(s) are and the rich interdisciplinary literatures that might be leveraged to deepen and expand our understanding of borders. There are diverse, multifaceted meanings for those interacting with borders, whether they be crossers themselves or the scholars who study them. Just as a spectacle seeks an audience, and without it is not a spectacle, so borders rely on human consideration and deference to solidify their significance. As this fluid and contextually, as well as geographically, disparate, process of "making" the border continues, we hope our contributions open new avenues for exploration. We, ourselves, have more questions than when we began writing this chapter. In the dialogue about border experiences and theorization we hope to have provoked richer, more meaningful questions.

References

Barry, Andrew. 2001. *Political Machines: Governing in a Technological Society*. London: Bloomsbury Academic.

Boltanski, Luc. 1999. *Distant Suffering: Morality, Media and Politics*. Translated by Graham D. Burchell. New York: Cambridge University Press.

Brighenti, Andrea. 2007. "Visibility: A Category for the Social Sciences." *Current Sociology* 55, no. 3 (May): 323–342. https://journals.sagepub.com/doi/10.1177/0011392107076079.

Brković, Čarna, and Stef Jansen. 2018. "A Lively Border: Bosnia and Herzegovina and Serbia on the Shifting Banks of the Drina." In *Everyday Life in the Balkans*, edited by David Montgomery, 230–238. Bloomington: Indiana University Press.

Butler, Judith. 2010. *Frames of War: When is Life Grievable?* London: Verso.

Canadian Press. 2009. "Refugee Free After 4 Years in Montreal Church." *CBC*, October 26, 2009. https://www.cbc.ca/news/canada/montreal/refugee-free-after-4-years-in-montreal-church-1.850001#:~:text=The%20moment%20of%20triumph%20came,to%20elude%20deportation%20since%20Jan.

Chakrabarty, Dipesh. 2000. "Subaltern Studies and Postcolonial Historiography." *Nepantla: Views from South* 1 (1): 9–32. Project MUSE.

Chibber, Vivek. 2013. *Postcolonial Theory and the Specter of Capital*. London: Verso.

Chouliaraki, Lilie. 2006. *The Spectatorship of Suffering*. London: Sage Publications.

Demetriou, Olga. 2019. "Materiality, Imbrication, and the Longue Duree of Greco-Turkish Borders. In *The Political Materialities of Borders: New Theoretical Directions*, edited by Olga Demetriou and Rozita Dimova, 16–35. Manchester: Manchester University Press.

Desroches, André. 2015. "Le réfugié Abdelkader Belaouni obtient sa citoyenneté canadienne." *Métro*, February 18, 2015. https://journalmetro.com/local/sud-ouest/717696/le-refugie-abdelkader-belaouni-obtient-sa-citoyenete-canadienne/.

Dimova, Rozita, and Olga Demetriou. 2019. Preface to *The Political Materialities of Borders: New Theoretical Directions*, edited by Olga Demetriou and Rozita Dimova, xi–xvii. Manchester: Manchester University Press.

Foucault, Michel. 1986. "Disciplinary Power and Subjection." In *Power*, edited by Steven Lukes, 229–242. Oxford: Basil Blackwell.

———. 1978. *The History of Sexuality*. Translated by Robert Hurley. London: Penguin Books.

Gregory, Derek. 2004. *The Colonial Present*. Malden, MA: Blackwell Publishing.

Green, Sarah Francesca. 2019. "Lines, Traces, and Tidemarks: Further Reflections on Forms of Border." In *The Political Materialities of Borders:*

    New Theoretical Directions, edited by Olga Demetriou and Rozita Dimova, 67–83. Manchester: Manchester University Press.
Guha, Ranajit. 1983. *Elementary Aspects of Peasant Insurgency in Colonial India*. Delhi: Oxford University Press.
Hameed, Ayesha. 2011. "Borders in the City." In *Imagining Resistance: Visual Culture and Activism in Canada*, edited by J. Keri Cronin and Kirsty Robertson, 121–140. Waterloo, ON: Wilfred Laurier University Press.
Hobsbawm, Eric J. 1978. *Primitive Rebels: Studies in Archaic Forms of Social Movement in the Nineteenth and Twentieth Centuries*. Manchester: Manchester University Press.
Keenan, Thomas. 2002. "Publicity and Indifference (Sarajevo on Television)." *PMLA* 117, no. 1 (January): 104–116. https://www.mlajournals.org/doi/abs/10.1632/003081202X63555.
Kurasawa, Fuyuki. 2009. "A Message in a Bottle: Bearing Witness as a Mode of Transnational Practice." *Theory, Culture and Society* 26, no. 1 (January): 92–111. https://journals.sagepub.com/doi/10.1177/0263276408099017.
Latour, Bruno. 2004. "From Realpolitik to Dingpolitik or How to Make Things Public." In *Making Things Public: Atmospheres of Democracy*, edited by Bruno Latour and Peter Weibel, 14–43. Cambridge, MA: MIT Press.
Mielke, Anelynda. 2017. "Objectifying the Border: Symbolism and Subaltern Experience of Borders in Palestine and Canada." *Borderlands* 16, no. 1 (May): 1–25. http://www.borderlands.net.au/vol16no12017/mielke_objectifying.pdf.
Nayar, Paramod K. 2009. "Scar Cultures: Media, Spectacle, Suffering." *Journal of Creative Communications* 4, no. 3 (March): 147–162. https://journals.sagepub.com/doi/10.1177/097325861000400301.
Pohran, Nadya. 2020. "Inviting the Other: An Ethnographically-informed Social History of Sat Tal Christian Ashram." PhD diss., University of Cambridge.
Rancière, Jacques. 1999. *Disagreement: Politics and Philosophy*. Translated by Julie Rose. Minneapolis: University of Minnesota Press.
Rygiel, Kim. 2013. "Mobile Citizens, Risky Subjects: Security Knowledge at the Border." In *Mobilities, Knowledge, and Social Justice*, edited by Suzan Ilcan, 152–176. Montréal: McGill-Queen's University Press.
Scott, James C. 1987. *Weapons of the Weak: Everyday Forms of Peasant Resistance*. New Haven, CT: Yale University Press.
Scott, Marian. 2015. "Refugee Claimant Who Sought Sanctuary in a Church for Four Years Gets Canadian Citizenship." *Montreal Gazette*, February 6, 2015. https://ccrweb.ca/en/refugee-claimant-who-sought-sanctuary-church-four-years-gets-canadian-citizenship.
Shohat, Ella, and Robert Stam. 1994. *Unthinking Eurocentrism: Multiculturalism and the Media*. London: Psychology Press.
Sliwinski, Sharon. 2011. *Human Rights in Camera*. Chicago: University of Chicago Press.

Solanki, Gopika. 2007. "Adjudication in Religious Family Laws: Cultural Accommodation, Legal Pluralism, and Women's Rights in India." PhD diss., McGill University.

Sontag, Susan. 1977. *On Photography*. New York: Picador, Farrar, Strauss and Giroux.

Stasiulis, Dalva. 2013. "Contending Frames of 'Security' and 'Citizenship': Lebanese Dual Nationals During the 2006 Lebanon War." In *Mobilities, Knowledge, and Social Justice*, edited by Suzan Ilcan, 23–58. Montréal: McGill-Queen's University Press.

Torchin, Leshu. 2012. "The White Band's Burden: Humanitarian Synergy and the Make Poverty History Campaign." In *Sensible Politics: The Visual Culture of Nongovernmental Activism*, edited by Meg McLagan and Yates McKee, 589–612. Cambridge, MA: MIT Press.

Walters, William. 2014. "Parrhēsia Today: Drone Strikes, Fearless Speech and the Contentious Politics of Security." *Global Society* 28, no. 3 (May): 277–299. https://doi.org/10.1080/13600826.2014.900741.

CHAPTER 4

Border Cultures: A Retrospective
Part 1. A Context for *Border Cultures* and Conversations with the Curator

Victor Konrad

In the years 2013, 2014, and 2015, the Art Gallery of Windsor featured consecutive exhibitions of *Border Cultures*, a landmark series of forty-five artist projects and essays on the "real, imagined, physical, political and conceptual" role of borders in everyday life. The three iterations of *Border Cultures* were "homes, land" (2013), "work, labour" (2014), and "security, surveillance" (2015). This chapter combines an overview and retrospective of the exhibitions and the exhibition catalogue with a contextual essay and introduction by Victor Konrad. In these two parts, the chapter offers a retrospective essay with a synopsis of the exhibitions, a selection of representative works of art in the exhibitions, and a brief comment on the contribution of the exhibitions. The overall aim is to allow the exhibitions to speak for themselves. This final chapter of the first section of the book, like chapter 8 at the end of the second section, and chapter 12 at the end of the third section, are all conveyed, in part, as essays, but also in the formats associated with the practitioners of the curatorial, policy, and management portfolios associated with borders and culture. We begin with viewing border culture, and specifically border art, through the eyes of both the curator and the border studies academic.

This chapter offers a brief overview of the exhibitions and a review of the book published on the occasion of the completion of the *Border Cultures* program (Mitra 2015). The overview and review in part 2 of this chapter draw extensively on Srimoyee Mitra's purpose and vision for the exhibitions, and the excerpted text from *Border Cultures* is contextualized in part 1 by Victor Konrad.[1] The primary contribution of the chapter is to assess the impact of the exhibitions. What did the exhibitions contribute to understanding the meaning of the border, and how this meaning has changed in the twenty-first century? How did the exhibitions change the way in which the border is viewed? What images of the border and the processes of bordering are conveyed by the art works in *Border Cultures*? How does "border art" expand our appreciation of border work, border processes, border security, and, ultimately, border life? How has *Border Cultures* impacted the border communities in the Detroit-Windsor cross-border region? What is the legacy of the *Border Cultures* project?

The chapter begins with a brief discussion of imaging and imagining the border between Canada and the United States. This context draws comparisons with other "border art" projects, both in a contemporary and a historical perspective. Also, the context places the Detroit-Windsor border region at the forefront and edge of the Canada-US encounter both before and after the events of 9/11. This is a creative edge, enlivened by the intermingling of American and Canadian lives advancing industry and technology, addressing ethnic, racial, and social issues; exploring cultural expression in architecture, music, theatre and the other arts; and forming ideas and attitudes about the border that linked and separated city, region, and nation. The contextual perspective offered by the editor includes a very brief overview of how art meets the border between Canada and the US. This introduction is followed by the editor's assessment of the contribution of the *Border Cultures* project as it relates to border studies. The assessment is informed by conversations with the curator Srimoyee Mitra. It includes an outlook on the contribution and significance of border art for humanizing the border between the US and Canada. Part 2 of this chapter, authored by the curator Srimoyee Mitra, is a detailed overview of the *Border Cultures* project, highlighting the exhibitions and the publication.

---

1   The editors wish to acknowledge the comments and suggestions of Lee Rodney and Michael Darroch in helping to envision and prepare this chapter, and reading drafts of the text.

Border Cultures in Perspective

Imaging and imagining the border between Canada and the United States has long inspired exhibitions of photographs, paintings, and sculpture, as well as installations of art at or near border crossings and places. The iconographic power of Niagara Falls alone has generated countless images and imaginaries of the border as a place of connection and division (McGreevy 2009). Since Canada evolved from France and Great Britain in the eighteenth and nineteenth centuries, caricatures have conveyed the border in politics, trade, and everyday life (Nicol 2012, 2015), and artists have captured the significance and meaning of the border in their works (Amilhat Szary 2012a). In the twentieth century, the border was celebrated for its benign nature. *Between Friends/Entre amis* (Canada, NFB 1976), Canada's gift to the United States on the occasion of the US bicentennial, depicted local ties, cross-border linkages, cooperation, mutual interests, and intertwined identities at places all along the thousands of kilometres/miles of the boundary. The border was envisioned as an entity, from sea to sea and north into the Arctic. Yes, there were regional components based on compartmentalization of this seemingly endless boundary across the continent, but the celebration of the border, either in *Between Friends/Entre amis* or in the bright palette of illustrations by Peter Max at US border crossings to Canada, was intended to convey consistency and unity along the line.

On September 11, 2001, the border re-emerged as a barrier with a sudden flourish of security and insecurity that still prevails. Not only did the events of 9/11 herald the end of an era of extensive cross-border integration and mutual respect between Americans and Canadians, but they also mark a massive shift in the imaginaries of the border and the cross-border relationship by people in the United States and in Canada. Artists in both countries were quick to take the pulse of these changes and to express the nature of the changing border and borderlands. Some of these artists are featured in *Border Cultures*. The exhibition program, associated activities, and publications are among the most ambitious and successful efforts to gauge the new meaning and impact of the changing border between the United States and Canada as well as the consequences generally of re-bordering the continent. Although other exhibitions after the events of 9/11 have focused on the Canada-US border, these have tended to be associated with specific localities along the border, as in the case of the *Stanstead Project, or How to Cross the Border*, or with particular cultural groups, such as Indigenous peoples in *Border Zones* at the UBC Museum of Anthropology (Amilhat Szary 2012a). Such a focus is desirable given the extensive and regional nature of the Canada-US border and the complexities of dealing with the broad range of issues that vary from region to region and from place to place along the border. Yet the border has itself grown to be a more formidable and common foe in the psyche of Canadians and borderland Americans, thus adding a similarity and sameness to border concerns across the continent and calling for artistic production to address these issues. *Border Cultures* responds to this call and in doing so establishes a framework for extensive artistic reaction to a growing presence of borders and bordering.

Anne-Laure Amilhat Szary (2012b) has noted that art production at borders and boundaries is a fast-growing expression. She states that art displays at borders, and those that focus on politically sensitive places such as borders, affect the meaning of art works as well as the meaning of place (Amilhat Szary 2012b, 213). "Border art is being strengthened by the harshening of border politics and this factual coincidence lays the ground for a geopolitical analysis of a renewed display of art" (Amilhat Szary 2012b, 219). This may be a new kind of art, an art that combines fusion and displacement and shatters the distorting mirrors of the "Western avant-garde" (Gómez-Peña 1991). For Amilhat Szary, and for a growing number of border specialists, the border art scene renews the debate on the display of art, questions public and private modes of display in disputed places, and contributes to the emergence of art geopolitics (Amilhat Szary 2012b, 222).

"Can cultural production be more than a side issue in border studies?" (Dell'Agnese and Amilhat Szary 2015, 4). Anne-Laure Amilhat Szary suggests that it can and should be more than a side issue or "soft" side of border studies (Amilhat Szary 2012a). Yet, according to Lee Rodney and Srimoyee Mitra, although there are some important border artworks and projects, conversations specifically about the Canada-US border in the contemporary art world are quite limited. So, even though visual arts on the Canada-US border (Amilhat Szary 2012a), and elsewhere that people engage and cultural productions about the border (Schimanski and Wolfe 2017), has increasingly called attention to the border, there remains an immense potential and need to explore the Canada-US border, and borders in

Canada more generally, through art. Also, it is important to connect the insights on the Canada-US border with those gained through such works as those, for example, appearing in the Way Past Kennedy Road Collective's exhibit *Sanctuary Inter/rupted*, which explores issues of internal bordering and unbelonging in Toronto (Fakhrashrafi, Kirk, and Gilbert 2019). In these works, Black, Indigenous, and other racialized women artists raised issues of everyday deportability, the ways that illegalization is mapped on the body, and the consequent refusal to reaffirm the multicultural nation.

Cultural production is essential to respond to borders of all kinds, and understanding this cultural production is fundamental to understanding borders. As the works featured in *Border Cultures* attest, cultural production at and about the border is linked to mobilities, agency, and citizenship. All of these human concerns and rights are now in question at the Canada-US border and at borders around the globe. They are at the heart of geopolitics in a world that is changing rapidly. Cultural production at and about borders is a rich and resonant expression of how we view the border and how we deal with it. This cultural production must be understood to inform our various perspectives—security, sustainability, trade, migration, governance—surrounding borders.

The Contribution of *Border Cultures*

Border Cultures has done the important cultural work of putting borders into perspective, and the exhibitions have established a model for engaging cultural productions at and about the border, specifically the border between the US and Canada. Yet the work is not done; there is so much remaining to reveal about how our border, and borders generally, operate and perform, and what they mean. *Border Cultures* is, then, a challenge and a call for more attention by artists, curators, and arts institutions to the borders that both separate and join people. Exploring the culture of borders and bordering, particularly in the variation and dislocation of globalization, requires the insight of the arts community. Moreover, it requires the interaction of artists, the public, and scholars to share our views of the border, discuss these views, debate them, and, hopefully, address both the negative impacts and positive interactions at the border.

In preparing the text for this chapter, Victor Konrad worked with Lee Rodney and Michael Darroch to develop several questions to explore the impact and contribution of *Border Cultures*. A conversation was initiated with curator Srimoyee Mitra to explore the questions. Although this conversation was very preliminary, and a more thorough retrospective is planned, the following discussion begins to examine the development, reception, and implications of the *Border Cultures* exhibition series. This brief discussion may help the reader to look behind the scenes of the exhibitions to understand more fully the curatorial process underlying the exhibitions and, in this way, broaden both their understanding of border culture and their empathy for its impact.

The challenges and obstacles faced by a gallery in developing and convening any exhibition are usually daunting and extensive. Once a vision for the exhibition is developed, the curatorial team needs to research ideas and themes, identify and engage artists, find and solidify funding, work out logistics, arrange public programs associated with the exhibition, and deal with a myriad of details surrounding the exhibition and associated programs. *Border Cultures* was a three-stage exhibition convened over three years. Consequently, the challenges were multiplied and sustained. Nevertheless, the Art Gallery of Windsor, the curatorial team, the associated arts communities, and, of course, the artists prevailed and, indeed, excelled in convening a highly visible and successful set of exhibitions. According to the curator, Srimoyee Mitra, this was accomplished with a small curatorial team. Mitra acknowledged: "My position as the only full-time curator at the Art Gallery of Windsor limited my capacity to deepen my research by travelling and visiting artists experimenting with these ideas and themes. As a result, I was very dependent on Skype and available resources to connect with artists to bring their projects to Windsor. By this token, our budgets were also very tight and this prevented me from developing some of the more ambitious projects and works for the exhibition that I had imagined, for example, with Canadian artists such as Abbas Akhavan and international artists such as Victoria Lomasko." Another challenge involved the public programs: "Each exhibition included a robust suite of public programs. Due to the limited budgets for marketing and publicity, we were not able to publicize the programs as widely nationally and internationally as we would have liked to, specifically in southeast Michigan and southwestern Ontario." Yet the exhibitions were reported by media on both sides of the border, particularly by the national media in

Canada. Prominent among the other challenges and obstacles were the tight timelines. Srimoyee Mitra recalled: "The *Border Cultures* series of exhibitions took place every twelve months. In retrospect, if we had eighteen months it would have been easier so that we would have had a little more time to develop new projects with artists. However, due to various programming decisions, we had to organize the exhibition every January to March from 2013 to 2015, respectively. On the other hand, the predictability of these exhibitions every winter season did help us plan with community partners and this boosted audiences."

An important measure of the success and impact of *Border Cultures* is associated with the exhibitions' resonance with local audiences. How did various local audiences respond to the exhibitions? Did you find that the response changed with each year's exhibition? Mitra responded:

> Among our core audiences for this exhibition were the students and faculty from the University of Windsor. We benefited from the faculty members of the University of Windsor's School of Creative Arts, and specifically Lee Rodney and Michael Darroch, with whom we developed a major cross-border conference in 2013 called Diversions: Detroit-Windsor Conversations on Borders, Traffic, and Circulation, which drew together a range of internationally acclaimed artists and urban scholars to consider the conditions and challenges posed by transborder urban environments in a global context. Another common audience group were students and faculty from the University of Windsor's Faculty of Law as well as social workers and organizers from non-profit organizations such as Windsor Women Working with Immigrant Women and organizers from Windsor Action Centre, to name a few. With each edition, I had a different set of local community partners whom we worked closely with to develop and present a socially edged project.

Mitra continued:

> For Part One, we worked with the Turtle Island Education Centre at the University of Windsor to develop the Indigenous youth project with Métis artist and scholar Dylan Miner. For Part Two, we worked with organizations such as the First Baptist

Church and Windsor Women Working with Immigrant Women, as well as the campus community radio station CJAM, to develop Reena Katz's collaborative projects with these organizations and the marginalized communities they represent. During Part Three, we partnered with Windsor's Downtown Farmer's Market, as well as the Multicultural Centre in Windsor and Salt and Cedar in Detroit to develop Tintin Wulia's project. In addition to this, each edition brought out different audiences: During Part One we did tours for educators and university students from Windsor and Detroit. Part Two drew more attendees who were activists and organizers, and Part Three garnered a lot of interest specifically from the Faculty of Law, students, and human rights organizations.

Finally, we asked Mitra about how the tenor of the discourse around bordering practices has changed since the conclusion of the *Border Cultures* exhibitions in 2015 and whether the choice of exhibits and artists would be different in the context of today's political climate. Srimoyee Mitra suggested: "The change in leadership of nations in North America has transformed the rhetoric around the border dramatically. The rise of the Right internationally (US, Europe, Latin America, Middle East) has made 'Walls' and 'Refugees' synonymous with the notion of the national boundary. While we have witnessed many of the issues around illegal human trafficking, war, environmental and economic crises that force people to move for some time, their urgency has intensified. So, I would not necessarily change the artists in the show. Yet," she continued, "I would probably include some [new] artists who were dealing with many of the issues in the news." Srimoyee Mitra concluded: "*Border Cultures* was deeply concerned with national boundaries as they are linked to mobilities, to agency, and to citizenship. We explored and examined what these may mean from the perspectives of diverse artists living across Canada and beyond. There is a lot of scope for examining the environmental impact on migration and belonging in future projects surrounding borders.

Part 2. *Border Cultures*: The Exhibitions

Srimoyee Mitra

Border Cultures was envisioned as a multi-year exhibition-in-process that would transform, respond to, reflect, and mobilize discussion and recognition of compelling and diverse artworks, practices, and subjectivities that "attest to the epistemological shift from the modern to the postmodern era of art and politics" (Shiekh 2009, para 3). While I was aware of the long lineage of artists' involvement in actions and activism that were pivotal in the formation of various modern art histories, I was keen to investigate the shift toward relational, collaborative and collectivist projects in contemporary art and the ways in which artists reinvent forms of representation and address vital questions of materiality in the turbulent, post-9/11 world. The exhibition was staged inside the white cube gallery spaces of the Art Gallery of Windsor. The task of the exhibition, in my perspective, was to restage the space to connect the past with the present (the history of modern art with contemporary spatial practices) (Shiekh 2009), the inside with the outside (by employing an expansive notion of place prior to selecting artists; Doherty 2007), where the gallery space itself is "able to morph around the artists' work" providing spaces for active rather than passive viewing and participation, collaboration, contemplation and imagination (Doherty 2004, 7). As I wrote in the volume documenting the exhibition:

> Here, artists are the key agents who use the exhibition platform to expand research and present ongoing bodies of work at various stages of completion and becoming. The exhibition-in-process is non-directive and thus placed in a heterogeneous space where artworks produced across diverse temporal and spatial registers enact a dialogue with each other in playful, compelling and chaotic ways, activating critical understandings of borders. The militarized divisions between places, which became the point of departure for the exhibition, were critically reimagined over and over again. In contrast to the homogeneous visual regimes of mass media that emphasize the fixity of the border, the exhibitions

> repeatedly staged it as an uneven, transformative and luminal space for the articulation of agency, pain, fear, desire and social justice. Keeping with the open-ended spirit of the exhibition, *Border Cultures* brought together local, national and international artists in no hierarchical or linear order to avoid the lazy and stereotypical recirculating of well-rehearsed artworks by star artists. (Mitra 2015, 12)

My aim in the research, and in the final exhibitions, was to build, instead, multilayered and multicentred dialogues by bringing together artworks of recognized and emerging artists from different places, of various races and genders. Altogether, the exhibitions presented "borders as complex sites of confluence and difference, where new subjectivities and identities can emerge and resist the colonial paradigm, while activating vernacular aesthetics within international contemporary art discourse" (Mitra 2015, 12).

As an exhibition-in-process, *Border Cultures* reimagined borders in three iterations: (homes, land), (work, labour), and (security, surveillance). These iterations offered lenses through which to address research questions about multiple, changing national and international boundaries; they were ways of thinking through ideas, testing and rehearsing artist-led strategies and proposals for reimagining borders. Below, I use excerpts from the introductory essay to the 2015 publication *Border Cultures*, "Sensing Borders," to highlight three projects and artworks; although these works do not necessarily represent the works of the forty-five artists featured in the exhibitions (a full illustrated catalogue is available in the book), they are touchstones and points of departure for me to explore deeper, situated, ongoing, and meaningful questions of homes and land, work and labour, and security and surveillance in the context of multiple and changing boundaries (Mitra 2015, 12). Each of the three works discussed below is representative of one of the exhibition's iterations and, in order to relate to the aims and scope of this book, is situated in the Canada-US borderlands. The works are Dylan Miner's *Together Forever/Never Apart* for Part One; reproductions from Detroit's *Inner City Voice* during the 1967 riots for Part Two; and Rebecca Belmore's *The Named and the Unnamed* for Part 3.

Part One (Homes, Land)

The first exhibition of the series began with an investigation of the multiple meanings of home: "Is it a geographical space, a historical space, an emotional, sensory space?" (Mohanty 2003). As Mohanty has insightfully pointed out, notions of home, identity and geography are infinitely complex for nomads, migrants, refugees, and workers across the globe today (Mohanty 2003, 126). In this context, the condition of statelessness or "refugeeism" is not a temporary problem, but a permanent characteristic of the twenty-first century (Minh-ha 2011). And, thus the idea of home is profoundly personal and political. In the Americas, for example, the discourses of transnationalism and globalization have consistently overlooked the habitual movement of Indigenous peoples across American, Canadian, and Mexican borders. Asserting the right to ancestral homelands in the Americas is intrinsically linked to ideas of belonging, self-determination, and fundamental human rights. In Part One, I was interested in artists who explored strategies of homemaking located in specific geopolitical sites and ongoing struggles against coloniality that challenge the dominant homogeneous narratives of nation(ality) and belonging while "mobilizing an image and imaginative possibilities that await potential realization" (Demos 2013, xxii). Thus the exhibition explored ways in which formal strategies and tactics in contemporary art, such as social practice, documentary realism, and media-based immersive installations interrupted the seamless image of the "nation."

Dylan Miner is one of the first artists I met when I moved to Windsor. He was born and raised in various cities across Michigan and lives in Lansing, Michigan, where he also teaches at Michigan State University. We quickly became friends, and through his prolific art practice I learned a great deal about Indigenous migrations between Windsor and Detroit. I invited him to develop a multi-year project for the *Border Cultures* series. For Part One we worked with First Nations' youths on both sides of the Detroit River to remap the borderlands with mobile print labs. For months leading up to the exhibition, Miner worked with young people in Windsor and Detroit to collectively build a cargo tricycle in each city and embellish them with culturally symbolic materials such as elk hide, horse hair, and beads mixed with graffiti and street art iconography. Equipped with a screen printer, the young people ranging from ages 8 to 18 remapped their city based on personal and Indigenous sites of significance. The colonial border was drafted with the establishment of the Treaty of Ghent in 1814, and restricts Indigenous mobility to this day. Unfortunately, the young people that Miner collaborated with were not permitted to cross the Canada-US border to work as one group, thereby inadvertently elucidating the colonial structures that continue to divide, alienate, and assimilate Indigenous peoples, as they have for generations. Meanwhile, Miner organized decolonial mapping projects that emphasized sites of personal and Indigenous significance on both sides of the river. He facilitated dialogues, providing tools for exchange and commonality that were also embedded in the aesthetic of the trikes. In the gallery, Miner invited audience members to participate in printing and distributing t-shirts and posters with Anishinaabeg iconography stating "no borders." Upon completion of Part One, the tricycle-print labs were returned to the partnering community centres in Windsor and Detroit where they continue to activate Indigenous knowledge systems and decolonizing practices that are invisible in the hegemonic framework of Canada and US relations (Mitra 2015, 12–13).

Dylan Miner and the Broken City Lab (BCL), a Windsor-based artist collective, generated a range of playful and poetic strategies to subvert the increasing social distance between Detroit and Windsor. Since the events of 9/11, mobility between the cities has changed radically. In an effort to draw attention to these attenuations, and to ameliorate them, BCL sought to reveal ways in which a renewed relationship between the cities could be imagined and enacted. In Together Forever/Never Apart (2012), the familiar elementary schoolyard term "best friends forever" (BFF) is contained and displayed in fractured hearts located in neighbourhoods in the cross-border cities. The gesture comes out of a nostalgic place to convey how it feels to be in Windsor and Detroit.

From a focus on the Detroit and Windsor border, the exhibition expands its scope and scale outward to the greater region, the continent, and beyond. Yet the themes of Indigenous knowledge systems and decolonizing practices are recurrent throughout the exhibition.

This condition of non-recognition is part of everyday life for refugees across the world. Since the 1948 Nakba, the forced expulsion of Palestinians for the establishment of the state of Israel, millions of people have become refugees and taken shelter in mass-produced refugee camps originally conceived as temporary solutions to emergency conditions. Now, more than six decades later, generations of refugees have been born and raised in the terrible conditions of these precarious camps—their "homes." Campus in Camps, a collective of artists, architects, urban planners, and social workers, reimagined the "temporary" and precarious sites as spaces that can challenge the status quo of nationhood, citizenship, and safety. Their project *School of Exile* was a proposition for the first girl's school in Shu'fat refugee camp that responded to the complex social, spatial, and psychological experiences of the community living in the camp. For the exhibition, Campus in Camps developed a larger-than-life photographic mural of a panoramic aerial view of the Shu'fat refugee camp, surrounded by the occupied city of Jerusalem. The image foregrounded the unruly, excessive architecture and chaos of the camp while the neat suburban homes from the occupation are captured looming in the horizon. The image confronted audiences with the messy details of the living conditions in a refugee camp in the twenty-first century and a distant view of Jerusalem from the position of a refugee, who does not have mobility or access to global economic advantages. The artists interrupted the passive spectatorship of this image with text panels that contextualized the site, only to abstract it with a three-dimensional architectural model that asked audiences what they would do if charged with redesigning/reimagining the space. By transforming the two-dimensional image into an interactive work, the artists and audiences participated in the "remaking" of the piece—albeit from distinct and diverse subjectivities and positions—thereby collectively connecting the experience of refugees with the public imagination (Bishop 2011).

Conversely, Northern Irish artist Willie Doherty's muted and haunting black-and-white photographs of Londonderry's built environment composed of intimidating walls and barbed wire fences, hidden alleyways and narrow bridges, captured the colonial repression, unspeakable violence, and devastation that ravaged the lives of so many young men and women during "The Troubles." The starkness of these images is exacerbated by their life-sized proportions, implicating the viewer's bodies while drawing them in with the bold text on its surface. Doherty exercised restraint in visualizing the conflict that was highly mediatized, and instead invited the viewers to listen to the silenced voices behind the barricades and across the fences. Toronto-based Taiwanese artist Ed Pien expressed his anxiety of dispossession through an immersive and site-specific installation where he explored the plight of undocumented migrants who travel vast territories to work in better-off economies as invisible and "illegal" people struggling to make ends meet. In *Memento* every audience member was invited to traverse through, under, and over layers of nets, intricate and fragile paper cuttings that created shadows of bold and tentative lines. Layered with discrete sound and video, the installation created dreamlike, haunting sequences of images that resembled spider webs, fishing nets, chain-linked fences. Pien paid homage to human survival in extreme adversity while experimenting with the affective possibilities of elemental drawing and mark making. The latter has served as the sign of life and a testament to the human creativity for centuries (Mitra, 2015, 13–14).

Part Two (Work, Labour)

The precarity of the global labour force and the experience of displacement are both commonplace and more complex in the twenty-first century (Papastergiadis 2000). As Niko Papastergiadis observes: "Every nation-state is at once seeking to maximize the opportunities from transnational corporations and, yet, closing its doors to the forms of migration that these economic shifts stimulate" (Papastergiadis 2000, 3). As goods move flow more easily than people, the proliferation of borders can be understood by analyzing contemporary patterns of migration and migrant workers, where only certain groups are allowed to enter in a selected and controlled manner. The border functions as a filter, "establishing multiple points of control along key lines and geographies of wealth and power" (Mezzadra and Neilson 2013, 7). Here inclusion exists in a continuum with exclusion. The communities of undocumented and so-called "illegal" migrants are a demonstration of the deep stratification and disparities in the border complex that impact multiple aspects of contemporary society such as labour, space, time, law, power, and citizenship (Mezzadra and Neilson 2013, 7). Part Two drew inspiration from the specific labour histories and social struggles of enslaved peoples, the anti-segregation movement, and wildcat strikes by black autoworkers in Windsor and Detroit. The inquiry extended into notions of work and labour that explored menial and invisible women's work and migrant labour, which are all embedded within the present-day neoliberal capitalist framework.

Marian McMahon was a Windsor-born artist, filmmaker, and scholar, who despite her early death in 1996, made significant contributions to Canadian film and video art practices in her short-lived career that remain overlooked in the canons of Canadian media art. Drawing from her archives, renowned filmmaker Philip Hoffman developed the major installation—*Dialogic Illuminations of Marian McMahon*—not only as a tribute to her life and work but also as a meditation on memory, the social production and distribution of images, and the complexity of subjectivity. McMahon's unfinished work, *Racing Home* (rough cut), 1994, highlighted her autodidactic, self-reflexive strategy in filmmaking that was unconventional among academic and formal filmmaker circles in the 1980s. Growing up across the Detroit River and in the wake of the civil rights movement, the Detroit race riots in 1967, and the Canadian Centennial celebrations that took place the same year, she nevertheless turned her gaze inwards in the film, questioning the formation of her own identity, which in turn comments on the dominant monolithic narrative of the Canadian nation. Through her autodidactic narration she aptly observes: "Focusing on raced identity I wanted to know how I have been taught to see myself as white, what were the specific dimensions of this identity and how were they shaped in this specific landscape—a border town facing a large US city and separated by a river. To get caught up in histories which we are largely unaware is inevitable. Yet we have a historical responsibility—the past shapes us in ways that are still with us" (McMahon 1994). Albeit unfinished, *Racing Home* was prescient and prophetic, as McMahon pairs her own footage of walking along the railroad tracks to symbolize the Underground Railroad, used by enslaved peoples in the US to escape to Canada where they could be free, with the startling found footage of the American National Guard targeting civilians and protesters during the Detroit race riots in 1967. All the while overlapping the moving images with her voice, as she narrates anecdotes and poems from fleeing slaves, reads public notices by slave owners offering rewards for those who escaped or ran away, to her meditations on the precedence of the economy and the auto industries in the late twentieth century that had become the dominant narrative on Windsor-Detroit relations. The video reflected on the systemic erasure of the painful social struggles experienced by thousands of people (Mitra 2015, 14).

Border Cultures: Part Two (Work, Labour) included reproductions of several issues of *Inner City Voice* that illustrated strategies and tactics for coping with and organizing against substandard healthcare and housing for the poor, police brutality and profiling, and the pervasive, systemic racism within the workplace and throughout the urban area. The words and pictures in these pages continue to resonate in Detroit, and throughout the United States and worldwide, as Black Lives Matter and other movements continue to work toward equality for Black Americans and racialized peoples everywhere.

Two decades later [after McMahon's work in the 1990s], Toronto-based artist Reena Katz explored the latent racial and gendered hierarchies in multifarious ways. Katz's performative installation *midnight down 20-10-10* cut across time and space to record, stage, and re-enact the living histories of labour-based social movements with human migration. For a year leading up to Part Two, Katz spent weeks in Windsor and Detroit, visiting community organizations, and meeting social workers and educators to learn about sociocultural-economic gaps their programs addressed. Based on this knowledge, Katz developed a complex installation composed of modular stages, Risograph posters, field recordings, reproductions of archival documents, objects, and ephemera that symbolized Windsor-Detroit tunnels and the multiple, shared cross-cultural and cross-border histories and memories of the Underground Railroad, labour and cultural histories that have been connecting people from both cities for centuries. She met youth, social workers, actors, singers, and radio broadcasters from four organizations—Windsor Women Working with Immigrant Women's Newcomer Art Program, the Sandwich Singers choir from the First Baptist Church, local labour organizer and radio show host Paul Chislett, and the New York Field Street Collective in Detroit. Katz invited them to use her installation in ways that would help them expand the reach of their respective projects among AGW members and patrons. Thus the installation was transformed every month from a rehearsal space to a safe intimate space for sharing difficult experiences of struggles with poverty, racism, and violence, to a live studio audience for a radio show. The labour of Katz's work activated collaborations and participation with these marginalized communities, on both sides of the Detroit River, and elucidated the elitist tendencies and legacies of the white cube gallery space that perpetually excluded them, while situating the historical struggles of enslaved peoples and indentured labour in the contemporary context.

This engagement of lesser-known histories of labour and peoples in contemporary society is echoed in the selection of work in Part Two. Works by Martha Rossler, Marisa Jahn, Min Sook Lee and Deborah Barndt, and Margareta Kern examined the multiple, divergent histories of women migrant workers in the US, Canada, and Germany respectively. Each deployed a distinct approach to the moving image, creating documentary fictions of diasporic identities of women migrant workers. Meanwhile, artists such as Andrea Slavik, Ken Lum, and Sam Durant played with the aesthetic of advertising billboards, electrical signs, and interactive digital boards to explore complicit consumption and individual agency. Dylan Miner and CAMP in turn activated narratives of migration and labour of Indigenous communities on Turtle Island and a seafaring Gujarati community in India through performative, media-based installations. Finally, the remarkable photographs of David Taylor examined the border patrol along the US-Mexico border, a multi-million dollar industry that more than doubled between 2007 and 2011, the period during which he made the work. Taylor's unprecedented access to the activities of the US Border Patrol—everything from performing mundane office tasks and fingerprinting people repeatedly to negotiating the complex issues of crime and justice within border security—highlight the various forms of precarity surrounding the everyday lives of migrants, border crossers as well as the border guards. Altogether the series cultivates a sense of empathy and respect (Mitra 2015, 14–15).

Part Three (Security, Surveillance)

The final iteration of *Border Cultures* pays critical attention to the manifold artistic reactions and responses to the human costs of US immigration policy and the "war on terror" since 9/11 that radically impacted people's lives and the urgency of art practice worldwide. The dispersal of the militarized armature across sectors, the culture of suspicion and fear perpetuated through censorship and surveillance tactics, and the ongoing mass disappearances, detentions, and deportations in North America that target Aboriginal women, black men, low-income migrant, refugee communities, and activists became the centre of investigation for Part Three (security, surveillance).

Rebecca Belmore has reclaimed, remembered, and re-enacted the violence of assimilation and erasure that continues to play out on Native women's bodies in Canada in her landmark video installation *The Named and the Unnamed*. Based on the footage of her seminal and disturbing performance *Vigil* that took place on June 23, 2002, she addressed the disappearance of more than fifty women (the numbers were underdetermined at that time) from Vancouver's Eastside.

Belmore started her performance by testing the audience's expectations of a Native artist as simply enacting embodiments of traditions. She employed elements of a classic ritual, cleansing and washing the street corner to establish a bounded luminal space before abruptly interrupting the meditative actions by shouting out the names of the missing and murdered women one by one, and decapitating a rose with thorns, swallowing and spitting out the petals. Moments later in the video, Belmore donned a red dress and nailed the ends of the fabric into the wood. As she struggled to detach herself from the nails, the fabric ripped and tore. She repeated this violent action of nailing her dress and struggled to release it over and over again. The performance and tattered fabric embodied an unbearable tension that can be read as symbols of pain, anger, ferocity, and grief about the violence of assimilation and erasure inflicted on the body, the Native body, and women's bodies. All the while, Belmore has agency, her performance resists the simplistic binaries of the oppressive colonizer and the colonial subject as a victim (Townsend-Gault 2002, 19). Her installation shocked viewers' minds and rational sensibilities by immersing them in a visceral and intuitive experience that activates the senses and creates a bodily knowledge (Garneau 2013). Here the artist was a provocateur, a necessary agent that transcends the boundaries of the teacher, spectator, and perpetuator of customary culture "to create startling non-beautiful, needful disruptions, and to build hybrid possibilities that resist containment by either colonial designs or Indigenous traditionalism" (Garneau 2013, 15).

New York–based artists Chitra Ganesh and Mariam Ghani have developed an extensive and evolving archive *The Index of the Disappeared*, which attempts to create a collective history of individual disappearances in the US since September 11, 2001, as a counterpoint to acknowledge the limited representation by the law and media of immigrants caught in the system. Comprised of official documents, secondary literature, and personal notes, portraits, postcards, neon signs, paintings, drawings, an online database, and a travelling library, the *Index* presented a counter-representation of the overlooked and hidden narratives and experiences of migrants, and in particular, those that were detained, deported, and profiled. While the *Index* enacts the processes of collecting, ordering, displaying, and narrating histories as in official museums and archives, it fosters an inclusive and discursive approach by incorporating multiple voices, experiences and subjectivities. The *Index* is a discursive platform that is site-specific and consistently reconfigured based on the physical and virtual spaces in which it is presented. At the AGW, audiences "come face to face with specific details of lives that are impacted by post-9/11 disappearance, but must also engage with the core cultural and systemic breakdowns that lie beneath the current events" when they mine the website and documents (Ganesh and Ghani 2005). The *Index* created space for interaction and reflection, where information could be read and considered without being reduced to simplistic images or raw data. Thus the ever-changing archive of the *Index* was as much a site of encounter with the structures of censorship as it is a space for the exploration of a visual language of resistance.

Renowned artist Trevor Paglen's work staged encounters with the American surveillance state—its structures of secrecy, surveillance, and its operations dispersed across the nation. In a large-scale floor-to-ceiling installation Paglen listed the code names of some 4,000 active military sites spread across the US. The absurd and nonsensical names obscure any connection to the programs they designate. Referencing the minimalist traditions of conceptual art, the starkness of the text-based work, simply titled *Code Names*, took on maximalist proportions as the unending list hints at the enormity of the US surveillance state apparatus. The installation was affective, confounding, and transgressive. The raison d'être of Paglen's rigorous research-based practice is to "expand the visual vocabulary we use to 'see' the US intelligence community" (Paglen 2014). He challenges the organizing logic of America's surveillance institutions based on invisibility and secrecy. For him, visualizing the infrastructure is a way of activating democratic values and mobilizing a public discussion on the ethical, legal, economic, social, and cultural benefits and costs of the militarization and surveillance which has resulted in so many lost lives on "home ground" and internationally.

Patrick Beaulieu, Yto Barrada, Tintin Wulia, Victoria Lomasko, Mahwish Chishti, Sharlene Bamboat, and Alexis Mitchell use playful and contemplative interventions and material manifestations to counter-survey institutional infrastructures and policies that restrict mobility, deepen hierarchies, and demonize marginalized border crossers. The deeply personal and poetic works by Camille Turner and Camal Pirbhai, Tory James and Alex McKay, Dylan Miner, Osman Khan, Tazeen Qayyum, and Jose Seone move back and forth between the historical processes of colonial exploitation and the new forms of domination they produce. These works can be understood as decolonizing practices resisting the reproduction of colonial taxonomies and vindicating a radical multiplicity as the basis of any imagination of the social. And, the projects by Harun Farocki, Hito Steyerl, Charles Stankievech, and Syrus Marcus Ware are at once acts, actions, and responses to the systems of power and authority vested in multinationals, museums, and border patrol that perpetuate standardization and homogeneity while obscuring the vitality and complexity of the global public sphere (Mitra 2015, 15–16).

Border Cultures brought together no less than forty-five artists in three separate exhibition platforms over a three-year period, to experiment with ideas and issues related to the complexity of national boundaries in the twenty-first century. What does it mean to be a border city in the world today, characterized by the movement of thousands of refugees, the proliferation of the processes of neoliberal globalization, and anti-globalization and decolonial struggles that are intertwined within economic, political, and social spheres? This question was the primary impetus for the exhibition series, reflecting strategies of place making and unsettling, and it was also an exploration of the ways in which artists participate in "informal politics" (Lynn and Papastergiadis 2014), reinvent new artistic strategies to mobilize the image as well as imagine mobility, statelessness, and coloniality (Demos 2013). Recent shifts in contemporary art toward collaborative, relational, and collectivist projects make evident that art and politics cannot be seen in binary terms such as "political/non-political, withdraw/participate, support/protest, silence/activism" (Lynn and Papastergiadis 2012, 15). Okwui Enwezor argued almost two decades ago that "the visual practices that emerged in the context of debates on multiculturalism and postcolonialism were not only instrumental in radically revising the parameters of modernist subjectivity, but he also acknowledged that they played a role in reconfiguration of the museum as a platform for cross-cultural exchange" (Lynn and Papastergiadis 2012, 15). To this paradigm-shifting observation, I would like to add that the processes of globalization and decolonizing practices that have together decisively transformed art history since the 1980s, and have led to significant efforts in rethinking of the context of art and identity and the multiple cultural spheres in visual production (Lynn and Papastergiadis 2012, 7). Grounded by this emergent understanding of the role of art today, I positioned *Border Cultures* as an ongoing discursive platform for contemporary art dialogues that were situated, and specific, but simultaneously resonated with the interstitial perspectives, experiences, and art histories of other regions and subjectivities. The exhibition energized, multiplied, and reconfigured the gallery space as an active, malleable, and responsive participant in creating a vernacular, decolonizing public space. At once immersive and disruptive, hospitable and exilic, this exhibition attempted to initiate visual experiences that were pedagogical and rational, as well as sensorial, intuitive, and emergent. Artists in the exhibition have made enriching connections, and reinvented forms of belonging and encounter that are fractured, flexible, and rooted in the jagged realities of the contemporary moment (Mitra 2015, 16).

References

Amilhat Szary, Anne-Laure. 2012a. "The Geopolitical Meaning of a Contemporary Visual Arts Upsurge on the Canada-US Border." *International Journal: Canada's Journal of Global Policy Analysis* 67: 951–962.

———. 2012b. "Walls and Border Art: The Politics of Art Display." *Journal of Borderlands Studies* 27 (2): 213–228.

Bishop, Claire. 2011. "Participation and Spectacle: Where are We Now?" Lecture for Creative Time's Living as Form, Cooper Union, New York, May 2011. http://dieklaumichshow.doragarcia.org/pdfs/Bishop.pdf.

Canada, NFB (National Film Board of Canada). 1976. *Between Friends/Entre Amis*. Toronto: McClelland and Stewart.

Dell'Agnese, Elena, and Anne-Laure Amilhat Szary. 2015. "Borderscapes: From Border Landscapes to Border Aesthetics." *Geopolitics* 20 (1): 4–13.

Demos, T. J. 2013. *The Migrant Image: Art and Politics of Documentary During Global Crisis*. Durham, NC: Duke University Press.

Doherty, Claire. 2007. "Curating Wrong Places…or Where Have All the Penguins Gone?" In *Curating Subjects*, edited by Paul O'Neill, 100–108. Amsterdam: DeAppel.

———. 2004. "The Institution is Dead! Long Live the Institution! Contemporary Art and New Institutionalism." *Art of Encounter*, no. 15 (Summer): 1–9.

Fakhrashrafi, Mitra, Jessica Kirk, and Emily Gilbert. 2019. "Sanctuary Interrupted: Borders, Illegalization, and Unbelonging." *The Canadian Geographer/Le Géographe canadien* 63 (1): 84–99.

Ganesh, Chitra, and Mariam Ghani. 2005. "Towards a Visual Language of Resistance: Notes on the Disappeared." In *Sarai Reader 05: Bare Acts*, 154–161. New Delhi: Centre for the Study of Developing Societies.

Garneau, David. 2013. "Extra-Rational Aesthetic Action and Cultural Decolonization." *Fuse Magazine* 36 (4): 14–22. https://e-artexte.ca/id/eprint/25209/1/FUSE_36-4.pdf.

Gómez-Peña, Guillermo. 1991. "A Binational Performance Pilgrimage." *TDR* 35 (3): 22–45.
Lynn, Victoria, and Nikos Papastergiadis. 2014. "Art as Action." *L'Internationale Online*. https://www.internationaleonline.org/research/alter_institutionality/11_art_as_action/.
———. 2012. "Art as Action." In *Cosmopolitanism and Culture*, edited by Nikos Papastergiadis. Cambridge: Polity.
McGreevy, Patrick. 2009. *Imagining Niagara: The Meaning and Making of Niagara Falls*. Amherst: University of Massachusetts Press.
McMahon, Marian. 1994. *Racing Home* (rough cut). https://vimeo.com/channels/879409.
Mezzadra, Sandro, and Brett Neilson. 2013. *Border as Method, or, the Multiplication of Labor*. Durham, NC: Duke University Press.
Minh-ha, Trinh T. 2011. *Elsewhere, Within Here: Immigration, Refugeeism and the Boundary Event*. New York: Routledge.
Mitra, Srimoyee. 2015. *Border Cultures*. London: Black Dog Publishing.
Mohanty, Chandra. 2003. *Feminism Without Borders: Decolonizing Theory, Practicing Solidarity*. Durham, NC: Duke University Press.
Nicol, Heather N. 2015. *The Fence and the Bridge: Geopolitics and Identity along the Canada-US Border*. Waterloo, ON: Wilfrid Laurier University Press.
———. 2012. "The Wall, the Fence, and the Gate: Reflexive Metaphors along the Canada-US Border." *Journal of Borderlands Studies* 27 (2): 139–166.
Paglen, Trevor. 2014. "Overhead: New Photos of the NSA and Other Top Intelligence Agencies Revealed." *Creative Time Reports*, February 10, 2014. http://creativetimereports.org/2014/02/10/overhead-new-photos-of-the-nsa-and-other-top-intelligence-agencies-revealed-trevor-paglen/.
Papastergiadis, Nikos. 2000. *The Turbulence of Migration: Gloablization, Deterritorialization and hybridity*. New York: Polity.
Schimanski, Johan, and Stephen F. Wolfe. 2017. *Border Aesthetics: Concepts and Intersections*. Oxford: Berghahn.
Shiekh, Simon. 2009. "Positively White Cube Revisited." *e-flux Journal*, no. 3 (February). http://www.e-flux.com/journal/positively-white-cube-revisited/.
Townsend-Gault, Charlotte. 2002. "Have We Ever Been Good?" In *The Named and the Unnamed*, edited by Rebecca Belmore. Vancouver: Morris and Helen Belkin Art Gallery, University of British Columbia. Exhibition catalogue.

BORDERS AND CULTURE IN MOTION

CHAPTER 5

The Snowbirds

A Cultural Movement across Borders

Melissa Kelly

It has become increasingly common for Canadian retirees to pursue a lifestyle that allows them to spend their winters in a warmer climate. There are destinations that lure Canadian retirees throughout the world: Mexico, Costa Rica, and even places as far as Thailand and Australia. For Canadians, however, there is one country that draws more retirees than any other, and that is the United States. Proximity and similarity to Canada are some of the key factors that make the US a popular choice for Canadian snowbirds. According to the Conference Board of Canada (2016), the United States is currently the destination of over half of snowbird trips and is likely to become even more popular with time, as baby boomers age and seek out what they perceive to be comfortable and convenient winter destinations.

According to Statistics Canada and Conference Board of Canada estimates, 1.7 million snowbird trips were made in 2015 (Conference Board of Canada 2016). A "snowbird trip" is defined, in the Conference Board of Canada (2016) *Canadian Snowbird Travel Market Annual Report*, as "a trip of 31 or more nights by Canadians aged 55 or older." According to the report, Canada's aging population has led snowbird trips to increase by over 305 percent in the years between 2000 and 2015. This can be compared with a growth rate of just 87 percent for outbound leisure trips.

It is difficult to classify Canadian retirees moving to the US temporarily each year. Canadian snowbirds spend too much time in the

US to be considered tourists, but neither are they full-time residents. Instead, their lifestyle is characterized by the back and forth migrations they make; most snowbirds return to the same snowbird destination every year, while maintaining strong links to their communities in Canada. Moreover, unlike other categories of temporary migrants such as labourers and students, they are motivated by leisure pursuits and the desire to build idealized lifestyle communities, often in partnership with American snowbirds of a similar demographic. As Ken Coates, Robert Healy, and William Morrison (2002) have postulated, snowbird migration represents the largest case of sustained face-to-face interaction between Americans and Canadians. It is therefore possible to argue that snowbird migration may be contributing to a new form of continental integration.

The influx of hundreds of thousands of Canadians into states like Florida, California, and Arizona for extended periods of time each winter has raised questions concerning the meaning of citizenship, borders, and belonging in the North American context. By actively participating in the formation and development of snowbird communities in the US, Canadian snowbirds' connections to their home communities in Canada are changing, as is the way they view their Canadian identity and citizenship. Through a qualitative exploration of the subjective experiences of Canadian snowbirds living in integrated snowbird communities in Florida, this chapter goes beyond a discussion of the economic implications of snowbird migration to consider the sociocultural impacts of this cross-border movement and its implications for citizenship, belonging, and people's participation in society.

The chapter begins by providing a theoretical overview of how migration and borders have changed in the context of a globalizing world, how seasonal snowbird migration has emerged, and how this migratory movement has played out in the context of the Canada-US border. This is followed by an overview of the study's methodology and the presentation of the findings. The chapter ends with a concluding discussion.

Migration and Borders in a Globalizing World

As succinctly stated by Steger (2013), "Globalization refers to the expansion and intensification of social relations and consciousness across world-time and world-space" (15). While the world has long been connected, developments in communication and transportation technologies have heightened space-time compression, leading to increased flows of ideas, people, and capital. As a result of these flows, culture has moved across borders in new ways, sometimes redefining the purpose and meaning of borders in the process. Alexander Rudolph (chapter 7, this volume) argues that a new common discursive space has been created between Canada and the United States as a result of Internet websites such as Netflix, where the same cultural content may be consumed by both Americans and Canadians, regardless of whether the content was produced in the United States or Canada. The flow of culture by way of the Internet has therefore heightened opportunities for regional integration and in some ways made the Canada-US border less significant.

The intensification and diversification of human migration is another way that culture is moving across borders in novel ways. Many researchers have considered how globalization has changed the scale and scope of international migration (Sheller and Urry 2004). Not only are more people moving, but they are creating new migration patterns. While in the past migrants moved to a place only to stay there, this understanding of migration is increasingly being challenged by new migration trajectories wherein people move between one or more destinations without staying permanently in any one place (Ahrens, Kelly, and van Liempt 2016; Jeffery and Murison 2011). This has made it harder to distinguish between categories such as temporary and permanent migrants, and between tourists and residents (Paasi et al. 2019).

Transnational theory was introduced in the 1990s (Basch, Glick-Schiller, and Blanc 2005) to explore people's shifting relationships to places and the new cultural forms that are taking shape as a result. The focus initially was on how people build relationships to multiple nation-states simultaneously, but recent contributions to the theory have explored how people forge attachments and develop a sense of belonging at a range of geographical scales, including the regional level, the city level, and the community level (Gustafson 2009; Caglar and Glick-Schiller 2011).

In border studies, this theoretical shift has led to a new focus on how borders have become increasingly relational, processual, and multiscalar (Paasi et al. 2019; Laine 2016). People interact across borders in various ways, thereby making connections that link localities, regions, and nation-states. As Laine (2016, 466) notes:

> The territorial rearrangements implied by globalization force us to rethink our layered analysis and seek to understand how borders contribute to a nested system of territoriality produced by various actors on different scales: at the global (through globalization), national (through the rules established by the state system), or regional and local levels (through the geographical characteristics of territories and societies).

This has implications not only politically and economically, but also for people's spatial identities and sense of belonging. For example, in their 2011 study on transnational identities, border security, and cross-border socio-economic integration in the United States borderlands with Canada and the British Virgin Islands, Victor Konrad and John Everitt found that "people in border regions balance their belonging to the cross-border region and to their respective nation-states in notions of regionalism (which often involves a theorization of region in transnational terms) and nationalism" (Konrad and Everitt 2011, 290). In specific contexts, local and regional dimensions of belonging may therefore intersect with national modes of belonging.

While geographical affiliation is often seen as having a monopoly on people's sense of belonging, it has been argued that people increasingly have choices concerning how they relate to other people and build a sense of community (Castles 2002). Elective forms of belonging based on, for example, lifestyle and religious affiliations, have gained importance, reducing the power of geography (and particularly the nation-state) to define people's identities and social lives (Agnew 2008). Increased access to travel as well as the development of Internet and communication technologies such as Skype have played an important role in facilitating this. Interestingly, however, these same technologies have also contributed to the maintenance of national affiliations and ethnic ties (Alonso and Oiarzabal 2010). Many migrants maintain strong connections to their countries of origin, participating in long-distance nationalism through their daily activities and their social ties. Others similarly identify strongly with those who share their ethnicity and culture, even when living abroad. In this context, there is a need to better understand the extent to which people maintain national, ethnic, and other types of spatial identities and to analyze the new forms of belonging that are emerging due to the technological and social changes wrought by globalization.

The concept of citizenship is an interesting angle from which to consider these phenomena, insofar as it incorporates not only the economic but also the emotive and the legal aspects of belonging. As more and more people acquire multiple citizenships or live in a country outside their country of citizenship, the classic link between territory, identity, and citizenship has been called into question (Carens 2016). At the same time, citizenship remains important insofar as it guarantees rights and access to goods, with no other global institution replacing it. As Agnew (2008) puts it, "Democratic theory and practice is not yet up to dealing with the complexities of a world in which territories and flows must *necessarily* co-exist" (186). Some countries have responded to this by broadening the scope for who can be a citizen or by granting specific rights to citizens from certain countries. In the Schengen area of Europe, for example, citizens of one Schengen country are permitted to take up employment and residency in another Schengen country. Agreements of this kind are often fraught and contradictory, however, as is evidenced by Britain's recent decision to leave the EU; Brexit was, to some extent, a result of concerns the British government had over its ability to control migration across its borders, although there were (and continue to be) many British citizens living in other parts of the EU. Borders remain very powerful and reinforce rules concerning what rights and opportunities people of specific citizenships can enjoy and access in a given state. Understanding how globalization and new migration patterns have impacted the concept of citizenship is therefore an important pursuit.

Seasonal Snowbird Migration as a Cultural Movement

Retirement migration is one of the many new forms of mobility to arise from globalization (Castles 2002). The expansion of transportation technology has led to increased connectivity between places, making it easier than ever before for people to travel (Sheller and Urry 2004). Communication technologies (mostly Internet-based) have helped to spread the word about different places and the lifestyles available and have made mobility easier by offering people a way to keep in touch with family and friends, regardless of their physical location. These developments have been accompanied by cultural shifts. Compared to their parents' generation, retirees in many parts of the world today are more familiar and comfortable with the idea of travel and transnational lifestyles. Other factors, such as the widespread promotion of physical fitness and sociability among retirees in many societies, have also contributed to increased lifestyle migration flows. For many, retirement signifies a period wherein one can have increased control over where and how to live, and with whom (O'Reilly and Benson 2015). A rise in individualism has made it rather unexceptional that people should want to seek out leisure and a better quality of life. It has therefore become common for retirees to move to places that can facilitate this desired lifestyle (Torkington 2010; Hayes 2018).

According to the Canadian Snowbird Association, snowbirds are people who spend at least one month or more in a location down south and return there regularly. Through their southern migrations, retirees have changed the physical nature of places by increasing the demand for new housing, infrastructure, and services (Castles 2002). Because many retirees spend significant amounts of time outside their country of citizenship, their mobility patterns have raised questions concerning the relationship between residency, belonging, and citizenship. Some retirement communities are constituted by a common demographic background or the values and interests of their residents rather than the residents' nationalities. These communities are indicative of new social, cultural, and spatial formations created by globalization and emerging mobility patterns.

While the factors driving the formation and growth of snowbird communities and the associated lifestyle may seem innocent and insignificant, the impact of the snowbirds' migratory movements should not be underestimated, especially in terms of policy. As community builders who spend part of their time in one local community and part of their time in another (in some cases crossing an international border as they move between the two), these migrants are challenging how people's relationships to places, borders, and citizenship status are understood. Their migratory patterns have raised questions, for example, concerning whether people who spend long periods of time outside their country of citizenship should be granted or denied the right to vote in elections in their country of citizenship, and whether they should be able to retain access to healthcare benefits in their country of citizenship, even after spending long periods of time outside it.

Snowbirds and the Canada-US Border

Every year, thousands of Canadian snowbirds cross the Canada-US border. While detailed measures of snowbird migration are difficult to obtain, it can be inferred that snowbirds make up the majority of people going on extended stays to the US. Overall, the number of Canadian retirees going to the United States each winter has increased steadily over time. This trend has occurred concurrently with the aging of the Canadian population (Conference Board of Canada 2016). Florida, California, and Arizona, are all known for attracting large numbers of Canadian snowbirds (Coates, Healy, and Morrison 2002). Based on data from 2014, these three states are among the top fifteen states visited by Canadians overall, and rank first, second, and third respectively for total number of nights spent.

TABLE 5.1.
Travel by Canadians to the United States in 2014

State	Number of Nights (x 1,000)	Number of Trips (x 1,000)
Florida	91,012	4,015
California	17,951	1,666
Arizona	16,226	909

Source: Statistics Canada 2016.

Other destinations, such as Texas, do not rank as high among Canadian travellers overall, but are nevertheless places that attract significant numbers of Canadian snowbirds (Simpson 2018).

From many points of view, Canada and the United States have long been closely linked, sharing a long land border, many cultural features and, with the exception of Canada's province of Quebec, the same language. Hence, it is not surprising that there has been a great deal of tourism and retirement migration from Canada to southern states such as Florida since the early 1900s (Jarvis 2002). Large numbers of students and workers have also moved between the countries over the years (Hardwick and Smith 2012; Tremblay, Hardwick, and O'Neill 2014).

Despite the high level of integration between Canada and the United States, there are a number of political and cultural differences between the two countries. The American Revolution that divided

Canada and the United States in the late eighteenth century has had a lasting impact on how each country defines itself. While Americans tend to focus on an individualistic ideology of liberty, Canadians have historically prioritized a stronger state (including the ongoing recognition of the British monarchy) and the recognition of group rights as is exemplified by the country's multicultural policy (Lipset 1990). These differences have become more visible in recent years as the two countries' political positions on border security and migration have diverged.

Following the events of 9/11, Canada was perceived by the United States as being "too soft" and was accused of allowing terrorists to enter the United States via Canada (De Eyre 2011). This led to heightened border security between the two countries that has yet to abate (Konrad and Nicol 2008). More recently, tensions have emerged over the two countries' very different positions on the reception of Syrian migrants (Carlier 2016) and the undocumented migration of several Haitian migrants from the United States to Canada following President Trump's cancellation of temporary protection for Haitians in the United States. This has made it challenging for Canada and the US to coordinate and integrate their policies, especially those in the domain of border security and migration.

Canadian snowbirds appear to have disassociated themselves from these negative discourses concerning migrants in the US. They have instead come to be regarded as an exceptional group of migrants, warranting special considerations and additional privileges. The United States has long recognized the benefits of having Canadian snowbirds flock to its Sun Belt every winter; the sales and property taxes they pay, as well as the money Canadian snowbirds spend, help to support the American economy. Moreover, unlike other migrants, Canadian snowbirds are generally uninterested in working in the United States and arrive with adequate medical insurance and enough funds to support their stay. They may also be perceived, on account of their demographic background, as being non-threatening and similar to middle-class Americans. In a study conducted by Smith and House (2006), it was noted that snowbirds in Florida are predominantly White, with relatively high levels of income and education.

Canadians are currently entitled to spend 182 days in the country (in contrast to the 90 days granted to people from other countries). A Canadian Retiree Visa has been proposed that would extend the number of allowable days to 240 for Canadian citizens over fifty years of age who meet certain requirements. This may only serve the needs and interests of Canadian snowbirds, however, if they are also given the right to be outside Canada for a similar length of time without losing access to their medical benefits.

Provincial policies in Canada concerning access to healthcare play an important role in influencing snowbird migration patterns and lifestyles. Maintaining residency in a specific province is often a prerequisite for accessing healthcare services. Requirements vary from province to province, but most provinces require that people be resident for at least five months out of twelve. Given the challenges of accessing affordable medical care in the United States, most Canadian snowbirds ensure that they maintain strong ties to their home provinces in Canada, returning there each spring or summer to stay for the requisite amount of time.

TABLE 5.2.
Maximum amount of time permitted abroad (to maintain healthcare benefits)

Province	Length of Time
British Columbia	7 months a year
Alberta	7 months a year
Saskatchewan	7 months a year
Manitoba	7 months a year
Ontario	7 months a year
Quebec	6 months a year (plus short trips of 21 days or less)
New Brunswick	7 months
Nova Scotia	7 months
Prince Edward Island	6 months minus a day
Newfoundland and Labrador	8 months
Yukon	6 months (but those absent from 6 to 12 months maintain access to physicians and hospitals)
Northwest Territories	7 months
Nunavut	Healthcare available to all permanent residents

Source: Canadian Snowbird Association 2019.

The Business and Tourism Research Center at the University of Texas Rio Grande Valley put some of the information they collected through a survey conducted with "Winter Texans" in 2016 on their website (https://www.utrgv.edu/tourism/_files/documents/reports/what-are-winter-texans-saying-report.pdf). According to the survey, some of the issues that Canadian snowbirds in the Rio Grande Valley would like to see addressed in order to make their time in Texas more satisfactory include making health insurance affordable, extending the number of days they can stay outside of Canada, and managing currency exchange rates (University of Texas Rio Grande Valley 2016).

The Canadian Snowbird Association (CSA) is an organization that exists to support the interests of Canadian snowbirds living abroad. The organization has been lobbying both the Canadian and the American governments to change their policies so that Canadian snowbirds can spend more time in the United States. The organization has also devised other ways to help Canadian snowbirds conveniently move between Canada and the United States, for example, by creating a system wherein participating Canadian snowbirds can collectively exchange Canadian currency for US dollars at a reduced exchange rate. Moreover, as is evident from the organization's website (www.snowbirds.org), the CSA has also had a cultural influence, by actively promoting a cross-border "snowbird lifestyle" through the publication of its magazines and newsletters and the staging of lifestyle conventions and events. Through their participation in the CSA, Canadian snowbirds are exposed to different snowbird lifestyles, such as various snowbird destinations and the different housing and recreational opportunities on offer in them. They are also introduced to certain types of messaging concerning what constitutes a desirable snowbird lifestyle and even the benefits of Canada-US integration created through snowbird migration. It would seem that, through their individual choices and their collective involvement in organizations like the CSA, Canadian snowbirds have become a driving force, challenging taken-for-granted conceptions of how borders are typically navigated and creating a new cross-border cultural movement in the process.

One reason for the strength of the CSA is the inability of nation-states to meet the needs of snowbird migrants. The Canadian and American governments, for example, have not devised a bilateral approach toward snowbird migration, despite the large numbers of Canadians crossing the border each year. The CSA has therefore been an important player in making snowbird interests visible and, where applicable, a focus of policymakers. Moreover, policies concerning the rights of Canadian snowbirds in the United States are often ambiguous and in flux. In addition to its political, social, and cultural influence, the CSA therefore plays an important role distributing information. By sharing up-to-date information about the policies impacting snowbirds on their website and in other publications, they make it easier for snowbirds to carry out their chosen lifestyles.

While the presence of Canadian snowbirds in the United States has been recognized by the media, researchers, and governments, much of the focus until now has been on the economic and logistical implications of snowbird migration, and less on the culture that is being produced in snowbird communities, and the perspectives and experiences of the snowbirds themselves. In order to broaden current understandings of snowbird migration, this paper therefore focuses on the experiences and narratives of retired Canadians living in various Floridian communities.

Methodology

In order to gain a deeper understanding of snowbird communities that have brought American and Canadian snowbirds together, this study adopted a decidedly qualitative approach. The focus was on the agency of snowbirds as active community builders who have used the opportunities available to them to develop a transnational lifestyle spanning two countries. The goal of the study was not to generalize but to gain insights from the experiences of individual snowbirds living in a cross-section of communities in southern Florida.

There are strong regional dimensions to snowbird migration patterns, and most Canadian snowbirds who go to Florida are from Ontario and Quebec. While Ontarians have, overall, been more numerous (Desrosiers-Lauzon 2011), Québécois migrants have received more attention. French-speaking snowbirds are more visible; on account of being a linguistic minority, they have been more inclined to form relatively distinct Francophone communities (Tremblay and Chicoine 2011). They have also been known to make performative displays of Québécois culture through the staging of festivals, concerts, and events (Desrosiers-Lauzon 2011). Anglophone Ontarian snowbirds, on the other hand, have blended in more with their American counterparts. While chain migration has led to pockets of snowbirds from similar parts of Canada moving to the same communities in Florida, it is still common for Ontarian snowbirds to live alongside American retirees as well as Canadians from other parts of Canada. In order to gain a more in-depth understanding of how Anglophone snowbirds experience the cross-border snowbird lifestyle and how their daily interactions with Americans may contribute to sociocultural integration at the continental level, I decided to focus the study on Anglophone snowbirds from Ontario.

The information used for this study was collected through fieldwork visits to specific adult-lifestyle communities in southern Florida. It was known at the outset of the research that while Québécois snowbirds have shown a tendency to settle on Florida's east coast, their Ontarian counterparts have shown a preference for the state's west coast (Coates, Healy, and Morrison 2002). Communities located in four urban areas on the west coast—Naples, Fort Myers Beach, Clearwater, and Port Charlotte—were therefore selected. Communities in two urban areas on the east coast—Boca Raton and West Palm Beach—were included to ensure a diversity of perspectives and experiences were included in the study.

There are many different types of communities in southern Florida that cater to snowbirds. Each one has its own characteristics; while some communities emphasize athletic activities, for example, others are known for their social activities. Moreover, while some communities consist of "permanent" housing such as houses, condominiums, prefabricated dwellings, or trailers, others are comprised of mobile homes. There is housing available across the income spectrum, and residential communities vary in terms of size, layout, and the amenities they offer.

Taking the different types of communities in Florida into account, it was decided that this study would focus on "permanent" communities as it was thought that they may have a stronger base of return visitors and be more stable than more transient-style communities and would therefore yield more insights on how Canadian snowbirds have developed relationships to Florida over time. The communities under study consisted of prefabricated homes and/or condominium-style housing and could be described as "middle class" insofar as they were typically in the middle of the economic spectrum of available housing in their respective locations in Florida. The minimum age for ownership in each community was typically fifty-five years. Almost all of the communities studied were in segregated spaces outside of urban centres. It was common for the communities to have a pool and clubhouse, and most had their own golf course. The communities under study organized activities for their residents, with golf, tennis, bocce ball, square dancing, and quilt making being some of the popular offerings available. However, the number of activities offered varied from community to community. While one community offered few organized activities, another offered their residents access to more than ninety activities. All of the communities included in the study had a combination of American and Canadian residents, although the balance differed between them.

Prior to visiting each fieldwork site, I arranged interviews with resident Canadian snowbirds. In order to participate in the study, individuals had to be fifty-five years of age or older, retain residency in Ontario, and spend at least two months in Florida every winter. Participants were initially recruited by way of my personal networks, various Canadian Clubs in Florida, and various Internet websites catering to snowbirds in the region. Once a group of participants was established, a snowball sample method was used wherein research participants referred me to additional participants.

Most of the participants owned properties in Florida and had been living there for several years. They came from all over Ontario, including Sudbury, Thunder Bay, Ottawa, Toronto, and numerous small towns. The majority of the study participants were married or common law, and gay and lesbian couples were included in the study. A minority of the participants were widowed or divorced. In total, thirty-nine participants were included in the study (twenty-one males and eighteen females). They ranged in age from their mid-fifties to their mid-eighties.

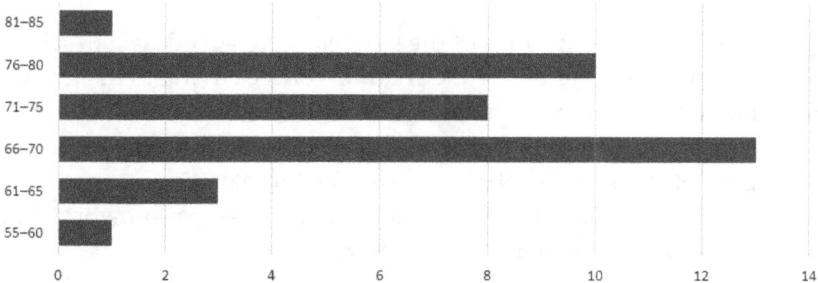

FIGURE 5.1. Participants by age group. *Source:* Melissa Kelly.

There were very few non-White residents living in the retirement communities under study. It is therefore not surprising that all of the participants in the study were White.

There was plenty of interest in participating in the study, and identifying participants was not difficult. It was, however, sometimes challenging to schedule interviews with the participants given their busy schedules. Participants were given the flexibility to set the time of the interview and were interviewed in a place of their choice, usually their homes or in the common areas of their residential communities. They were interviewed either alone or together with their partner. Participants were asked about how they came to be snowbirds in Florida, their experiences of moving back and forth between Canada and the United States each year, and their plans for the future (see appendix).

Each interview was identified by a number rather than a personal identifier (such as a personal name). The material was analyzed thematically. This process was carried out, in nearly half of the cases, with the help of NVIVO, a qualitative software that assists with the classification and analysis of large amounts of unstructured textual data. The software was used to help identify themes in the interviews and to draw connections between them.

There are multiple ways to be a snowbird in Florida. The findings generated by this study do not, therefore, claim to be representative of all Canadian snowbirds or all lifestyle communities in Florida. In focusing on the experiences of individuals living in selected lifestyle communities, however, the study has led to new insights on how American and Canadian snowbirds come together in residential spaces to create and share an active and enjoyable lifestyle.

Findings

In what follows, the findings of the study are presented. The first section explores the experiences of Canadian retirees living in integrated retirement communities. This is followed by an analysis of how the time spent in these spaces has affected the participants' sense of belonging at the community level. Finally, the participants' national attachments are discussed, as are the ways that being a snowbird has changed how they view being Canadian.

Integrated Border Spaces

A survey of American and Canadian snowbirds living in the Rio Grande Valley (Simpson 2018) found that the desire to live in a nice climate and engage with friendly people were among the top reasons retirees chose to winter in the southern US. These motivations are the same for American and Canadian snowbirds, and apply to Florida as much as they do to Texas. According to the participants in this study, the desire to lead the same lifestyle as their American counterparts has made it easy for Canadians and Americans to come together in shared residential spaces in Florida.

In addition to having shared lifestyle objectives, participants found that linguistic and cultural commonalities that extend across the border made it easy for them to mix with their American neighbours. In general, the US was viewed favourably in comparison to other possible snowbird destinations on account of its similarity to Canada. As one participant noted: "I always wanted to come someplace warm and prefer coming to the US as opposed to Mexico or Central America and so on. This is much more....We've travelled to those places or some of those places, but this is much more, I guess our lifestyle and sort of what we're accustomed to. It's just like living at home" (Interview 15).

While there are many cultural and linguistic similarities between Canada and the US, as already noted, snowbird migration is also largely a regional phenomenon, with retirees tending to move between their home province (or state) in the north, to the southern state that is most accessible to them. The Floridian communities studied here, for example, were mostly comprised of retirees originating from the province of Ontario and adjacent US states (such as New York and Michigan). This further contributed to a sense among the study participants that they had much in common in terms of language and culture with other members of their Floridian communities. Furthermore, it was common for friends and relatives to follow one another to the same retirement communities over time. This led to the formation of communities within communities, as some people knew each other very well even prior to becoming snowbirds.

It is important to point out, however, that despite the ease with which community residents came together, the residents of retirement communities in Florida could not be considered representative of the diverse populations on either side of the Canada-US border. Instead, like most snowbird communities in the United States, the communities under study were visibly dominated by White North Americans with European origins. The communities were also naturally sorted by class, since people typically chose their Floridian communities based on what kind of housing they could afford and the kind of activities they were interested in. Many of the participants therefore felt that they had a great deal in common with their neighbours, and had similar understandings of what a desirable retirement lifestyle should be. It would seem that having a common language and ethnic background, and being of a similar class and age made other differences, such as nationality, former occupation, or religion, less significant. As one participant eloquently put it when speaking of his community: "We're all birds of a feather in here. We all have what we have in common: We're all within a few years of age, we all want to be active, we all love the sun, we all love being outside, doing things" (Interview 18).

Despite the emphasis participants placed on their similarities to other snowbirds, there were also differences between them which they regarded as significant. Participants across the various communities mentioned the importance of avoiding certain topics in conversation. As one participant explained: "One of the things we do not discuss is politics, especially this year [the year of Trump's election]. So that's one of the things… [Maybe] if we're in our own little home and it's Canadians or Americans that we know" (Interview 23). It was also common for the participants to comment on how, in comparison to Canada, they found the US to have a number of undesirable characteristics. Some of the things that made them uncomfortable included the relatively higher rate of gun ownership, what they perceived to be reckless driving, and the prevalence of certain political and religious views. In order to maintain community cohesion, however, efforts were made to downplay these real or perceived differences between Canadians and Americans, and focus on what they had in common. As one participant noted: "We want to sort of mesh together to the greatest extent possible and I think we do pretty well" (Interview 20).

Another factor that contributed to cohesion in the communities under study was the expectation that residents engage fully in the snowbird lifestyle. According to the participants, this involved demonstrating a high level of sociability: attending dinner parties, wine and cheese nights, and other events, as well as participating in the organized activities on offer and volunteering for the community when necessary. From the perspective of some participants, the presence of "rounders" (Americans who lived year-round in a community that was otherwise dominated by seasonal snowbirds) was perceived as threatening to community cohesiveness. Rounders were often younger and still working, and therefore did not necessarily have the time or interest to participate in the community in meaningful ways. As one resident stated, in reference to her community: "[Americans] are snowbirds, too, and that was the goal: to have everyone snowbirds. Too bad some of that is changing. It's a very new place for couples to come. We don't want younger couples who work; we want people who are retired and want to volunteer and who have a vested interest in the activities. These people you never see them, because they're living here, but they're working in the community and they're just buying it because it's a great bargain" (Interview 20). Hence, it was considered important that community members be physically present and engage with the community and not simply live there while maintaining a work and social life off-site.

Although some of the study participants enjoyed volunteering or taking part in activities in their wider local community, the majority spent their time engaging with people and activities on-site in the residential community. The fact that the majority of the communities were situated outside of urban centres, and the extent to which residents were encouraged and given opportunities to engage with other residents, seemed to discourage community members from getting too involved in activities in the wider society. As one woman pointed out, in snowbird communities, individuals could feel like they were in an "alternate reality." As she experienced it, "It's kind of like when you come through the door, everything else stays out" (Interview 29). The precise location of these communities, therefore, did not matter as much as the social opportunities and lifestyle that they made available to their residents.

In spending most of their time in their residential communities, study participants were able to avoid what they regarded as some of the more negative aspects of both Canadian and American society such as inequality and crime. Most participants emphasized how they felt relatively comfortable and safe in their respective communities and attributed this to the similarities they shared with their neighbours as well as the security mechanisms that were in place to protect them. Several of the communities were gated, while others had arranged for paid or voluntary security staff to monitor the community streets at night.

The communities that the study participants formed with their American counterparts could be considered spaces of Canada-US integration, albeit on a very limited geographical scale, and involving only a segment of the North American demographic. While the Canada-US border was effectively transcended by bringing residents together across the geopolitical divide, other criteria, such as the age of the community residents and their lifestyle preferences, made these communities distinguishable from the outside world. In the process of forming these transnational communities, new criteria for belonging was generated and new borders, in the form of community boundaries, were drawn.

Shifting Modes of Belonging to Community

Given the high level of social cohesiveness and community involvement encouraged in the communities studied, it is not surprising that the study participants found it very easy to develop a strong sense of belonging to their Floridian communities. As one participant put it, "The thing that's special about the life here is that you have more friends than you ever had in your whole life. And you see them every day" (Interview 31).

These sentiments were repeatedly expressed by the study participants, who regarded their Floridian community (but not necessarily the state of Florida or the US as a whole) as a place to which they had a high level of belonging and attachment. It was primarily the people and the social relationships they had developed through interacting with their neighbours that made these spaces feel like "home." Residents served as a valuable support network for one another, and many commented on how efforts were made to ensure that the elderly, vulnerable, and single members of their communities were given extra care and attention if they were in need of it.

Interestingly, the value they placed on their face-to-face interactions with other snowbirds in Florida had important implications for how study participants interacted with people in their home communities in Canada. While they looked forward to the time they would spend with their families when they returned to Ontario for the summer holidays or when their families visited them in Florida, most of the participants did not question their decision to be away from their families for several months each winter. As one participant put it: "If the family wants to see me, they can come here. You've got FaceTime and Skype and that sort of stuff, so you can see them. You don't have to physically be there" (Interview 21).

The close relationships they had with other members of their snowbird communities, coupled with access to new technology, played a role in reducing their need to see family members in person. Studies conducted on snowbirds prior to the 2000s emphasized the conflicted feelings many snowbirds had over being away from their families for extended periods of time. It would seem that the advent of advanced and widespread communication technology and the shift toward a more globally connected social world has made it easier for snowbirds to pursue their lifestyle goals while still maintaining relationships with their family members, regardless of their physical location.

Technology can only do so much to keep people connected to their communities of origin over time, however. Aside from the strong ties most snowbirds maintained to their extended families through regular telephone, Skype, and FaceTime conversations, many participants felt that their relationship to their home communities had weakened since they first started making the regular sojourn to Florida. As one participant pointed out: "We're less and less involved as we stay down here. We get less involved up there....Because here you're involved so much because you're so close and when you're... It's not like when you're in the subdivision up there. When you're here and it's close and it's a walking distance. I think we found we're spreading thinner and thinner up there, as far as the local community goes" (Interview 19).

As several of the participants noted, it is difficult to maintain commitments such as work or voluntary positions when one is not consistently in a place, unless that place is based on a seasonal schedule (as is the case with most snowbird communities in Florida). Hence, many participants felt less involved in their Canadian communities than they had previously and instead felt increasingly connected to their neighbours and communities in Florida as they spent more time there.

Many of the participants interviewed highlighted how, as the number of seasonal visits they made to Florida increased, often their number of commitments did, too. They typically engaged in volunteer maintenance of the grounds, raised money for on-site projects, and were members of several clubs. Many had to return to Florida by a certain date each year due to the commitments they had to various sports teams, clubs, or governing boards.

Interestingly, the participants' ties to their Floridan communities also affected the way they viewed their properties and homes in

Ontario. Several participants had decided to downsize their northern homes. One motivation for this was to release funds that could be used to support their lifestyle in Florida. Another major reason for downsizing was to allow for easier property maintenance during the extended periods of time they spent away. As one participant explained when reflecting on the sale of his house: "The fact that we were spending our winters here pushed that sale forward faster than maybe not because we would come down here and we were always worried whether the kid that we had hired to shovel ... and if the house was okay and all of that and so, we were actively looking for a place where all the stuff would be looked after. Where we could come down here and not worry about somebody breaking into the house because it looked like nobody was there" (Interview 30).

On account of their experiences in Florida, the participants also began to reconsider what kind of community they wanted to live in up north. Through their time in Florida, many had found that they enjoyed interacting regularly with and participating in activities with their neighbours, and preferred being around people their own age; they were therefore hoping to find an adult-lifestyle community in Ontario that would meet their needs in a similar way. As one participant put it: "Everybody is looking for a community like this in Canada. And everybody is trying to share what they find. But it's not coming up yet." As he continued, "Because you're looking to get rid of the big houses but all be in something where there's so many people around and lots to do and stuff" (Interview 19). Spending winters in Florida clearly meant more to the participants than simply enjoying time in the sun. It also gave them the opportunity to explore new lifestyles and develop new perspectives on community life. Residential arrangements that brought similarly minded retirees together into closely knit communities was, in fact, a concept that many wanted to see replicated in Canada.

New Meanings of Being Canadian

The participants' changing conceptions of community raise questions concerning their attachments at other levels of geographical scale, particularly at the level of the nation-state. Since they started going to Florida in large numbers in the 1920s, Canadian snowbirds have been accused of losing their loyalty to Canada (Jarvis 2002). In his historical analysis of Canadian snowbirds in Florida, however, Godefroy Desrosiers-Lauzon (2011) challenged this view by postulating that

Canadian snowbirds are highly patriotic toward Canada, and that the time they spend in the United States does not change this. The findings of this study would support this argument.

While most of the participants acknowledged the cultural similarity between Canada and the US, they also openly expressed how happy they were to be Canadian and how, from many points of view, they saw Canada as a superior country. For example, they frequently remarked how they believed Canada was more open to diversity and better at providing for its citizens, with Canada's universal healthcare system standing out as a particular point of pride. As one participant noted: "I just love singing the praises of our country and I do it down here because, god, they don't know how good we have it up north. We have the best healthcare going and these poor people down here, it's just…it's sickening" (Interview 23).

Several participants also referenced how their British roots, the presence of family in Canada, and their ties to local places or homes made them value their Canadian citizenship and identity. Few had an interest in becoming American citizens, unless they had family in the United States. The participants enjoyed the sunshine and lifestyle on offer in the US, but their legal and emotional sense of belonging to Canada remained very solid.

In his 2011 book, Desrosiers-Lauzon argues that snowbirds emanating from both Quebec and Ontario maintain strong ties to their home communities in Canada and engage in similar community-building practices in Florida. However, they typically relate to Canada differently as a nation. While Ontarian snowbirds typically adopt a generalized "Canadian" identity rather than a regional identity, the opposite is true of Québécois snowbirds, who more often embrace their regional and linguistic identities as Francophone Canadians. Historically, tensions between Francophones in favour of separating from Canada and those in favour of staying in Canada played out in Florida, further complicating how Québécois snowbirds viewed their relationship to Canada (Desrosiers-Lauzon 2011). Today, there are a number of Québécois snowbirds in Florida that actively embrace the idea of being both Canadian and Québécois. While carrying out the fieldwork for this study, I met some bilingual snowbirds who had chosen to live in communities inhabited primarily by Anglophones, thereby breaking down barriers between Anglophone and Francophone snowbird communities in Florida and contributing to a broader sense of Canadianness in the process. It may be interesting to see if, over time, snowbird communities play a role in bridging the cultural and linguistic divide that exists between Anglophone and Francophone Canadians.

While the study participants were generally in agreement that they would prefer to avoid crossing an international border in order to reach their winter destinations, the border did not deter them from going to Florida each year. They were prepared to deal with such inconveniences as fluctuating currency exchange rates between the Canadian and American dollar, limitations on their business activities in the US, and the (sometimes) stressful crossings at the physical border. What most of the participants were hoping for, however, was an extension in the number of days that they could spend in the United States and away from Canada. Some felt that the winters in Canada were too long to be away only for the allowable 182 days per year. Others felt that they needed to be in Florida for this entire period of time because of their commitments there, which limited the time they could spend in the United States at other points during the year; having more days in the US would allow them to visit the American friends they had met during their time in Florida, shop, or carry out tourist activities. As one participant put it:

> It would be nice if I could come down for two or three weeks in the summer or the spring or you know, at a different time of the year, but when you get five months down here, you're restricted. You only have four other weeks to play with so you don't use them to come down here other than those four to five months. So, I said I'd like to have up to nine months because one year we might want to come down in October and come home in April. Well, that's your whole six months right there. (Interview 13)

A related concern of the participants was the challenge of maintaining their medical care in Canada. The participants had very carefully calculated the number of days they could spend away from Ontario in any given calendar year without losing their residency (and hence, their medical care), and were sure not to go over it. In addition to this, they had to purchase top-up medical insurance for the days they spent in the United States, with many paying thousands of dollars for this over the years they spent going to Florida. They were acutely aware that developing a serious condition may lead to an increase in the cost of insurance, to the point that they may no longer be able to afford it. Some participants had already refused to purchase insurance and simply planned to return to Canada at their own expense in case of an emergency.

While the participants understood that restrictions on the time they could spend outside Ontario were partly in place to ensure that they were contributing to the province's economy, they defended their right to stay in the US longer by pointing to the social and financial contributions they had made to Canada throughout their working lives. Furthermore, they believed that the health and psychological benefits of the snowbird lifestyle were significant, and many hypothesized that they would use the medical system more if they stayed in Canada throughout the winter and would therefore present a bigger cost to Canada's social resources if they lived in Ontario year-round. They hoped for the innovation of a better insurance system that would allow them to access medical care in the US at a reasonable cost.

The participants' narratives point to a new understanding of what it means to be Canadian. While they enjoyed the lifestyle in Florida and were very attached to their communities there, they identified strongly with Canada, and what they regarded as "Canadian values." They made an effort to remain connected to Canada, and they appreciated and wished to maintain access to all of the benefits of the Canadian welfare state, even if they felt that the time they were allowed to be in the US each year was insufficient for achieving some of their objectives. It would seem that the current policies concerning healthcare, residency, and citizenship do not fully align with the cross-border lifestyle that the snowbirds have created.

Conclusion: Snowbirds and Continental Integration

Changes typically attributed to globalization, such as the expansion and transformation of communication and transportation technologies, have led to a world characterized by increased flows of people. The new migratory patterns, routes, and lifestyles resulting from these flows have transformed the world, creating new relationships between places, as well as new ways of understanding borders. Rather than being viewed as sharp lines on a map representing the geopolitical order, borders are increasingly seen as dynamic and shaped by a range of multiscalar social processes (Brambilla et al. 2015; Laine 2016). As some of the other chapters in this volume also illustrate (Rudolph, chapter 7; Grudzien, chapter 8), borders are not static, they are in motion. Studying the retired Canadians that cross the border into the United States and spend extended periods of time there each winter provides new insights on how borders between Canada and the US are being rescaled and how a form of continental integration is being formed through this process.

Snowbird migration is unequivocally multiscalar. The face-to-face interaction that occurs between Canadian and American snowbirds has created new spaces of North American integration at the localized level. As the study findings have shown, commonalities in language and culture on both sides of the border have made it possible for North American snowbirds to come together in integrated communities in southern Florida, where they can enjoy a shared retirement lifestyle. However, this is not a permanent arrangement, and, by definition, snowbirds live between two localities throughout the year: their homes in Florida and their homes in the north. The cities and towns they come from are situated in specific provinces, states, and geographical regions that further shape their identities and the way they relate to one another. It could be said that the phenomenon of snowbird migration is therefore simultaneously constituted by local, regional, and transnational linkages across borders that lead to complex encounters between people in which both cultural similarities and differences come into view.

As the study findings show, in coming together in the pursuit of a desired lifestyle, it is the similarities between snowbirds living in integrated communities that are meaningful. A local sense of belonging is created that allows for differences in nationality and ignores differences in political and religious affiliation. Communities are further solidified by a seemingly natural sense of affinity between residents. This may, in part, be attributed to the residents being of a similar age, but also to similarities in their racial, ethnic, and class backgrounds (even if these similarities are for the most part not explicitly acknowledged). The communities under study are a product of globalization; they have redefined conventional understandings of the relationship between belonging, citizenship, and geography by bringing people from both sides of the Canada-US border together in defined spaces where daily social interactions occur face-to-face and a new culture is produced. In rescaling the border, however, new borders have been created that clearly distinguish between those who belong to the physical and social spaces of the community and those who do not.

One might expect that in the process of developing new community bonds and creating new borders, the snowbirds' attachments to Canada might wane. The findings of this study, however, would suggest otherwise. Instead, for the study participants, maintaining a strong national identity was a compatible if not a fundamental part of being a snowbird. Despite the extended periods of time they had spent in Florida, the majority of the study participants remained staunchly Canadian in outlook and allegiance. Many drew on strong national tropes and nationalist discourses to make sense of their circular migrations, thereby demonstrating that even though they spend extended periods of time in the US, the border between Canada and the US remains significant to them. As Lipset (1990) has noted, Canadian identity is shaped primarily in relation to the United States; to be Canadian is to not be American. This thinking has only been reinforced for snowbirds who have a particular dislike of the recent resurgence of nationalism in the US, and President Trump's policies concerning borders, security, and migrants. It could be said, then, that continental integration is occurring through the large-scale migration of Canadians to the US each winter, but this integration is very much mediated by the snowbirds' ongoing identification with Canada and the value they continue to place on their Canadian citizenship.

The snowbird movement has many important implications for policy. While businesses and non-governmental organizations such as the Canadian Snowbird Association have been quick to adapt to the snowbird migration trend, governments have found it more challenging. Presently there are no bilateral agreements concerning snowbird migration between Canada and the United States, and the two countries continue to view snowbirds according to existing policy frameworks that clearly distinguish between resident citizens and migrants when concerning who is and is not allowed access to certain rights. Given the large number of snowbirds crossing the border each year, there is clearly a need for more innovative policy thinking concerning the management of seasonal migration flows. The snowbird phenomenon may also provide an impetus to consider innovations in other policy fields. The snowbird movement has highlighted some of the challenges emerging in a globalizing world where people may not always be physically present in their country of citizenship. How to effectively provide necessary services such as healthcare to nonresident citizens or temporary migrants may be a topic worthy of further exploration. Finally, the communities Canadian snowbirds build with their American counterparts have much to teach us about how people develop place attachments and cultivate a sense of belonging. This knowledge may be important for policymakers and others interested in understanding what motivates people to contribute to specific places through investments, philanthropy, voluntary service, and other types of sociocultural activities.

References

Agnew, John. 2008. "Borders on the Mind: Re-framing Border Thinking." *Ethics and Global Politics* 1 (4): 175–191.

Ahrens, Jill, Melissa Kelly, and Ilse van Liempt. 2016. "Free Movement? The Onward Migration of EU Citizens Born in Somalia, Iran, and Nigeria." *Population, Space and Place* 22, no. 1 (January): 84–98.

Alonso, Andoni, and Pedro J. Oiarzabal. 2010. Preface. In *Diasporas in the New Media Age: Identity, Politics and Community*, edited by Andoni Alonso and Pedro J. Oiarzabal, ix–xii. Reno: University of Nevada Press.

Basch, Linda, Nina Glick-Schiller, and Cristina S. Blanc. 2005. *Nations Unbound: Transnational Projects, Postcolonial Predicaments, and Deterritorialized Nation-States*. London: Routledge.

Brambilla, Chiara, Jussi Laine, James W. Scott, and Gianluca Bocchi. 2015. "Introduction: Thinking, Mapping, Acting and Living Borders Under Contemporary Globalization." In *Borderscaping: Imaginations and Practices of Border Making*, edited by Chiara Brambilla, Jussi Laine, James W. Scott, and Gianluca Bocchi, 1–12. London: Routledge.

Caglar, Ayse, and Nina Glick-Schiller. 2011. "Introduction: Migrants and Cities." In *Locating Migration: Rescaling Cities and Migrants*, edited by Nina Glick Schiller and Ayse Caglar, 1–19. Ithaca, NY: Cornell University Press.

Canadian Snowbird Association. 2019. "The Canadian Travellers' Report Card: An Evaluation of Government Policy and Practice for Canadians Who Travel (Seventh Edition). Accessed November 5, 2020. https://www.snowbirds.org/publications/travellers-report-card/.

Carens, Joseph. 2016. "In Defense of Birthright Citizenship." In *Migration in Political Theory: The Ethics of Movement and Membership*, edited by Sara Fine and Lea Ypi, 205–224. Oxford: Oxford University Press.

Carlier, Melissa. 2016. "Explaining Differences in the Canadian and American Response to the Syrian Refugee Crisis." *Virginia Policy Review* 9 (2): 56–82.

Castles, Stephen. 2002. "Migration and Community Formation Under Conditions of Globalization." *International Migration Review* 36, no. 4 (Winter): 1143–1168.

Coates, Ken, Robert Healy, and William Morrison. 2002. "Tracking the Snowbirds: Seasonal Migration from Canada to the U.S.A and Mexico." *American Review of Canadian Studies* 32, no. 3 (Autumn): 433–450.

Conference Board of Canada. 2016. *Canadian Snowbird Travel Market Annual Report*.

De Eyre, Steve. 2011. "The Prospects for a North American Security Perimeter: Coordination and Harmonization of United States and Canadian Immigration and Refugee Laws." *Canada-United States Law Journal* 35, nos. 1-2 (Spring-Fall): 181–207.

Desrosiers-Lauzon, Godefroy. 2011. *Florida's Snowbirds: Spectacle, Mobility, and Community Since 1945*. Montréal: McGill-Queen's University Press.

Gustafson, Per. 2009. "Mobility and Territorial Belonging." *Environment and Behavior* 41, no. 4 (July): 490–508.

Hardwick, Susan, and Heather Smith. 2014. "Crossing the 49th Parallel: American Immigrants in Canada and Canadians in the U.S." In *Immigrant Geographies of North American Cities*, edited by Teixiera, Carlos, Wei Li, and Audrey Kobayashi, 288–311. Don Mills, ON: Oxford University Press Canada.

Hayes, Matthew. 2018. *Gringolandia: Lifestyle Migration Under Late Capitalism*. Minneapolis: University of Minnesota Press.

Jarvis, Eric. 2002. "Florida's Forgotten Ethnic Culture: Patterns of Canadian Immigration, Tourism, and Investment Since 1920." *The Florida Historical Quarterly* 81, no. 2 (Fall): 186–197.

Jeffery, Laura, and Jude Murison. 2011. "The Temporal, Social, Spatial, and Legal Dimensions of Return and Onward Migration." *Population, Space and Place* 17, no. 2 (March/April): 131–139.

Konrad, Victor, and John Everitt. 2011. "Borders and 'Belongers': Transnational Identities, Border Security, and Cross-Border Socio-Economic Integration in the United States Borderlands with Canada and the British Virgin Islands." *Comparative American Studies: An International Journal* 9 (4): 288–308.

Konrad, Victor, and Heather N. Nicol. 2008. *Beyond Walls: Re-Inventing the Canada-United States Borderlands*. London: Routledge.

Laine, Jussi. 2016. "The Multiscalar Production of Borders." *Geopolitics* 21 (3): 465–482.

Lipset, Seymour M. 1990. *Continental Divide: The Values and Institutions of the United States and Canada*. New York: Routledge.

O'Reilly, Karen, and Michaela Benson. 2015. "Lifestyle Migration and the Pursuit of Successful Ageing." In *Handbook of Cultural Gerontology*, edited by Julia Twigg and Wendy Martin, 420–427. Abingdon, UK: Routledge.

Paasi, Anssi, Eeva-Kaisa Prokkola, Jarkko Saarinen, and Kaj Zimmerbauer. 2019. "Introduction: Borders, Ethics, and Mobilities." In *Borderless*

Worlds for Whom? Ethics, Moralities and Mobilities, edited by Anssi Paasi, Eeva-Kaisa Prokkola, Jarkko Saarinen, and Kaj Zimmerbauer. New York: Routledge.

Sheller, Mimi, and John Urry. 2004. "Places to Play, Places in Play." In *Tourism Mobilities: Places to Play, Places in Play*, edited by Mimi Sheller and John Urry, 1–10. New York: Routledge.

Simpson, Penny. 2018. "The Winter Texan 2017-18 Survey Report." The University of Texas Rio Grande Valley, Robert C. Vackar College of Business and Entrepreneurship, Business and Tourism Research Center. Accessed July 5, 2020. https://www.utrgv.edu/tourism/_files/documents/reports/winter%20texan%20survey%20report%202017-18.pdf.

Smith, Stanley K., and Mark House. 2006. "Snowbirds, Sunbirds, and Stayers: Seasonal Migration of Elderly Adults in Florida." *Journal of Gerontology: Social Sciences* 61B, no. 5 (September): S232–S239.

Statistics Canada. 2016. Table 24-10-0039-01 "Travel by Canadians to the United States, Top 15 States Visited." Accessed November 5, 2020. https://www150.statcan.gc.ca/t1/tbl1/en/tv.action?pid=2410003901.

Steger, Manfred B. 2013. *Globalization: A Very Short Introduction*. Oxford: Oxford University Press.

Torkington, Kate. 2010. "Defining Lifestyle Migration." *Dos Algarves* 19: 99–111.

Tremblay, Rémy, and Hugues Chicoine. 2011. "Floribec: The Life and Death of a Tourism-Based Transnational Community." *Norwegian Journal of Geography/NorskGeografiskTidsskrift* 65 (1): 54–59.

Tremblay, Rémy, Susan Hardwick, and Jamie O'Neill. 2014. "Academic Migration at the Canada-US Border." *American Review of Canadian Studies* 44, no. 1 (March): 118–134.

University of Texas Rio Grande Valley. 2016. "What are Winter Texans Saying?" Accessed November 5, 2020. https://www.utrgv.edu/tourism/_files/documents/reports/what-are-winter-texans-saying-report.pdf.

APPENDIX

Interview Schedule

The questions below in the left-hand column were used to loosely guide the interviews discussed in chapter 5. Please note that in each interview an attempt was made to avoid interrupting the natural flow of conversation. When necessary, different probes were used in order to ensure that key topics relevant to the study were adequately addressed.

Topic	Examples of Follow-Up Questions
Demographics and Personal Biographies	
Please tell me a little bit about yourself and about your background.	How old are you? Where did you grow up? What did you do for work and when did you retire?
Please tell me the story of how you came to be a snowbird in Florida.	Did you know anybody in this community when you first arrived? How did you choose to come to Florida? Did you consider other destinations?
Please tell me more about your experience of living in this community.	How many years have you been wintering in this community? What was the community like when you first arrived? How has your experience of living in the community changed over time?
Current Lifestyle	
Please tell me a little more about your lifestyle here.	What do you like about this community? How do you spend your time? Which community activities do you participate in? Are you involved in activities outside of the community? For what purposes do you leave the community?

Topic	Examples of Follow-Up Questions
Current Lifestyle (continued)	
Please tell me more about your experience of moving between Ontario and Florida every year.	How do you divide your time between Ontario and Florida? How would you compare your current lifestyle in Ontario with your current lifestyle in Florida? Are there any challenges associated with moving back and forth between two places? How do you maintain two homes? For how long do you plan to maintain this lifestyle, and what are your future plans?
Social Relationships	
Please tell me about your social life in Florida.	Who are your friends here? What kind of informal social activities do you participate in? Are there any social divisions in the community?
How does your social life in Florida compare to your social life in Canada?	Do you engage in different social activities in the two places? Are there friends that you see in both Florida and in Ontario?
How do you maintain relationships with friends and family in Ontario and Florida throughout the year?	What kind of communication do you have with friends and family throughout the year? Do you receive visitors from Canada in Florida and do your American friends visit you in Canada?
Crossing the Border	
Please tell me about your experiences with crossing the border between Canada and the United States.	Is it easy for snowbirds to cross the border? Have you experienced any challenges? Do you find it convenient/inconvenient moving between the two countries?
What do you think of the policies concerning the number of days snowbirds can spend in the United States and away from Canada?	Is the time you are allowed to spend in the United States each year sufficient? In addition to wintering in Florida, do you visit the US for other purposes during the year? Given the choice would you consider relocating permanently to the US?
Have your views on the US or Americans changed as a result of the time you have spent in Florida?	Have you learned things about the US that you did not know before? Have you come to see Americans differently?
Attachments to Canada	
Do you consider it important to stay up to date on what is happening in Canada when you are in Florida?	What kind of Canadian news and media do you read/watch? Do you vote in Canadian elections?

Topic	Examples of Follow-Up Questions
Attachments to Canada (continued)	
Do you actively seek out other Canadian snowbirds in Florida?	Are you part of Canadian-focused clubs and activities? Do you find that you socialize more with Americans or Canadians? Are you a member of the Canadian Snowbird Association and do you participate in their events?
What does your Canadian citizenship mean to you?	What do you value about Canada? Do you identify strongly with being Canadian when you are in Florida? How does it feel to return to Canada each spring?

CHAPTER 6

Passing Through or Living Here

Body and Self In-Between and On Edge in the Borderland Region of Stanstead, Quebec, and Derby Line, Vermont

Sandra Vandervalk

In the fall of 2015, I spent several months doing ethnographic fieldwork in the borderland communities of Stanstead, Quebec, and Derby Line, Vermont. I was drawn to the area by news reports that reflected a wide curiosity about these communities that had been purposefully settled along the Canada-US border. At the time, much was being made of how changes to the structure and functioning of the border were affecting the region. In particular, locals argued that increased security was driving a wedge through the heart of what had formerly been a singular albeit cross-border community. The intended purpose of my research was to consider the impacts of processes initiated outside this borderland region on relations within it. As an anthropologist, I realized that I could only do this by reflecting on another question: what it might mean to live in such a perpetually in-between place? In what follows, I explore what it is to be an embodied self in this borderland region. It might be more accurate to say that this is an account of the process by which I came to understand that there is a way of being in the world unique to this on-edge and in-the-middle place. The local meaning and significance of the border betrays itself in a certain style of being in the world evident among borderlanders, and with this style of being, borderlanders manage to trouble the non-borderlander assumption of the border as a line that divides and separates.

In this chapter, I will introduce the communities of Stanstead and Derby Line and a particular and uncomfortable zone that exists along the border between them. My experiences in this zone gave me an unexpected glimpse into the contradiction between my body's understanding of my world and the world I encountered in this new and complicated place. I will explore this contradiction by considering the concept of liminality, as fleshed out by Victor Turner. As we shall see, my understanding of what it means to be in a threshold place fails me in the borderlands. I have chosen to use the phenomenology of Maurice Merleau-Ponty to assist me in framing how I have come to inhabit the world I know: how my bodily experiences in the liminal zone might enable me to better understand something of the presubjective world that I inhabit even as my natural attitude puts me in a subject-object relation with a particular social and cultural reality. I will then turn my discussion to the intersubjective space shared by the people who live in what we on the outside experience as an in-between place. In particular, I will discuss how, just as snowbirds, through their cross-border lifestyle, seem to develop a unique perspective on their Canadian identities (Kelly, chapter 5, this volume), the lived experiences of borderlanders also yields a unique manifestation of national identity. I will argue that life in this place where one is always both on the edge and in the middle has fostered a particular style of being in the world that embraces and reflects the peculiar kind of in-betweenness that inhabits and is inhabited by the selves who live here.

There have been many ethnographic approaches to contending with the relationships among how the border is a manifestation of the nation-state, how it is enacted on the ground, and how it impacts lives of local borderlanders. Early border ethnography tended to be concerned with the border as an enactment of the central state, with its political and economic priorities portrayed in opposition to the interests of individual migrants and borderland dwellers (Grimson 2012, 198). Alejandro Grimson argues that this led to borderland inhabitants being treated as either "patriots" or as culturally contaminated and "insufficiently patriotic" (2012, 199). He identifies a more recent trend in border anthropology that sees "the root of all evil in the state—imagining and implementing an artificial homogeneity onto its territory—and idealized border populations as 'noble savages' who had best been able to resist it" (199). Such an approach makes it much easier to characterize those impacted by border policy as powerless victims or, as Joel Robbins (2013) would put it, "suffering subjects." Thomas Wilson and Hastings Donnan identify another trend in which focus on the role of the state and border in a borderland region is minimized in order to concentrate on the particularities of a community (1998, 6). Grimson suggests that such studies risk other kinds of essentialism: "One can fall into believing in an essential brotherhood or essential hybridity among all border dwellers" (2012, 200). A more recent theoretical approach in border anthropology sees the goal of the anthropologist as "simply to understand the borders, those who live on each side of them and the actors who interact with them" (201). The strength of such an approach is that it complicates the picture created of the people who live in borderland regions, accounting for their agency while also acknowledging that they live in a situation not entirely of their own making. Additionally, from outside the discipline of anthropology, and with an acknowledgement that the processual nature of borders has long been recognized in border studies literature, a recent trend in interdisciplinary border studies has been to more fully flesh out a theory of borders in motion (see Konrad and Kelly, introduction, this volume; Konrad 2015). While not quite a unifying theory of borders, this offers a framework for border research that accentuates the dynamic nature of borders as they are created and enacted, as they function on a day-to-day basis, and as they respond to both internally and externally generated challenges (Konrad 2015, 11). While this chapter may first and foremost be an ethnographic exploration of what it means to live in the borderlands of Stanstead and Derby Line, its emphasis on the border as something that is performed and, as a result, something that can never be static, fits well with the borders-in-motion framework.

Much important recent work has been done on the changing Canada-US border (Bhandar 2004; Conway and Pasch 2013; Helleiner 2007, 2009, 2010, 2013, 2016; Konrad and Nicol 2008). And several scholars have written specifically about the borderland area of Stanstead, Quebec, and Derby Line, Vermont (Hataley and Mason 2018; Lasserre, Forest, and Arapi 2012; Thibault 2008). Much of this work has been based on interviews. My work in the region included interviews, but also added participant observation to my methodological toolkit. Through this approach, I greatly expanded my access to the local life-world.

Stanstead and Derby Line

The town of Stanstead is located in the Eastern Townships of Quebec, approximately 160 kilometres southeast of Montréal. According to the town of Stanstead's website (http://www.stanstead.ca/en/welcome.htm), its population is approximately 2,850. Stanstead is the product of the 1995 amalgamation of the three villages of Rock Island, Stanstead Plain, and Beebe Plain. Locals still tend to refer to the different villages individually. Just south of Stanstead (the Rock Island sector)—down the road, across the street, and occasionally as near as the other side of the room—is the village of Derby Line, Vermont. Derby Line boasts a population of under 700 (Census Viewer, n.d.).

On both sides of the border, the median age of residents is 45.6 years, three to three and a half years older than their state and provincial counterparts.[1] Just over 50 percent of the residents of Stanstead identify English as their first language, and 44 percent identify French as their first language. In Derby Line, almost a quarter of residents claim French Canadian ancestry. A large percentage of those on the Canadian side of the border hold dual citizenship. The nearest hospital is in Newport, Vermont, so every baby born here from the time women began going to the hospital to give birth (locals point to the 1930s) until the introduction of socialized medicine in Quebec in 1969, was born in the US—and each was granted dual citizenship. Canadians now must travel to Sherbrooke to give birth in a hospital. Stanstead and Derby Line share well water, sewage treatment, maintenance of shared roads, and firetrucks when necessary. They also share the Haskell Library and Opera House, which is built on the line and funded by both Quebec and Vermont. A portion of one road runs along the border between communities for a kilometre. Homes on one side of this road are in the US, and those on the other are in Canada.

There are three border crossings between Stanstead and Derby Line—a major one on the expressway east of the communities and two smaller ones within the communities. In recent years, all local roads that cross the boundary without an associated port of entry

---

1 Statistics Canada, https://www12.statcan.gc.ca/census-recensement/2011/dp-pd/prof/details/page.cfm?Lang=E&Geo1=CSD&Code1=2445008&Geo2=PR&Code2=24&Data=Count&SearchText=Stanstead&SearchType=Begins&SearchPR=01&B1=All&Custom=and City-Data.com 2020, http://www.city-data.com/income/income-Derby-Line-Vermont.html.

have been blocked by gates except one. The one remaining open road is used by patrons of the Library and Opera House who are permitted to walk on the sidewalk from Canada to get to the building's entrance on the American side. A US Border Patrol or Royal Canadian Mounted Police (RCMP) vehicle usually idles near the building, with officers keeping a watchful eye on patrons. Although the rules for movement in this little area are well marked, missteps by a number of Canadians have led to detentions and large fines. In 2010, much to the consternation of some locals who felt that the road should remain open, even if just symbolically, the mayor of Stanstead placed large ornamental planters across it in order to prevent people from accidentally crossing into the US via the road rather than the sidewalk.

Prior to 9/11, the communities on either side of the line, while perhaps not thriving, were nonetheless surviving. Many more businesses could be found in the zone between the two ports of entry in the Rock Island sector and Derby Line. Americans crossed to play hockey or go curling, or to pick up quick emergency groceries. Canadians bought gas and went to the post office on the other side. They also shopped and dined in the US. In the immediate aftermath of 9/11, security at the border dramatically tightened in the short term. The US government tripled the number of border guards, and adopted a "militarized stance" (Konrad and Nicol 2004, 17). Lineups and excessive delays at the border resulted from "increasingly onerous border checks" (18). By 2004, border delays of commercial traffic were costing both sides billions of dollars. The move to expedite the flow of goods while minimizing the flow of terrorists expedited the shift in border management toward a strategy of high technology surveillance (Konrad and Nicol 2008, 164). The US government began upgrading its ports of entry. The US border patrol was given an enhanced mandate—by 2005, they were patrolling everywhere within one hundred miles of the boundary (Grant 2011, 5). By 2009, the gates were erected across the two ports of entry. For border crossers, passports became mandatory in 2008. A number of informants from both sides indicated to me that acquiring a passport was too expensive for many area residents, and that the requirement had therefore torn apart cross-border families. The passport requirement has also curtailed the cross-border use of sports and recreational facilities. A disturbing development for many of my informants was the concurrent rise of a militarized attitude among American border guards.

Discombobulation and Bewilderment in the Liminal Zone

There is a mysterious bit of geography that exists between the Canadian and American ports of entry at Rock Island and Derby Line—a part of the borderland region that during my fieldwork I began to refer to as the "liminal zone." The ports of entry in this area are located approximately 100 metres north and south of the border. Sizable chunks of the downtowns of both communities therefore exist in the area between entry ports, making this area something of a no man's land. Within this zone, people are required to report to the appropriate customs port to cross the border, even if they intend to stay between the two border ports. Those who travel into this in-between place technically should not have to report to customs if they do not intend to cross the border, although occasionally, US border patrol officers insist that they do.

One of the most important experiences that I had in the region involved moving through the border in the company of a local borderlander. Her comfortable movements made me aware of how something as mundane and everyday as my "knowledge" of the structure and functioning of a port of entry was particular to my own history and experience—in other words, it was an interpretation that reflected my point of view—and that this knowledge was also something that had been carved into my body. To begin to get a sense of what it means to live in a place defined by the boundary in its midst, this little, almost insignificant event drew my attention to a most simple idea—the communicative relationship between body and world, and how that might be shaped in such an extraordinary place. The description that follows is from my field notes (September 15, 2015):

> Today I went through the entry point in the Rock Island/Derby Line sector as a passenger in Kelly's car. Kelly was born in Newport and holds dual citizenship. The officer on duty at the US border kiosk asked for our passports. Kelly thrust hers in her left hand out the car window and then grabbed mine with her right hand to offer it. "No," he said, "Both at the same time." Kelly put both hands out the window, a passport in each. "No," he said, "Put them together." Kelly rolled her eyes and gathered the passports together and handed them over. The officer was annoyed, but proceeded with the traditional questions: "Where are you from? Where are you going?"

While this interaction gave me a taste of how bizarre things can get in the border-crossing process, what happened next shocked me.

> Kelly drove forward and stopped at the road, but instead of turning right and continuing deeper into the US, she turned left and headed back in the direction from which we had just come, back into the ill-defined, liminal, in-between Canada and the United States space. It was a jolt to both my mind and body. I felt like I had hit a wall of impossibility. "We're going back?" I asked. "No," she replied, "I'm just heading over to the interstate. That'll get us to Newport faster." And off she drove, with me, dumbfounded in the seat beside her. Just before the boundary with Canada, she turned the car right onto a road halfway down the hill. Before this moment, I hadn't noticed the road there. For Kelly, this was obvious and natural. For me, it made no sense. A border, in my experience equated with the port of entry, is something to be crossed and put behind oneself. I was seized with shock.

I was disturbed by the violent physical response I felt in my body to a kind of movement that seemed outside of the realm of possibility for me, someone with a good deal of border-crossing experience. To begin the process of teasing apart what happened to me in this moment, I feel I must engage with the idea of liminality as fleshed out by Victor Turner.

The Border as Experienced by an Outsider: A Threshold

Liminality is a word encountered in many different contexts in anthropology. The idea of liminality originated with Arnold van Gennep, who used the words "liminal" or "threshold" to represent the middle phase of what he identified as the tripartite ritual structure of *rites de passage* (van Gennep [1960] 1992). Rites of passage are ceremonies that mark the transition from "one situation to another or from one cosmic or social world to another" (10). A rite of passage is a ritual event that symbolically marks and facilitates transitions of "place, state, social position and age" (Turner [1969] 2011, 94). Rites of passage often include a movement through geographical space that parallels the passage to a new status.

The first phase of a rite of passage is separation—marked by the symbolically mediated detachment of an individual or group from a former social condition and a separation of time and space from the ordinary and profane (Turner 1982, 24). Next, a liminal phase puts its participants into an ambiguous state of being that bears little resemblance to either the former or the anticipated future status. Liminality, according to Victor Turner, is a "betwixt and between" period, and liminal beings are between categories of being—" neither here nor there" ([1969] 2011, 95).

Liminality is a place between places and a time between times. Liminal people in a group are often reduced to a low common status—as though dead or not yet born. Participants in this phase are often physically removed from nonparticipants and are ground-down and weakened (Turner 1982, 26–27). They may experience homogeneity and a deep camaraderie with fellow participants (Turner [1969] 2011, 96). Finally, participants are reintegrated back into society in new social roles or positions—with clearly understood responsibilities and behavioural standards.

The work of any rite of passage is accomplished through the use of symbols. Turner understands symbols to be living events rather than fixed things. He argues that the social and psychological meanings behind symbols and the work they might accomplish can only be evaluated "in relation to other events" (Turner 1982, 21). He states that symbols are "social and cultural dynamic systems, shedding and gathering meaning over time and altering in form" (Turner 1982, 22). They might appear in one ritual performance and then reappear somewhere else—moving from ritual to myth, for example. Their use is open-ended—their meaning and form are subject to shifts over time and, in many ways, from person to person. Turner (1982) points out that the symbols employed in rites of passage of traditional societies tend to be aspects of "relatively stable, cyclical, and repetitive systems" and have a more literal link to the changes they facilitate in bringing about compared to the more metaphorical sense that they tend to hold in large-scale, complex societies (29).

While it is clear that the process of border crossing and the changes that may result from such a crossing do not perhaps belong in the same category as the traditional rites of passage with which we are familiar (weddings, etc.), it nonetheless seems reasonable to claim that there are parallels between border crossing and these kinds of rites of passage. Border crossing, for most of us, is a three-part process laden with symbols that speak to us and change us, if even for just a short time. Border crossing (of the legal kind) happens at well-defined, prescribed sites. At land crossings, we pass the Canadian port of entry as we leave Canada. Beyond this point we become separated from our fellow citizens. The gap between the Canadian port of entry and the actual boundary line is an uncomfortable no man's land. Another eerie gap exists between the boundary line and the American port of entry. This is betwixt and between, neither here nor there, yet both here and there. The boundary lies in the middle and belongs to neither country even as it also belongs to both. This is a liminal place and time for those passing through. It is not a place to linger. Already in this place, we are outsiders to our own country.

As the border crosser approaches the border kiosk on the other side, he or she is subjected to warning signs and other symbols of the state and its authority (flags, surveillance equipment, and vehicles) and then must perform appropriately for the agent of the state in order to be allowed to move out of the in-between place. These interactions are more or less scripted, but the demands of the border officer dictate the responses given by the crosser. We see this in the interaction between Kelly and the border agent as she attempts to hand over our passports. He dictates the terms of the transaction, and although she does not appreciate his tone or attitude, she ultimately complies. The border crosser becomes separated from his or her everyday life identity, and for a few moments becomes a suspect—a person with no citizenship or status. This is a place where one does not have recourse to the rights and privileges that one held prior to this and that one might hold anew once through. Usually, having met the required conditions, the border crosser becomes transformed into a recognizable entity: either a legitimate stranger or the home comer.

This is the border as I have experienced it many times. I am familiar with the symbols, the rules, the procedures, and the feelings of vulnerability that one experiences when being scrutinized by a border agent. When I am told I am free to move on and into whichever country lies before me, I do so without hesitation. Until the moment that Kelly turned her car and drove us back the way we had come before entering the port of entry, such a movement for me was unthinkable, unimaginable. Liminality is an in-between state, an in-between place, but it should not be without a time limit. It is part of a process that moves forward, or cycles—it changes people, if only just temporarily. It is not something that stands still. In the car with Kelly,

I began to catch sight of something different about her relationship with this threshold place, and I began to question how I had come to have the understanding of it that I had. Furthermore, given the violent physical response I felt to what was for me an impossible, yet evidently very possible movement, it became clear that my understanding of this world was not simply a product of my mind but was something that had been carved into my body.

In this early moment during my time in the region, I began to wonder what it might mean to always live in an in-between place and how that might be inscribed in body and mind. How does it shape one's way of being in the world to have dual citizenship? To speak and understand two languages? To not just venture across an international boundary for major shopping or travel adventures, but to do so sometimes many times in a single day in order to pick up mail, or buy gas, or eat at a fast-food restaurant, or do any of the other mundane activities we non-borderlanders do not think twice about doing within the confines of our own communities? Oscar Martinez argues that "many borderlanders live and function in several different worlds: the world of their national culture, the world of the border environment, the world of their ethnic group ..., and the world ... on the other side of the boundary" (1994, 20). My research question shifted. I began to ask myself what it might mean to inhabit different worlds simultaneously.

Embodiment and Liminality

It is clear to me that I had brought a particular world with me into this borderland region. Even though my geographical location had changed, my body nonetheless situated me in this new place within the world that I knew, given my previous life experience. Through my experience with Kelly, I began to understand that the border as I experienced it was not, and could not be, the same as the border experienced by locals who crossed regularly. This brings me back to my original research interest—but from a slightly different angle. The changes that are constantly implemented in the functioning of the border are put in place by those from without, people who do not have the embodied knowledge of living in-between that local borderlanders have. There is a disconnection between the world of locals and the world of policymakers, journalists, and fellow countrymen who live elsewhere. It is, I believe, important to consider at this point how we come to inhabit the worlds that we do in order to do justice to the claims of borderlanders that the tightening of the border is wreaking havoc on a way of life, and perhaps a way of being in the world.

"Being in the world" is a phrase often deployed in anthropology, perhaps not always in the sense that phenomenologists use it. In the phenomenological sense, it represents a style of existence—a certain kind of coherence in the way our body opens to the world. It also encompasses the reality that arises for us as a result of the communication between the body and the indeterminate world in which we live. It captures the idea that our reality is neither initiated by nor built upon by purely physiological or cognitive processes but instead emerges from an indeterminate place that underlies, or is prior to, the differentiation between I, the subject, and me, the object. In what follows, I will expand on some of the ideas captured by this phrase.

In *Phenomenology of Perception*, Maurice Merleau-Ponty's project was to break free of the dichotomies that have historically shaped both science and philosophy—to underscore the unity that underlies the appearance of subject and object, and mind and body. We are embodied, our bodies are in constant movement toward a world that is given to us by our senses, preobjectively and in fullness. In other words, our bodies exist in relation to the world—have a perspective on and in the world—without the mind as intermediary. This preobjective world is the complex upon which personal existence is built.

Phenomenologists aim to "bracket" off, or disconnect from, the assumptions that underlie our natural attitude toward the constitution of our world. As Merleau-Ponty (2012) writes: "Our perception ends in objects, and the object, once constituted, appears as the reason for all the experiences of it that we have had or could have" (69). Our perceptions are therefore always already interpretations. For example, when objects appear to us, we experience them as complete despite the fact that we can only ever have partial experiences of them at any given time. There is always something more available in any object that presents itself to consciousness—there is always something more to be grasped. This is indeterminacy.

We experience objects as existing independently of our perception of them, and we expect to be able to experience them from different perspectives. If we move, we expect to see an object from the new vantage point, even if we only have a general sense of what we might see from that new position. We are oblivious to the communicative processes between our bodies and the world that give rise to the appearance of objects, that give us the distinction between self and other, subject and object. It is in moments such as the anecdote I shared above, in which something as simple as a left turn was able to completely disorient me, that one realizes that there might be glitches in our natural attitude toward the world, glitches that provide clues to help us understand how our experiences of the world are structured by the ongoing communicative relationship between body and world, a relationship that is always subject to shifts in perspective as we move through both time and space.

Merleau-Ponty shows us that objects do not exist in and of, or for, themselves—they always emerge out of contexts. The horizon metaphor captures this idea and is useful not only for considering our relationship with objects that arise through perceptual experience but also for more abstract and ethereal objects. If we look up and out toward the edge of the visible horizon, we see that its edge is ill-defined and indeterminate. Keeping our gaze on the edge, the field within the horizon swirls with vaguely meaningful yet indefinite shapes and colours that our body has a sense of but that are not given the appearance of full objects unless we consciously attend to them. The thing, the object, comes to us out of the indeterminate field. It looms on the fuzzy edge, part of nondescript nothingness and every-thingness until it suddenly appears in focus, bringing with it a sense that "announces more than it contains" (Merleau-Ponty 2012).

An object is manifested in a spatial horizon, but its appearance is also woven into a temporal horizon. That is, the glass presently on the table occupies a point in time that remains in communication with past moments but is also evocative of possible futures—all of which allow a moment to rise up as "an identifiable point in objective time" (Merleau-Ponty 2012, 72). Objects that spring into being are accompanied by wisps of the past: memories arise out of experiences with like objects. The mind does not think its way through sensations and perceptions to yield the objects that appear before us. Rather, edges, colours, textures, and sounds suddenly spring into being as objects according to "present givens" and "acquired experiences" (Merleau-Ponty 2012, 15). Knowledge is pulled forward into the present from the past and pushes into possible futures.

Merleau-Ponty (2012) would argue that my body has a world that it spreads out around me, anchoring me in the richness of my personal history as a body in the physical world and also as a body in relation to other bodies that live in the same physical world. The body gives us natural objects whose fullness bear witness to the threads of the very existence that reaches into them. The first objects that necessarily appear in consciousness must be composed of properties that avail themselves to the senses, which function pre-personally (Merleau-Ponty 2012). These become the building blocks that allow other, more abstract objects to come into awareness, including language. Our sense of every object is changed every time we encounter it, if only ever so minimally. These changes are registered in the body as our understanding of the world is continually etched upon it, adjusted and re-etched. Knowledge and language, always anchored in the body, are no different: They grow out of and build upon previous encounters between body and world. Sensing then is not the presentation of reconstructions of things in the world outside of our bodies to our minds so that they can be identified by cross-checking against catalogued ideal types (Merleau-Ponty 2012). Things in the world have meaning and sense because we have bodies, and our bodies place us in the thing we perceive and incorporate a temporal perspective into our experience, which carries with it our past experiences and future expectations. My body has been the foundation for an accumulation of experiences that, layer by layer, have structured my understanding of the world. My reach into the world continues to stretch outward toward the horizon, but my point of view necessarily limits me. There is always something more than I can see. Anything new that presents itself must be understood through the structures of my prior experiences.

If one side of experience is perception, the other is the movement of my body toward the world. Merleau-Ponty (2012) refers to naturalized forms of movement as habit and argues that they are neither "a form of knowledge nor an automatic reflex"; instead, they are indicative of the understanding that the body has of its world (145). Acquired habits, he argues, are no different from other movements such as touching our nose or toes. Movements like these are reflections of intention: the body's movement into the world. When our body has learned to do something, when that something has become second nature to us, it is because our body has grabbed the significance of what we are doing and has "dilat[ed] our being in the world" (Merleau-Ponty 2012, 146). This kind of understanding is held in the body and does not enter conscious awareness. The body is the starting place for our world. It is the foundation for everyone, for everything, and this world that we inhabit is not simply a world we sense, it is a world we act on. Our body situates us in the world it knows—an indeterminate, never fully graspable, but fully human world. And the body, through the course of its existence as a movement toward the world, accumulates a certain style of being in the world.

Intersubjectivity and Identity in an In-Between Place

Merleau-Ponty (2012) reminds us that just as we are born into a physical world so we are also born into a social world. Other people are present in the objects we use and are evident in the structures that surround us or in the way the land has been altered or shaped. When I see another face, I understand that I am in the presence of a consciousness not unlike my own, who is also situated in the world with a point of view (Merleau-Ponty 2012). I understand that this point of view may or may not overlap with my own. An object or thing in view presents itself to both of us, but we experience it from different angles. When I perceive another body in action, I have a sense of that body's intentions because I have a sense of my own. From infancy, I have communicated in this way with others who share my world—I see them act on objects and I learn to do likewise because I understand the correspondence between my body and theirs. We are both in the world, and in our communication, we construct a shared world—this is intersubjectivity. That is not to say that our worlds are exactly the same: when I perceive a living being like myself acting, the action reveals another subjectivity to me. Like all other perceptions, this one is anchored in a context: each of our perceptions arise from unique points of view and reflect the indeterminacy of the fields of our own beings (Merleau-Ponty 2012). Anelynda Mielke and Nadya Pohran (chapter 3, this volume) argue that the border emerges out of a field of symbolic *things* that are not necessarily proximal to a borderline. In this chapter, I argue that the meanings held by those symbols have been uniquely shaped according to the life histories and encounters of their beholders. The border as an object (concrete or abstract) must arise for each of us out of the horizons of our own experiences. We enact it in the space between us, and as Alfred Schütz points out, we can usually take it for granted that our worlds coincide adequately enough for us to relate to one another (Schütz and Luckmann 1973). Schütz stresses that the intersubjective world, the life-world, as he refers to it, is "not my private world nor your private world, nor yours and mine added together, but rather is the world of our *common experience*" (Schütz and Luckmann 1973, 68).

I would like for a moment to consider my private world—the starting point of my particular sense of the border. This means thinking about it in terms of my identity as a Canadian. My Canadianness undoubtedly began with the rudimentary sense of belonging that I experienced first as a physical participant in a mother-infant dyad, then as a member of a family, and then as a member of ever-widening circles of community. It must have been and continues to be shaped by interactions with family members, friends, and teachers; by news reports, celebrations of national holidays, and beer commercials; as well as by the occasional venture beyond Canada's boundaries. My awareness of what it might mean to be Canadian has always been tied to an equally important awareness of what it might mean to not be Canadian. For the most part, exposure, proximity, and a sense of powerlessness in the shadow of such a powerful country as the US have ensured that it has usually been the entity against which I define my Canadianness. My point is that there is a line that defines my identity as a Canadian. It has perhaps become more sophisticated and reflects the broader perspective I have gained over the years—but as a person who has only ever lived in Canada, there is a line, and I define myself as much by difference from what is on the other side as I do by what makes me similar to my fellow countrymen. This is the way the world has presented itself to me—slowly, in incremental steps. The world has come to me through my body, and ultimately, through my body, I know and continue to learn about my world.

For me, the border is the physical manifestation of the line between the essence of what it is to be Canadian and what it is to be American. It is not that I think this, it is more that my being understands it to be so. The entity that I am insists on choosing sides. Border crossing remains an unsettling process that always highlights the precarity of my own existence. My name, where I live, my citizenship—all these things that I have accumulated and that anchor me in the world I know seem less real when a border officer has my passport in his or her hand. I either want to be a legitimate visitor to the US or I want to be home. I do not want to be in between. My body knows, and a shock runs through it when Kelly's car turns and takes us back into the liminal zone. For my informants in the borderlands, the same things are at stake, are they not? When I arrive in Stanstead, it does not occur to me to think otherwise. My experience with Kelly in the car throws a wrench in the works. What does the border represent to borderlanders? Their movements tell me that even though I believe we are sharing a world when I interact with them, there is something different about what the border means for many of the people who live along it.

I would argue that for borderlanders, who together share a particular kind of intersubjective space, a particular life-world, the border does not represent national identity or citizenship in the way it does to those from away from the border. Borderlanders certainly identify as citizens of one country or the other, but that citizenship is not so tightly confirmed by geography as it is for outsiders, even as it is perhaps more tightly confined by that same geography. I would argue that borderlander markers of national and ethnic identity are necessarily more nuanced and complicated than for those of us for whom such identity is not always in question. Here it seems prudent to turn to Fredrik Barth.

Although national and ethnic identity are not quite the same thing for those of us who live away from the border, I believe for borderlanders they are necessarily closely linked. Barth ([1969] 1998) asserts that what matters in the formation of ethnic identity is ascription: self-identification and classification. Cultural differences matter, but only the ones most meaningful to the players. Aspects of culture that are likely to be woven into ethnic identity are those that might function as "overt signals and signs," such as "dress, language, house-form, or general style of life," as well as value standards by which an individual's identity performance may be judged (Barth [1969] 1998, 14). Ethnic identity is not a representation of culture but rather a performance that signals belonging. Barth argues that the genesis and persistence of ethnic identity require the existence of boundaries between ethnic groups. The groups are defined by these perceived boundaries rather than by the cultural content contained on either side of boundary lines. The lines are social, not territorial, geographical, or biological. They are conjured, affirmed, and maintained each time there is an interaction between different groups.

For those of us who live away from the border, the degree of one's Canadianness does not matter on a day-to-day basis. The border serves to place us well inside of Canada, well beyond the need to perform Canadianness. For borderlanders however, the situation is more complex. Regular movement back and forth through the port of entry demands the performance of national identity while also ensuring that at any given time, on either side of the line, there is a vexing mixture of Canadians and Americans. There is a high rate of dual citizenship amongst Stansteaders, many of whom were born in the nearest hospital in Newport, Vermont, prior to the advent of socialized medicine in Quebec. Those with dual citizenship almost universally identify as Canadians, but this is not an identity confirmed by the side of the border they are on. Through intermarriage and employment, Canadians and Americans live on both sides of the line. The border does not act to differentiate what it is to be Canadian from what it is to be American, but its presence makes it necessary for locals to know how to differentiate themselves. Borderlanders have become skilled at identifying who is who—they have learned to deploy and read identity markers, regardless of which side of the border they happen to be on in any given moment. Informant Bruce illustrates my point: "The other day I was down on the street here, and there was two ladies… and I say, 'You are ladies from the States for sure, eh?' 'How do you know that?' 'Well,' I said, 'just, you know, it was your look.' I love Vermonters, they're very friendly. She says, 'Yep, we always know when Canadian women are in Newport.' And I say, 'What makes you say that?' She says, 'They're always better dressed than we are'" (B. K. 2015). Here Bruce identifies several important markers of citizenship and also informs me that people on both sides of the line can read them: Vermonters are friendly and outgoing, and Canadians are well dressed. Most of my informants were clear in telling me about other people's national identities. Sometimes I would ask how they know, and I was often told, "I can just tell." Citizenship was usually the first thing I was told about any person who came up in discussion.

The border insists on an identity from borderlanders and makes national citizenship a salient and important identity claim, but being on one side or the other has little to do with the claims one makes as a borderlander. For borderlanders, there is a very real distinction between Canadians and Americans, but the distinction is not determined by the border, even as the process of crossing the border demands the performance of citizenship. My point here is that while the line to me is an intimidating threshold that marks the outer limits of two different countries populated by different, yet similar peoples, for borderlanders, the border is not a site of differentiation, even as it makes it necessary to perform difference. For borderlanders then, the border is not a threshold. Every person who crosses it is confronted by their own identity claims, and those identity claims are important to borderlanders, but the border itself does not have the transformative power for locals that it has for those from away. For locals, it functions more as an irritating and inconvenient stop light that slows down movement in and through a place that feels like home.

While the border may not be experienced as a threshold in the same way for locals as it is for outsiders, I believe that for locals the border does nonetheless point to another. Strangely, it can only do this by highlighting the common experiences of those who live on either side of it. All locals on either side routinely suffer its insults. Everyone on either side lives on the edge and in between. For most borderlanders, the border does not point to the other on the other side of the line at all, but in fact points to another other: the non-borderlander—the policymakers, journalists, and outsiders who constantly interfere in the day-to-day functioning of the ports of entry. In this way, when locals claim that they share a community, they are expressing something legitimate about their reality. The sense of what they have in common is their shared experience of this thing that they maneuver around and through and with as part of their daily existence, this thing that is always imposed on them from the outside and that is now increasingly being managed from afar.

I would argue that this similarity that I claim exists across the border in the borderlands reflects more than simply a way of life. It reflects a way of being in the world. Above, I have been writing about identity as something that emerges in the intersubjective spaces between people, as an aspect of a life-world. Identity therefore speaks to social organization and a way of life rather more than it does to a way of being in the world, although the two are connected. Through Merleau-Ponty, we are able to consider another side of the social world. We can put together how as a group we come to share (more or less) a particular way of experiencing and responding to the world that might be called culture. In the next section, I will consider how living in an in-between place might give rise to a particular style of responding to the world.

An In-Between Way of Being in the World

In the borderlands, my body placed me in the world that it knew until the moment in Kelly's car when I was jarred from complacency and forced to respond to something that made no sense to me. Until that moment, turning back into the liminal border area was inconceivable. It was not that I thought that it was unacceptable or even illegal to navigate the border the way Kelly did; rather, it was that such movement was outside the realm of possibility for me. I was in an intersubjective moment in which the world Kelly and I were attempting to share was showing some cracks.

Like every other aspect of our experience as embodied beings, perspective, incompleteness, and fullness also structure our cultural worlds (Merleau-Ponty 2012, 374).

Our body opens us to physical, temporal, spatial, historical, and social horizons that exist prior to our births, the edges of which continually expand and shift according to our perceptual engagements. We are immersed in social worlds from our birth that our bodies come to know and that give us, as collectivities, particular views of the world and therefore particular styles of engagement with it. One might call this culture—culture not as a thing but as an embodied style of being in the world, a way of responding to the demands of any situation. Culture is necessarily open-ended and therefore frames the possibilities for how a situation might unfold while never with certainty limiting its meaning or sense (Leistle 2015, 295). And of course, just as two people may interact in a constructed and shared intersubjective world, each with the appearance of fullness, yet neither being totally graspable by the other, so too is it possible for shared spaces to open between two different "experiential regions"—an intercultural space (Waldenfels 2011, 74). Neither side will be able to fully grasp an understanding of the other in such a space—for each side, something of the other always remains beyond comprehension, beyond imagination, outside the realm of possibility.

Phenomenologist Bernhard Waldenfels (2011) refers to the inconceivable, the unimaginable, the thing beyond our ken, as the alien and argues that when the unknowable alien grabs our attention, we must respond and make sense of it, but by doing so, something of the alien always escapes. To make sense of the incomprehensible, we domesticate it so that it shifts into alignment with our understanding of the world—which does indeed broaden, even as the alien runs off. Everything that has become part of our understanding of the world since our birth has come to us in this way. We embody what comes to us in a way that makes sense to us given our accumulation of experiences. The physical jolt I felt when Kelly turned her car around and drove back into the liminal zone was an alien call. After the fact, looking at maps and coming to terms with the rules that dictate movement through the murky area between the ports of entry helped me to "make sense" of what had happened, but I also know that something escaped my understanding that day. I have come to believe that despite my sense-making processes, and as much as I have grasped what it might mean to be a Stanstead–Derby Line borderlander, I nonetheless have not quite caught hold of a particular way of being in the world that has not been years in the making in the experiences of my own body.

Yet I did catch glimpses of our different worlds. Toward the conclusion of an early interview, an informant remarked that he "loved living at the edge of a country" (S. N. 2015). This remark seemed important. It seemed representative of the feelings of most borderlanders with whom I spoke. The Stanstead and Derby Line region is remarkable in that it is bisected by a line that is incredibly solid and real to those of us who do not live beside it but that is not quite so solid or real for those whose everyday lives are wrapped around it, even as authorities are literally and physically hardening it up. But the border is not the only identifiable boundary in the region. This is a place where two countries meet, but it is also a place of two languages, and historically the intersection of two, arguably three, cultures. People whom I met in the region were quick to claim and proclaim identities. Americans were Americans. Those with dual citizenship always declared one country or the other as their home or place of origin. Canadians either identified as "English" or "French," even if they were completely bilingual. How do people in this region come to feel at home in such a liminal place? I do not claim that by virtue of their proximity to so many borders and boundaries that they have somehow become immune to the effects of liminality. As Waldenfels argues, humans are liminal beings—always subject to transformation by experiences that come from beyond the limits of our understanding. The people of this region can be no different.

I would like to bring back into play a question that I posed earlier in this chapter. I asked what it means to inhabit different worlds simultaneously. In hindsight, that was a poor question. Borderlanders do not inhabit two worlds simultaneously. The question reflects my response to a situation that I can only make sense of in my own way. I experience the border as an entity that creates two sides, two places, but this cannot be their sense. Borderlanders have for centuries been comfortable dancing along the lines that in theory should divide, and that do in fact divide many of us. They are comfortable in those in-between places that make most of the rest of us nervous, if not totally uncomfortable, *because this is their world*. The line that divides us, unites them. They are and always will be, like the rest of us, liminal beings who adapt and expand as they deal with confrontations with the unknown. Borderlanders, like everyone else, must grapple with the eerie objects that take shape along the murky edges of their being. They respond in ways that make sense to them given the world they inhabit. And the world they inhabit is a place between places—it is both Canadian and American. For borderlanders, the unimaginable is not what lies on the other side of the line or the other side of town. It's the aftermath of the events of September 11, 2001. It's the unanticipated changes to the way the line works—such as when the bodily inscribed geography of one's community is violently and unexpectedly altered by fences and gates. Borderlanders are troubled by the barrage of changing rules imposed from outside the region that affect their ability to move freely in the border zone. This indicates a uniquely in-between way of being in the world: borderlanders inhabit the middle space, they dwell in the in between, moving backward and forward, in and out of it in ways that defy the understanding of those of us who do not live on the edge and in the middle. The back-and-forth web of existence that borderlanders have knit for themselves is their taken-for-granted world. That embodied knowledge of their world comes into question through interference from outside forces.

Conclusion

We are fascinated by places like Stanstead and Derby Line when they turn up in media stories precisely because the people who live there show us something real about ourselves and our relationship with the world—something that defies our understanding of how borders should work and what they do. Those of us who do not live in the borderlands rely on the border to contain us as a nation. We use the border to define ourselves against those on the exterior. And we use the border to create that exterior. We expect the border to be enacted cleanly and decisively. We take comfort in neat categories of binary opposition that serve to organize our thinking. Borderlanders unsettle us by comfortably inhabiting both sides of the line. They unsettle us through their claims of a shared life-world, despite differing national identity claims—claims they must make in order to inhabit their life-world, in order to live on both sides. They unsettle us, because they proclaim difference in order to proclaim similarity.

They show us something about ourselves that we all must recognize somewhere in the bottom of our beings: that we all live in the middle all the time.

Acknowledgements

This research was made possible in part through a Social Sciences and Humanities Research Council of Canada J. A. Bombardier Canada Graduate Scholarship as well as an Ontario Graduate Scholarship.

References

Barth, Fredrik. (1969) 1998. Introduction to *Ethnic Groups and Boundaries: The Social Organization of Culture Difference*, 9–38. Long Grove, IL: Waveland Press.

Bhandar, Davina. 2004. "Renormalizing Citizenship and Life in Fortress North America." *Citizenship Studies* 8 (3): 261–278.

B. K. 2015. Interview by author. Voice recording. Stanstead, QC, September 24, 2015.

Census Viewer. n.d. "Derby Line, Vermont Population: Census 2010 and 2000 Interactive Map, Demographics, Statistics, Quick Facts." Accessed September 29, 2020. http://censusviewer.com/city/VT/Derby%20Line.

Conway, Kyle, and Timothy Pasch. 2013. *Beyond the Border: Tensions across the Forty-Ninth Parallel in the Great Plains and Prairies*. Montréal and Kingston: McGill-Queen's University Press.

Grant, Julie. 2011. "U. S.-Canadian Border Changes since 9/11." North Country Public Radio, September 9, 2011. http://www.northcountrypublicradio.org/news/story/18372/20110909/u-s-canadian-border-changes-since-9-11.

Grimson, Alejandro. 2012. "Nations, Nationalism and 'Borderization' in the Southern Cone." In *A Companion to Border Studies*, edited by Thomas M. Wilson and Hastings Donnan, 194–213. Chichester, UK: Wiley-Blackwell.

Hataley, Todd, and Scott J. Mason. 2018. "Collective Efficacy across Borders: The Case of Stanstead, Quebec, and Derby Line, Vermont." *Journal of Borderlands Studies* 33 (3): 433–444.

Helleiner, Jane. 2016. *Borderline Canadianness*. Toronto: University of Toronto Press.

———. 2013. "Unauthorized Crossings, Danger and Death at the Canada-US Border." *Journal of Ethnic and Migration Studies* 39 (9): 1507–1524.

———. 2010. "Canadian Border Resident Experience of the 'Smartening' Border at Niagara." *Journal of Borderlands Studies* 25 (3–4): 87–103.

———. 2009. "'As Much American as a Canadian Can Be': Cross-Border Experience and Regional Identity among Young Borderlanders in Canadian Niagara." *Anthropologica* 51 (1): 225–238.
———. 2007. "'Over the River': Border Childhoods and Border Crossings at Niagara." *Childhood* 14 (4): 431–447.
Konrad, Victor. 2015. "Toward a Theory of Borders in Motion." *Journal of Borderlands Studies* 30 (1): 1–17.
Konrad, Victor, and Heather N. Nicol. 2008. *Beyond Walls: Re-inventing the Canada-United States Borderlands*. Aldershot, UK: Ashgate.
———. 2004. "Boundaries and Corridors: Rethinking the Canada–United States Borderlands in the Post–9/11." *Canadian–American Public Policy* 60: 1–51.
Lasserre, Frédéric, Patrick Forest, and Enkeleda Arapi. 2012. "Politique de sécurité et villages-frontière entre États-Unis et Québec." *Cybergeo: European Journal of Geography*. Posted online on March 2, 2012. https://doi.org/10.4000/cybergeo.25209.
Leistle, Bernhard. 2015. "Otherness as a Paradigm in Anthropology." *Semiotica*, no. 204 (April): 291–313.
Martinez, Oscar J. 1994. *Border People: Life and Society in the U.S.-Mexico Borderlands*. Tucson: University of Arizona Press.
Merleau-Ponty, Maurice. 2012. *Phenomenology of Perception*. Translated by Donald A. Landes. London: Routledge.
Robbins, Joel. 2013. "Beyond the Suffering Subject: Toward an Anthropology of the Good." *Journal of the Royal Anthropological Institute* 19, no. 2 (September): 447–462.
Schütz, Alfred, and Thomas Luckmann. 1973. *The Structures of the Life-World*. Evanston, IL: Northwestern University Press.
S. N. 2015. Interview by author. Voice recording. Stanstead, QC, September 22, 2015.
Thibault, Pierrette. 2008 "How Local is Local French in Quebec." In *Social Lives in Language—Sociolinguistics and Multilingual Speech Communities: Celebrating the Work of Gillian Sankoff*, edited by Miriam Meyerhoff and Naomi Nagy, 195–219. Amsterdam: John Benjamins Publishing Company.
Turner, Victor. 1982. *From Ritual to Theatre*. New York: PAJ Publications.
———. (1969) 2011. *The Ritual Process: Structure and Anti-structure*. New Brunswick, NJ: Aldine Transaction.
van Gennep, Arnold. (1960) 1992. *The Rites of Passage*. Translated by Monika B. Vizedom and Gabrielle L. Caffee. Chicago: The University of Chicago Press.
Waldenfels, Bernhard. 2011. *Phenomenology of the Alien: Basic Concepts*. Translated by Alexander Kozin and Tanja Stähler. Evanston, IL: Northwestern University Press.

Wilson, Thomas M., and Hastings Donnan. 1998. "Nation, State and Identity at International Borders." In *Border Identities: Nation and State at International Frontiers*, edited by Thomas M. Wilson and Hastings Donnan, 1–30. Cambridge: Cambridge University Press.

CHAPTER 7

North American Cyber New Regionalism in Canada

Online Cultural Borderlands and Change through New Media

Alexander Rudolph

Canada is among the most wired countries in the world and was among the quickest to adopt broadband Internet. This rapid adoption has resulted in approximately 90 percent of Canadian households having Internet access and becoming "ubiquitous" (BTLR 2020, 119). Canadians have been eager to take advantage of Internet media and entertainment. The use of the Internet for media and entertainment represents not just a trivial pastime for Canadians; rather, it exists as an extension of the cultures from which they originate. As a result of its distinct cultural role, mass culture functions to preserve, perpetuate, ingrain, and innovate upon the common culture of peoples. The growing popularity and use of the Internet, and with it the consumption of new media, will contribute to shifts in how individual Canadians and Canadian society view themselves. Recognizing that new media will influence Canadian self-definition raises some questions: How will the lack of domestic control over the Internet contribute to Canadian culture? What are the implications of any possible changes in Canadian culture?

The start of any discussion about new media begins with traditional media[1] in Canada, which has long had regulations that require a specific amount of Canadian content to be broadcast on Canadian airwaves to promote and preserve the domestic film and television industry and advance Canadian mass culture. These regulations ensure that Canada has unique forms of cultural expression for Canadian citizens to consume, but they also guarantee adequate funding for Canadian productions by requiring broadcasters to devote a portion of their revenue to the creation of domestically produced content. Canada has not enacted the same content regulations regarding the Internet and new media, in no small part due to the Canadian public's opposition to such legislation.

Previous studies of Canadians' engagement with American mass culture noted that the preferred consumption of American materials did not shift Canadian cultural views to align with Americans (Rutherford 1993, 270). Paul Rutherford argues that American mass culture does not present a threat to Canadian national identity because the Canadian sense of self is safeguarded through an ingrained resistance to any attempt to curtail an independent and self-directed destiny for the country. This resistance is bolstered by what Rutherford refers to as "the Victorian and British" qualities in Canadian identity and history (278). Though Rutherford remains confident about the strength of the unique character of Canadian identity in his assessment of historic trends in Canadian mass culture consumption, recent trends in consumption of mass culture in cyberspace suggest a shift in the attitudes and interpretation of online cultural products.

Theories of new regionalism are used to demonstrate that the transformation of Canadian mass culture consumption and interpretation may be part of a greater process of North American regionalization. The lack of action by the Government of Canada to address the role of cyberspace in mass culture is tacitly supporting a gradual cultural shift among Canadians due to the growing reliance on American mass culture on the Internet. An outcome of new regionalism is a homogenization of North American society, built from the political, security, economic, and cultural integration of the region. While the consumption of non-Canadian forms of cultural expression through the Internet promotes a common identity, this communal

---

1   Traditional media refers to nondigital formats of media, including, but not limited to, movies, television, radio, newspapers, magazines, and other print media.

identity formation—heralded by changes in the norms and standards advocated in digital media—is likely to erode the independent basis of Canadian national identity.

Is there Canadian Culture?

This exploration of the role of cyberspace in the development of Canadian mass culture can be understood as a challenge to Rutherford's (1993) exploration of American mass culture's influence in Canada. Writing of the formation of Canada following confederation, Rutherford (1993) portrays Canadian mass culture as already tacitly "Americanized" when compared to the Indigenous, British, and French cultural influences on Canada. Rutherford's conceptualization of Canadian culture is comparable to that of Seymour Martin Lipset (1986), who argued that Canada and the United States have divergent developmental and cultural origins resulting from the American Revolutionary War. The divergent origins led Canada's founders to be concerned with "peace, order, and good government" while the American Founding Fathers, imbued with a revolutionary spirit, focused the American national discourse on the precept of "life, liberty, and the pursuit of happiness" (Lipset 1986, 128). Similar to Lipset, Rutherford (1993) argues that Canadian culture demonstrates a "Victorian" spirit that resisted any potential influence of American mass culture. I suggest, however, that since the publication of *Made in America: The Problem of Mass Culture in Canada* (1993), the Canadian media landscape has greatly shifted with the inclusion of new media and the Internet, which did not become culturally prevalent until the 2000s. Accordingly, the purpose of this chapter is to evaluate and challenge Rutherford's conclusions by examining the role of new media and the Internet as part of mass culture, which he (1993, 261) situates as fundamental to community discourse and supportive of "a separate national existence." The notion of sharing is noteworthy as it embodies much of the role of the Internet and the development of Web 2.0,[2] and Canadians' heightened engagement in this process is a defining quality.

Despite previous efforts to define the character and canon of Canadian culture, some note a "national cultural incoherence" in

---

2   Web 2.0 refers to a shift of the World Wide Web to a more participatory environment for its users, which led to the rise in user-generated content and social media.

Canada that resists a clear encapsulation of the core of Canadian culture (Acland and Wagman 2017). Edward Grabb and James Curtis (2005) even suggest that there is little difference, if any, between what they refer to as the culture of "English Canada" and the "northern United States."[3] Nevertheless, I begin from the assumption that a distinctly Canadian culture does exist in some form and is relevant to Canadian self-assessment and the Canadian political climate. This conclusion is informed by the position of Canadians themselves; 2015 and 2016 Angus Reid Institute polls found that 76 and 83 percent of Canadians believe that there is a unique Canadian culture (Angus Reid Institute 2015, 1; 2016, 1). The surveys show that despite fluctuations that occur from year to year, there is a high level of consistency, if not growth, in the belief that there is a Canadian culture. This belief in a uniquely Canadian character and philosophy leads to conscious and subconscious behaviour by citizens to embody what it means to be Canadian and to national legislation by the Canadian government to define and protect Canadian culture. In this way, culture functions as a constraining norm that guides and determines how a state acts in response to citizens' expectations that the behaviour of the national government comports with the norms and values of society. Regardless of what Canadian culture *is*, the fact that Canadians and their government acknowledge and publicly strive to perform what it means to be Canadian signifies that the boundaries and strictures of Canadian national belonging are an important consideration in the study and analysis of Canadian civic behaviour and self-definition.

The focus of this chapter will be on how a national society identifies with that nation's culture, how policies work to support and shape culture, and the subsequent expression of that culture through its interactions in online borderlands. Specifically, I examine the role of the United States and associated sub-state actors on the Internet in contributing to a changing environment for engagements with a mass culture increasingly defined by new, rather than traditional, media. Human beings are fundamentally active in shaping and providing meaning in their social environment (Charon 2010, 29). Consequently, in the last two decades, the Internet, part of the expansion of sources of culture, has changed how Canadians shape their social environment. Accordingly, it is necessary to understand the consequences of

---

3   Grabb and Curtis (2005) argue that the US South and Quebec function more as sub-societies within a broader North American culture.

Canadians' engagement with cyberspace as a crucial and pervasive discursive space of cultural creation and contention. Canadians, in believing they are Canadian and embodying Canadian culture, interact with fellow Canadians in the social environment, contributing to the broader meaning of what it means to be Canadian as part of a broader relational process of being a social person in a society built through social interaction (Charon 2010, 28). In the borderlands of cyberspace, which Canadians increasingly occupy, social interaction with non-Canadian culture will increase and challenge the intellectual and emotive core of Canadian self-definition. This recurrent challenge has the potential to reshape the context of Canadians' self-definition and relation to the institutions and norms that currently represent Canadian cultural values (28).

The Canadian Response to American Mass Culture

Canada has traditionally looked toward the production of Canadian content as a counter to the significant influence and presence of American mass culture. Canadian content is Canadian-produced material that meets the requirements set by the Broadcasting Act (1991) to ensure the support for Canadian cultural expression. The Broadcasting Act (1991) and the Canadian Radio-television and Telecommunications Commission (CRTC) have determined that Canadian networks must encourage the "development of Canadian expression" via three methods: (1) "Providing a wide range of programming that reflects Canadian attitudes, opinions, ideas, values, and artistic creativity"; (2) "Displaying Canadian talent in entertainment programming"; and (3) "Offering information and analysis concerning Canada and other countries from a Canadian point of view" (CRTC 2020b).

These regulations have ensured that Canadians have been able to choose between media made in Canada for Canadians and media produced outside of Canada. Despite these regulations, time and the growth in communications technology have dismantled the traditional gatekeeping role that broadcasters have served in showing Canadian content and contributing to Canadians becoming active viewers. In this instance, I diverge from John Fiske's (2010) definition of active viewers, instead defining active viewership with reference to the viewer's activity in seeking out the content they prefer. Barry Brown and Louise Barkhuus (2006) identified this selection process as even occurring in television, a traditional media, through the adoption of personal video recording devices (PVRs) and the downloading of related video from the Internet. With the growing selection of channels and programs, and the ability to download videos or record programs for later viewing, individuals possess greater agency in how they engage with mass culture (Brown and Barkhuus 2006). Canada and the CRTC are forced to adapt and to make Canadian content competitive in a market that has more content to compete with, particularly American content. Instead of using the same methods they have always used, the CRTC is working to adapt and expand content availability and selection, but it may not be enough to prevent the cultural shifts already underway.

In 1999, the CRTC issued an order that exempted new media from regulation, which was supplemented in 2009 to include media available through the Internet and mobile devices (Dewing 2014, 2–3). Most notable for Canadian cultural expression is the exemption of new media from regulations related to Canadian content in the Broadcasting Act (1991; CRTC 1999). Canadian media corporations would come to view this as an unfair advantage for Internet-based media companies, specifically Netflix, which entered the Canadian market in 2010 (Acland and Wagman 2017). The exemption is due in part to convergence—the transmission of digital information over the same networks that transmit analog information (Dewing 2014, 6)—which makes it difficult to distinguish between broadcasting and telecommunication signals. Despite this, each medium is governed differently through the Broadcasting Act (1991) and the Telecommunications Act (1993).

Convergence has been a point of contention for some cultural advocacy groups, who argue that digital media should not be exempt from Canadian content regulations (Dewing 2014, 7). Internet service providers (ISPs) have countered that instead of being "broadcast undertakings," which are subject to regulations in the Broadcasting Act (1991), they are better defined as content-neutral services that provide access rather than content (Dewing 2014, 7). Compared to broadcast networks, ISPs do not sell time or schedule specific programs to be viewed on the Internet; instead, they serve as an intermediary between users and the content available on the Internet. The CRTC, the Federal Court of Appeal, and the Supreme Court of Canada have agreed with ISPs, confirming that they are not broadcast undertakings and are considered content-neutral services (Supreme

Court of Canada 2012). The Supreme Court's recognition of this difference between content producers and mediums for content transmission cements the conditions that turn Canadians into active viewers.

As active viewers, Canadians look for the best content for their needs and wants, which often means that they are turning to non-Canadian content. Rutherford (1993) notes that this has long been the case; however, the demands of Canadian media consumers are now shaped by their active engagement with and greater exposure to non-Canadian content on the Internet. Two of the most visited websites in Canada—YouTube[4] and Netflix—are both based in the United States and have no obligation to provide Canadian content ("Top Sites in Canada" 2020). Further, Amazon, also among the most visited websites in Canada, launched its video service on December 14, 2016, further supplementing the already American-dominated online video service market. By the end of 2019, Netflix reported that approximately 50 percent of Canadian households had a Netflix subscription (Netflix 2019). The dominance of US mass culture means that Canadians have become reliant on non-Canadian sources for their cultural entertainment, which allows for a greater penetration of American mass culture. As Canadians come to rely more on American online streaming and video services, the Canadian sociocultural environment will become increasingly Americanized, and this will shape the context in which social interactions between Canadians and Americans occur. Joel M. Charon (2010, 28) describes how humans define their actions and identity in the context of their environment, which ultimately creates society. Understanding this process is important to thinking through how the environment of online cultural borderlands occupied by Canadians influence their identity formation.

A 2016 Angus Reid Institute survey found that while Canadians are open to adopting online media, they retain a strong belief in the need to protect Canadian culture. This is in keeping with the 70 percent of Canadians who a year prior felt that Canada "needs specific protection policies and support from the government for Canadian culture to survive" (Angus Reid Institute 2015, 3). The 2016 survey, however, also showed that 56 percent of Canadians were not in favour

---

4 Among the dominant video services, YouTube is unique as a video-sharing platform that hosts content from all over the world, and thus content can be produced by Americans and Canadians alike. The unique position that video-sharing platforms like YouTube occupy will be explored later.

of subjecting online media to the same Canadian content regulations as traditional media (Angus Reid Institute 2016, 4). These responses suggest some level of cognitive dissonance among Canadians with regard to what they believe is needed to preserve Canadian culture in the media. It also suggests, however, that although Canadians want Canadian culture protected, they either do not know how it can be protected in this new age of media or believe that such protections must be different than those for traditional media. There is also the possibility that Canadians do not see streaming services as cultural products. It is thus no surprise that the Canadian government has been hesitant to respond to a public that is sending mixed messages.

The Future of Canadian Adaptation

The Canadian government has taken notice of the possible existential threat cyberspace poses to Canada's mass culture environment. In response, the Department of Canadian Heritage initiated a consultation process with Ipsos that resulted in the report *What We Heard across Canada: Canadian Culture in a Digital World* (Ipsos Public Affairs 2017). This report acknowledges many of the challenges, both implicit and explicit, presented in this chapter. The report states: "As a culture next to a juggernaut like the United States, Canadian talent requires more support rather than less" (12). This juggernaut already has a head start, so the question, then, is how can Canada compete and offer Canadian cultural options to consumers who are seeking both Canadian content and the best quality content. Canadians are interested in Canadian content—61 percent of Canadians who watch videos online seek out Canadian content at least occasionally—which suggests that there is an underdeveloped market for Canadian online content (CIRA 2020).

According to the Ipsos consultation report (Ipsos Public Affairs 2017), one difficulty that Canadian content creators face is the Canadian content certification system. Since the 1920s, Canada has had some form of criteria to define a broadcasting initiative as "Canadian." The CRTC created the Canadian Program Certification system in 1984 to enable producers to easily establish and certify their productions as Canadian productions (CRTC 2016a). This system classifies Canadian content according to four criteria: (1) the producer must be Canadian and responsible for decisions of the program; (2) the program's key creative functions must score between 6 and 10 points;[5] (3) at least the director or screenwriter and at least one of two lead performers must be Canadian; and (4) at least 75 percent of program and post-production expenses must be for services provided by Canadians or Canadian companies (CRTC 2016a). The Ipsos consultation report correctly notes that this system can only work with traditional media and that it favours producers rather than content creators (Ipsos Public Affairs 2017). Due to the absence of traditional producers in many forms of new media, which rely instead on content creators, existing Canadian content structures are completely obsolete for regulating new media. Some have argued that the solution to this new media issue is to increase access to funding for Canadian content creators on new media platforms. This, however, would open up the question of Canadian content and funding to an even bigger debate in Canadian culture creation: cultural value versus profit (11). How exactly should such funding be distributed? There is disagreement over how the Canadian government should fund projects based on their cultural value or their ability to be successful (17–18). Regardless of the model used, existing models will not provide a sustainable future for Canadian new media content.

Canadian Mass Culture Consumption: Where are We Now?

Chairperson and chief executive officer of the CRTC Jean-Pierre Blais stated that "both the broadcasting and telecommunication sectors are at important crossroads that are determining their futures" (CRTC 2016b). The viewing and usage habits of Canadians are rapidly changing and adapting to the digital age, which requires the Canadian government and private sector to also adapt. This shift has significant implications for how Canadians consume entertainment, for the future of the Canadian communications sectors, and for how Canada supports its mass culture. One of the CRTC's stated missions is to support the creation of content that "reflects Canada's diversity and enables Canadians to participate in their country's democratic and cultural life" (CRTC 2018). Canadian content serves an important role in promoting and preserving Canadian culture as both a

---

5 The CRTC awards points based on key creative functions being performed by Canadians. Canadian directors and screenwriters are worth 2 points; Canadian first and second lead performers, production designers, director of photography, music composers, and picture editors are worth 1 point.

touchstone of Canadian identity and a means of cultural engagement. Further, mass culture imported from the United States may not reflect the diversity of Canada or promote identity construction, which have been vital functions of Canadian mass culture (Acland and Wagman 2017).[6]

Since the adoption of the Canadian Broadcasting Act in 1936,[7] the Canadian government has nurtured, supported, and protected the expression of Canadian culture through various regulations and organizations. Many of these regulations have ensured that Canadians experience, view, and listen to content created for Canadians and by Canadians and that represents Canadian culture. Although Canada has retained its cultural expression over the airwaves with this system of regulations, the Internet provides a challenge to the status quo. If the purpose of such regulations is to ensure that Canadians are exposed to and enjoy aspects of their culture, what does it mean if Canadians become less exposed to such expressions of Canadianness?

The future of Canadian media and entertainment consumption is not with traditional media but with the Internet and new media. Overall, the Canadian Internet Registration Authority (CIRA) found that Canadians across the board are making use of the Internet for all aspects of life, with 66 percent of Canadians saying they watch television and movies online (CIRA 2020). Most applicable to this study are the mediums that the CRTC regulates via Canadian content regulations, which includes movies, television, and radio. Challenging traditional media is new media, which encompasses the same types of mediums—films, television, and radio—but in digital formats, which are predominantly distributed and available on the Internet. Traditional media and broadcasting corporations should be concerned as this shift to new media is occurring at an increasingly rapid pace. In 2018 and 2019, Canadians TV subscribers declined, on average, 2.5 percent per annum, with the decline anticipated to continue through 2022 (Convergence Research Group Ltd. 2020, 13). In 2019, approximately 32.5 percent of Canadian households did not have a TV subscription (6). In contrast, in 2011, nearly 90 percent of Canadian

---

6 Acland and Wagland (2017) do acknowledge and problematize the ways in which "diversity" can mask the "tacit hierarchies of power" that marginalize or disenfranchise certain peoples.
7 While the Broadcasting Act originally received royal assent in 1936, it was subsequently updated in 1958, 1968, and 1991.

households had a paid TV subscription and approximately 10 percent had subscriptions to "foreign on-demand Internet video and audio services" (BTLR 2020, 120). In 2018, these same TV subscriptions declined to 72.5 percent and the foreign on-demand Internet video and audio services jumped to 61 percent (120). These trends mean that it will only be a few years until more Canadians are subscribing to foreign Internet video and audio services than to traditional TV.

In the United States, the rate of decline is even faster. Overall, 36.1 percent of American households are without a traditional TV subscription, which is well ahead of Canadian cordcutting numbers (Convergence Research Group Ltd. 2020, 11). The rate of decline of traditional TV subscriptions in the United States is also well ahead at 7.1 percent compared to 2.5 percent in Canada (Convergence Research Group Ltd. 2020). As new media becomes the primary form of mass culture, it is also the principal form of shared cultural expression and engagement. The growing convergence of Canadians and Americans operating in this shared online cultural borderland is important as it produces a common discursive space. The common space of an online borderland increases the ability of both Canadians and Americans to engage and share experiences with mass culture, which Rutherford (1993) points to as integral to the development of community discourse and a national experience.

Cultural-Semantic Modelling and Online Cultural Borderlands

To understand how this lack of clear online Canadian presence develops, it is necessary to conceptualize the borderlands of information and culture across cyberspace and what these spaces mean for governance and the role of the state. One of the most developed models for understanding how the Internet operates is the physical-syntactic-semantic model (Libicki 2009). Martin Libicki asserts that cyberspace exists on three levels of reality, from the bottom most physical layer to the virtual semantic layer. The physical layer contains the machines and networks that make up the whole of the hard infrastructure of cyberspace. The syntactic layer is the software and protocols that give order and structure to the use and control of physical infrastructure. Last and most important to understanding culture in cyberspace is the semantic layer, which contains all the information a machine possesses. While this layer contains the code used for syntactic purposes, it also contains all information that is visible to and shared by users.

The interaction between users and cultures is isolated to the semantic layer, where mass culture is shared and thus the space in which online cultural borderlands exist.

The relationship between these layers of cyberspace and borderlands requires further expansion and elaboration. Although the physical layer seems the most obvious to address through an understanding of borderlands as having a strict physical ontology of space and time, it is not, however, conducive to discussions of culture and Internet content, which, though located on physical servers, can usually be accessed regardless of its physical location and that of the user. Although certain restrictions can be placed on access to online content, this is done at the syntactic or semantic layers. Thus the location of someone accessing online content is not a physical or technical impediment in and of itself, although a user may be denied access to content as a by-product of their spatial position and not because of their location. The reduced importance of the spatial position of actors or objects in the physical layer reifies a non-physical understanding of borderlands in cyberspace based in the syntactic and semantic layer.

An engaged discussion of culture in an online borderland requires a focus on the semantic layer; this is where social interaction and engagement occurs. Although the syntactic layer affects engagement in the semantic layer and remains important, it provides only a foundation for online social interactions. The mechanisms for interaction and engagement in cyberspace are a natural parallel to human geography's conception of "borderlands" as a discursive normative space where the interactions between normative regimes under different political systems occur (Wastl-Walter 2009). Drawing on this idea of borderlands, I theorize the semantic layer of cyberspace as a complex borderland where cultures encounter each other and transfer values through virtual, incorporeal social interactions. Doris Wastl-Walter (2009) notes that at physical borders and in physical borderlands, cultural values and norms are manifested through practices and the use of such material objects as signs. The semantic layer of cyberspace and its nonmaterial borderlands also contain instruments and practices that manifest culture.

Given the unregulated nature of the Internet, the territorial and physical location of the servers and information matter less than the accessibility of content. This principle is of crucial importance for the semantic layer, where ideas and information in the form of created content are shared; content creation and sharing is what delineates the expressive form of cyberspace. Barring intervention from third parties, language then is the most significant gateway controlling access to content, content that, among other things, is a representation of a creator's or a people's culture. If one is unable to understand the content on a website or in a video, this effectively denies access to the cyberspace which that culture occupies. Expressions of culture are thus not isolated within a state's physical and syntactic layers; rather, content on the Internet represents a creator's cultural influence and is their cultural product, be they state or non-state actors. It is for these reasons that the dominance of English in new media is an important issue for minority-language groups, as it supports the disenfranchisement of these people within the broader culture of a state. This also means, however, that language could unite previously distinct cultural traditions and create fusions or "hybridities" that were previously unlikely, thus raising questions about the ability of Canada or any government to serve as a cultural gatekeeper. These potential fusions are discussed in greater detail later in examining the role of Mexico in North American regionalization.

The Internet allows actors through media to share their culture and identity with audiences around the world, but the act of sharing is part of a greater sociocultural process in the context of the unique nature of the Internet. Sharing and producing for audiences on the Internet has less to do with the audience itself than with the context of the actor within that audience (Poole 2011). On the Internet, it is not only important whom actors share information and content with but also who they share as. A humorous video shared by a Canadian on a platform dedicated to content about terrible food could be shared and understood across multiple cultures. However, a video about terrible poutine shared by the same Canadian will mean much more to that Canadian and other Canadians who watch the video.[8] Due to the strong association of poutine with Canadian culture, the second scenario makes for a more personal shared cultural experience as it speaks specifically to a product of that culture in a way that is less accessible to non-Canadians. These scenarios also demonstrate the dialectic that exists in the production of media that is culturally specific but that is absent when Canadians make or share generically cute dog or cat videos, for instance. The identities one may assume,

---

8   It does not escape the author that this could be further broken regionally between Québécois and non-Québécois.

express, or seek out are near limitless; they are not singular or binary states of identity but more prismatic in representing the multiple faces and identities that individuals and groups have.

Due to the existing physical, governmental, historical, linguistic, and cultural linkages with Americans, Canadians may find it easier to relate and identify with their fellow North Americans in the United States than those in Mexico. For this reason, a North American culture comprised of elements and input from Canadians and Americans, and not Mexicans, is likely to emerge. This process is currently underway through the confines of cyberspace and the use of new media, but Americans currently dominate this process. By dominating online mass culture, and the subsequent consumption of these media by Canadians, Canadians' ability to participate in this process of shared meaning making is circumscribed in an already crowded and highly competitive environment. Instead of participating in a mutually negotiated cultural product and discursive space, Canadians will be obliged to rely on American forms of expression and will begin to identify with a North American identity that is not entirely representative of the core norms and values of Canadian national identity. It is important to understand that these influences and the emergence of an online cultural borderland does not exist in a social, cultural, or political vacuum; rather, they must be understood as part of a broader regional shift in North America.

New Regionalism Approach and North American Culture

Theories of regionalism provide a useful analytical lens through which to understand the potential cultural shifts in Canada because they address the roles of state and sub-state actors in processes of cultural narration and re-narration. New regionalism is a complex and varied process whereby a region experiences homogenization within multiple dimensions, the most important being culture, security, economy, and politics (Hettne and Söderbaum 1998). This homogenization can often create ambiguity about the role of state apparatuses. The new regionalism approach is significant in the context of this study for its inclusion of culture as a critical component in regional integration processes (Hettne and Söderbaum 1998). Canada is already significantly integrated with the United States in terms of security, economy, and politics. This chapter incorporates new regionalism into its consideration of the ways in which cyberspace influences the development of common cultural practice and identity in Canada and North America.

In their foundational work on new regionalism, Björn Hettne and Fredrik Söderbaum establish that the process of regionalization, characterized by an increased sense of "regionness," has three stages (1998). The first and second stages address the geographical and social dimensions of North America (stage 1) and its formal structures and institutions (stage 2). They describe the third stage as an outcome of the regionalization process: "[T]he region acting as subject, with a distinct identity, institutionalized actor capability, legitimacy, and structure of decision-making, in relation with a more or less responsive regional civil society, transcending the old state borders" (6). The recognition of identity and culture in the new regionalism approach supports the incorporation of an online cultural borderland into political analysis as but one variable in this process. Despite the Canadian government's opposition to cultural regionalization, as evident in Canadian content regulations, cultural integration due to new media and online cultural borderlands is already occurring at an increasing rate and supporting the outcome of this third stage. The convergence and interaction of Canadians and Americans in the comparatively unregulated and deterritorialized online cultural borderlands simultaneously increases the points of interaction between the two cultures and reduces points of contention by increasing familiarity. These processes of interaction between Canadians and Americans are a product of both cultures mutually living within the online cultural borderlands that increasingly define mass culture.

Regionalization in new regionalism occurs through both natural processes and active political steering of state actors, and Canada and the United States, at all levels, are a prime example of this process (Hettne and Söderbaum, 1998). Canada and the United States have a long history of actively seeking integration to address a multitude of issues. Some politically or geographically steered institutional attempts to build regional cooperation and community include the North American Aerospace Defense Command (NORAD), North American Free Trade Agreement (NAFTA), the Permanent Joint Board on Defense, the Regulatory Cooperation Council, and the Great Lakes Commission. Current regionalization trends in mass culture through new media could be described as a natural process as they lack any political steering from either Canada or the United States. The weak action, or lack of action, by the Canadian government regarding

Canadian cultural content in new media serves to undermine the production and distribution of expressly Canadian cultural expression in new media and thereby inadvertently supports the natural process of cultural convergence with the United States, the principal author of this shared North American identity.

The new regional convergence of US and Canadian cultures stands in stark contrast to the process of integration that is occurring between the United States and Canada and Mexico. Although Mexico has similar formal institutional arrangements with both the United States and Canada and has the geographic proximity to make cultural diffusion possible, it has not experienced a similar cultural integration with Canada and the US. Overall, Mexico does not have the same level of cultural, security, and political integration that Canada has with the United States, though there are many indicators suggesting a significant cultural regionalization between the United States and Mexico, including cultural hybridization[9] (Dear and Burridge 2005, 302). Michael Dear and Andrew Burridge (2005) point to the development of "Spanglish" as the most obvious hybridized product of this process, but the integrative cultural relationship between the US and Mexico goes well beyond hybridized language products to affect the way individuals identify with their respective cultures, national governments, and territorial neighbours. Dear and Burridge (313) note that the effects of cultural hybridization and integration between the United States and Mexico on identity are perhaps most profound in the territorial borderlands region in the United States. Specifically, the authors refer to an increasing number of individuals who identify as Hispanic and express mixed national and racial identification, which highlights the power of the hybridized and contested interstitial space of the border in creating new interpretations and understandings of identity and culture. This powerful process across the territorial US-Mexico border pales in comparison to cyberspace, which has no limits posed by geography, time, or space; there is no switch to turn off content creation or distribution in the online cultural borderlands.

The new regionalism that occurs between the United States and Canada, however, is an even more complicated and complete process. In the United States border territories, integration depends on overcoming a language barrier and cannot by definition incorporate the

---

9   Cultural hybridization refers to the creation of different cultural forms or practices through the merging of two separate cultural entities.

entirety of either country, so the formation of a shared identity is both temporally and territorially bound, producing not a common identity but a regionally distinct variant of American identity. New regionalism in the semantic layer of cyberspace, where the online cultural borderland is situated, is rooted in a shared language. The dominance of English in Canada and the United States—not to mention their shared identities as predominantly White and Protestant (Lipset 1986; Rutherford 1993)—and on the Internet as a whole, logically leads to a more complete interaction between Canadian and American cultures in the online cultural borderlands. In the end, this is not to say that it is not possible for Mexico to become culturally integrated into North America, like Canada and the United States, through new regionalism, but a cultural convergence will prove more difficult than the economic, security, or political convergence resulting from political steering. The lack of a shared common heritage, history, and culture with their neighbours to the north make cultural regionalization a slower and potentially more difficult process for Mexico; the lack of a common language is the greatest obstacle to regionalization in the online cultural borderlands. And now that new regionalism is well underway in the online US-Canada cultural borderlands, Mexico will find cultural integration with both countries even more difficult.

What Is Ahead for Canada?

What becomes the future of Canadian cultural expression in the age of new media? The exemption of new media from broadcasting regulations, particularly Canadian content regulations, has significant and far-reaching sociopolitical implications for Canada. With the increasing influence of American mass culture accessible online, Canadians as a whole risk having their sense of national identity subsumed by a homogenous, new regional identity. The trend toward homogeneity in new regionalism presents a challenge to already disenfranchised communities, such as Indigenous groups, who now face further marginalization. French Canadians and French Canadian content now face an even stronger English mass culture environment. These changes and shifts emerging from the rise of new media are not inherently negative, but they do present new and challenging opportunities, to which the Canadian public, corporations, and government must adapt. For those seeking the preservation of their culture in the face of regional cultural integration, however, this cultural whitewash can be understood as inherently negative and representative of an existential threat to the survival of Canadian culture. However, with emerging technologies come new methods of distribution to reach audiences previously unheard of with traditional media.

The Regionalization of Mass Culture in Cyberspace

In the United States, the status of traditional media is no less secure than in Canada. Just over 36 percent of American households are without a traditional TV subscription, which is well ahead of Canadian cordcutting numbers (Convergence Research Group Ltd. 2020). The rate of decline of traditional TV subscriptions in the United States is also higher than in Canada, 7.1 percent compared to 2.5 percent (Convergence Research Group Ltd. 2020). As the consumption of new media increases, it becomes the principal form of cultural expression and engagement. Even without broadcasting regulations similar to Canada's to promote American cultural expression, there is a growing shift away from traditional to digital media (Convergence Research Group Ltd. 2020). But unlike in Canada, where this shift potentially limits the market for Canadian cultural products, in the US it means an even greater global reach for US media and culture. The reach of new media platforms such as YouTube and Netflix has only increased the cultural influence of the US in the online cultural borderlands.

Even when a video service makes a commitment to produce Canadian content and invest in the Canadian film and television industry, such a commitment may not produce the desired results or be followed through with action. This has been the case with Netflix, the most popular Internet-based on-demand video service in Canada (Acland and Wagman 2019). In 2017, Heritage Canada and Netflix announced an agreement to create Netflix Canada, which was to be Netflix's first production company outside of the United States, and invest at least "$500 million in original productions in Canada over the next five years" (Department of Canadian Heritage 2017). The agreement with Netflix was originally lauded as progress in regulating online streaming services, but the agreement shows little substantive progress and is less a regulatory action than a public relations initiative. Charles Acland and Ira Wagman (2019) note that the agreement was "not enforceable, had no specific language commitments, had no way to measure the expenses on various kinds of productions, and didn't specify anything on Canada's part, [and] though unstated was presumably the continuation of the current non-regulation approach to international streaming services at the federal level." Just over two years after the initial agreement between Heritage Canada and Netflix, the Broadcasting and Telecommunications Legislative Review Panel unveiled its report *Canada's Communications Future: Time to Act* (BTLR 2020). Perhaps in response to the issues highlighted by Acland and Wagman (2019), the review panel recommends the classification of Netflix and similar new media as "content curators" that would be required to contribute to Canadian content through spending and "discoverability requirements…consistent with [Canada's] legislative framework" (BTLR 2020, 18).

In the lead up to the BTLR report, Canada and the CRTC's response to the growing competitive environment from online streaming services has been to adjust the requirements of traditional media, for instance reducing daytime Canadian content requirements from 55 percent to zero and exploring reductions to required revenue contributions for Canadian productions (Acland and Wagman 2017, 2019). These changes reveal that even if American influence in the cultural borderlands of cyberspace remains minimal, there is a concern that the likes of Netflix pose an existential threat to the Canadian content system that has helped to sustain Canadian mass culture for nearly a hundred years. Nevertheless, as Acland and Wagman (2019) argue, even if Canada was to legislate the production of such content as a requirement, it is more complicated than simply bringing Netflix and "content curators" into the traditional institutional structures, which may not work as they did with traditional media.

Among online video services, YouTube is unique in that it is a video-sharing platform that hosts content from all over the world, including Canada and the United States. Researchers out of Ryerson University's Audience Lab found that Canadians are the top exporters of content, with 90 percent of their views coming from outside of Canada[10] (Berkowitz, Davis, and Smith 2019, 62). The chief viewers of Canadian content are located in the United States, France, and Australia, supporting the notion of shared cultural and language borderlands in cyberspace (62). Furthermore, while a portion of the viewers

---

10 By contrast, the average percentage of views from outside the host's home country is 50 percent.

of Canadian Francophone YouTube creators are located in Quebec, the rest is located in France, Belgium, and Switzerland (62). As much as the discussion here shows an overwhelming influence of American mass culture in this regionalization, Berkowitz, Davis, and Smith (2019) show that Canadians do have a role in cultural content production and are not completely subsumed by American mass culture.

Despite the fact that the bulk of Canadian content creators' viewers are Canadian, 88 percent of Canadians do not actively seek Canadian content and 65 percent noted that they value the ability to "watch the same content as audiences anywhere else in the world" (Berkowitz, Davis, and Smith 2019, 104). Moreover, 60 percent of Canadian YouTube creators stated they wanted to reach an international audience, 50 percent wanted to reach a North American (Canada and the United States) audience, and just under 30 percent wanted to reach a Canadian audience (64). These findings support the idea that Canadians continue to adopt, and value, active viewership habits and reinforce the supposition that Canadian culture faces an increasingly competitive environment. Stuart Cunningham and David Craig (2019) note that YouTube is in a unique position as a new media platform with regard to existing traditional media content producers. While the influence of traditional media—especially Hollywood in Southern California and Silicon Valley in Northern California—is felt across new media, there are differences in revenue models; Netflix, for instance, innovates on existing models used by traditional media by negotiating licences with intellectual property rights holders to stream content on their platform, whereas YouTube has created a new partnership model by splitting advertising revenue (Cunningham and Craig 2019, 49; see also Berkowitz, Davis, and Smith 2019, 92). The agency of users to choose content on YouTube has been dubbed "MeTube," which signifies the greater choice available on, the instantaneous quality of, and ease of use of YouTube, and this agency effectively increases the value of YouTube for Canadian users (Berkowitz, Davis, and Smith 2019, 91). Although the active viewership entailed in "MeTube" is not exclusive to cyberspace—Brown and Barkhuus identified this sort of agency in 2006—the traits of cyberspace have provided mechanisms that significantly bolster active viewership.

The increase in active viewership is integral to the cultural dimension of new regionalism insofar as regionalization marks a region's transition from passive object to coherent subject. Hettne and Söderbaum (1998) refer to this "process whereby a geographical region is transformed from a passive object to a subject with capacity to articulate the interests of the emerging region" by the term "regionness," which can increase or decrease through the regionalization process itself. As regionalization across various dimensions increases, regionness grows. As a region, North America exhibits high levels of regionness in terms of the economic, political, and security dimensions of its formal structures and institutions (stage 2); this level of regionness is even greater when looking at just Canada and the United States. What is left is the emergence of the third stage, that of a shared cultural identity and tradition. The use of new media in promoting this cultural evolution is aptly identified by Hettne and Söderbaum (1998) when they state that "culture is not given, but continuously created and recreated" (6). Söderbaum (2013) states that the formation and functioning of a region is intrinsically dependent upon identity formation and is socially constructed. The unfettered access to online media from other cultures encourages there-creation and amalgamation of Canadian and American cultures. Active viewership and greater agency provide the means for the public to become active participants in this re-creation in the shared online cultural borderlands that Canadians and Americans occupy.

The Challenges

Although the regionalization of Canada and the United States is not inherently negative but rather a culmination of the new regionalism, there are repercussions that are harmful to some groups, specifically those who already exist in a subordinate or contested cultural space. The dismantling of existing cultures and languages is not an explicit goal of regional integration, but the conditions of new regionalism produce challenges to minority languages and cultures that do not integrate easily with the dominant Anglophone cultures of Canada and the United States. The outcome of a homogenous society and culture that is rooted in new regionalism poses an existential challenge to cultures that are already marginalized. Although the mechanisms of the regionalization process encompass Canadian culture broadly, the most vulnerable are minority and disadvantaged groups that do not have the same level of privilege to make use of the mechanisms and systems in play as the dominant culture in the online borderlands.

Canadians broadly believe that Canadian culture needs protection, but this is especially true in Quebec, where 70 percent—compared to the national average of 60 percent—are in favour of government policies to protect and support Canadian content to ensure the survival of Canadian culture (Angus Reid Institute 2016). Quebec residents are also the most likely to seek out Canadian content online (CIRA 2020). Because French-language programming is more dependent on government support and promotion, Francophones and Francophone Québécois have the most to lose if Canadian funding, support, and policies protecting Canadian content in traditional media disappear in this age of new media (BTLR 2020, 139). These are among the reasons why Acland and Wagman (2019) are especially concerned about the lack of recognition for non-official languages in Canada in the original deal between Heritage Canada and Netflix.

French is the ninth-most-used language on the Internet, which translates to significantly less French-tailored, let alone Canadian Francophone or Québécois, content (Internet World Stats 2020). Compared to their Anglophone compatriots, Canadian and Québécois Francophones are at a disadvantage in terms of the limited availability of non-domestic French-language or culturally-related content. Canadian Anglophones not only have an easier time finding English content but find it easier to relate to the cultural expressions of American new media. Data also shows that Anglophones are much more likely to exclusively watch content online than their Francophone compatriots (CRTC 2020a, 205). There is a prominent language divide in the consumption of digital content in Canada: 60 percent of Anglophones subscribed to Netflix in 2018 versus only 33 percent of Francophones (BTLR 2020, 119). Furthermore, residents of Quebec are most likely to seek out Canadian content online (CIRA 2020). Despite this, Francophones in Canada end up spending five fewer hours per week online than their Anglophone counterparts, which is four hours less than the national average (CIRA 2020, 119). This is not to say that only Francophones live in Quebec, but their large demographic and specific cultural identity in the province makes this noteworthy and the prime case study to explore potential cultural erosion due to regionalization. Although Netflix is only one new media provider, their status as the dominant online video streaming service means that subscriptions are an important indicator of how Canadians are adapting to trends in new media.

Video-sharing platforms such as YouTube exemplify the opportunities for public-private partnerships that can support Canadian expression in new media. These services provide a platform for the Government of Canada and Canadian content creators or producers to upload competing Canadian content. Also, there is potential that the existing Canadian content certification system can apply to such services by either using the already established criteria or creating new ones unique to new media and content-sharing platforms. Most of all, such ventures have significant potential to benefit minority and disenfranchised peoples and increase representation and voice of those communities in the online space by expanding their influence and reach to broader audiences.

Given the low cost of entry for creators and the ease of access for consumers, online video-sharing platforms present a unique space for consumers, one that allows them to search for and be introduced to linguistic and cultural material that is comparatively unavailable through traditional media platforms. As well, if such content gains an audience, services such as YouTube that split advertising revenue could generate revenue for these groups and support the continued efforts to promote and preserve their cultures. This is potentially an even more profound benefit to significantly marginalized and disenfranchised groups, such as Indigenous peoples in Canada, as it provides a funded platform that can give voice and visibility to communities that are otherwise excluded from high-dollar production companies and online content curators' algorithms. In addition to reaching greater audiences, these methods help groups to preserve their culture and language by uploading them to the Internet. Posting such content online ensures the digital permanence of the content and the survival of their culture, barring deletion or removal of said content. Significant potential thus exists for Indigenous peoples that are at risk of losing their languages and cultures due to a decline in the rate of learning and adoption.

Canadian Content Funding

While the CRTC and Canadian broadcasting corporations may be able to adapt to emerging trends with the Internet and new media, there potentially exists significant contribution and funding gaps to the production and creation of Canadian content. Cable, IPTV, and satellite companies in Canada are required to spend 5 percent of annual broadcast-related revenue on the creation and production of Canadian programming. In addition to various independent funds, these contributions largely come from thirteen Certified Independent Production Funds and the Canada Media Fund. According to the CRTC's 2019 monitoring report, contributions to Canadian content have increased an average of 2.4 percent over the past ten years, reaching $3.47 billion in 2018. Despite this trend, however, current legislation is insufficient to ensure the sustainability of these contributions once broadcasting profits begin to decline. Most recent trends forecast a decline in revenue growth in traditional media (CRTC 2020a).

Since Canadians do not want to see the same regulations applied to the Internet as traditional broadcasting, the decline in revenues in traditional media producers becomes a death sentence for Canadian content unless the Government of Canada responds as suggested by the Broadcasting and Telecommunications Legislative Review Panel. The 5 percent of broadcast-related revenue spent on the creation and production of Canadian programming does not apply to revenue obtained online. The CRTC (2017) states that "gross revenues derived from broadcasting activities exclude revenues earned from telecommunications services"; telecommunications services are instead regulated under the Telecommunications Act (1993). Due to this limitation in Canadian content funding, it removes one of the major support instruments that ensure adequate funding for Canadian content. The outcome of this gap in financing is that corporations will have to look at what incentives and markets exist to produce and fund specific Canadian content on the Internet. As shown previously, a market for Canadian content does exist, but this content must compete with an increasingly crowded cultural marketplace (CIRA 2020; Berkowitz, Davis, and Smith 2019). In the United States, traditional content producers are largely safe as they have been able to adapt to the new environment by innovating to mitigate the disruptive nature of new media and working with platforms to provide content with little to no loss of revenue (Cunningham and Craig 2019, 49). It is no longer enough that such Canadian content exists and is available, but it must be able to compete in availability and quality with American-produced content. With a lack of sustainable funding available to Canadian content producers, there is a justified concern for the persistence of support for Canadian cultural expression.

Conclusion

Despite the differing environments and postures of the governments, there is a trend in North America away from traditional media (Convergence Research Group Ltd. 2020). While this means different things for Canada and the United States, one central aspect of this trend is a greater mass culture convergence of the two states, which supports regionalization within new regionalism. Researchers have shown that with the introduction of the Internet, and the greater agency that comes with it, individuals' viewing habits change significantly, including what services they use (Brown and Barkhuus 2006; Berkowitz, Davis, and Smith 2019). The BTLR Panel (2020, 120) has taken notice of this shift and has warned the Government of Canada of the significant impact this will have on Canada. The impact in question is not just isolated to Canada's creative sectors, but—by the review panel's own admission that broadcasting and telecommunications are essential "in the maintenance of Canada's identity and sovereignty"—impacts the self-definition of Canadians insofar as the creative sector is a key part of Canada's social fabric (BTLR 2020, 113). However, as the new media landscape has cemented viewing habits online, is it too little, too late for Canada to respond accordingly?

The implications drawn from the review panel's report is that if Canada does not ensure the protection of its broadcasting and telecommunications mediums, it comes at a serious risk to Canada's identity. Almost two decades ago, Paul Rutherford (1993) addressed many commonly held assumptions and myths about the influence (or lack thereof) of American mass culture on Canadian culture and identity. Although many arguments made by Rutherford hold, he would disagree with many arguments made in this piece and by the review panel. However, we are now in a new century and contending with a new form of mass culture that has changed Canadian habits (Brown and Barkhuus 2005; Berkowitz, Davis, and Smith 2019; CIRA 2020; BTLR 2020). Long-held assumptions must be problematized and the emergence of an online cultural borderland, and how it impacts Canadian identity, must be reckoned with in discussions about media and identity in Canada.

The online cultural borderlands in the semantic layer of the Internet is a new vector of influence by all cultures for good and bad, and thus far the United States is significantly ahead of the curve in dominating this space (Acland and Wagman 2017, 2019; Berkowitz, Davis, and Smith 2019; BTLR 2020). Canadians operating in this space, particularly on YouTube, have shown a level of adaptability to thrive on these platforms and a quintessential Canadian spirit in punching above their weight (Berkowitz, Davis, and Smith, 2019). Nevertheless, further research is required to understand the degree of Canada's impact in this online cultural borderland and if Canadians' influence in this space provides a balance to the influence of others. In the current environment, Canada and Canadians have limited means to project their mass culture and identity in the online borderlands, which are broadly dominated by American producers and corporations (Acland and Wagman 2019; Berkowitz, Davis, and Smith 2019). The oversaturation of American mass culture in this space, along with the increasingly active viewership by Canadians, increases the influence of American culture on Canadians, thus promoting regionalization under new regionalism.

References

Acland, Charles, and Ira Wagman. 2019. "Canada – Update (March 2019)." Global Internet TV Consortium. March 2019. https://global-internet-tv.com/canada-update-march-2019/.

———. 2017. "Canada." Global Internet TV Consortium. May 2017. https://global-internet-tv.com/netflix-country-reports/canada/.

Angus Reid Institute. 2016. *Not Netflix, Sans Spotify: Canadians Back Continued CRTC Regulation, but Not for Online Content*. http://angusreid.org/wp-content/uploads/2016/06/2016.06.02-CanConHeritage.pdf.

———. 2015. *Culture, the CBC and the CRTC: Both Institutions Get Good Marks, but Future Relevance Seen as a Challenge*. http://angusreid.org/wp-content/uploads/2015/03/2015.03.CRTC_.CBC_.pdf.

Berkowitz, Irene S., Charles H. Davis, and Hanako Smith. 2019. *Watchtime Canada: How YouTube Connects Creators and Consumers*. May 22, 2019. Ryerson University, Faculty of Communication and Design, Audience Lab.http://audiencelab.fcad.ryerson.ca/wp-content/uploads/2019/05/YouTube-Full-Report-FINAL_V7_May21.pdf.

Brown, Barry, and Louise Barkhuus. 2006. "The Television Will Be Revolutionized: Effects of PVRs and Filesharing on Television Watching." In *Proceedings of the 2006 Conference on Human Factors in Computing Systems, CHI 2006, Montréal, Québec*, 663–666. New York: Association for Computing Machinery.

BTLR (Broadcasting and Telecommunications Legislative Review). 2020. *Canada's Communications Future: Time to Act*. Ottawa: Innovation,

Science and Economic Development Canada. https://www.ic.gc.ca/eic/site/110.nsf/vwapj/BTLR_Eng-V3.pdf/$file/BTLR_Eng-V3.pdf.

Charon, Joel M. 2010. *Symbolic Interactionism: An Introduction, an Interpretation, an Integration*. 10th ed. Boston: Pearson.

CIRA (Canadian Internet Registration Authority). 2020. *Canada's Internet Factbook2020*(website).https://www.cira.ca/resources/factbook/canadas-internet-factbook-2020.

Convergence Research Group Ltd. 2020. *The Battle for the North American (US/Canada) Couch Potato: OTT and TV*. April 2020.

CRTC (Canadian Radio-television and Telecommunications Commission). 2020a. *Communications Monitoring Report 2019*. Ottawa: CRTC. https://crtc.gc.ca/pubs/cmr2019-en.pdf.

———. 2020b. "Content that Meets the Needs and Interests of Canadians." CRTC (website). Last modified January 28, 2020. http://www.crtc.gc.ca/eng/cancon/mandate.htm.

———. 2018. "Our Mandate, Mission and What We Do." Last modified May 11, 2018. http://www.crtc.gc.ca/eng/acrtc/acrtc.htm.

———. 2017. "Broadcasting Glossary." Last modified September 26, 2017. http://www.crtc.gc.ca/eng/dcs/glossaryB.htm.

———. 2016a. "So What Makes it Canadian?" Last modified October 13, 2016. http://www.crtc.gc.ca/eng/cancon/c_cdn.htm.

———. 2016b. "Communications Monitoring Report 2016: Executive Summary" CRTC (website). Last modified September 12, 2018. https://crtc.gc.ca/eng/publications/reports/policymonitoring/2016/cmrs.htm.

———. 1999. "Public Notice CRTC 1999-1997: Exemption Order for New Media Broadcasting Undertakings." December 17, 1999. http://www.crtc.gc.ca/eng/archive/1999/pb99-197.htm.

Cunningham, Stuart, and David Craig. 2019. *Social Media Entertainment: The New Intersection of Hollywood and Silicon Valley*. New York: New York University Press.

Dear, Michael, and Andrew Burridge. 2005. "Cultural Integration and Hybridzation at the United States-Mexico Borderlands." *Cahiers de géographie du Québec* 49 (138): 301–318.

Department of Canadian Heritage. 2017. *Launch of Netflix Canada: A Recognition of Canada's Creative Talent and Its Strong Track Record in Creating Films and Television*. Government of Canada (website). September 28, 2017. https://www.canada.ca/en/canadian-heritage/news/2017/09/launch_of_netflixcanadaarecognitionofcanadascreativetalentandits.html.

Dewing, Michael. 2014. "Canadian Broadcasting Policy. Library of Parliament Background Paper, Publication No. 2011-39-E, revised August 6, 2014. https://lop.parl.ca/staticfiles/PublicWebsite/Home/ResearchPublications/BackgroundPapers/PDF/2011-39-e.pdf.

Fiske, John. 2010. *Television Culture*. New York: Routledge.

Grabb, Edward, and James Curtis. 2005. *Regions Apart: The Four Societies of Canada and the United States*. Don Mills, ON: Oxford University Press.

Hettne, Björn. 2005. "Beyond the 'New' Regionalism." *New Political Economy* 10 (4): 543–571.

Hettne, Björn, and Söderbaum, Fredrik. 1998. "The New Regionalism Approach." *Politeia* 17 (3): 6–21.

Internet World Stats. 2020. *Internet World Users by Language* (website). https://www.internetworldstats.com/stats7.htm.

Ipsos Public Affairs. 2017. *What We Heard across Canada: Canadian Culture in a Digital World. Consultation Report*. February 21, 2017. http://www.canadiancontentconsultations.ca/system/documents/attachments/82eb44ca377ab94e80535ee617d129c8841dab18/000/005/629/original/PCH-DigiCanCon-Consultation_Report-EN.pdf.

Libicki, Martin C. 2009. *Cyberdeterrence and Cyberwar*. Santa Monica, CA: RAND Corporation. http://www.rand.org/content/dam/rand/pubs/monographs/2009/RAND_MG877.pdf.

Lipset, Seymour Martin. 1986. "Historical Traditions and National Characteristics: A Comparative Analysis of Canada and the United States." *The Canadian Journal of Sociology* 11 (2): 113–155.

Netflix, Inc. 2019. Letter to Shareholders. October 16, 2019. https://s22.q4cdn.com/959853165/files/doc_financials/quarterly_reports/2019/q3/FINAL-Q3-19-Shareholder-Letter.pdf.

Poole, Chris. 2011. "'High Order Bit' Talk—Web 2.0 Summit 2011." October 18, 2011. YouTube video, 8:03. https://www.youtube.com/watch?v=e3Zs74IHomc.

Rutherford, Paul. 1993. "Made in America: The Problem of Mass Culture in Canada." In *The Beaver Bites Back? American Popular Culture in Canada*, edited by David H. Flaherty and Frank E. Manning, 260–280. Montréal: McGill-Queen's University Press.

Söderbaum, Fredrik. 2013. "Rethinking Regions and Regionalism." *Georgetown Journal of International Affairs* 14 (2): 9–18.

Supreme Court of Canada. 2012. *Reference re Broadcasting Act*. [2012] 1 SCR 142. https://scc-csc.lexum.com/scc-csc/scc-csc/en/item/7989/index.do.

Surlin, Stuart, and Barry Berlin. 1991. "TV, Values, and Culture in U.S.-Canadian Borderland Cities: A Shared Perspective." *Canadian Journal of Communication* 16 (3–4): 431–439.

"Top Sites in Canada." 2020. Alexa.com. https://www.alexa.com/topsites/countries/CA.

Wastl-Walter, Doris. 2009. "Borderlands." In *International Encyclopedia of Human Geography*, edited by Rob Kitchin and Nigel Thrift, 332–339. Amsterdam: Elsevier.

CHAPTER 8

#WelcomeRefugees
A Canadian Phenomenon That Illustrates the Temporal Dimension of Border Constructs

Renata Grudzien

Every year Immigration, Refugees and Citizenship Canada (IRCC) issues Canada's benchmarks for refugee resettlement. In the past, Canada has committed to resettling twenty-five thousand refugees *per year* from all over the world (IRCC 2014); however, after the international outcry over three-year-old Alan Kurdi's body washing up on Turkey's shores in September 2015, IRCC significantly decreased expected processing times for refugee resettlement in order to increase that number in response to the Syrian refugee crisis. By November 2015, IRCC had initiated a five-phase plan to resettle twenty-five thousand Syrian refugees by the end of February 2016. The plan was branded with the #WelcomeRefugees hashtag. Despite domestic and international scepticism, Canada successfully resettled twenty-six thousand Syrian refugees in just four months (IRCC 2016c).

The #WelcomeRefugees plan was an unprecedented development in Canadian immigration history. Compared to the mainstream view of borders as lines demarcating where one state's territory ends and another's begins, the language of "phases" in the #WelcomeRefugees plan suggests a new dimension to Canada's *border construct*: time. The phases of the #WelcomeRefugees plan were as follows: (1) identify Syrian refugees to come to Canada; (2) process Syrian refugees overseas; (3) transport refugees to Canada; (4) welcome refugees to Canada; and (5) settle and integrate refugees into the community. Because of how much emphasis was placed on the precision of timing, #WelcomeRefugees illustrates a Westernized version of time as linear; each phase was sequential and the process had a beginning and an end. Recognizing that there are many theories about the shape of time, this chapter will use the linear lens to explore the temporal dimension of Canada's border construct. The temporal dimension is always present, though it is made more obvious during times of crisis, such as the Syrian refugee crisis. I posit that the hegemony of the territorial dimensions of border constructs has already been challenged in the literature on border laws and policies, borderlands cultures, the environment, and so forth. The temporal dimension, however, is largely missing from the existing literature.

This chapter will be organized in five parts. Part I is a literature review on the notion of the border construct and its various dimensions, as well as existing literature on time-space theory. Part II will explore time as a valid measurement in and addition to border construct theories. Part III will explore the temporal dimension of Canada's border construct as exemplified by the five phases of the #WelcomeRefugees plan. Part IV will discuss Canada's border construct vis-à-vis that of the United States. It will also identify areas for further study. Ultimately, this chapter seeks to add to the mounting notion in territory and territorialisation literature that the border is a fluid, living organism (Konrad 2015).

Part I. Dimensions of Borders and Border Processing

Definition of Border Construct

For the purpose of this chapter, *border construct* refers to all concepts relating to borders, including but not limited to borderlands, border regions, and border processes. Holistically discussing the border as a construct of many different things allows us to be critical of its composition, identifying significant gaps in the way we describe, discuss, and comprehend it. In addition, border constructs should be considered in the abstract, beyond the brick and mortar of borders; to do so helps us to see what we might not expect to see—that border constructs are organisms with constantly evolving genetic compositions (Konrad 2015).

Dimensions of Border Constructs

Generally, borders emerged as a way for states to protect their territorial hegemony from competing claims. They demarcate where a state has the right to the use of force (Weber 1946). In addition, they outline the shape of landmasses to which people feel connected. As a result, border placement has been an unending source of conflict between nations and states (Anderson 2006). However, this Westphalian idea of the state has deteriorated with the emergence of pivotal theories reconceptualizing territory, such as Agnew's (1994) piece on the "territorial trap" and Newman's (2010) notion that "our understanding of the lines which demarcate these territories moved beyond the fixed and absolute" (773). Recent works on territory and territoriality incorporate discourses of power to examine the social, political, and economic dimensions of borders in order to better describe the border construct.

Marcela Alvarez Perez and Mark T. Berger (2009) examine the US-Mexican border to highlight how a border's physical dimensions, its appearance, and the feeling of crossing it depends on the standards of the states that shape it. One side of the border can appear very different than the other. In the case of the US-Mexico border (in 2009), the requirement of a passport to enter the US from Mexico but not Mexico from the US fundamentally shaped the lead-up to and experience of crossing that border. The authors describe the US-Mexico border as "a border in one direction" (Alvarez Perez and Berger 2009, 1). Of course, much has changed in border crossing between the US and Mexico since their writing, including the election of President Trump, who ran on a platform of building a wall along the US-Mexico border.

Mark B. Salter's (2012) suture theory suggests that borders are comprised of evolving sociopolitical discourses. He argues, specifically, that borders are a symbolic manifestation of "a division and a unity between the inside and outside" (Salter 2012, 734) of a state. Borders can be symbols and physical reminders of such historical processes as colonialism, war, and secession, where conflict is rich and the redrawing of state lines can be traumatic (Salter 2012). His theory touches on the temporal dimension of borders as sutures—the stitches or scars of historical events—that emerge over time.

Gabriela Valdivia, Wendy Wolford, and Flora Lu (2013) examine the relationship of humans and nature to the internal borders on the Galapagos Islands. The authors examine how farmers and conservationists compete for land resources, continually drawing and redrawing internal borders (Valdivia, Wolford, and Lu 2013). It becomes apparent that the border is an entity constructed by humans for humans and that flora and fauna defy borders and move easily between realms. This raises questions about the design of borders and why efforts to reduce processing times and improve immigration experiences, such as with the #WelcomeRefugees plan, have not always been at the forefront of state immigration policies.

Konrad (2015) explores the evolutionary potential of border constructs with his "borders in motion" theory. He suggests that the border is a living organism "born in motion" (Konrad 2015, 2). They are sites of numerous overlapping processes, relationships, exchanges, and developments. He uses the Pacific Northwest border region to illustrate that "the border system needs to accommodate greater or lesser volumes of movement, sudden changes of flow characteristics, enhanced impediments to predictable flows, and changes in barrier configuration" (Konrad 2015, 9). It is this constant need to accommodate evolving processes that constitutes and reconstitutes the border over time, maturing it like any other living organism.

Stuart Elden's (2013) three-dimensional theory of the border informs my thinking about the temporal dimension of the border construct. He states that "territories are bordered, divided and demarcated, but not understood in terms of height and depth" (Elden 2013, 35). And so, if we can explore borders two dimensionally, like on a map, or three dimensionally, as Elden suggests, then so too should we be able to explore a fourth dimension of borders: the temporal.

Efforts to illustrate the relationship between time and space—not exactly time and borders—exist. Agnew (2005) discusses the concept of "time-space compression," the notion that globalization has shortened time and shrunk space. He argues that "fixed territorial spaces of modernity no longer match a new world of kaleidoscopic and jumbled spaces where speed conquers established geopolitical representations" (Agnew 2005, 159). We will revisit the idea that speed—or the sense of urgency to fit the government's resettlement deadline—had the power to change the nature of the Canadian border process during the #WelcomeRefugees plan.

The literature mentioned above exemplifies that borders are so much more than lines on a map, but maps are still the easiest way to illustrate territory. Perhaps one reason why the temporal dimension of borders has remained largely unexamined in the border studies literature is because it is difficult to visualize time on a map.

Klaus Spiekermann and Michael Wegener (1994) provide a solution to this problem by highlighting an unconventional map—the "time-space map"—that uses a temporal rather than territorial lens to describe global spaces: "Short travel times between two points result in their presentation close together on the map; points separated by long travel times appear distant on the map. The scale is ... in temporal units" (654). The authors compare travel times in 1985, 1993, and projected travel times for 2010 and plot geographical distance based on those travel times as opposed to distances. Therefore, the map areas appear enlarged along routes that take longer to travel and condensed along routes that take less time to travel.

Speikermann and Wegener's (1994) method of time-space cartography is a solution to illustrating time quantitatively and qualitatively. The maps depict how long it would take for an individual to travel somewhere, and, simply by looking at the map, they could opt to travel a route through the shrunken areas of the map since those would take the least amount of time to travel along. Later on, I will discuss Spiekermann and Wegener's method as an opportunity to further our understanding of differences between Canadian and American border constructs in the context of the Syrian refugee crisis.

Part II. Exploring Time as a Measurement

Discussions of the territorial dimensions of borders frequently reference time as a characteristic of the border construct. For example, David Newman (2010) says borders determine "places at which transition from one entity or space into the next takes place, either as a sharp movement from one to the other, or as gradual process of transition through spaces which have become known as frontiers, borderlands, border regions and the like" (774). This sense of the border as a process implies a temporal dimension in the movement from one state of being to the next. In addition, when we describe the border as a process, it is natural to contemplate the length of time a process will take. We already regularly use a temporal lens to contemplate the border construct.

Still, how do we discuss and develop time as a characteristic of the border construct? Time is an elusive entity. The most common way to discuss it is by using quantitative measures such as rate, or milestones, timelines, deadlines, and phases. These measures standardize the passage of time, which makes it easier to organize and categorize events (Fraisse 1984). In addition, these measures allow us to visualize the passage of time and help us identify how an organism has changed.

Such measurements standardize the passage of time, but as the saying goes, time is relative. We often perceive time to move quickly when we are having fun and slowly when we are not, so objective measures are not always the most appropriate way to temporalize "gradual processes." Rate is another measurement unit to denote time. Newman (2010) uses rate to describe frontiers, borderlands, and border regions, which require time to reach their current form.

By contrast, Aleksandra Galasinska (2003) explores how time can be measured qualitatively by collecting and examining personal accounts of the *feeling* of its passage. Galasinska presented people with historical photographs of Zgorzelec, a Polish border town, and asked them to reflect on its history. She found that, "even presented with the relatively specific historical time of the photograph, the informants' narratives invariably tended to hover around the very concrete temporal dimension of the present day" (Galasinska 2003, 42). Participants described Zgorzelec through the lens of the present day. Her investigation also challenges the temporal dimension of border constructs because it suggests that time can feel irrelevant to describing a place since the effect of the present moment on one's experience can be overpowering. However, the same could be said for someone looking at an old photograph and being launched back into the past. In either case, Galasinska helps us to see the importance of subjective language, perceptions and feelings to considering the temporal dimension of border constructs. We can identify both quantitative and qualitative measures of time in Canada's #WelcomeRefugees plan.

Part III. Temporal Challenges to the Territorial Hegemony of Border Constructs

The #WelcomeRefugees plan illustrates how territory only plays a partial role in the genetic makeup of a border construct. In response to the Syrian refugee crisis, the border was no longer simply a line to cross between states, guided by lane dividers and border officials; rather, the #WelcomeRefugees plan transformed Canada's border into a guide for people moving from the source country to the destination country.

The plan's phases are arranged along a clear timeline, which presents a more realistic depiction of the Canadian border process and helps to dispel the image of Canada's border simply being a line on a map. Even without words, this image alludes to the bureaucracy, transportation factors, and length of time inherent in the resettlement process. It provides a good starting point from which to explore the Canadian border construct through the temporal lens.

In order to understand the evolution of Canada's border construct, it is first necessary to understand Canada's refugee policy: who qualifies as a refugee and what are the standards for refugee resettlement? With regard to the former, the main piece of legislation governing refugee resettlement is the Canadian Immigration and Refugee Protection Act 2001. It stems from the Convention and Protocol Relating to the Status of Refugees, which states that a refugee is someone who, "owing to a well-founded fear of being persecuted for reasons of race, religion, nationality, membership of a particular social group, political opinion, is outside the country of his nationality, and is unable to, or owing to such fear, is unwilling to avail himself of the protection of that country" (UNHCR [1951] 2010, 14). With regard to the latter, there are two ways for refugees to resettle in Canada: they must either (1) travel (legally or illegally) to Canada to claim asylum once they reach Canadian territory or (2) apply for resettlement selection from within the country wherein they first sought asylum (Ostrand 2015). The second option was the foundation for the #WelcomeRefugees plan as Syrian refugees were selected to come to Canada from Jordan and Lebanon, the countries where they first sought asylum.

In the past, Canada's border process has been criticized for its complexity and lethargic pace (Ngugi 2007). Kamau Ngugi noted that official wait times listed on the IRCC website were anywhere between thirteen and eighteen months. Even still, according to some personal accounts, resettlement could sometimes take up to three years. In the meantime, refugees were living in a figurative limbo, receiving only a small stipend while unable to officially gain employment and housing (Ngugi 2007).

By contrast, in November 2015, the government promised to resettle twenty-five thousand Syrian refugees in just four months. The #WelcomeRefugees plan was a five-phase approach that irrevocably changed the nature of the Canadian border construct.

Comparing the Phases of Canada's #WelcomeRefugeesPlan

Phase 1: Identifying Syrian Refugees to Come to Canada. "Canada will work with the United Nations Refugee Agency (UNHCR) to identify people in Jordan and Lebanon, where they have an extensive list of registered refugees" (IRCC 2016b).

This phase perhaps most clearly challenges the border as primarily a territorial entity by demonstrating the *point in time at* which refugees began the Canadian border process. "As refugees in Jordan and Lebanon are identified, the UNHCR will be contacting them by SMS (text message) to determine if they are interested in being resettled to Canada" (IRCC, n.d.a). Thus, the border began not at the end of the person's journey, but rather at the beginning. Moreover, the border did not begin at a specific territorial point, but rather it began psychologically at the time that the person had to respond to the text message with their decision as to whether or not they would be immigrating to Canada (van der Velde and van Naerssen 2011). Instead of passing through a physical border crossing, Syrian refugees entered into a much more abstract process, defined not by distance but by phase. In this abstraction, the border becomes a blend of timed administrative, psychological, and transit processes in separate places—quite the jumble of space and time.

Phase 2: Processing Syrian Refugees Overseas. "Interested refugees will be scheduled for processing in dedicated visa offices in Amman and Beirut" (IRCC 2016b).

To meet its formidable deadline, Canada needed to maintain a rapid rate of processing. In the end, the Canadian government deployed officials to not only Jordan and Lebanon, but also to Turkey and Egypt, to process Syrian refugees in the countries where they first sought asylum (IRCC 2018). In doing so, Canada prioritized the temporal integrity of its border over its territorial integrity—it did not matter that border officials sat somewhere upwards of nine thousand kilometres away from Canada's land border, it only mattered that refugees were processed as quickly as possible. Typically, immigration screening processes—such as the full medical examination, collection of biographical information, biometrics, and the visa issuing process—occur on Canadian soil. But as these processes were exported abroad, it heavily suggests that Canada's border process evolved into something more distant yet more flexible, mobile, and efficient.

Phase 3: Transportation of Syrian Refugees to Canada. "Beginning in December, transportation via privately chartered aircraft, with military aircraft assisting if needed, will be organized to help bring refugees to Canada" (IRCC 2016b).

The transportation phase illustrates how the temporal and territorial dimensions of a border construct intersect. A series of decisions were made about transit type and location not for proximity, though that might have been an ancillary outcome, but because they would lead to faster processing times. First, a combination of private airplane charters, military aircraft, and loaned airplanes from Jordan were commissioned (Boutillier 2015). Second, the landing locations— Montréal and Toronto—were specifically chosen because "[t]hese cities naturally have the capacity to accept a large number of flights daily, and the necessary facilities and services available to process this volume of refugees for a short time" (IRCC, n.d.b). In this case, decisions about which land border to use were chosen tactically, specifically to cater to the #WelcomeRefugees deadline. So while we can look at territorial and temporal dimensions separately, often they are interdependent and evolve in relation to one another.

Phase 4: Welcoming Syrian Refugees to Canada. "Upon arrival in Canada, all refugees will be welcomed and processed by Border Services Officers for admission into Canada. This will include final verification of identity" (IRCC 2016b).

Phase 4 bears the closest resemblance to what we typically expect of a border crossing—with a twist, though, because all of the major administrative parts had already been completed. Refugees met the Canadian land border crossing but, like previous phases, the processing was expedited: "Refugees who come to Canada as privately sponsored refugees will then continue directly to the community where their private sponsor is located" (IRCC, n.d.c). Long processing times at the border characteristic of the refugee process were virtually nonexistent (Ngugi 2007). The government had already pre-empted this process, and refugees were only faced with one final screening to verify their identity before they were admitted to Canada.

Phase 5: Settlement and Community Integration. "Syrian refugees will be transported to communities across Canada, where they will begin to build a new life for themselves and their family. They will be provided with immediate, essential services and long-term settlement support to ensure their successful resettlement and integration into Canadian society" (IRCC 2016b).

Unlike the average border-crossing experience, the #WelcomeRefugees plan included a phase for the government to follow up on the status of newly resettled people. The temporal theory—or perhaps sociopolitical theory—is useful in explaining this part of the border construct, where attention to only the physical dimensions of the border would fall short. IRCC described this phase as follows: "Immigration, Refugees and Citizenship Canada is working with settlement partners, private sponsors, provincial, territorial, and municipal government to coordinate and welcome these refugees into their new communities. Support that will be available includes orientation to life in Canada, access to healthcare, permanent housing, counselling, language services, schooling and other federal, provincial, territorial and municipal support services" (IRCC, n.d.d). The final phase extends far further into time than an average border crossing, which would have ended around phase 4. These services would normally exist in Canadian society for migrants and refugees regardless of the border construct; however, during the Syrian refugee crisis, these services were *subsumed* and therefore became part of the Canadian border construct as soon as they were made part of the #WelcomeRefugees plan.

Part IV. Further Areas for Study: The Canadian versus American Border Construct for Syrian Refugees

Canada and the United States had opposite approaches to Syrian refugee resettlement. Whereas Canada expanded its refugee intake numbers and expedited resettlement, the US House of Representatives passed a bill that would require the secretary of Homeland Security, the director of the Federal Bureau of Investigation, and the director of National Intelligence to certify that a person was not a threat before they could enter the resettlement process (Jacobs 2015). An analysis of why and how Canada and the US differed in their refugee resettlement policies is beyond the scope of this chapter. However, it is fair to say that whereas Canada's #WelcomeRefugees plan, in promoting inclusion, temporally shrank, even as it geographically expanded, the Canadian border to create a more streamlined border process for Syrian refugees to navigate, US policies that fostered exclusion lengthened, widened, and burdened its border construct with barriers that rendered it impassable in a short period of time and without significant administrative assistance. By November 2016, approximately sixteen thousand Syrian refugees were resettled in the United States, a year after the #WelcomeRefugees plan was initiated and ten months after it was successfully executed (Statista, n.d.).

It would also be possible to extend the analysis of the temporal dimension of Canada's border construct during the Syrian refugee crisis even further (but that was also beyond the scope of this chapter) by applying Speikermann and Wegener's (1994) method and mapping the estimated resettlement time for Syrian refugees based on political factors. The factors could have included administrative processing times, physical distance from Syria, and whether the state was open to resettling Syrian refugees at all. Given the different political factors between Canada and the US in November 2015, the time-space map might have depicted the distance between Syria and Canada and Syria and the US quite differently. Processing time was integral to the #WelcomeRefugees plan, and I could imagine a time-space map being a valuable aid in decision-making for refugees everywhere. In addition, it could serve as a visual aid to global decision makers when assessing how inclusive versus exclusive their state's borders and resettlement policies are compared to other states. Perhaps such an understanding and visualization would be instrumental in helping refugees overcome the psychological threshold that holds them back from decisions that might improve their lives and in helping policymakers make more inclusive policy decisions during both ordinary times and times of crisis.

Conclusion

Before the #WelcomeRefugees plan (and indeed, for refugees who were not of Syrian origin), the Canadian border has been described as a monolith of indeterminate processing. Leading up to Ngugi's (2007) study, one Venezuelan refugee waited four years for her resettlement claim to be processed once she arrived in Canada. In these cases, Canada's border construct is less streamlined than it was for Syrian refugees between November 2015 and February 2016, creating an indeterminate limbo that traps refugees without social insurance numbers, employment prospects, adequate income, and housing. Evidently, without clearly outlined phases, like those of the #WelcomeRefugees plan, the border construct stretches on in uncertainty.

By thinking in terms of rapid rates and deadlines, we bring the temporal dimension to the front of discussions about the border. At the centre of these discussions, you'll find something that is less prominent in discussions of borders in terms of territory or political standards, that is, how the border *feels* to a person. A greater evaluation of the #WelcomeRefugees plan, including personal accounts of refugees, is made by Zyfi (2016), but still, we can ask, how does the person perceive of and feel during the border process? Was the process quick, efficient, and transparent? When discussing the border using the language of territory or politics, the discussion changes. We might say that the border is long or disputed, but do these terms mean anything to the average person trying to cross it? The border can be long on a map, but so long as the process to cross it is quick at one critical point, the length might not matter to a person. The border might be disputed at certain points, but if there are inclusive policies to safeguard the free flow of people, that might not matter to a person. Therefore, when a state emphasizes the temporal dimension of its border construct, we can immediately see that it has prioritized the feel of the border experience.

As of February 2016, with the successful execution of the #WelcomeRefugees plan, Canada's border construct was different than its previous versions owing to the emphasis on processing rates and its four-month deadline. Indeed, the #WelcomeRefugees plan fundamentally altered the genome of Canada's border construct. Afterward, Parliament pushed to resettle future refugee groups using its blueprint (Levitz 2016). Granted, not every future border construct will take the same shape as #WelcomeRefugees moving forward (for example, chartered flights for each group may be unfeasible). However, there will hopefully be uptake of transferable elements, such as expedited processing in transit countries.

But expediting resettlement through the #WelcomeRefugees plan was not without challenges. Phases 1 through 4 were implemented so quickly, and Canada suddenly took in such a large number of refugees, that phase 5 (long-term settlement) was criticized for not being as robust as promised. Moreover, Saskatchewan's premier raised concerns that cities would be unprepared to resettle families so quickly, which might lead to strain on infrastructure and the families themselves. (CBC News 2015) Indeed, in some cases, refugees found that their living stipend ran out after four months instead of five, and that long-term employment was more elusive than expected.[1] These are, without a doubt, significant considerations for the Canadian government—or any state—should they plan to use the #WelcomeRefugees blueprint for resettlement moving forward.

Finally, in a world where globalization has shortened time and shrunk distance, it is necessary that we internalize different perspectives, such as the temporal dimension, of border constructs. This understanding is critical for emergency management planning and for optimizing the experience of borders for most vulnerable populations during times of crisis. In addition to being a well-executed plan, the #WelcomeRefugees plan acutely brings to our attention how borders truly are evolving organisms. It has become a part of Canada's immigration history, where we now can point to a precedent—an imprint—of resettlement acceleration on Canada's border genome.

References

Agnew, John. 2005. *Hegemony: The New Shape of Global Power*. Philadelphia, PA: Temple University Press.

———. 1994. "The Territorial Trap: The Geographical Assumptions of International Relations Theory." *Review of International Political Economy* 1 (1): 53–80.

Alvarez Perez, Marcela, and Mark T. Berger. 2009. "Bordering on the Ridiculous: Mex America and the New Regionalism." *Alternatives* 34 (1): 1–16.

Anderson, Benedict. 2006. *Imagined Communities: Reflections on the Origin and Spread of Nationalism*. London: Verso Books.

Boutillier, Alex. 2015. "Liberals Look to Private Aircraft, Military Planes to Transport Syrian Refugees." *The Star*, December 1, 2015. https://www.thestar.com/news/canada/2015/12/01/refugee-crisis-a-defining-moment-for-canada-johnston.html.

CBC News. 2015. "Sask. Premier Brad Wall asks Ottawa to Suspend Refugee Plan." November 16, 2015. https://www.cbc.ca/news/canada/saskatoon/sask-premier-brad-wall-asks-ottawa-to-suspend-syrian-refugee-plan-1.3321159.

Elden, Stuart. 2013. "Secure the Volume: Vertical Geopolitics and the Depth

---

[1] A greater evaluation of #WelcomeRefugees can be found in Zyfi (2016).

of Power." Political *Geography* 34 (May): 35–51.

Fraisse, Paul. 1984. "Perception and Estimation of Time." *Annual Review of Psychology* 35 (February): 1–37.

Galasinska, Aleksandra. 2003. "Temporal Shifts in Photo-elicited Narratives in a Polish Border Town." *Narrative Inquiry* 13 (2): 393–411.

IRCC (Immigration, Refugees, and Citizenship Canada). 2018. "Syrian Refugees Horizontal Initiative." Government of Canada (website). Last modified December 20, 2018. https://www.canada.ca/en/immigration-refugees-citizenship/corporate/publications-manuals/departmental-performance-reports/2016/section-4.html.

———. 2016a. "Check Application Processing Times." Government of Canada (website). Last modified March 3, 2016. http://www.cic.gc.ca/english/information/times/index.asp.

———. 2016b. "#WelcomeRefugees: How It Will Work." Government of Canada (website). Last modified March 15, 2016. http://www.cic.gc.ca/english/refugees/welcome/overview.asp.

———. 2016c. "#WelcomeRefugees: Milestones and Key Figures." Government of Canada (website). Last modified March 21, 2016. http://www.cic.gc.ca/english/refugees/welcome/milestones.asp.

———. 2014. *Annual Report to Parliament on Immigration*. October 31, 2014. http://www.cic.gc.ca/English/resources/publications/annual-report-2014/index.asp.

———. n.d.a. "#WelcomeRefugees: Phase 1."Government of Canada (website). Accessed April 1, 2016. http://www.cic.gc.ca/english/refugees/welcome/phase1.asp.

———. n.d.b. "#WelcomeRefugees: Phase 3." Government of Canada (website). Accessed April 1, 2016. http://www.cic.gc.ca/english/refugees/welcome/phase3.asp.

———. n.d.c. "#WelcomeRefugees: Phase 4." Government of Canada (website). Accessed April 1, 2016. http://www.cic.gc.ca/english/refugees/welcome/phase4.asp.

———. n.d.d. "#WelcomeRefugees: Phase 5." Government of Canada (website). Accessed April 1, 2016. http://www.cic.gc.ca/english/refugees/welcome/phase5.asp.

Jacobs, Ben. 2015. "House Passes Bill Adding Barriers for Syrian and Iraqi Refugees Entering US." *The Guardian*, November 19, 2015. https://www.theguardian.com/us-news/2015/nov/19/house-passes-bill-adding-barriers-for-syrian-and-iraqi-refugees-to-us.

Konrad, Victor. 2015. "Toward a Theory of Borders in Motion." *Journal of Borderlands Studies* 30 (1): 1–17.

Levitz, Stephanie. 2016. "Canada Syrian Refugees Program Sparks Political Push for Other Refugee Resettlement." *Huffington Post*, July 17, 2016. https://www.huffingtonpost.ca/2016/07/17/syrian-refugee-program-sparks-political-

push-for-other-humanitarian-settlement_n_11042814.html.
Newman, David. 2010. "Territory, Compartments and Borders: Avoiding the Territorial Trap." *Geopolitics* 15 (4): 773–778.
Ngugi, Kamau. 2007. "Long Walk to Safety: Experiences of Refugee Claimants with Canada's Refugee Policies and Practices." Master's thesis, Ryerson University. https://digital.library.ryerson.ca/islandora/object/RULA%3A709/view_premis.
Ostrand, Nicole. 2015. "The Syrian Refugee Crisis: A Comparison of Responses by Germany, Sweden, the United Kingdom and the United States." *Journal on Migration and Human Security* 3 (3): 1–25.
Salter, Mark B. 2012. "Theory of the /: The Suture and Critical Border Studies." *Geopolitics* 17 (4): 734–755.
Spiekermann, Klaus, and Michael Wegener. 1994. "The Shrinking Continent: New Time-Space Maps of Europe." *Environment and Planning B: Planning and Design* 21 (6): 653–773.
Statista. n.d. "Syrian Refugee Arrivals in the United States from 2011 to 2019." Accessed July 1, 2020. https://www.statista.com/statistics/742553/syrian-refugee-arrivals-us/.
UNHCR (United National High Commissioner for Refugees). (1951) 2010. *Convention and Protocol Relating to the Status of Refugees.* Geneva: UNHCR. http://www.unhcr.org/3b66c2aa10.html.
Valdivia, Gabriela, Wendy Wolford, and Flora Lu. 2013. "Border Crossings: New Geographies of Protection and Production in the Galapagos Islands." *Association of American Geographies* 104 (3): 686–701.
van der Velde, Martin, and Ton van Naerssen. 2011. "People, Borders, Trajectories: An Approach to Cross-Border Mobility and Immobility in and to the European Union." *Royal Geographical Society* 43 (2): 218–224.
Weber, Max. 1946. *Essays in Sociology.* New York: Oxford University Press.
Zyfi, Jona. 2016. "Syrian Refugee Resettlement in Canada: An Autoethnographic Account of Sponsorship." Canadian Association for Refugee and Forced Migration Studies Working Paper no: 2016/2, May 2016. https://doi.org/10.13140/RG.2.2.23991.11686.

PLACING AND REPLACING BORDER CULTURE: INDIGENOUS PERSPECTIVES

CHAPTER 9

Across Borders and Cultures
Thomas King's Artistic Activism

Evelyn P. Mayer

Borders are multifaceted and their meaning is attributed and inscribed by different actors. Borders can be understood in terms of their restrictive function, and yet they also remain a reassuring or grounding presence for many people during times of great transition—including those associated with security, migration, and climatic conditions—in society and in the world at large. Against this backdrop, it is worthwhile to closely look at the representation of various borders and borderlands in Canadian and Native author Thomas King's most recent works and to compare pertinent aspects of those works with his earlier novel *Truth & Bright Water* (1999) and his emblematic border-related short story "Borders" ([1993] 1999). *The Back of the Turtle* (2014) and *The Inconvenient Indian* (2013) are both critically acclaimed and underline King's status as one of the leading literary voices in Canada. King's 2003 CBC Massey Lecture, published as *The Truth About Stories: A Native Narrative* and delivered as the first Native person (King 2003), are another significant contribution to Canadian literature and the discussion of Native cultures, including storytelling and the arts.

This chapter analyzes the aforementioned works by King in terms of their diverse cultural expressions, border representations, and identity negotiations in figurative borderlands settings. It draws on ideas about artistic activism, motion and fluidity, subversion, resistance, and survival—or, in Gerald Vizenor's (2008) terms, "survivance"

(1)—and liminality (Turner 1979) as a space of opportunity oscillating between, on the one hand, complexity and multiplicity and, on the other, identity and belonging to think through how King's descriptions of concrete border crossings illustrate the "porosity and selectivity of borders to flows of goods, people and ideas" (Konrad 2014, 42).

King's historical and political narrative *The Inconvenient Indian*, as a work of creative non-fiction, epitomizes an artistic activist stance. He himself practices in real life what his main characters endorse as invented representatives in fictional realms. King the writer and writings by King are two sides of the same coin, as he walks the talk in terms of writing with a message. Artistic activism comprises writing back in such a way that it undermines expectations, reimagining circumstances and characters. Such an activism in an Indigenous context is linked to resistance, resilience, and survival, in short to "survivance" (Vizenor 2008). Vizenor (2008) defines "Native survivance" as "an active sense of presence over absence, deracination, and oblivion" (1). This active attitude and practice can merge into a more programmatic activist stance. Vizenor (2008) postulates that "survivance is the continuance of stories" and that "survivance" comes to the fore "in narrative resistance" (1). Artistic expression in its manifold forms—this chapter focuses on painting and the arts as depicted in King's narration—is a means for righting the wrongs of the past, seizing the present, and, in so doing, creating hope and a new vision for the future. Eve Ensler (2011) describes artistic activism, what she calls "artivism," as an alternative to the opposing forces of "power" and "passion," "a third way, ... a kind of escalated passion" and "a creative energy" (Ensler 2011). She further posits that artivism is "where edges are pushed, imagination is freed, and a new language emerges altogether" (Ensler 2011). In this sense, in King's narrative art, his artivism transcends boundaries and builds bridges between the past and the future, beyond present conditions and divisions, and thus something new arises. A beacon of hope emerges, mirroring the beach tower built in King's *The Back of the Turtle*.

Juxtaposing King's fiction and non-fiction is revelatory and highlights King's twin strands of narrative art. King could be described as a borderlands author, straddling the line between writing and righting the wrongs of the past in an activist stance, but he does not stop there. He questions border binaries: "Conjoining in himself the two partly collapsed dichotomies of Native and non-Native, Canadian and US, King regularly portrays how racial and national dividing lines work—and do not work" (Davidson, Walton, and Andrews 2003, 122). Beyond being a borderlands author in terms of both his biography (he has US and Canadian, Greek, and Cherokee roots) and his oeuvre's frequent settings in the borderlands between countries, cultures, and mixed characters (Sadowski-Smith 2008, 87), King is also a professor, literary critic, and intellectual, reflecting on a range of issues from storytelling to stereotyping. Reading King's *The Inconvenient Indian* in this context, it becomes even more apparent that addressing the lingering issues of land, culture, identity, belonging, social injustice, colonial history and oppression, discrimination, and institutionalized racism is paramount in a North American setting. In Canada, the urgent social justice issues are the missing and murdered Indigenous women, the history and legacy of residential schools, the taking and misuse of Native land, Indigenous people's physical and mental health, and future prospects for Indigenous youth (Gray 2016, 262).

Multicultural Canada increasingly tries to assume responsibility for its role in past injustices and to embrace a Native presence and future by, for example, appointing Native members of Parliament "to key cabinet positions" in Prime Minister Justin Trudeau's government, or through the work of the Truth and Reconciliation Commission, or in an official apology regarding residential schools by then-Prime Minister Stephen Harper (Ray 2016, xiii). However, as King (2013) posits in *The Inconvenient Indian*, a lot remains to be done and he is often sceptical of the prospects for real change in the present and future: "The history I offered to forget, the past I offered to burn, turns out to be our present. It may well be our future" (192). Nonetheless, historian Charlotte Gray (2016) observes a recent shift and expanding phenomenon in Canada of recognizing "First Peoples' presence in our national life" (266) and describes how territorial acknowledgments have become prevalent, for example, at public gatherings or such events as the swearing-in ceremony of Prime Minister Trudeau's cabinet in November 2015. Arthur J. Ray (2016) shares a holistic yet hopeful view: "For the First Nations, Inuit, and Métis of Canada, justice and reconciliation with the Government of Canada remain unfinished projects, but the signs are hopeful" (xv). Beyond the political realm, public territorial acknowledgments of Indigenous lands can serve as a call to reflection or even action on the part of the non-Indigenous audience members and reaffirm, to a certain extent, Native presence. Métis public intellectual, educator, and writer Chelsea Vowel (2016) published the following thoughts on territorial acknowledgments in her blog *âpihtawikosisân*: "If we think of territorial acknowledgments as sites of potential disruption, they can be transformative acts that to some extent undo Indigenous erasure. I believe this is true as long as these acknowledgments discomfit both those speaking and hearing the words. The fact of Indigenous presence should force non-Indigenous peoples to confront their own place on these lands." These acts of transformation are instances of activism, voicing past wrongs and absent discourses that can bring about change, as long as territorial acknowledgments maintain their disruptive nature.

The powerful narrations in *The Inconvenient Indian* and *The Back of the Turtle*, published a couple of years apart, can fruitfully be read as two sides of the same artivist coin; they are examples of overt and covert artistic activism in the realm of literature and narration. Their artistic expression starts with the imagination, knowledge, and the mind and appeals to readers' more noble instincts by employing humour, fact, and fiction. The activist author straddles a line in "writing back," balancing activism and the writing in order to reach readers; thus the activist author must maintain a border, only at times blurring it, between authoring a story and trying to right certain wrongs as an activist. King successfully negotiates that line, and as a reader, one primarily follows King the author, while more or less subtly also experiencing King the artistic activist. As a reflection on King's life and an analysis of selected King works, this chapter addresses the crossing of geopolitical, ethnic and cultural, and utopian borderlines, as well as the related notion of borderlands.

King's Storytelling in "Borders": Geopolitical Boundaries Versus a Native Presence

Thomas King himself is a border crosser. He is of mixed heritage and has lived in both the United States and Canada. King's oeuvre comprises a number of works dealing directly or indirectly with geopolitical and cultural borders, as well as the liminal space between them. In "Borders," King contrasts the fluidity of a seemingly natural geopolitical border with the determinacy of a land border enforced by both American and Canadian border guards. At the land border, the prospective border crosser is forced to imbue her nation-state nationality with meaning despite self-identifying tribally as Blackfoot. For the short story's Native protagonist, her Blackfoot identity supersedes any national affiliation as Canadian or American; she "aligns herself with her own conception of nation, not with the Euro-North American nation-states" (Roberts 2013, 130). From her perspective, tribal identity comes first, whereas the opposite is true for the border guards, who would like her to abide by the superimposed nation-state designations, whether American or Canadian. By refusing to do so, the Native mother and her son are stuck in a liminal space, quite literally "in between" the two nation-states, in the no-man's land of a duty-free shop and parking lot, seemingly devoid of any deeper meaning. Only after the media publicize her several failed attempts to cross the border as "Blackfoot" rather than "Canadian" or "American" are the border guards able to reinterpret the geopolitical boundary and allow the Blackfoot mother and her son to finally cross into the United States to visit the daughter or, from the young I-narrator's perspective, sister.

Borderlands scholars have written extensively about the complexities of geopolitical borders and how the significance of those borders varies depending on one's perspective. For instance, in "Culture at the 49th Parallel: Nationalism, Indigeneity, and the Hemispheric," Gillian Roberts and David Stirrup posit that the international boundary between Canada and the United States is "a site of cultural defence for Canadian identity against US hegemony" (1). They then discuss the asymmetric perception of the border by contrasting the (mostly Anglophone) Canadian perspective with the American perspective on the Canada-US border (Roberts and Stirrup 2013, 5–6). The discussion raises certain questions, however: Who counts as Canadian and features as part of the Canadian mosaic? How important is the Canada-US border for Québécois, Francophone minorities in other provinces, Indigenous peoples, and immigrants to Canada from all over the world compared to the Anglophone majority in Canada outside of Quebec?

Roberts and Stirrup note that "cultural texts continue to invoke the Canada-US border" and, in doing so, enumerate the border's several functions: "a protective barrier," "a site of policing bodies and identities," "a threat to Indigenous sovereignties," "a dividing line," a cultural zone, and a "contact zone" (Roberts and Stirrup 2013, 1–2). Furthermore, they describe a "tension between the arbitrariness of the line and the determinacy of what it represents" (Roberts and Stirrup 2013, 5). In King's short story "Borders," the prospective Native border crossers experience just that. The "determinacy" comes to the fore and prevents the Native mother and son from crossing the line after the Blackfoot mother refuses to provide the standard answers in the discourse of power between border guard and prospective border crosser. What is more, the border guards themselves acknowledge that there are Blackfoot people on both sides of the geopolitical boundary, hence inadvertently paying tribute to the arbitrary and artificial nature of the borderline. Roberts and Stirrup (2013) state that "the Canada-US border continues to operate as a colonial imposition and contributes to attempts to impose nation-state citizenship on Indigenous communities" (6). The border bisects Indigenous communities and land, thus complicating notions of belonging and identity. The Natives in King's short story value their Blackfoot tribal affiliation above the designations associated with Western nation-states and societies linked to a "settler-invader" (Sugars 2004, xiii) paradigm. In the same vein, Roberts points out that "[i]n Indigenous contexts, the Canada-US border figures as a settler-colonial scar bisecting Indigenous territories" (2018, 15). The image of the border as a "scar" highlights Indigenous peoples' painful past and its lingering repercussions in the present.

Reingard M. Nischik (2016) also turns her scholarly analysis toward border narratives situated along and across the Canada-US border. In her *Comparative North American Studies: Transnational Approaches to American and Canadian Literature and Culture*, she states that the Canada-US border is increasingly taken into account not only by "politicians, political scientists, and economists, but also literary and cultural critics" (Nischik 2016, 61). Nischik postulates that short stories are "particularly suited to border narratives, especially when it comes to stories dealing with the crossing of the border as such" (64). For Nischik, the form of the short story is better suited to addressing borders than that of the novel because the short story is characterized by "the significant moment, of initiation, transition, being on the threshold, liminality, indeed of crossing the border between two 'states' (here applicable in more than one sense of this word)" (64). Moreover, Nischik claims that "crossing the border of political states is often paralleled with metaphysical, metaphorical, or mental states" (74). She refers to the ambiguity, indeterminacy, and liminality of the border region as "a threshold situation" (Nischik 2016, 74), echoing Victor Turner's definition of liminality as "literally 'being-on-a-threshold'" (Turner 1979, 65). The significance of the threshold experience of border crossing, Nischik argues, is that it "makes a memory space of the border" (2016, 82). Quoting Herb Wyile's commentary on King's "Borders," Nischik states that "these border narratives are a 'literalization of liminality (1999, 120)'" (Nischik 2016, 91). As a type of fiction, the short story is itself liminal, falling somewhere between a novel and a poem, and when used to convey stories about border crossings or set in a borderlands or at a geopolitical boundary line, liminality, as "place between places, and a time between times" (see Vandervalk, this volume, chapter 6) is present both formally and thematically.

King's ([1993] 1999) "Borders" epitomizes crossing "states," nation-states, states of identity, and states of affiliation. Mother and son are stuck in a liminal space, neither allowed to cross back into Canada nor to continue their journey into the United States due to the Native "mother's insistence on her Blackfoot identity—indeed, on a Blackfoot citizenship" (Roberts 2015, 127): "'Blackfoot side,' she said." (King [1993] 1999, 138). Border literature and culture scholar Gillian Roberts argues that, "although the Canadian and American nation-states do not recognize a 'Blackfoot side' of the border, the mother demonstrates that *both* sides of the border are in Blackfoot territory" (2015, 127–28). However, the border guards on both sides of the international boundary want to force her to comply with official definitions of nationhood and self-identify as either Canadian or American. Nischik adds both a national and gendered perspective in this regard, thus underscoring the underlying complexity of the short story. She focuses her analysis beyond the Indigenous protagonists in examining the role of the border guards, arguing that King "characterizes them contrastively according to national stereotypes: the female Canadian border patrol is much nicer, more polite, and more communicative with the travelling Natives than the American border guards, who, with their weapons, their swagger, and their eventually rather rough treatment of the Natives remind the youthful narrator of American cowboys" (2016, 90). These clichés are perpetuated in King's text. Nischik further alludes to "the catalyzing behaviour of the often identity-challenging 'border guards'" (91). It is at the border that one needs to decide and give name to one's identity and nationhood. The boundary is inscribed with state power and mechanisms of control, and it is there that "questions of whether, how, for whom, and when the border signifies" (Roberts 2015, 148) come to the fore.

The subtitle of King's *The Inconvenient Indian: A Curious Account of Native People in North America* signals King's broader understanding of North America in terms of a Native presence transcending the geopolitical and colonial boundary between Canada and the United States. He contests the appropriate use of terminology, noting that differences lie in the eye of the beholder. King uses North American in the non-NAFTA sense of the word, comprising only Canada and the United States of America. He concedes: "Someone will wonder why I decided to take on both Canada and the United States at the same time, when choosing one or the other would have made for a less involved and more focused conversation" (King 2013, xv–xvi). King (2013) explains his choice to take on both Canada and the United States in the following way: "While the line that divides the two countries is a political reality, and while the border affects bands and tribes in a variety of ways, I would have found it impossible to talk about the one without talking about the other" (xvi). For King, the tribal presence needs to be seen as one, despite the border's divisive consequences for the lived realities of Native people in both nation-states. King claims: "For most aboriginal people, that line doesn't exist. It's a figment of someone else's imagination" (xvi). In noting that "stories go wherever they please" (King 2013, xvi), King contrasts the limits of Indigenous mobility when people such as himself might be stopped at the border with the transcendent power of storytelling to convey a shared experience and humanity beyond borders.

King's writing highlights Indigenous persons' experiences at the crossroads, in the borderlands, or in the liminal space of being Native, Canadian, or American, or all or none of the above. Tribal homelands, such as those of the Blackfoot or the Akwesasne along the St. Lawrence River (Konrad and Nicol 2008, 297; Rouvière, this volume, chapter 10), were bisected by the superimposition of the international boundary line. The Canada-US border means different things to different border crossers or borderlands dwellers depending on, for instance, ethnicity, nationality, mother tongue, or the economic situation. Sometimes the border functions as a marker of identity and at other times it demarcates economic or legal differences. Historically, this legal dimension has been instrumental for people seeking freedom as well as fleeing persecution or legal prosecution, for instance, in the cases of Loyalists during the American Revolution, African Americans making their way north on the Underground Railroad, or the "draft dodgers" and Vietnam War resisters going to Canada (Nischik 2016, 72–73). For Native peoples, the Canada-US border used to be a "medicine line" due to opportunities related to the legal differences between the two nation-states such as in the times of

Sitting Bull (Sadowski-Smith 2008, 86). The Canada-US border needs to be seen from multiple perspectives—Anglophone Canadian, Francophone Canadian, First Nations and Indigenous peoples in Canada, Euro-American, African American, and Native American—to fully comprehend its significance and its treatment or lack of treatment in literature and culture.

Borders are often mobile themselves but can also restrict the mobility of prospective border crossers. Mobility studies as well as border and transnational American and transnational Canadian studies focus on borders. Indigenous studies cannot ignore the international boundary as it is marked by a "tension between the arbitrariness of the line and the determinacy of what it represents" (Roberts and Stirrup 2013, 5). Although Native peoples have special Jay Treaty border crossing rights (Konrad and Nicol 2008, 297), the use of passports issued by Indigenous Nations, such as the Haudenosaunee passport, for international travel has proved to be a very complicated undertaking (Weigand and Howell, this volume, chapter 11), reminiscent of the Blackfoot mother's border crossing experience in King's short story "Borders" (Roberts and Stirrup 2013, 6–8). Sid Hill (2015), "a citizen of the six nation Haudenosaunee," insists on Indigenous sovereignty: "Too often, our passports are denied by the very countries that took our land. They call them 'fantasy documents,' but they are not." King (2013) also emphasizes the linkage between the issuing of passports and sovereignty, writing: "The issuing of passports is a legitimate exercise of sovereignty" and that the "Iroquois have been practising sovereignty by issuing and using their own Haudenosaunee Confederacy passports" (195).

In *The Inconvenient Indian*, King postulates that there are three types of Natives: there is the "bloodthirsty savage," the "noble savage," and the "dying savage" (34). He contrasts these stereotypical types of Natives in "North American popular culture" with seemingly "Dead Indians, Live Indians, and Legal Indians" (King 2013, 53). In explaining his terminology, King writes, "'Indian,' as a general designation, remains for me, at least, the North American default" (xiii). Nonetheless, he maintains that there is value in the Canadian terminologies "First Nations" and the American "Native Americans" (xiii). In addition to the First Nations, King also mentions Inuit and the Métis as the two other peoples comprising Canada's Indigenous peoples (xiii). He uses "Whites" (xiv) but also discusses "Native–non-Native relations" (xv). For him, "terminology is always a rascal" (xiii).

Furthermore, King contrasts the differing Native and non-Native perspectives on the current situation of Indigenous peoples in North America: "For Native people, the distinction between Dead Indians and Live Indians is almost impossible to maintain. But North America doesn't have this problem. All it has to do is hold the two Indians up to the light. Dead Indians are dignified, noble, silent, suitably garbed. And dead. Live Indians are invisible, unruly, disappointing. And breathing. One is a romantic reminder of a heroic but fictional past. The other is simply an unpleasant, contemporary surprise" (King 2013, 66).

After this excursion to the borderlands between King's authorship and humanity, read in conjunction with his fictional realms, it is enlightening to return to King's main characters in "Borders." The Native mother epitomizes a "Live Indian," as she refuses to play along with the expectation that she should behave more like a "Dead Indian," in King's sense above. Eventually, after sharing creation stories about the trickster figure coyote with her son in the parking lot, gazing at the stars, and receiving media attention, the mother and her son are allowed to enter the US even though she continues to describe herself solely as Blackfoot. This is an instance of the power of storytelling and to transform "the stasis of being stuck between two geopolitical entities into an Indigenous interstitial space of Native identity, survivance, and opportunity" (Mayer 2015, 272). Vizenor's notion of survivance comes to the fore in King's oeuvre and becomes a leitmotif. Several of his main characters, such as Monroe Swimmer in *Truth & Bright Water*, explicitly exhibit survivance.

Beyond Reserves: The Art/s of Survivance in King's Recent Fiction and Non-Fiction

King's novels *The Back of the Turtle* (2014) and *Truth & Bright Water* (1999) can be read through the lens of King's non-fiction text *The Inconvenient Indian* (2013). In these works, King calls attention to the negotiated border between the White and Native worlds and the tension between economy and ecology through a focus on the repercussions of colonial pasts, individual action, and corporate policy for Native people, their livelihoods, and the lands they inhabit. Traces of the colonial legacy persist, often as glaring examples of social injustice. King, however, and his characters, assume a stance of survivance (Vizenor 2008) rather than victimization.

Survivance is present in *Truth & Bright Water* on multiple levels. One practitioner of survivance is the trickster-like character Monroe Swimmer, a Native artist coming home from his arts-related journeys in the world at large. He uses multiple media to express his artistic identity and—in a survivance-like, active as well as activist stance—to undo the lingering repercussions of the colonial past. His survivance and artivist practices include repainting the Native presence into Western landscape paintings, painting a Methodist church out of the surrounding landscape, reintroducing artificial buffalo—and, by extension, Native livelihood—into the prairie environment, and even repatriating Native remains taken from Western anthropological museums. He is an explicit activist by artistic means, one who could truly be called an "artivist." In addition to Monroe Swimmer's explicit activism as a means of "survivance," *Truth & Bright Water* also depicts a more personal form of "survivance" in artistic expression; the character Helen practices life quilting, which is analogous to life writing (Mayer 2014, 96). The quilt she creates represents places and events of her life, and her inclusion of unusual objects such as razor blades (King 1999, 62) and porcupine quills (61) are a means of survivance, of quilting back, of exhibiting resistance, survival, and artistic as well as enigmatic presence in the face of adversity.

Artistic practice and, by extension, artistic activism are crucial in both *Truth & Bright Water* and *The Back of the Turtle*. In fact, activism is linked to artistic expression instead of big political revolutionary actions. The forms of art range from quilting, painting, sculpture, and performance art to acting, storytelling, and such musical forms as singing and drumming. Kinship ties and a sense of community, in addition to personal connections between the characters, are at the fore in both. King the writer addresses family and community tragedy, the basis for characters' survivance and artivism, by using irony, sarcasm, and above all humour. In an interview published in *The Inconvenient Indian*, King (2013) underlines that humour is "the only way to deal with tragedy" (284). In a subversive stance, he claims that "sometimes a little satire goes a long way. Sometimes looking at a tragic moment through a particular angle provides a bit of humour and deepens the tragedy at the same time. Makes it more powerful" (King 2013, 285). For King, comedy and tragedy are interrelated and can be employed effectively to create a memorable reading experience and ideally produce a more lasting effect on the reader. King (2013) wants to engage in a dialogue with, and not against or about, the reader: "You have to work with your reader, and not just brutalize them with facts, even if the facts are legitimate concerns" (285). King himself, like the arts-oriented characters in his books, engages in powerful storytelling in order to ultimately get his message across, a message of Native "survivance."

Borders are usually in flux and meaning is attributed to them by social practices, political processes, and a seeming need for them on the part of citizens on both sides of a geopolitical boundary. The ascribed meaning and ensuing functions can vary depending on the cultural group, place, times, stakeholders involved, and overarching aims. Sometimes the gate-keeping function of the border is emphasized and at other times the commonalities between people residing in the borderlands. The fluid nature of the border and its significance are subject to change and are socially constructed. King highlights the fluidity and mobility of the border by choosing, for instance, to set the border along the Shield River in *Truth & Bright Water*. The Shield River does not stay in place; it floods and thus blurs the fluvial line. Nonetheless, the border river has also become a burial ground for repatriated Native remains taken by Monroe Swimmer from anthropological museums and a means to make money by depositing toxic and hazardous waste in the water. The Shield is thus "figured as both boundary and bin" (Bates 2013, 146) and "is reminiscent of the mythological river Styx, a border and concomitant connection between the realms of the living and the dead" (Mayer 2014, 73). In *Truth & Bright Water*, King, in his storytelling, shows how the fictional characters are often forced to put their own economic well-being ahead of ecological concerns and the needs of future generations. The landfill waste washes up on the shore of and is even actively dumped into the river; this is what the character Lum calls "landfill economics" (King 1999, 152). Lum underlines the necessity and pervasiveness of these economics by calling garbage "the new buffalo" (King 1999, 153). Yet again, in *The Back of the Turtle*, economic interests—not in terms of making ends meet or sustaining a livelihood but in terms of corporate greed and profit—surpass ecological and health issues. In *The Back of the Turtle*, the defoliant GreenSweep is deposited illegally and destroys the environment around Smoke River, driving away many of the community's residents—this is referred to in the novel as "The Ruin." The spectre of the ship *Anguis* (King 2014, 498), which carries the remains of the toxic GreenSweep and whose name echoes, in this context, the ominous word "anguish," haunts the narration of King's novel until the very end and represents the danger and social injustice that Native tribes face with regard to mining, landfills, and related issues. The natural environment, whether maritime or on land, is sacrificed for profit maximization by corporations. As in the contemporary world, "for non-Natives, land is primarily a commodity" (King 2013, 218). King contrasts this understanding and use of land with the Indigenous conception thereof: "Land contains the languages, the stories, and the histories of a people. It provides water, air, shelter, and food. Land participates in the ceremonies and the songs. And land is home" (King 2013, 218). Land is more than a commodity, as it provides a link to the past and creates a sense of belonging, of putting down, quite literally, roots.

The borders depicted in *The Back of the Turtle* differ from those in King's short story "Borders" or the international border river in *Truth & Bright Water*. In *The Back of the Turtle*, borders are less geopolitically explicit, transcending the dichotomy between the US and Canada. King places a greater emphasis on the divisions and overlap between the White and Native worlds and worldviews as well as on the urban-rural continuum. Geographic, ethnic, and cultural borders come to the fore in *The Back of the Turtle*. The Native protagonist, scientist Gabriel Quinn, embodies a belief in science that is pitted against a more community-oriented approach to life: "His life was a world of facts, of equations, of numbers. His family's world was made up of connections and emotions" (King 2014, 184). For Gabriel: "Stories were stories. They were not laws of the universe" (185). At the beginning of the novel Gabriel wants to commit suicide by letting himself be drowned by the tide, but instead he saves people from the sea and ultimately himself. This is an inexplicable event for him as a scientist, distanced from his family and Native community and made to function in a capitalist corporation based in the big city. From the first pages of the novel, the contrast or rather mysterious narrative presence quite literally emerges from the depths of the sea.

The seashore and the beach also become a liminal space. It is there that "community" is practiced, such as in the joint effort to deal with the washed-up *Anguis* toward the end of the novel (King 2014, 498–500). "'The Ruin,'" according to Mara, "sounds monumental....Biblical even" (248). Mara seems to have a negative impression of the Bible—God being a violent, vengeful, strict presence. She stereotypically equates the adjective "biblical" with the Old Testament, brimstone, and fire. King plays with these preconceived notions of the Bible and ultimately a philosophical or metaphysical worldview by contrasting Edenic settings with Anthropocene disasters. The protagonists must negotiate that tension and the borders between, for instance, Native and Western creation stories and traditional and seemingly more progressive, yet disastrous—both in terms of community and ecology—ways of living. King's critique of so-called Western progress and economic greed becomes apparent.

In King's works, several characters embody the characteristics of motion, resistance, and liminality all at once, including the trickster-like and seemingly shape-shifting Native artist Monroe Swimmer in *Truth & Bright Water*. Writing from a border studies perspective, Johan Schimanski and Stephen Wolfe have argued that "people engaged in cultural production can negotiate borders by providing new visions of what they may be, or even of what borders should not or cannot be" (2010, 39). They also highlight the subversive potential of those people engaged in cultural production: "Their cultural and aesthetic practices can disrupt expectations of what borders are, through the creation of imagined and imaginary borderlands" (Schimanski and Wolfe 2010, 39). This creative potential based on the imagination comes to the fore in King's works through his fictional characters. They transcend preconceived notions to allow the world to be imagined and represented in writing as it could or even should be. Aside from Monroe Swimmer in *Truth & Bright Water*, there are a number of characters engaged in cultural practices in *The Back of the Turtle* that overcome borders between the White and Native worlds or worldviews.

The Back of the Turtle echoes "Turtle Island" (Lischke 2008, 220), a Native expression designating North America. King also uses "North America" in a border-crossing sense to mean Canada and the United States. In *The Truth About Stories: A Native Narrative* (2003), a reflection on Native storytelling, King begins with the following words: "There is a story I know. It's about the earth and how it floats in space on the back of a turtle. I've heard this story many times, and each time someone tells the story, it changes" (King 2003, 1). Indeed, King practices exactly that approach, since each chapter of *The Truth About Stories* starts with a page-length variation of this basic story—the only difference between them is that the storyteller interacts with a different audience member. After this prelude, as of the second page of each chapter, the narrative evolves. All the chapters are interwoven. In the first chapter, King shares the creation story about "Charm," the "Woman Who Fell from the Sky" (21). She is pregnant and is put "on the back of the turtle" (16). The woman has her babies, twins: "A boy and a girl. One light, one dark. One right-handed, one left-handed" (18). Surprisingly enough, despite King's criticism of "dichotomy, the elemental structure of Western society" (King 2003, 25), this creation story also deals in such dualities as good and evil.

Truth & Bright Water and The Back of the Turtle also share a number of other themes, including concern for the environment, Native land, and Indigenous livelihoods, and the bordered and fractured relations between the White and Native worlds. Bright Water is the reserve in Truth & Bright Water, whereas Smoke River is the reserve in The Back of the Turtle. Water imagery in both—the name of the reserve or the border river between two nation-states in Truth & Bright Water and the ocean in The Back of the Turtle—underlines the fluidity and blurriness of borders. In The Back of the Turtle, the surf on the beach and the tides are liminal spaces between the solid and the fluid, between land and water. This inbetween space is symbolically charged: the river Shield in Truth & Bright Water can be read as a "Stygian" space (Mayer 2014, 70) and the ocean almost becomes a fluid grave for Gabriel Quinn in The Back of the Turtle. He wants to commit suicide by drowning, allowing the water to overcome him on one of the basalt columns known as the Apostles (King 2014, 33), which symbolically becomes his "rock of salvation" (Bible, n.d., Ps. 95:1). Despite being very critical of organized religion and the colonial past, which is evident in The Inconvenient Indian, King nonetheless presupposes the reader's familiarity with the tropes and symbolism of Christianity, and only with this familiarity would a reader comprehend the full extent of King's satire, critique, sarcasm, and irony regarding religion. King, in The Truth About Stories, contrasts Christian and Native stories: "So here are our choices: a world in which creation is a solitary, individual act or a world in which creation is a shared activity; a world that begins in harmony and slides toward chaos or a world that begins in chaos and moves toward harmony; a world marked by competition or a world determined by co-operation" (King 2003, 25).

King's naming practices, for instance Samaritan Bay (King 2014, 30) and character Sonny (a reference to Jesus, the Son) in The Back of the Turtle, testify to King's subversive stance toward Christian scripture and Christianity's role in European colonization. Moreover, King's use of the phrase "In the beginning was the salvage" (2014, 28) clearly echoes the language of the Gospel according to John ("in the beginning was the word"; Bible, n.d., John 1:1). Salvage and salvation appear to be related. Here, salvage is found at the beach and thus underscores the biblical words "seek and you will find" (Bible, n.d., Matt. 7:7) as well as "he was lost and is found" (Bible, n.d., Luke 15:24).

The lost son in *The Back of the Turtle* is Gabriel Quinn. He goes to the US and leaves part of his family, Canada, and his Native roots behind. Furthermore, he also gets lost in fog on the reserve and lost in life, as his suicide attempts attest to. Gabriel, however, literally calls the dog Soldier "the prodigal son" (King 2014, 309). In *Truth & Bright Water*, another dog named Soldier vanishes into the void, or rather the river Shield, with Lum. Therefore, Soldier does indeed exhibit a quality of the lost son returning home to Native land. Returning to *The Back of the Turtle*, Gabriel reunites himself with his Native roots and Native community. His negative deeds in terms of the ecological tragedy are eventually redeemed by the power of storytelling, love, and emerging forgiveness. The "ecocide" (King 2013, 220) links King's narration to the overarching theme of globalization, capitalism, and industrialization. The tension between the economy and ecology is illustrated by the ecological disaster destroying the reserve and making the turtles vanish.

The vanishing turtles call to mind the vanishing buffalo and, by extension, the stereotype of the vanishing Indian (Gray 2016, 93–94). However, the Indians are no longer vanishing. There is hope. The sea turtles return eventually, and so too does life (King 2014, 516). Resilience (King 2013, 266) and survivance (Vizenor 2008, 1) are a leitmotif in King's novel. Furthermore, not only in fiction, but also beyond, there is a renaissance in Native culture. Despite the ongoing struggles over land claims and for justice for the missing and murdered Indigenous women, or the seeming lack of opportunity for Indigenous youth, there is some progress. King (2013) singles out the creation of Nunavut, for example (263) and expresses his longing to know how Indigenous people will fare in the future: "Just to hear the stories" (266).

In his fictional writing, King employs powerful symbolism and tropes, the turtle being one of them. In addition to being referenced in the book's title, to being part of a creation story, to being echoed in the Native designation of North America as Turtle Island (Lischke 2008, 220), and to the actual sea turtles in the story, sea turtles are symbols of hope and of home. Not only do they eventually return after their vanishing following the ecological disaster in Samaritan Bay, but they also anchor Gabriel's relationship to his home and family through his sister, Lilly. Before Gabriel and his father cross the Canada-US border when the two move from Lethbridge, Alberta, to Minneapolis, Minnesota, when Gabriel was a boy, Lilly gives Gabriel "a laminated picture of a turtle" (King 2014, 259). She even describes Gabriel as a "turtle." For her: "Turtles carry their houses on their back.... Everything they need, they carry with them" (King 2014, 259). King interrupts the telling of the departure of Gabriel and his father several times, one time to note that "Minneapolis had been a world away from Lethbridge" (309). The contrast between Canada and the US becomes apparent to Gabriel. These settings are also part of King's own biography; he moved between Canada and the US and has taught at the University of Lethbridge in Alberta (Sadowski-Smith 2008, 87).

What is home and where is it? Borders can help to create a sense of home, belonging, and identity and ultimately even help someone to create roots. However, borders can simultaneously exclude and add to a sense of displacement by creating a home for one group of people at the expense of another group. The issue of home and belonging, of identity as such, is repeatedly addressed by King in *The Back of the Turtle*. The protagonist Gabriel sees home as a non-place: "Home wasn't a place. At best, it was a shifting illusion, a fiction you created to mask the fact that, in the end, you were alone in the world" (King 2014, 311). There are flashbacks to Minneapolis when he was mistaken for being White (314). Gabriel thinks back about his sister (312) and his nephew as well as Samaritan Bay and the Smoke River Reserve (314). His father, Joe, was "from Leech Lake in Minnesota" (314). In the story, there are negative father figures, such as Sonny's absent so-called Dad/God. Gabriel's mother was from Canada and his father from the US, both Natives. The family was divided, as Gabriel and his father are in the US after his father moved back there for his officer job and his mother and sister remained in Canada, first in Lethbridge and then in Smoke River (315). When Gabriel's father passed away, his mother did not want to go to the funeral (316).

The US is portrayed in negative stereotypes, as the father returns to his homeland for a job against the wishes of his Canadian wife. This is reminiscent of King's short story "Borders," where the family is also split, though the mother and son go to Utah to visit the daughter, Laetitia. In *Truth & Bright Water*, the town of Truth is in the US and Bright Water, yet again a water-related reserve name, is on the Canadian side (King 1999, 1). Stereotypes of the US as profit-oriented and domineering also come to the fore in a seemingly Americanized

Toronto, in which the fictional company Domidion, reminiscent of "dominion," is located on Tecumseh Plaza (King 2014, 14). When Dorian Asher, Domidion's CEO, inquires about the meaning or story of Tecumseh, his personal assistant, Lee Winter, fills him in, and Asher finds the naming of the plaza, given Tecumseh's biography, "ironic" (16). With King's witty sarcasm apparent, Winter responds: "There's a peace prize named after Alfred Nobel" (16). Tecumseh is also the name of the protagonist in *Truth & Bright Water*. King ostensibly likes to use names from history for contemporary people or places to highlight a tension or create irony. His narrative technique of multiple storylines that are all entangled turn out to be a coherent woven fabric when seen from above.

Regarding the artistic expression or artistic activism of painting, the foremost practitioner in *The Back of the Turtle* is a Native woman named Mara Reid. Mara paints back by composing portraits of those tribal members who perished in The Ruin herself and thus sharing her perception instead of an outsider's perspective (King 2014). Mara considers a painting "done" not "finished" (King 2014, 189). She is convinced that a "painting held its own" (King 2014, 189). The spirit or soul-like quality of her art lingers, always in flux: "Art was fluid and continuously full of potential" (King 2014, 189). This positive fluidity can also be observed in the borderlands, a space in between that can shift but that remains a space of possibility. Mara, by painting the portraits of the deceased, in the remnants of the community Samaritan Bay, on the edge of the former reserve, now a "ghost town," links both places. Indeed, she becomes a good Samaritan, not turning her back on the reserve and local community after The Ruin. She does not embrace a stance of victimization but instead uses painting to express herself and stay connected to the tribal past and, in so doing, the tribal present and future. She does so with a spirit of courage and daring, as symbolized in her use of a "palette knife" for "a bolder effect" (King 2014, 247).

Using her "memory" (King 2014, 248) to paint the locals who have perished in The Ruin, she honours them and the community. Her painting "dead people" (King 2014, 249) is both artivist practice and an example of Vizenor's concept of survivance. Quite literally, by painting her late fellow community members, she refuses to subscribe to the myth of the "vanishing" (Gray 2016, 93–94) or "dying Indian" (King 2013, 35). She embodies the "active sense of presence over absence" that Vizenor postulates. Mara keeps the connection to her family, the local community, her Native traditions and artistically and vividly renders the portraits of the community members. At the same time, she almost resuscitates them. This is reminiscent of Monroe Swimmer in *Truth & Bright Water*; just as Monroe makes the buffalo return or recreates a Native presence in nineteenth-century landscape paintings, Mara recreates a presence for her deceased neighbours and thus reunites with her past and present. She re-roots herself, claiming her Native identity and belonging. For her, people are "part of a larger organism" (King 2014, 189), and she therefore feels "diminished" (King 2014, 189) after the passing of her mother and grandmother.

In the end, the narrative strands of *The Back of the Turtle* come full circle: "A sea turtle. Dragging itself toward the water. A turtle with a depression in its shell and a blood-red slash across its neck" (King 2014, 492). Gabriel seems to recognize the turtle "from the tank in the lobby at Domidion, the turtle with whom he had shared his lunch all those years" (King 2014, 492), but is not sure (493). King leaves it to the reader's imagination. The story of the *Anguis*, along with the remaining toxic GreenSweep in its hold, also comes full circle. The broken ship returns and Mei-ling, one of the sea people rescued as the first people by Gabriel Quinn at the start of the story, recognizes it. It is also called "salvage" (King 2014, 497), and the newly emerging local community singing together is the transformative power in preventing another ecological disaster. Finally, in a symbolic gesture of generosity and community, Gabriel gives Sonny his drum and jacket: "Consider it today's salvage" (King 2014, 502). In *The Back of the Turtle*, King, as in "Borders" and *Truth & Bright Water*, uses the character of a young boy to signal the future. The novel closes with hopeful tones, illustrated by the return of the animals, the sea turtle laying her eggs again, and the sight of pelicans, a reminder of Lilly, Gabriel's sister and Mara's best friend. Moreover, Gabriel will put his trailer home right next to Mara's house, alluding to the possibility of a shared future. Lilly is their bond.

Conclusion: Utopian Borders
Related to Culture, Community, and Canada

At the end of *The Back of the Turtle*, survivance (Vizenor 2008) unfolds. Thanks to the community coming together, using the power of song and utilizing the tides, they push the broken ship back out into the ocean, where the waves carry it away. This means that the multicultural community reverses, as much as possible, the "ecocide" (King 2013, 220) from the past and, in so doing, prevents the repetition of The Ruin and thus saves the emerging community of Samaritan Bay and the Smoke River Reserve. There is rebirth and redemption, and ultimately hope. King closes his novel on an upbeat note, as he also does in *The Inconvenient Indian*, by referring to Native successes in reclaiming land. In *The Back of the Turtle*, the community reclaims land from ecological disaster and dereliction and in *The Inconvenient Indian*, King cites Nunavut a positive example and even a victory for Native people, first and foremost Inuit.

The Native situation as depicted in *The Back of the Turtle* after The Ruin is initially reminiscent of an apocalyptic dystopia. Singing and painting in *The Back of the Turtle*, cultural practices such as painting and art projects in *Truth & Bright Water*, and storytelling in "Borders" become the forces that, in their respective liminal spaces, subvert preconceived notions and create connections to the Native past and present, in short to a continued Native community. In the case of the protagonist Gabriel Quinn, Native survivance becomes literally manifest because he survives his suicide attempt. Thanks to artistic practice, resilience, and survivance, the novel exhibits some optimism toward the end. The dystopian realm of the ghost-town reserve is transformed by community and cultural practice into a utopian space of possibility. King describes Indigenous cultures as "tenacious" and "resilient" (King 1999, 266), hence echoing Vizenor's notion of survivance. King remains curious about the future of Native people. He stresses that Indigenous people would like to determine for themselves how they would like to live their lives.

King puts his vision of survivance, encapsulated in his writings, as follows: "Native cultures aren't static. They're dynamic, adaptive, and flexible, and for many of us, the modern variations of older tribal traditions continue to provide order, satisfaction, identity, and value in our lives" (King 2013, 265). The past influences the present and shapes the future. By adapting valuable Indigenous traditions to modern needs and lifestyles, Native presence and survivance is reaffirmed, showing the resilience, vibrancy, and relevance of Native cultures in the future.

References

Bates, Catherine. 2013. "Waste-full Crossings in Thomas King's *Truth & Bright Water*." In *Parallel Encounters: Culture at the Canada-US Border*, edited by Gillian Roberts and David Stirrup, 145–162. Waterloo, ON: Wilfrid Laurier University Press.

The Bible. n.d. NIV/New International Version. Accessed February 20, 2017.

Davidson, Arnold E., Priscilla L. Walton, and Jennifer Andrews. 2003. *Border Crossings: Thomas King's Cultural Inversions*. Toronto: University of Toronto Press.

Ensler, Eve. 2011. "Politics, Power and Passion." *New York Times*, December 2, 2011. https://archive.nytimes.com/www.nytimes.com/interactive/2011/12/02/opinion/magazine-global-agenda-big-question.html?_r=1#.

Gray, Charlotte. 2016. *The Promise of Canada: 150 Years—People and Ideas that Have Shaped our Country*. Toronto: Simon and Schuster Canada.

Hill, Sid. 2015. "My Six Nation Haudenosaunee Passport is not a 'Fantasy Document.'" *The Guardian*, October 30, 2015. https://www.theguardian.com/commentisfree/2015/oct/30/my-six-nation-haudenosaunee-passport-not-fantasy-document-indigenous-nations.

King, Thomas. 2014. *The Back of the Turtle*. Toronto: HarperCollins.

———. 2013. *The Inconvenient Indian: A Curious Account of Native People in North America*. Toronto: Anchor Canada.

———. 2003. *The Truth About Stories: A Native Narrative*. Toronto: Anansi.

———. 1999. *Truth & Bright Water*. New York: Grove Press.

———. (1993) 1999. "Borders." In *One Good Story, That One*, 131–147. Toronto: Harper Perennial Canada.

Konrad, Victor. 2014. "Borders and Culture: Zones of Transition, Interaction and Identity in the Canada-United States Borderlands." *Eurasia Border Review* 5 (1): 41–57. http://hdl.handle.net/2115/57845.

Konrad, Victor, and Heather N. Nicol. 2008. *Beyond Walls: Re-Inventing the Canada-United States Borderlands*. Farnham, UK: Ashgate.

Lischke, Ute. 2008. "'This Is a Pipe and I Know Hash': Louise Erdrich and the Lines Drawn upon the Waters and the Lands." In *Lines Drawn upon the Water: First Nations and the Great Lakes Borders and Borderlands*, edited by Karl S. Hele, 219–231. Waterloo, ON: Wilfrid Laurier University Press.

Mayer, Evelyn P. 2015. "Indigenous Interstitial Spaces: Liminality in Thomas King's 'Borders.'" In *Liminality and the Short Story: Boundary Crossings in American, Canadian, and British Writing*, edited by Jochen Achilles and Ina Bergmann, 263–273. Abingdon-on-Thames, UK: Routledge.

———. 2014. *Narrating North American Borderlands: Thomas King, Howard F. Mosher, and Jim Lynch*. Frankfurt: Peter Lang.

Nischik, Reingard M. 2016. *Comparative North American Studies: Transnational Approaches to American and Canadian Literature and Culture.* New York: Palgrave Macmillan.

Ray, Arthur J. 2016. "Preface to the Fourth Edition." In *An Illustrated History of Canada's Native People: I Have Lived Here Since the World Began*, 4th edition, by Arthur J. Ray and Sam Benvie, xi–xviii. Toronto: Key Porter Books.

Roberts, Gillian. 2018. "Introduction—Cultural Production and Consumption across the 49th Parallel: Negotiating Material Citizenship. In *Reading between the Borderlines: Cultural Production and Consumption across the 49th Parallel*, edited by Gillian Roberts, 3–37. Montréal and Kingston: McGill-Queen's University Press.

———. 2015. *Discrepant Parallels: Cultural Implications of the Canada-US Border.* Montréal and Kingston: McGill-Queen's University Press.

———. 2013. "Strategic Parallels: Invoking the Border in Thomas King's *Green Grass, Running Water* and Drew Hayden Taylor's *In a World Created by a Drunken God.*" In *Parallel Encounters: Culture at the Canada-US Border*, edited by Gillian Roberts and David Stirrup, 127–143. Waterloo, ON: Wilfrid Laurier University Press.

Roberts, Gillian, and David Stirrup. 2013. "Introduction: Culture at the 49th Parallel: Nationalism, Indigeneity, and the Hemispheric." In *Parallel Encounters: Culture at the Canada-US Border*, edited by Gillian Roberts and David Stirrup, 1–24. Waterloo, ON: Wilfrid Laurier University Press.

Sadowski-Smith, Claudia. 2008. *Border Fictions: Globalization, Empire, and Writing at the Boundaries of the United States.* Charlottesville: University of Virginia Press.

Schimanski, Johan, and Stephen F. Wolfe. 2010. "Cultural Production and Negotiation of Borders: Introduction to the Dossier." *Journal of Borderlands Studies* 25 (1): 39–49.

Sugars, Cynthia. 2004. "Introduction: Unhomely States." In *Unhomely States: Theorizing English-Canadian Postcolonialism*, edited by Cynthia Sugars, xiii–xxv. Peterborough, ON: Broadview Press.

Turner, Victor. 1979. "Frame, Flow and Reflection: Ritual and Drama as Public Liminality." *Japanese Journal of Religious Studies* 6 (4): 465–499.

Vizenor, Gerald. 2008. "Aesthetics of Survivance: Literary Theory and Practice." In *Survivance: Narratives of Native Presence*, edited by Gerald Vizenor, 1–23. Lincoln: University of Nebraska Press.

Vowel, Chelsea. 2016. "Beyond Territorial Acknowledgments." *Âpihtawikosisân: Law. Language. Culture* (blog). September 23, 2016. https://apihtawikosisan.com/2016/09/beyond-territorial-acknowledgments/.

CHAPTER 10

In the Space between Aboriginal Sovereignty and National Security

Re-engaging Border Security and Mohawk Culture at Akwesasne

Laetitia Rouvière

The border between Canada and the United States cuts across various ancient Aboriginal territories and divides communities that have maintained close links across time. Since 2001, the deep transformations within the border security policies of both countries have worsened the daily relationship between customs authorities and Aboriginal people who cross the border on a regular basis. However, these changes have also meant an increasing inclusion of Aboriginal border communities in the implementation of border security policies. In this context, the border situation can paradoxically be a strong political resource for local Native leaders who take a stand on border policy issues and play an active role in the implementation of such policies: border security and cross-border culture can be conceived of as co-constructed rather than diametrically opposed. Thus, this chapter considers the contributions of local leaders and communities to the ways that borderlands become "secured," not only in the literal sense of security measures but also in the sense of being "securitized" through the institutionalization of First Nations' participation in the implementation of these policies.

The increasing inclusion of cultural concerns in the implementation of security policies turns the border into a resource in the maintenance and rebuilding of cultural specificities, identities, and claims for nationhood. By considering Indigenous territorialities as spatial strategies that affect the implementation of border policies without disturbing the policies' contents, the goal is to apprehend the potential changes that arise both from and on the territorial and sociopolitical margins: how do Indigenous authorities take over security imperatives on borderlands while affirming cultural specificities?

The Mohawk territory of Akwesasne, wedged between Ontario, Quebec, and New York State, is a useful case study in this regard. The Mohawks are renowned for their activism in defending their territory (Pertusati 1997; George-Kanentiio 2008) and for their implication in cross-border smuggling (Daudelin, Soiffer, and Willows 2013; Spencer 2011). Beyond the periods of political crises that have arisen since the 1990s, the judicial conflicts and any "romance of resistance" (Sparke 2008), I aim at exploring the various forms of dialogue that Mohawk leaders and external agencies have engaged in together. The regeneration of border security policies has resulted in significant disturbances in Akwesasne residents' daily lives. Nonetheless, the affirmation of Aboriginal sovereignty when addressing such concerns specifically impacts the political positioning of borderland leaders on issues of the border. After questioning the meaning of Aboriginal sovereignty within the borderlands, I observe how sovereignty is projected within border security policies. I focus especially on identification requirements, cultural sensitivity training of border officers, and, finally, cooperation between law enforcement agencies. The perspectives, analysis, and conclusions that are reached in this chapter point to the potential for border security policies to be built from the bottom-up.

Indigenous Sovereignty and Cross-Border Territoriality in Akwesasne

The Recognition of Indigenous Sovereignty as a Securitization of Borders

The territorial component of Indigenous cultural affirmation in North America rests in the presence of the reserve. The reserve was created by European states as a concrete limitation to Indigenous power in a historical process of "internal colonization" (Tully 2000) and even finds continuity within the broader politics of recognition

(Coulthard 2007). But the reserve has also become a basis for political autonomy and cultural affirmation, especially over the last few decades with the constant reaffirmation of Aboriginal sovereignty. This term, "Aboriginal sovereignty," is used by stakeholders as a way of affirming a political stand in a day-to-day practice, not only to refer to the most spectacular mobilizations, radical discourses, or Indigenous activism. Sovereignty is also part of the discourses about and within cooperation with external agencies. This is all done following a specific way of addressing diplomacy and affirming cultural differences. Sovereignty is not only the capacity to dictate selfhood when faced with external powers, but also a way to render Indigenous peoples visible (Byrd 2014, 131). Although it has been characterized as a Western concept inappropriate for Indigenous governance (Alfred 1999, 59), sovereignty is part of a political game and must be used as a category of analysis rather than a category of practice (Brubaker 2001, 69).

Aboriginal sovereignty is closely linked to the spatial strategy of territoriality (Sack 1986, 1–2). Thus, cross-border Indigenous territoriality differs from state territoriality, but the paradox is that it does not necessarily challenge it in the end (Paasi 1998; Taylor 1994). Indeed, cross-border territoriality can result from a local appropriation of the national government of territories through its reinterpretation and through local uses of the existing institutional frameworks. Cross-border territoriality may be defined as a strategy of adaptation and negotiation resulting from a combination of various territorial referents: border territoriality is always "flexible" (Novak 2011). Cross-border activities, claims, and cultural practices can sometimes contribute to the enhancement of state territory as a political referee, in a game of interaction between centre and peripheries that allows local leaders to take over some national norms while, at the same time, using cultural specificities as a political resource (Rouvière 2012). This reflection ensues from a broader perspective on the participation of border communities in the construction of borders. Various scholars have acknowledged how borderland practices and culture help to shape the very definition of borders (Brunet-Jailly 2005; Konrad and Nicol 2008; Sahlins 1991; Pratt and Allison 2000). Borders are not only political institutions but also processes (Anderson 1996; Newman 2006) that evolve over time according to the perceptions of different stakeholders who are either affected by the border or involved in shaping its definition. Borders are always in motion (Konrad 2015). Borderland communities, their culture, their constructed identity, and their practices of power all wholeheartedly lend themselves to the definition of borders.

The study of Aboriginal territorialities, which are the dynamic and evolving result of a complex interaction between values, norms, and interests from the centre and from the peripheries, can thus be helpful in understanding how border administration is defined and how it is concretely practiced in borderlands. This approach allows us to question potential changes that can arise on and from the territorial and sociopolitical margins, sites of interaction where the change within any action occurs (Parker 2009). The role of these margins may be observed not only in the historical construction of borders but also in the definition of border policies.

Territorial margins are places where changes occur and where cross-border dynamics can paradoxically contribute to reinforcing the boundary line. Securitization can thus be defined as the recognition and support of cross-border dynamics at the margins as a way to better regulate those margins. Rather than a response to an exceptional situation following a "sudden rupture" in daily life (Gruszczak 2010; Huysmans 1998, 571) that is rhetorically coded as a threat to the survival of the group (McDonald 2008, 567), securitization can be defined as a set of norms that have been constructed—cooperatively and through negotiation—as implicit or explicit codes of behaviour (Paasi 1998, 82). Beyond exceptional security measures or their periodic contestation through demonstrations and conflict, these codes of behaviour define "correct" discourses and practices for Indigenous people and leaders to address border issues. The Foucauldian way of analyzing the government of marginal spaces certainly does not only refer to borderlands; it encompasses a broader situation in which borders can be qualified as "mobile" (Amilhat Szary and Giraut 2015), their location blurred by traceability and processes of de/re-bordering. Nonetheless, borderlands are of increasing interest to policymakers: not only for reasons such as the implementation of high technology, sensors, and cameras in some of those areas but also because of the involvement of borderland peoples in the generalization of surveillance.

Akwesasne: Two Reserves, One Territory

The case of Akwesasne is particularly instructive in tackling questions of securitization and Aboriginal sovereignty. Its geographical situation is quite unique in that this Mohawk territory literally straddles the international boundary between Canada (Ontario and Quebec) and the US (New York), which makes Akwesasne different from the territories of many other Aboriginal communities whose members cross the border on a regular basis. With the exception of the two official ports of entry, most border crossings have always been so informal that visitors barely know whether they are in Ontario, Quebec, or New York. Half of the radio building is located in Canada, while the other half is on American soil. Border markers are covered with vegetation; the only signs of border crossing are changes in pavement and, sometimes, mobile phone networks. During the winter, the "ice bridge" is the easiest way to cross from the US to Quebec. The boundary line separates the Canadian and the American official reserves, with a consequent diversity of legitimate authorities (table 10.1), but both reserves constitute only one territory.

This geographical situation is a strong basis to the claim for sovereignty—even for the reification of sovereignty (Kalman 2016)—and Akwesasne has a strong reputation of political resistance against external imperatives. When the Canada-US boundary was drawn across the territory of Akwesasne in 1842, the Akwesasne Community Proclamation affirmed the maintenance of unity within the territory regardless of jurisdictional and international boundaries (MCA 2013, 23). Despite institutional and political complexity, this affirmation of unity has been maintained, sometimes through the spectacular demonstrations that have occurred since the 1960s. In 2009, for instance, the community mobilized against the Canadian Border Services Agency (CBSA) plan to arm Canadian border officials, forcing the Canadian government to remove the port of entry from Cornwall Island and build a new one outside the reserve (see figure 10.1). The impression that everyday life in Akwesasne revolves around border crossings has become stronger since 2009. To reach the Mohawk Council of Akwesasne's building in Quebec from Cornwall, Ontario, by land, people need to cross the border at the Massena, New York, port of entry, go through the United States, and enter Quebec once in the reserve. Mohawk people who live on Cornwall Island and work in the American part of the reserve must cross through the island, report to CBSA at Cornwall and come back again to return home, which has resulted in significant traffic issues on the bridge. These changes have made daily life in the reserve even more complex; nonetheless, this event has also been perceived as a manifestation of complete Mohawk sovereignty.

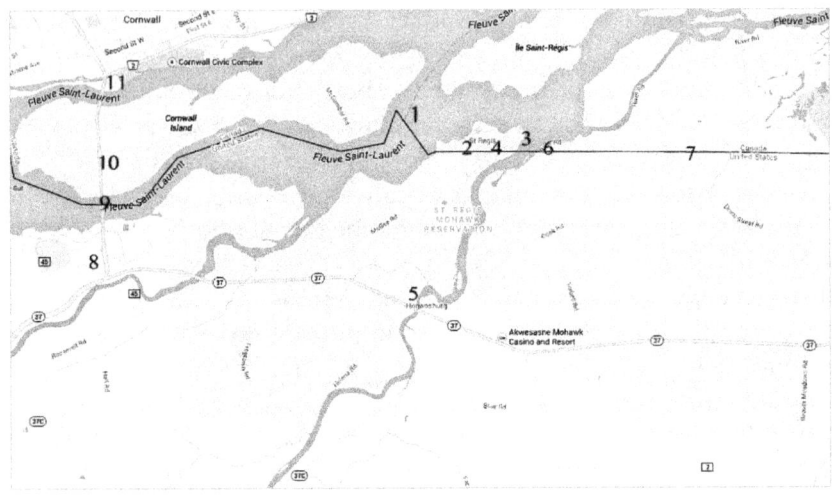

FIGURE 10.1. Map of the border in Akwesasne. *Source:* Mohawk Council of Akwesasne, Map of Akwesasne Borderlands, September 2014.

TABLE 10.1.
Sources of authority in Akwesasne

Name	Mohawk Council of Akwesasne	Mohawk Tribal Council of Saint Regis	Council of Chiefs of the Mohawk Nation	Haudenosaunee Confederacy
Space of Influence	Reserve, Canada	Reserve, United States	Mohawk people	Six Nations of the Iroquois Confederacy

Source: Laetitia Rouvière.

Claiming Aboriginal Sovereignty In Between: Resistance and Diplomacy

In Akwesasne, the most obvious version of cultural affirmation against divisive securitization policies has been through demonstrations, bridge blockades, and activism. Nonetheless, the Akwesasne leaders also affirm Aboriginal culture across the international boundary through specific forms of mobilization, negotiation, and cooperation, opening a dialogue with external authorities on border security policies. Both are manifestations of sovereignty that must be understood by taking into consideration the way in which public action is legitimized within the territory.

The various manifestations of Aboriginal sovereignty in Akwesasne rely on the complex structure of power within the reserve. In addition to the multiple jurisdictions in which Akwesasne is situated, traditionalist and Catholic sources of power in Akwesasne also inform the behaviours of local leaders in their interactions with external agencies. Although most of the population, as well as the elected Chiefs, are Catholic, traditionalist voices emerged in the 1930s (Frisch 1971, 75). The traditionalists claim to be followers of the Longhouse religion, or the Handsome Lake Code and the Great Law of Peace (Venables 2010). The Great Law of Peace is an old agreement defining a clanic organization between the Six Nations (Mohawk, Onondaga, Oneida, Cayuga, Seneca, and Tuscarora nations) that form the Iroquois Confederacy, or Haudenosaunee (Fenton 1998). Traditionalism has a strong role in the political thinking within Akwesasne, especially since the 1970s, when it was recovered by the Warrior movement (Alfred and Lowe 2005). The Warrior Society has provided significant contributions to internal debates about the "correct" way to deal with external agencies. This division of power sources continues to impact the different leadership styles among the Iroquois:

> The difference between the two is that a traditional chief would be quieter; he would definitely speak his language and know a lot about the culture; he would not make a snap decision or be very emotional; he would analyze things, there could be people yelling at him or in his face and in Mohawk you'd say his skin is more than seven spans thick. Well, he would just not react. He would listen to you, he would listen to other people. He would go and consult with his clan and his clan mothers. He would think about it for a while. Maybe a week later, he'd come to a decision. That's a traditional chief. An elected chief would end up on the podium, talk to the crowd, say, "This is what we're going to do right away, this is how we're going to try and resolve it." It's two different leadership methods. (Intergovernmental liaison officer, MCA, interview with author, Akwesasne, October 25, 2014)

In particular, the concept of Aboriginal sovereignty relies on historical diplomatic practices and on the inheritance of the Great Law of Peace (Bedford and Workman 1997). The Kaswentha Wampum Belt symbolizes ancient diplomatic practices as well as the first treaties with colonial powers, supporting the idea that the Mohawk and the

European descendant are two different peoples. The two parallel rows on the Wampum Belt are meant to symbolize an Iroquois canoe and a European ship: the boats travel in the same direction, but never meet each other, like two nations working together as neighbours. The claim for recognition of nationhood and autonomous governance relies on this historical and political background. The idea of sovereignty is part of a political argumentation that confers legitimacy within the community by mixing Catholic and traditionalist thought. Some of the current elected Chiefs—and Grand Chief of the MCA Mike Mitchell (1984–2015), the first to be elected—represent this mix. While preserving the Mohawk traditions, these leaders have learned all the codes to communicate and cooperate efficiently with external agencies.

Toward a Local Appropriation of Border Security Policies

From Space of Exception to Space of Experimentation

If borders and borderlands are generally in "permanent states of exception" (Salter 2006, 169), borderlands can also appear as "spaces of refusal," as alternatives to the domination-resistance binary (Jones 2012, 687; Simpson 2014). Indeed, exceptional measures exist in Akwesasne as well as in other border areas, but practices of refusal of the state's imperatives are taking place within an acceptance of those measures. It is at the margin of the exceptional measures and, at the same time, at the margin of the refusal, that changes occur. The issue of controlling the modalities of security implementation within the reserve is mostly addressed through processes of negotiation and cooperation rather than through opposition. Between the state of exception and a space of refusal, Akwesasne could be qualified as a space of political experimentation: a specific target of border policies that simultaneously serves as a laboratory for the affirmation or the inclusion of Aboriginal positions on border policies. From my point of view, those actions are completely part of the affirmation of sovereignty within this territory. Cooperation is one element of local strategies to affirm cultural specificities and political autonomy. It is a way to survive and a way of finding the margin within which negotiation can take place.

Local leaders' willingness to cooperate with external agencies is illustrated by the organization of local forums that deal with border security. Although national authorities actually organize most of the events, they are local in character. Among them, the MCA has organized two Border Security Summits. These meetings were designed to gather representatives from various government agencies as well as Aboriginal leaders in order to allow everyone involved to express concerns over border security policies and practices. The first summit was held in March 2006 in the town of Cornwall, off reserve, and the second took place in September 2014 within the territory, at the Mohawk Casino of Akwesasne.

Despite the fact that only representatives from the US, not Canada, attended the 2014 summit, these events are illustrations of local leadership's commitment to taking a stand on national border security policies. They are arenas of political visibility in which issues specific to Akwesasne can be addressed, as well as broader concerns regarding Aboriginal rights. This local event could be a model for other political arenas: the National Congress of American Indians expressed their interest in reproducing the experience in other places, and in July 2017, the Kootenai Tribe of Idaho and the Saint Regis Mohawk Tribe organized a Northern Tribal Border Summit in Shakopee, Minnesota. The confrontation of border issues within borderlands thus creates a space of discussion with the governments and leads to a broader mobilization based on Aboriginal rights to cross the border freely. In the following sections, I will analyze the three main themes that were addressed in the forums—identification measures for Indigenous people, cultural sensitivity training for border officers, and law enforcement cooperation—in terms of building border security from the bottom-up.

Bordering Mohawk Identity

One of the main border security issues that Indigenous people currently face concerns specific identification documents required at ports of entry. As a consequence of the Jay Treaty of 1794, Aboriginal people are allowed to cross the Canada-US border with their Certificate of Indian Status or status card. In the Iroquois case, the Haudenosaunee passport was first used in 1923, but the long struggle for its legitimacy has been reactivated recently by new identification requirements (see Weigand and Howell, this volume, chapter 11). Under the Western Hemisphere Travel Initiative (WHTI), every traveller has to cross the border with a passport (Tolazzi 2011). For North

American Indians, a new card is required: the Secure Certificate of Indian Status (SCIS) in its "border-crossing format," which contains a Machine Readable Zone. These recent changes have raised the issue of citizenship and sovereignty among Aboriginal people. In Akwesasne, many members of the community refuse to be defined as Canadians or Americans when they cross the border: their belonging is closely tied to the cross-border territory (Grinde 2002).

Consequently, identification was the first theme that was addressed during the Border Security Summit in September 2014. Representatives of the Pascua Yaqui Tribe in Arizona presented their "Enhanced Tribal Card Program," which was the first of its kind to be financed by the US Federal Emergency Management Agency. The program was implemented between 2009 and 2011; in 2014 about three thousand cards were held by members of the tribe. This program was presented as a model for other Aboriginal groups, but many questions arose among the participants about the use of data and the potential for profiling and discrimination based on individuals' past criminal activities. A great deal of apprehension relating to the use of data and the declaration of citizenship remains within the community: "We want to control our information. We actually don't want anyone else to have access to it. The big part of it was the question of citizenship. There's a lot of people, including myself, who believe that we are Mohawk citizens who happen to live in the United States, but we also are Mohawk citizens of the Mohawk nation. The same thing on the other side" (Chief, Saint Regis Mohawk Tribe [US], interview with author, Saint Regis, October 25, 2014). How does one find a secured status card that would not only fulfill security requirements but also maintain Akwesasne's sovereignty? This is a sensitive subject and a source of internal debate, as it would require tribal members to choose one of the three Mohawk Councils to make the new card. Who should define the Akwesasne identity: the Canadian, the American, or the traditional Mohawk council?

> To get our local chiefs to agree with three councils together (a US council, a Canadian council, the traditional council), getting them to agree on one swipe card is a tricky thing. For me, if you had the symbol of the tribal council for the US, the technology on the back would be the exact same. It's just the design of it, let's say the tribal council emblem for those that would like to follow the US elected council, you had a Mohawk council emblem for

those that follow that system. And you had a traditional council, let's say a five-nation council, on the front. If you had the same technology, it's the exact same card, just a different colour and design, then I think we could agree. (Assistant to the Grand Chief of the MCA [Canada], interview with author, Akwesasne, October 29, 2014)

In addition to the symbolic aspect, the cost to create such a document is another issue of debate. Contrary to the Canadian government, the US government offers financial support for the tribes to create their own card, as they did for the Pascua Yaqui. This could be the easiest way to create a secured card for Mohawk citizens, but this option would mean that the Council of Saint Regis in the American region would need to lead the process. At the time of my fieldwork, the three councils were having internal debates about the common design and the visual aspect of the card. Finally, the Haudenosaunee Confederacy, through a documentation committee, announced that new cards would be available soon for Iroquois citizens. The symbolic choice of logo and visual appearance of the future card is a source of much debate, as it will ultimately determine whether the Mohawk people of Akwesasne identify themselves with the Iroquois Confederacy only or more specifically with either the American or the Canadian parts of the Mohawk territory. Notwithstanding the future card's visual composition, all councils agree with the need to create a secured card in order to fulfill the new requirements.

The practice of Indigenous sovereignty does not rely upon a radical opposition to external imperatives. Instead, it hinges on the definition of a specific way to fulfill sovereignty requirements while respecting the community's integrity, as defined by local leaders. This is another illustration of the negotiated way in which Mohawk identity is defined and bordered. The potential traceability of Akwesasne residents that could result from such security requirements is a real concern that has been expressed within the community, but the most current discussion in the community deals with the way in which Mohawk identity will be recognized in the midst of the changes.

Performing the Border Mohawk Style

The reinforcement of controls, especially those at the Canadian border, affects cultural practices that involve gatherings, such as powwows and other ceremonies. The transportation of sacred items to these events has been increasingly problematic within the last few years. The use of eagle feathers, sweet grass, sacred medicine bundles, and ceremonial tobacco in the ceremonies that take place on either side of the border is not specific to Mohawk people; yet, the practice is more visible and common in such a borderland community. No specific rules have been implemented to more strictly control these sacred items. On the contrary, the transportation of eagle feathers to or from either country is no longer illegal as of February 2003. However, broader practices of control at the border have been affecting those activities in a different way. Some objects considered sacred are normally handled by certain individuals only. And tobacco pouches that are transported for ceremonies cannot be opened:

> The reason behind that is that because it takes many years of working with that tobacco pouch. If you open that pouch, that fellow has to start all over again and he's going to be mad. But you're not going to understand why he's mad... [A]nd you're going to arrest him....It may have taken him 7, 10, 15 years of work behind that tobacco pouch to make it powerful and all of a sudden you're going to open it to see what's in it and all of the power is gone. (Chief, MCA [Canada], interview with author, Akwesasne, October 9, 2014)

For many border officers, anyone who carries objects that cannot be touched or opened is suspected of illegal activities. Although the activities are not comparable, the tobacco issue is particularly strong in this area as Akwesasne is often identified as a main corridor for smuggling. The tobacco contraband that escalated during the 1980s found continuity with drug, arms, and human trafficking in the following decades. It is extremely difficult for Mohawk authorities as well as for external law enforcement agencies to implement control over such activities in this territory. Nonetheless, although it has been proved that most of the smuggling leaders come from outside of the reserve (Poiret and Beylier 2016), members of the community are often targeted as potential smugglers or criminals.

To avoid any conflation of the transportation of sacred items or other cultural practices with organized crime and to reconcile the CBSA and the Mohawk community after the events of 2009, some dialogue between "security" and "culture" has taken place. Some negotiations took place "in between" to demonstrate the respect of cultural specificities in Akwesasne. First, the position of Aboriginal liaison officer was created in 2009 by the CBSA in order to facilitate dialogue between authorities about misunderstandings that have led to an increasing number of complaints of harassment from the members of the community. Second, cultural sensitivity training was arranged for CBSA officers. The three-day programs entailed courses given by Aboriginal Chiefs on cultural specificities that involve cross-border mobility. During an interview, a Chief from the Saint Regis Mohawk Tribe affirmed: "There's some cultural sensitivity. It's a true measure of sovereignty, where we are able to say to our community that we did this." Similarly, a Chief from the Mohawk Council of Akwesasne, who participated in this experience, asserted that, following 2009, the CBSA had no other option than this training to maintain links with the community of Akwesasne:

> [We said] we're going to be neighbours. You move to Cornwall, that's fine, we don't have a problem with that. But we still have to use the borders. We have to figure out some way of doing this that makes sense or our people aren't going to report. It's not that we're going to tell them not to report, it's the People: we know our People. If things don't change, they're just not going to report. And then what are you going to do? Are you going to arrest the whole community? (Chief, MCA [Canada], interview with author, Akwesasne, October 9, 2014)

Nonetheless, he has a nuanced appreciation of the results of this program. Although the border agents are more and more aware of Akwesasne's cultural specificities in their daily work, the general policy guidelines remain an issue: "That hasn't changed because that is dictated from operational policy. Their operational policies and their standard operating procedures tell them they have to do things this way, but when they're doing things, they are cognizant of some of the information we gave them" (MCA 2014a). This illustrates the contingent way in which public policies are implemented not only according to the agents in the field (Muller 2000) but also according to the cultural context. The involvement of Mohawk Chiefs in the local adjustments that are made to implement security policies at the port of entry is a way to create links or to improve the mutual understanding between the community and CBSA agents, through reaffirming the legitimacy of Aboriginal cross-border practices and to support a more effective implementation of national policies.

Even though the cultural sensitivity programs do not radically change the Mohawks' daily experiences at the border, the programs are components in the evolving definition of Aboriginal sovereignty. The reinforcement of controls is an opportunity for the leaders to take a stand on an older concern regarding Aboriginal rights to cross the borders, especially with regard to the transportation of goods and taxation. At the same time, the recognition of cultural identity in the concrete implementation of border policies involves local leaders in the securitization of the border and in the erosion of Aboriginal sovereignty as a practice of decision-making in the territory.

Implementing Security Through Law Enforcement Agencies' Cooperation

The increasing inclusion of the Mohawk police in the implementation and regulation of border security within the territory could be interpreted as another way of affirming sovereignty in Akwesasne. In Akwesasne, despite the existence of different policing units in both the Canadian and American areas, Indigenous policing remains a symbol of autonomy and a contributor to border security issues. Since the 1990s, there has been increasing cooperation between Indigenous police forces and external law enforcement agencies. Self-directed police services were created in Akwesasne in 1989 (Clairmont 2006), before any governance agreements between different law enforcement agencies (Stenning 1996). Cooperation between Indigenous police and external law enforcement agencies, however, did not start until after 9/11. Although "sovereignty issues" and the consequent necessity of cooperation were a concern for the US government from the 1990s (US Congress 1999, 72), cooperation has only been formalized more recently in Canada, through such agreements as the Akwesasne Partnership Initiative in 2002, which created a joint investigative team between the Akwesasne Mohawk Police and the RCMP. Other initiatives in this regard include the Integrated Border Enforcement Team (IBET), which is made up of, among others, the CBSA and US Customs and Border Protection (CBP), and the Border Enforcement Security Task Force (BEST), which, in the case of the Massena, New York, task force, includes the Akwesasne Mohawk Police and the Saint Regis Tribal Police in addition to Canadian and

American law enforcement agencies. The main goal of BEST is training and information sharing, as the different agencies each have their own unique types of information. At first, Mohawk authorities had very little information about the activities of other agencies surrounding Akwesasne. So, with this initiative, they are becoming more and more informed about and involved in those activities and in information sharing. Second, because the Mohawk police are community-based, their officers can help external law enforcement agencies to understand Mohawk cultural dynamics. But questions remain: How is this cooperation perceived in the community, and what is the concrete impact on security issues? As one of the public reports (Public Safety Canada 2012) outlines, there is a risk of stopping only the "couriers" and not more important criminals.

The Akwesasne Mohawk Police first engaged in agency cooperation, according to its Chief, to access additional funding and to get involved in investigations that affected the territory. Interagency cooperation has also had the effect of strengthening policing within the community:

> There are certain reasons why we have agreements with outside agencies. It's for the protection of our community and the stability of our community. The last thing we would like is to have somebody else tell us how to take care of our community. That's not their right....We said, "You guys gotta behave when you come here. You know, because if you hit anybody, we cannot and will not guarantee your safety here because you've violated that trust." They understand that, so they don't fly up and down our roads like they used to. It's all about cooperation." (Chief, Saint Regis Mohawk Tribe [US], interview with author, Saint Regis, October 25, 2014)

Another compelling reason to cooperate is to change the perception that the Akwesasne community is involved in or supportive of criminal activities in their territory: "Like they say, this is the largest unmanned border in wherever, you know. We understand and take our security here very, very seriously. We don't want bad people coming through here and we don't want to be blamed for bad people coming through here and creating atrocities some place. We don't want to be known for that" (Chief, Saint Regis Mohawk Tribe, [US], interview with author, Saint Regis, October 25, 2014). Cooperation finally appears to be the last way to balance cultural affirmation with external security imperatives:

> I think, you know, in the art of cooperation, you get a lot of things done. It's easier when you're not adversaries, but you also don't want to be too friendly with them, because that creates another issue, too. To use that old saying, you keep your friends close and your enemies even closer. I'm sure they understand that phrase, too. They don't do things because they like us, but they know some time down the road they're going to need something from us. It works both ways and that happens over there all the time, too. I guess that's one of the uglinesses of government. It's give-and-take; it's compromise. I think that over the years we've become really good at it." (Chief, MCA [Canada], interview with author, Akwesasne, October 9, 2014)

Cooperation is thus a form of governance, for both Aboriginal leaders as well as for federal agencies. Local involvement in the enhancement of security measures might be the most productive way to control degree to which external agencies intrude into the community. In 2014, the RCMP announced the implementation of the Border Integrity Technology Enhancement Project (BITEP) to erect an electronic surveillance fence on the Canada-US border in Ontario and Quebec. The MCA (2014) responded: "Putting Akwesasne into a police state that is already surrounded by security cameras and a multitude of law enforcement agencies can be viewed as an attack on not only our sovereignty; but also on our human rights, mobility rights and privacy rights." Opposed to the BITEP, the leaders of Akwesasne focused on the necessity of law enforcement cooperation as well as funding for additional patrol officers and the creation of a full-time marine unit in the reserve: "At a time when Canada is planning to spend tens of millions more on law enforcement, Akwesasne continues to propose the least expensive path of partnerships and increased cooperation" (MCA 2014a). This pragmatic way of affirming the role of local authorities in the implementation of public policies demonstrates how cultural resistance to external imperatives can work, to some extent, through active participation in the redefinition and negotiation of national rules.

Building Border Security from the Bottom Up?

On the Canada-US border, two different federal strategies are illustrated in the case of Akwesasne: while there are exceptional instances of participation of local leaders in the implementation of security policies in Canada, this participation is part of a national policy design in the US. From a local perspective, the American strategy might be conceived as more inclusive, even if the potential effects in terms of privacy and autonomy are quite similar. The integration of Indigenous communities in federal strategies—and the fact that the relationship between the Mohawk leaders and federal authorities is marked by less conflict in the US than in Canada—is important when local leaders negotiate with Canadian agencies. Indeed, in reaction to the events of 2009, both the cultural sensitivity training program and the position of Aboriginal liaison officer position were created ad hoc for the Cornwall port of entry. These administrative positions and practices do not exist at other Canadian ports of entry; however, both have more systematic analogues at the federal level in the US since the creation of the Department of Homeland Security (DHS). On the American side, the Tribal Homeland Security Grant Program targets reservations located near strategic points to cooperate on the enforcement of security policies (DHS 2013). While cooperation between law enforcement agencies is part of a larger federal strategy for border security in the US (GAO 2013; NCAI 2013; ONDCP 2012), this level of cooperation is specific to the case of Akwesasne in Canada.

The involvement of First Nations in border security is much more institutionalized in the US and responds to a renewed vision of border security in terms of "perimeter" (*United States-Canada* 2011). In this sense, borderlands can be spaces where Indigenous leaders can use the national referents from both countries as local resources. At the same time, they can be spaces where the transfer of public policies from the US to Canada is concretely framed. In their struggle to affirm cultural specificities through cooperation with external agencies, Indigenous leaders can become agents for the circulation of American norms for security.

Conclusion

In Akwesasne, the right to move freely across the international boundary and the right to make decisions in the way border security is implemented within the territory are affirmed through cooperation with external agencies. In this context, the affirmation of cultural specificities and the involvement of the local discourses in security imperatives are not mutually exclusive. Borderlands thus appear as spaces of negotiation and laboratories of public policy. Therefore, beyond rules of security, what is at stake is the construction of norms of securitization? The enhancement of border security policies does not only work through the imposition of juridical rules produced by the state but also through the diffusion of norms. Those norms are not proposed, nor imposed, by a unique type of political stakeholder. Instead, security norms are taken over by each group of actors involved in the process; they are created and modified through the interactions and cooperation between those actors. The norms have an effect on the application and reinterpretation of security policies within Indigenous borderlands. They are constructed at every level, scale, and dimension of Indigenous border territorialities and contribute to the evolving definition of Indigenous (cross)border culture.

References

Alfred, Taiaiake. 1999. *Peace, Power, Righteousness: An Indigenous Manifesto.* Toronto: Oxford University Press.

Alfred, Taiaiake, and Lana Lowe. 2005. "Warrior Societies in Contemporary Indigenous Communities." Ipperwash Inquiry Research Paper. Policing Aboriginal Occupations and Aboriginal/Police Relations. http://www.attorneygeneral.jus.gov.on.ca.3pdns.korax.net/inquiries/ipperwash/policy_part/research/pdf/Alfred_and_Lowe.pdf.

Amilhat Szary, Anne-Laure, and Frédéric Giraut. 2015. *Borderities and the Politics of Contemporary Mobile Borders.* Basingstoke, UK: Palgrave Macmillan.

Anderson, Malcolm. 1996. *Frontiers: Territory and State Formation in the Modern World.* Cambridge: Polity Press.

Bedford, David, and Thom Workman. 1997. "The Great Law of Peace: Alternative Inter-Nation(al) Practices and the Iroquoian Confederacy." *Alternatives: Global, Local, Political* 22 (1): 87–111.

Brubaker, Rogers. 2001. "Au-delà de l'identité." *Actes de la recherche en sciences sociales* 13 (1): 66–85.

Brunet-Jailly, Emmanuel. 2005. "Theorizing Borders: An Interdisciplinary Perspective." *Geopolitics* 10 (4): 633–649.

Byrd, Jodi A. 2014. "Introduction: Indigeneity's Difference: Methodology and the Structures of Sovereignty." *J19: The Journal of Nineteenth-Century Americanists* 2, no. 11 (Spring): 131–136.

Clairmont, Don. 2006. "Aboriginal Policing in Canada: An Overview of Developments in First Nations." Ipperwash Inquiry Research Paper. Policing Aboriginal Occupations and Aboriginal/Police Relations. https://www.attorneygeneral.jus.gov.on.ca/inquiries/ipperwash/policy_part/research/pdf/Clairmont_Aboriginal_Policing.pdf.

Coulthard, Glen S. 2007. "Subjects of Empire: Indigenous Peoples and the 'Politics of Recognition' in Canada." *Contemporary Political Theory* 6 (4): 437–460.

Daudelin, Jean, Stephanie Soiffer, and Jeff Willows. 2013. *Border Integrity, Illicit Tobacco, and Canada's Security*. Ottawa: Macdonald-Laurier Institute.

DHS (US Department of Homeland Security). 2013. *FY 2013 Tribal Homeland Security Grant Program (THSGP)*. https://www.fema.gov/media-library-data/628ce627e2238ad34641d53f15321fad/FY_2013_Tribal_Homeland_Security_Grant_Program_Fact_Sheet+-+Final.pdf.

Fenton, William N. 1998. *The Great Law and the Longhouse: A Political History of the Iroquois Confederacy*. New York: Library of Congress.

Frisch, Jack A. 1971. "Factionalism, Pan-Indianism, Tribalism, and The Contemporary Political Behaviour of the St. Regis Mohawks." *Man in the Northeast* 2:75–81.

GAO (US Government Accountability Office). 2013. *Report to the Honourable John Teste, US Senate. Border Security: Partnership Agreements and Enhanced Oversight Could Strengthen Coordination of Efforts on Indian Reservations*. Report to the Honourable John Teste, US Senate, April 5, 2013. http://www.gao.gov/products/GAO-13-352.

George-Kanentiio, Douglas M. 2008. *Iroquois on Fire: A Voice from the Mohawk Nation*. Lincoln: University of Nebraska Press.

Grinde, Donald A. 2002. "Iroquois Border Crossings: Place, Politics, and the Jay Treaty." In *Globalization on the Line: Culture, Capital, and Citizenship at U.S. Borders*, edited by Claudia Sadowski-Smith, 167–180. New York: Palgrave.

Gruszczak, Artur. 2010. "The Securitization of the Eastern Borders of the European Union. Walls or Bridges?" Paper presented at the 40th Annual Conference of the University Association for Contemporary European Studies, Bruges, September 6–8, 2010.

Huysmans, Jef. 1998. "The Question of the Limit: Desecuritization and the Aesthetics of Horror in Political Realism." *Millenium* 27 (3): 569–589.

Jones, Reece. 2012. "Spaces of Refusal: Rethinking Sovereign Power and Resistance at the Border." *Annals of the Association of American Geographers* 102 (3): 685–699.

Kalman, Ian. 2016. "Framing Borders: Indigenous Difference at the Canada/US Border." PhD diss., McGill University.

Konrad, Victor. 2015. "Toward a Theory of Borders in Motion." *Journal of Borderlands Studies* 30 (1): 1–17.

Konrad, Victor, and Heather N. Nicol. 2008. *Beyond Walls: Re-inventing the Canada-United States Borderlands*. Farnham, UK: Ashgate.
MCA (Mohawk Council of Akwesasne). 2014. "MCA Responds to RCMP Surveillance Fence Announcement." *Indian Time*. November 20, 2014. https://www.indiantime.net/story/2014/11/20/news/mca-responds-to-rcmp-surveillance-fence-announcement/15998.html.
———. 2013. "Akwesasne Community Proclamation, June 14, 1842." *Onkwe'ta:ke, The Mohawk Council of Akwesasne's Monthly Community Newsletter*, November 11, 2013. http://www.akwesasne.ca/wp-content/uploads/Onkwetake/final_november_2013_onkwetake.pdf.
McDonald, Matt. 2008. "Securitization and the Construction of Security." *European Journal of International Relations* 14 (4): 563–587.
Muller, Pierre. 2000. "L'analyse cognitive des politiques publiques: vers une sociologie politique de l'action publique." *Revue française de science politique* 50 (2): 189–208.
NCAI (National Congress of American Indians). 2013. *Tribal Homeland Security, Border Issues, and Stafford Act Implementation. Tribal Leaders Briefing Book*. November 2013. http://files.ncai.org/broadcasts/2013/November/c6b%20-%20Homeland-Border-Stafford.pdf.
Newman, David. 2006. "The Lines that Continue to Separate Us: Borders in Our 'Borderless' World." *Progress in Human Geography* 30 (2): 143–161.
Novak, Paolo. 2011. "The Flexible Territoriality of Borders." *Geopolitics* 16 (4): 741–767.
ONDCP (US Office of National Drug Control Policy). 2012. *National Northern Border Counternarcotics Strategy*. January. https://obamawhitehouse.archives.gov/sites/default/files/ondcp/policy-and-research/national_northern_border_counternarcotics_strategy_.pdf.
Paasi, Anssi. 1998. "Boundaries as Social Processes: Territoriality in the World of Flows." *Geopolitics* 3 (1): 69–88.
Parker, Noel. 2009. "From Borders to Margins: A Deleuzian Ontology for Identities in the Postinternational Environment." *Alternatives: Global, Local, Political* 34 (1): 17–39.
Pertusati, Linda. 1997. *In Defense of Mohawk Land: Ethnopolitical Conflict in Native North America*. New York: State University of New York.
Poiret, Guillaume, and Pierre-Alexandre Beylier. 2016. "La réserve autochtone 'transfrontalière' d'Akwesasne entre Canada et États-Unis, zone de contrebande et faille dans la sécurisation de la frontière." *Territoire en mouvement*, no. 29. https://doi.org/10.4000/tem.3238.
Pratt, Martin, and Janet B. Allison. 2000. *Borderlands Under Stress*. London: Kluwer Law International.
Public Safety Canada. 2012. *2012–2013 Evaluation of the Akwesasne Partnership Initiative*. Final Report. December 10, 2012. http://www.

publicsafety.gc.ca/cnt/rsrcs/pblctns/vltn-kwssn-prtnrshp-2012-13/vltn-kwssn-prtnrshp-2012-13-eng.pdf.
Rouvière, Laetitia. 2012. "A la frontière de l'État : gouvernement et territorialités aymaras au Chili." PhD diss., Université de Grenoble, Institut d'Études Politiques.
Sack, Robert. 1986. *Human Territoriality. Its Theory and History*. Cambridge: Cambridge University Press.
Sahlins, Peter. 1991. *Boundaries: The Making of France and Spain in the Pyrenees*. Berkeley: University of California Press.
Salter, Mark B. 2006. "The Global Visa Regime and the Political Technologies of the International Self: Borders, Bodies, Biopolitics." *Alternatives: Global, Local, Political* 31 (2): 167–189.
Simpson, Audra. 2014. *Mohawk Interruptus: Political Life Across the Borders of Settler States*. Durham, NC: Duke University Press.
Sparke, Matthew. 2008. "Political Geography—Political Geographies of Globalization III: Resistance." *Progress in Human Geography* 32 (3): 423–440.
Spencer, Bree. 2011. "Akwesasne: A Complex Challenge to U.S. Northern Border Security." *The National Strategy Forum Review* 2 (3): 1–5.
Stenning, Philip C. 1996. *Police Governance in First Nations in Ontario*. Toronto: Centre of Criminology, University of Toronto.
Taylor, Peter J. 1994. "The State as Container: Territoriality in the Modern World-System." *Progress in Human Geography* 18 (2): 151–162.
Tolazzi, Sandrine. 2011. "'May These Gates Never Be Closed': L'initiative relative aux voyages dans l'hémisphère occidental et ses conséquences sur les Premières nations du Canada." In *A Safe and Secure Canada: Politique et enjeux sécuritaires au Canada depuis le 11 septembre 2001*, edited by Eric Tabuteau and Sandrine Tolazzi, 137–152. Brussels: Peter Lang.
Tully, James. 2000. "The Struggles of Indigenous Peoples for and of Freedom." In *Political Theory and the Rights of Indigenous Peoples*, edited by Duncan Iveson, Paul Patton, and Will Sanders, 257–288. Cambridge: Cambridge University Press.
United States-Canada Beyond the Border: A Shared Vision for Perimeter Security and Economic Competitiveness. Action Plan. 2011. https://www.dhs.gov/xlibrary/assets/wh/us-canada-btb-action-plan.pdf.
US Congress. House of Representatives. Committee on the Judiciary. 1999. *Law Enforcement Problems at the Border Between the United States and Canada: Drug Smuggling, Illegal Immigration and Terrorism. Hearing before the Subcommittee on Immigration and Claims of the Committee on the Judiciary*. 106th Cong., 1st sess., April 14, 1999.
Venables, Robert W. 2010. "The Clearings and The Woods: The Haudenosaunee (Iroquois) Landscape—Gendered and Balanced." In *The Archaeology and Preservation of Gendered Landscapes*, edited by Sherene Baugher and Suzanne Spencer-Wood, 21–55. New York: Springer.

CHAPTER 11

Sport, Globalization, and the Bordering Process

The Iroquois Nationals Lacrosse Team and the Issue of Contested National Identities

Heidi Weigand and Colin Howell

Sport in today's globalized world plays an especially significant role in nation building and the bordering process. It has done for centuries. As far back as the mid-nineteenth century, organized sport developed as a handmaiden of emergent industrialized nation-states in Europe and North America, and proponents believed that team sport enhanced "respectable" morality, healthy living, patriotism, and military preparedness (Metcalfe 1987; Kidd 1996; Pope 1997; Dyreson 1998; Howell 2001; Boucher 2003). In turn, games such as football, baseball, and hockey acted as unifying rituals, taking on the status of "national pastimes" in what Benedict Anderson has called the "imagined communities" of nationhood (Anderson 1983). With the revival of the Olympic Games at the end of the nineteenth century, sport became inexorably and institutionally linked to national rivalries, although Baron Pierre de Coubertin's original purpose had been to rise above the conflicts and disputes that accompanied an increasingly bordered and militarized world. Today, the Olympics, along with World Championships in a range of sports and games, reveal the extent to which globalization, the nation-state, and relentless international economic expansion contribute to and legitimize a powerfully interconnected transnational sporting culture (Martyn, Barney, and Wenn 2004; Maguire 2011).

It is important to remember, however, that sport then and now has always been contested terrain and debates about its social value and contribution to identity formation and national patriotism extend far beyond the sporting pitch or venue (Dyreson, Mangan, and Park 2012). Sportive nation building has faced particular resistance over the years from those struggling through the decolonization process, from others intent on reversing the process of cultural appropriation that accompanied the expansion of empire and its impact on Indigenous peoples (Downey 2012; Poulter 2010), and from local communities intent on shaping sport to serve their own needs and traditions. Sociologist Roland Robertson coined the term "glocalization" to describe the mitigation of tensions between globalizing influences and the requirements of hinterland, colonial, Indigenous, and borderland communities (Robertson 1995). Indeed, localized populations were not simply acted upon by relentless metropolitan and global influences but have found ways to exercise their own agency as well.

Understanding how sport operates in cross-border settings is a particularly valuable way to investigate the "glocalization" process. Test cases of how this works—like the one we offer here—are thus not only welcome and necessary but ubiquitous as well. Whether our focus is bullfighting on both sides of the Mexican-American border in the late nineteenth century (Beezley 1989), Aboriginal influences in the development of Australian football or rugby in New Zealand (Hay 2019), the blending of European and Indigenous traditions in Anaulataq or "Inuit baseball" throughout the circumpolar Arctic (Howell and Fletcher 1997), or in the multiplicity of transnational configurations of sporting culture around the world, borderland sports culture allows us to appreciate the tensions between metropolitan sporting influences and local needs. Seen from the borderland, sport takes on a vastly different meaning than from an imperial, national, or metropolitan perspective.

It is only in the last couple of decades that sports scholars have seriously confronted what Colin Howell and Daryl Leeworthy call the "metropolitan fallacy" (Howell and Leeworthy 2010). They have increasingly challenged the argument of scholars like Allen Guttmann who see modern sport as essentially a metropolitan creation exported to hinterland or colonial regions as part of a modernizing and globalizing process. In *Games and Empires*, Guttmann (1994) imagined a relatively benign and uncontested process of diffusion where sporting culture moved from cosmopolitan imperial centres to less modern hinterland regions and facilitated, in turn, a transition from traditionalism to modernity. Many scholars now suggest that this unidirectional model fails to capture the complexity of the process and describe diffusion as a multidirectional process of cultural exchange that accompanies the globalization process but is shaped and adjusted to reflect the particular experience and requirements of local communities (Van Bottenburg 2010; Reid and Reid 2015). In the Canadian context, for example, local settler colonies and Indigenous communities received games such as cricket, rugby, and football and put them to local rather than national or imperial purposes (Reid 2018; Leeworthy 2015). In the northeastern borderlands, moreover, games and pastimes like baseball, boxing, hockey, sailing, and long-distance running had little to do with nation-building or metropolitan power (Howell 1995, 2002; Holman 2004; Ross 2008; Dimmel 2010).

The question of how the experience of Indigenous people cuts across an older narrative of modernization and metropolitan authority is a particularly important one. As Bruce Trigger pointed out in *Natives and Newcomers* almost forty years ago, the modernization model exerted extremely deleterious effects on First Nations communities (Trigger 1986). It created a stereotype of static, unchanging communities, whose members lacked the capacity for adaptiveness and innovation. By extension, it was also assumed—and this without any grounding in research—that the inability of Indigenous communities to adjust to the modern world was the source of their continuing problems. Fortunately, recent scholarship has made the pejorative assumptions of the metropolitan thesis untenable (Forsyth and Giles 2013).

Informed in particular by Allan Downey's *The Creator's Game: Lacrosse, Identity and Indigenous Nationhood* and the work of others mentioned above, this paper focuses on the struggle of Indigenous communities to assert their identity(ies) within a contested northeastern borderland and under the influence of the globalizing processes involving sport (Downey 2018). More particularly, it addresses the restricted agency of the Iroquois Nationals lacrosse team and its hopes of representing its own nation at the 2010 World Lacrosse Championship in the United Kingdom. The case exposes modern day colonial power relationships involving Canada, the United Kingdom, and the United States, with the Haudenosaunee peoples and Iroquois Nation caught in a complex web of increasing national security concerns, international and nation-state conflicts, and the engagement of political voices raised through new media channels to support the goals and dreams of both communities and the athletes who represent them. The conflict also produces an opportunity to explore the intersectional dimensions of national identity and contested borderland communities through the prism of sport.

The Haudenosaunee Confederacy: Lacrosse and Collective National Identity

The Iroquois Confederacy, as referred to by the French, is properly known as the Haudenosaunee Confederacy (Ramsden 2006; Haudenosaunee Confederacy, n.d.). It is an example of a northern borderland nation with territories in Quebec and Ontario, and across the border in New York State, creating a unique national identity that crosses colonial borders. For the Haudenosaunee peoples, the traditional game of lacrosse has been central to their collective identity. The Iroquois Nationals lacrosse team, moreover, has been recognized as one of the best teams in the world, with a third place standing in the 2014 World Championship in Denver, Colorado. The team promotes the Indigenous origins of the game of lacrosse in many ways and through its website timeline. The website lists one of the first encounters with lacrosse by a colonial in 1636, when French missionary Father Jean Brébeuf described the game as "le jeu de la crosse." Later, in 1750, the Mohawks taught the game to the French Canadians in and around Montréal, and in 1844 the first official game was held between the Iroquois and Canadians, with the Iroquois producing a seventeen-year winning streak, demonstrating their strong command of the game. In 1867, lacrosse arrived in Britain when an eighteen-member team from Akwesasne, sponsored by the Montreal Lacrosse Club, toured Britain. Although the Iroquois Nationals website suggests that the first English lacrosse club was formed in Stockport in 1875, the impact of the 1867 tour was more immediate. A number of teams emerged in the fall of 1867, and a National Lacrosse Association was formed in London on January 15, 1868. A second tour followed in 1876, led by George Beers, who had codified the rules of the game and advocated for its adoption as Canada's "national sport." After this tour, the game spread across the United Kingdom to Scotland and Wales (Howell and Leeworthy 2017).

According to the Iroquois Nationals timeline, the Indians were banned from international play in 1880 with inferences to their natural ability, and for that reason they were not allowed to compete with those who adhered to the ideals of "gentlemanly" amateurism associated with the later Olympic Games ("Timeline," n.d.). Similarly, in 1932, the Iroquois Nation was banned from international competition as players were deemed to be professional based on their participation in various box lacrosse leagues (T. Smith 1998). Lacrosse was an Olympic sport in 1904 and 1908, with the Canadians winning gold both times. However, lacrosse has not been an official Olympic sport since 1908. As a result, in 1932, an Iroquois team participated in the Los Angeles games when it was a demonstration sport. In 1967, Canada hosted the first World Lacrosse Championship and in 1983 the Iroquois Nationals lacrosse team was formed ("Timeline," n.d.).

The Haudenosaunee Confederacy over time has been comprised of six nations: initially the Seneca, Mohawk, Oneida, Onondaga, Cayuga, and later joined by the Tuscarora Nation in 1722. The population is estimated at 125,000, with 80,000 within the United States' geographical borders and 45,000 in Canada (Haudenosaunee Confederacy 2016). The national flag represents unity among the members of the Haudenosaunee Confederacy. In keeping with the Haudenosaunee's emphasis on unity and peace, the game of lacrosse is regarded as the Creator's game, played to give thanks and praise to the gods (Calder and Fletcher 2011). The Iroquois Nationals lacrosse team embraces this spiritual heritage in every game and in many cases players are using wooden lacrosse sticks carved for them by their fathers. In an interview, Brett Bucktooth said: "My father put a wooden lacrosse stick into my crib when I was a baby, and now that I have a son, I put a lacrosse stick into his crib." He continued, "In our culture, we all start playing lacrosse young" ("Iroquois Lacrosse Team Denied" 2010).

The game of lacrosse is no longer an Olympic sport, but there is a movement led by the Federation of International Lacrosse (FIL) to reinstate the game in the Olympics. Acceptance as an Olympic sport requires a following of the sport on four continents, with seventy-five nations competing. There were twenty-nine competing teams in the 2010 World Championship, so the movement is progressing but will likely take some time. This leaves the World Championships as the pinnacle event, played every four years. The last World Championship was held in 2018 in the United Kingdom. The Iroquois, Canadian, American, and Australian teams continue to dominate the field, with a continuous presence in the top four when participating. The sport has helped the Iroquois Confederacy gain credibility as a nation on the world scene. Recognition as a nation in the eyes of the public seems to have been forged through sport: however, recognition through traditional national identity policies, procedures, and legislation has been far less evident. For example, the Iroquois Confederacy passport, although recognized in North America, is not recognized by all countries. One that does not is the United Kingdom.

Not all Identities are Created Equal: Indigenous Nationality in the International World Order

The debate over the Iroquois team nationality is part of a long-standing geo-cultural borderland dispute that was brought to the international stage when the Iroquois Nationals team was banned from travelling to the United Kingdom to play in the 2010 World Lacrosse Championship in Manchester, England. We explore the complex web of issues that ultimately led to the Iroquois Nationals players being excluded from the game their ancestors had brought to the world's attention so many centuries ago and the devastating impact on the players' hopes, dreams, and expectations to be included in the World Championships of a game pioneered by their ancestors. At the heart of the issue was the passport question (Kaplan 2010b).

As they began their journey to Manchester in early July 2010, the Iroquois Nationals lacrosse team players were grounded for days near the Kennedy International Airport in New York. They were waiting for three powerful nations—Canada, the United States, and Britain—to come to an agreement that would never materialize. Later, their hopes of representing their game and their nation on the national stage vanished and the team was sent home. The players' diminishing hopes and ultimate devastation were documented in various press interviews while waiting in the Hilton Hotel. Quotes in the media from team leaders and managers emphasize their commitment to the game and shock at the level of bureaucracy involved. "We'd rather be playing there than sitting here," said the team's captain, Gewas Schindler. "It's hard to talk about, really." (Kaplan 2010a, para. 7). Adding to the sense of frustration was the recognition that despite being the originators of the game, they were being excluded from competition, carrying on a history that began with racially based exclusionary practices in the late nineteenth century. Denise Waterman, a member of the team's board of directors, noted the hypocrisy that was contained in this bureaucratic morass. "Lacrosse is our game—we are the originators, we invented the game, there are 60 countries that play our game," said Waterman. "And now we can't go to a tournament that's honoring our game? It's almost unbelievable that this is happening" (Kaplan 2010a, para. 8).

On July 14, 2010, the CBC threw further light on the story, highlighting the three nation's positions ("Iroquois Lacrosse Team Denied" 2010). Canada and the United States were willing to send the players overseas with a one-time exception, but in the United States there remained an unresolved issue. Did the one-time exception mean that the United States would waive their entry requirement that players have a United States passport, or would the one-time exception leave the Iroquois in England with no ability to return to their home? Why was this question not answered in a timely fashion if an exception could be given? Was this a question of national security, which could be precedent setting? Was this just bureaucratic red tape? Was it a simply a continuation of colonial power? Or was it a combination of all of the above?

After 9/11, the Iroquois were welcome to travel, provided they identified as Canadian or American to meet international travel and security guidelines. As the passport issue arose with respect to the 2010 World Championship, officials at the US State Department were sympathetic. According to State Department spokesperson P. J. Crowley, "Documents that are necessary to facilitate travel within and outside the hemisphere have changed. We are trying to help them get the appropriate documents so they can travel to this tournament" ("Iroquois Lacrosse Team Denied" 2010). American authorities subsequently provided a temporary solution for the players born on the American side of the US-Canada border but indicated the Canadian-born players would need a similar exception from Canadian authorities ("Iroquois Lacrosse Team Denied" 2010). Canada was equally sympathetic; the problem was with the British. Canadian Minister of Indian Affairs Chuck Strahl told *The Globe and Mail* that there was little he could do "to help an aboriginal lacrosse team at the center of a passport dispute....Canada cannot force Britain to accept documents it doesn't recognize, and the government-issued passport is the only document guaranteed to be accepted" (*The Globe and Mail* 2010).

Although the United States and Canada were willing to create a temporary solution to allow the Iroquois to travel, a complication arose. Initially the United States government had required an American passport for re-entry, but at the behest of Secretary of State Hillary Clinton, it approved a one-time waiver to travel overseas. Unfortunately, the British had decided in the interim to require a universally recognized passport, and despite the Clinton waiver would not grant the necessary visas for entry into the United Kingdom. When British officials communicated their decision, it dashed the team's hopes of participating in the World Championship ("Iroquois Lacrosse Team Denied" 2010). In addition, it angered several American lawmakers, including house member Dan Maffei (Democrat, NY), who "called the situation an 'international incident' and went so far as to question England's ability to host the 2020 Olympics" (Kaplan 2010b, para. 11).

The guarantee of re-entry was not able to be resolved in time for the players to travel. It appears that there may have been a simple solution: ensuring the temporary travel permit included re-entry into the United States for the Iroquois Nationals' registered members. However, there are many underlying complications that may have been present. Was an international inspection needed for each player to help mitigate the risk of an international threat? Were all the appropriate departments consulted for the temporary solution? What national identity would the players have on their documents and would the United Kingdom recognize any unofficial document the American government administered?

Whatever the case, the Iroquois Nationals found themselves in a bureaucratic dilemma that they could not escape and eventually had to return home. One of the most disappointing aspects of the case, from the Iroquois point of view, was the lack of advanced warning about the change in requirements for the passports. This left a bad feeling with team members since they had been travelling on these passports since 1977, when they first travelled to Australia. "They pulled a bait and switch," Nationals executive director Percy Abrams said, "and they got us" (Hamill 2010, para. 15).

Indigenous Rights and Treaties Have Been Recognized in Both Canada and the United States in Areas Such as Nationhood, Land Rights, and Traditional Knowledge and Practices

In Canada, some of the First Nations that have become self-governing nations and many others are engaged in the process of working toward self-sufficiency and self-government ("Self-Government"

2010). While the literature around how much more can be done with regard to self-sufficiency of Indigenous peoples in North America is rich, the actual progress already made remains largely unrecognized. The emphasis on cultural heritage is at the crux of the debate on national identity. According to an article in the *Toronto Star*, Hemlock, a Mohawk from the Montréal community of Kahnwake, explained that "the notion of self-determination goes back to their first treaty with the Dutch government in the 17th century, called Guswhenta, or the Two Row Wampum Belt treaty" (J. Smith 2010, para. 13). In fact, there are many nations making great strides to develop self-sufficiency within Indigenous populations, including Australia, Canada, New Zealand, and the United States (Cornell 2006). New Zealand and the Māori have made significant progress in working together around ocean management and health priorities as examples (Houkamau and Sibley 2011; Schiffman 2013). An important component of the self-governing strategy is the ability to come together as one nation, shifting away from the distributed reservations/reserves across a colonized land mass. Many Indigenous peoples are taking advantage of the holistic nature of Web 2.0 to create networks across the five countries to discuss issues and opportunities common to their Indigenous communities (Harris and Wasilewski 2004). Within their existing national borders, these four countries are working with Indigenous populations shifting to self-governing nations, but outside the borders of these individual nation-states, Indigenous nations are not formally recognized. The Western Hemisphere Travel Initiative went into effect in 2009 and requires nations to carry high-tech documents or passports when crossing borders. This has created an intersection for national identity between established geographic borders by colonial nations and more fluid borders based on cultural heritage ("Iroquois Lacrosse Team Denied" 2010).

Internally, Canada, New Zealand, Australia, and the United States have made strides toward established national identities for their Indigenous populations. The intersectional dimensions of Aboriginal national identity include territorial identity, historical proof of residency on the land prior to colonization; cultural identity, practices, and traditions, including language; and biological identity, blood quantum, and family connections (Battiste 2014a).

While most of these elements remain unrecognized in the constitutions of the developed nations, the informal practices of recognizing Indigenous nationhood through cultural identity and biological identity are generally accepted practices within the borders of these nation-states. However, recent scientific literature has shown that many scientists see race not as a scientific or biological phenomenon but rather a cultural and social phenomenon (Battiste 2014b). For Indigenous populations interested in developing citizenship codes, biological identity has proven to be contentious, as an adopted child from birth would not meet the biological requirements in order to access services in the community, yet a person who has never lived in the community with no recent family connections can gain access to services based on blood quantum.

Territorial identity has traditionally proven challenging since both the non-Indigenous and the Indigenous lay claim to the land. This has meant lengthy land-claim applications and heated protests. Given the problems associated with biological and territorial expressions of identity, the cultural identity of the Indigenous peoples creates a common value and belief system on which to build a nation. "Your passport is kind of a means of showing who you are in the world and we're Haudenosaunee," said Kanen'tokon (Tyler) Hemlock, "so carrying our own passport, we're able to represent ourselves as such" (J. Smith 2010, para. 13).

The history of lacrosse is deeply rooted in the identity of the Haudenosaunee. One member of the Iroquois Nationals described the frustration surrounding the passport issue, especially since lacrosse plays such an important part of the hope of establishing and sustaining the Iroquois national identity now and for future generations. "It was frustrating," said Brett Bucktooth, a member of the 2010 team who was slated to play attack for the Iroquois in the UK. "But more importantly, we stood up for what we believed in. Representing ourselves, who we are as a people. Not just for that day, for the week, but for future generations. There was a bigger purpose at hand" (Chidley-Hill 2014, para. 7).

The entities that monitor the geographic borders place formal power and decision-making authority in their national officers to uphold entry into their nation based on a passport, but not all passports carry the same level of recognition. Although the first Haudenosaunee passport was issued in 1923, and Switzerland accepted the passports of Iroquois delegates to the United Nations in 1977, governments have been less lenient after the terrorist attacks of September 11, 2001 (Chidley-Hill 2014). British officials in 2010 would not accept tribal documents since they did not have the security features used in

Canadian and American passports. Iroquois passports are partly handwritten and lack the holograms and other technological features that guard against forgeries (Kaplan 2010b). The Iroquois Nation recognizes the security regulation changes and intends to make the required changes to the Haudenosaunee passports, but the technological features are not easily implemented as they are intended to prevent forgeries. As a result, the bureaucratic management of the sensitive cultural implications of national identity has restricted Haudenosaunee international travel. "It's a tough one," Chief Oren Lyons of the Onondaga Nation said. "We're dealing with new regulations that have come about since 9/11, and we understand that" (Kaplan 2010b, para. 10).

Despite all the efforts by the politicians and the eventual outcome of being denied entry to the world championships, the Iroquois Nationals did not see this as a total defeat. Instead, they took pride in the national exposure of the issue, which strengthened the Haudenosaunee long-standing claim of sovereignty. There were photos posted in social media and national newspapers with Hillary Clinton and other political legislators, and a $50,000 donation from James Cameron, director of the movie *Titanic*. As the controversy unfolded, New Mexico Governor Bill Richardson sent a letter to the State Department and the Department of Homeland Security on behalf of the Nationals raising his concern of the situation: "As a governor of a state with a significant Native American population, I know many tribes and pueblos will watch carefully how these young competitors are treated by the administration. As a signatory to the UN Universal Declaration of Human Rights, which includes the freedom to travel and return, I believe we have an obligation to assure these young men's rights are protected" (Hamill 2010, para. 22). He adds that Congress hoped to work with federal officials to develop a system of tribal identification documents that are deemed secure—an effort already under way in some Indigenous nations. Senator Kirsten Gillibrand, Democrat of New York, also made a similar request of Secretary of State Clinton. Clearly, the concerns of the Iroquois Nationals had received considerable attention at the highest levels of government, both in the United States and Canada, and this compensated to some degree for not being allowed to participate in Manchester. "You cannot buy that kind of publicity," said Percy Abrams, the team's executive director (Hamill 2010, para. 7). Iroquois Nationals midfielder Brett Bucktooth put it even more succinctly. In the end, he concluded, "It is a win" (Hamill 2010, para. 13).

The Aftermath

This chapter has addressed various issues related to the transnational diffusion of sporting culture over time and raises particular concerns about sport, borders, and Indigenous nationality in an increasingly globalized world. In outlining the difficulty that the Iroquois Nationals experienced with respect to travel on a Haudenosaunee passport, it underscores the complexities surrounding Indigenous peoples and their representation in international sporting events. For various peoples around the world—from the Sami in Scandinavia to Aboriginal peoples in Australasia, and those on other continents as well—sport has been a way to express identities and to further aspirations of self-determination. Obviously, sportive expressions of identity can be attached to a wide array of sports and games. At the 2012 Olympics Games, for example, Damien Hopper, an Indigenous Australian boxer raised initial concern with the International Olympic Committee (IOC) for wearing a sweater embellished with the Australian Aboriginal flag. "I'm an Aborigine representing my culture and my people here at the Games," he said ("Australian Boxer" 2012). In order to avoid sanctioning, Hopper eventually apologized for breaching Rule 50 of the Olympic charter and agreed not to wear the shirt again. Hopper nonetheless had made his point. The institutionalization of existing national borders through international competition by no means diminishes or expunges the reality of local and Indigenous cultural identities that transcend nation-state boundaries. Like most forms of cultural life, sport remains a continually contested realm that gives expression to a multiplicity of competing cultural identities. In our contemporary world, where concerns about threats to national security and the challenge of COVID-19 sharpens tensions around national identities, sport will continue to exemplify the interplay between metropolitan and local influences and the particular aspirations and agency of Indigenous peoples.

References

Anderson, Benedict. 1983. *Imagined Communities: Reflections on the Origin and Spread of Nationalism*. London: Verso.

"Australian Boxer May Be Punished for Wearing Aboriginal Flag at Olympics." 2012. *Indian Country Today,* August 3, 2012. https://indiancountrymedia network.com/news/australian-boxer-may-be-punished-for-wearing-aboriginal-flag-at-olympics/.

Battiste, Jaime. 2014a. "Defining Aboriginal Identity." *Mi'kmaq Rights Initiative*. http://mikmaqrights.com/wp-content/uploads/2014/01/Defining-Aboriginal-Identity-Final-draft-for-MMN.pdf.

———. 2014b. "What's in Our Blood?" *Mi'kmaq Rights Initiative*. http://mikmaqrights.com/whats-in-our-blood/.

Beezley, William. 1989. *Judas at the Jockey Club and Other Episodes of Porfirian Mexico*. Lincoln: University of Nebraska Press.

Boucher, Nancy B. 2003. *For the Love of the Game: Amateur Sport in Small-Town Ontario, 1838–1895*. Montréal and Kingston: McGill-Queen's University Press.

Calder, Jim, and Ron Fletcher. 2011. *Lacrosse: The Ancient Game*. Toronto: Ancient Game Press.

Chidley-Hill, John. 2014. "Creator's Game: Iroquois Nationals Return to World Field Lacrosse Championships." *City News*, July 9, 2014. https://www.citynews1130.com/2014/07/09/creators-game-iroquois-nationals-return-to-world-field-lacrosse-championships/.

Cornell, Stephen E. 2006. *Indigenous Peoples, Poverty and Self-determination in Australia, New Zealand, Canada and the United States*. Native Nations Institute for Leadership, Management, and Policy.

Dimmel, Brandon. 2010. "Bats along the Border: Sport, Festivals and Culture in an International Community During the First World War." *American Review of Canadian Studies* 40, no. 3 (Autumn): 326–337.

Downey, Allan. 2018. *The Creator's Game: Lacrosse, Identity and Indigenous Nationhood*. Vancouver: UBC Press.

———. 2012. "Engendering Nationality: Haudenosaunee Tradition, Sport, and the Lines of Gender." *Journal of the Canadian Historical Association* 23 (1): 319–354.

Dyreson, Mark. 1998. *Making the American Team: Sport, Culture and the Olympic Experience*. Urbana: University of Illinois Press.

Dyreson, Mark, J. A. Mangan, and Robert Park, eds. 2012. *Mapping an Empire of American Sport: Expansion, Assimilation, Adaptation and Resistance*. London: Routledge.

Forsyth, Janice, and Audrey Giles. 2013. *Aboriginal Peoples and Sport in Canada: Historical Foundations and Contemporary Issues*. Vancouver: UBC Press.

Guttmann, Allen. 1994. *Games and Empires: Modern Sports and Cultural Imperialism*. New York: Columbia University Press.

Hamill, Kristen. 2010. "Iroquois Lacrosse Team Still Caught in Bureaucratic Net," *CNN*, July 15, 2010. http://www.cnn.com/2010/SPORT/07/14/sport.iroquois.passport.controversy/.

Harris, Laura, and Jacqueline Wasilewski. 2004. "Indigenous Wisdom of the People Forum: Strategies for Expanding a Web of Transnational Indigenous Interactions." *Systems Research and Behavioral Science* 21 (5): 505–514.

Haudenosaunee Confederacy. n.d. "About the Haudenosaunee." Accessed May 15, 2015. http://www.haudenosauneeconfederacy.com/aboutus.html.

Hay, Roy. 2019. *Aboriginal People and Australian Football in the Nineteenth Century. They Did Not Come from Nowhere*. Newcastle upon Tyne, UK: Cambridge Scholars Publishing.

Holman, Andrew C. 2004. "Playing the Neutral Zone: Meanings and Uses of Ice Hockey in the Canada-U.S. Borderlands, 1895–1915." *American Review of Canadian Studies* 34 (1): 33–57.

Houkamau, Carla A., and Chris G. Sibley. 2011. "Maori Cultural Efficacy and Subjective Wellbeing: A Psychological Model and Research Agenda." *Social Indicators Research* 103 (3): 379–398.

Howell, Colin. 2002. "Borderlands, Baselines and Bearhunters: Conceptualizing the Northeast as a Sporting Region in the Interwar Period." *Journal of Sport History* 29 (2): 251–270.

———. 2001. *Blood Sweat and Cheers: Sport and the Making of Modern Canada*. Toronto: University of Toronto Press.

———. 1995. *Northern Sandlots. A Social History of Maritime Baseball*. Toronto: University of Toronto Press.

Howell, Colin, and Chris Fletcher. 1997. "Modernization Theory and the Traditional Sporting Practices of Native People in Eastern Canada." *Journal of Physical Education and Sport* 19 (2): 79–84.

Howell, Colin, and Daryl Leeworthy. 2017. "Playing on the Border: Sport, Borderlands and the North Atlantic, 1850–1950." *Sport in Society* 20 (10): 1354–1370.

———. 2010. "Borderlands." In *The Routledge Companion to Sports History*, edited by S. W. Pope and John Nauright, 71–84. Abingdon, UK: Routledge.

"Iroquois Lacrosse Team Denied Visas by U.K." 2010. *CBC*, July 14, 2010. https://www.cbc.ca/news/world/iroquois-lacrosse-team-denied-visas-by-u-k-1.869901.

Kaplan, Thomas. 2010a. "Bid for Trophy Becomes a Test of Iroquois Identity." *New York Times*, July 12, 2010. https://www.nytimes.com/2010/07/13/us/13lacrosse.html.

———. 2010b. "Iroquois Defeated by Passport Dispute." *New York Times*, July 16, 2010. https://www.nytimes.com/2010/07/17/sports/17lacrosse.html.

Kidd, Bruce. 1996. *The Struggle for Canadian Sport*. Toronto: University of Toronto Press.

Leeworthy, Daryl. 2015. "Skating on the Border: Hockey, Class, and Commercialism in Interwar Britain." *Histoire Sociale/Social History* 48 (96): 193–213.

Maguire, Joseph A. 2011. "Globalization, Sport and National Identities." *Sport in Society* 14 (7): 978–993.

Martyn, Scott G., Robert K. Barney, and Stephen R. Wenn. 2004. *Selling the Five Rings; The IOC and the Rise of Olympic Commercialism.* Salt Lake City: University of Utah Press.

Metcalfe, Alan. 1987. *Canada Learns to Play: The Emergence of Organized Sport, 1807–1914.* Toronto: McClelland and Stewart.

Pope, S. W. 1997. *Patriotic Games: Sporting Traditions in the American Imagination 1876–1926.* New York: Oxford University Press.

Poulter, Gillian. 2010. *Becoming Native in a Foreign Land: Sport, Visual Culture, and Identity in Montreal, 1840-85.* Vancouver: UBC Press.

Ramsden, Peter G. 2006. "Haudenosaunee (Iroquois)." *The Canadian Encyclopedia.* December 14, 2006. http://www.thecanadianencyclopedia.ca/en/article/iroquois.

Reid, John. 2018. "The Cricketers of Digby and Yarmouth Counties, Nova Scotia, 1871–1914: Social Roots of a Village and Small-Town Sport." *Histoire Sociale/Social History* 51 (103): 47–73.

Reid, John, and Robert Reid. 2015. "Diffusion and Discursive Stabilization: Sports Historiography and Contrasting Fortunes of Cricket and Hockey in Canada's Maritime Provinces, 1869–1914." *Journal of Sport History* 42 (1): 87–113.

Robertson, Roland. 1995. "Glocalization: Time-Space and Homogeneity-Heterogeneity." In *Global Modernities*, edited by Mike Featherstone, Scott Lash, and Roland Robertson, 25–44. London: Sage Publications.

Ross, Greggory MacIntosh. 2008. *Beyond the Abysmal Brute: A Social History of Boxing in Interwar Nova Scotia.* Master's thesis, Saint Mary's University.

Schiffman, Howard. 2013. "The South Pacific Regional Fisheries Management Organization (SPRFMO): An Improved Model of Decision-making for Fisheries Conservation?" *Journal of Environmental Studies and Sciences* 3 (2): 9–16.

"Self-Government." 2010. Indigenous and Northern Affairs. Last updated September 15, 2010. https://www.aadnc-aandc.gc.ca/eng/1100100022287/1100100022288.

Smith, Joanna, 2010. "Six Nations Passport More Than Travel Document, Say Users." *Toronto Star*, July 16, 2010. https://www.thestar.com/news/canada/2010/07/15/six_nations_passport_more_than_travel_document_say_users.html.

Smith, Timothy W. 1998. "Lacrosse; Another National Pastime," *New York Times*, July 24, 1998. http://www.nytimes.com/1998/07/24/sports/lacrosse-another-national-pastime.html.

The Globe and Mail. 2010. "No Help from Indian Affairs on Iroquois Nationals Passport Flap, Strahl Says." July 16, 2010. https://www.theglobeandmail.com/news/politics/no-help-from-indian-affairs-on-iroquois-nationals-passport-flap-strahl-says/article1368457/.

"Timeline." n.d. Iroquois Nation. Accessed May 15, 2015. https://iroquoisnationals.org/the-iroquois/timeline/.

Trigger, Bruce G. 1986. *Natives and Newcomers: Canada's Heroic Age Reconsidered*. Montréal: McGill University Press.

Van Bottenburg, Maarten. 2010. "Beyond Diffusion: Sport and its Remaking in Cross-Cultural Contexts." *Journal of Sport History* 37, no. 1 (April): 41–54.

CHAPTER 12

A Biocultural Planning Approach for Managing Transborder Cultural Heritage Landscapes

Scott Cafarella, Joel Konrad, and Rebecca Sciarra

This chapter explores the relationship between borders and the conservation of natural and cultural heritage resources in a municipal context. Intergovernmental researchers and policymakers have recently linked conservation of natural and cultural heritage to the protection of *biocultural diversity*, defined as "biological diversity, cultural diversity, and the links between them" (IPBES 2016, xxxi). The conservation of biocultural diversity requires the conservation of biocultural resources: the natural and cultural heritage of an area, people, and region. Biocultural resources are deeply defined by borders and boundaries that are concurrently shaped by ecological and political processes. Natural resources and landforms often transcend political boundaries; just as often, landscape features such as rivers, mountain ranges, or lakes become political boundaries. It is often this intersection of people and landscape along political and naturally occurring boundaries and borders that create unique or outstanding cultural landscapes. The transfer of cultural practices and knowledge along borders creates new regional identities, thereby affirming the importance of regions and sense-of-place in a globalizing world. In this way, the border becomes a resource, functioning as an economic and cultural driver in the region (Sohn 2014a, 2014b).

As historian Simon Schama notes in his book *Landscape and Memory:* "Landscapes are culture before they are nature; constructs of the imagination projected onto wood and water and rock"

(Schama 1996, 61). Culture mediates our understanding of the natural environment and gives it meaning. The notion that natural features or landscapes are culturally significant and should be legally conserved can be traced back to the nineteenth century in Euro-Canadian communities. Land management has a complicated history in Canada: in 1885, what would become known as Banff National Park was established through an order-in-council enacted by the federal government. Protection of the hot springs at Banff marked the creation of Canada's first national park and the third in North America, following on the heels of Yellowstone and Mackinac National Parks in the United States. The Rocky Mountains Park Act (1887) prevented settlement or occupation of any part of the park, resulting in the displacement and exclusion of the Nakoda (Stoney) First Nation from their traditional territory. Protection of nature and the existence of culture were seen as mutually exclusive by Canadian law, and the protection of natural areas was an instrument of colonization and subjugation of Indigenous peoples. In 1911, Canada's federal government passed the Dominion Forest Reserves and Park Act to establish a pan-Canadian framework for preserving the country's natural and cultural heritage. The most recent iteration of this law is the Canada National Parks Act (2000), which includes amendments that acknowledge the treaty rights of Indigenous peoples to "traditional renewable resource harvesting" within park boundaries (Canada 2019). Coexistence of culture and conservation of natural areas in Euro-Canadian land management follows developments in international policy and governance: by the 1970s, the United Nations Educational, Scientific and Cultural Organization (UNESCO) advanced discourse around human uses of, and relationships with, natural resources. The 1972 World Heritage Convention recognized the intrinsic link between human culture and nature, stating that "cultural or natural heritage should be considered in its entirety as a homogeneous whole": heritage cannot be "dissociated from its environment" nor from "community life" (UNESCO 1973, 148). In Ontario, various pieces of legislation have been enacted since the early twentieth century to conserve areas such as parks, watersheds, and large landforms like the Niagara Escarpment in relation to their natural and cultural heritage resources. While the idea that landscapes can be culturally significant has been advanced steadily over the last century, there are few established methodologies for meaningfully assessing, and therefore managing, a place so its culturally valued natural resources are appropriately conserved.

This chapter will explore the challenges of managing cultural assets on the borderlands and propose potential solutions to the cross-border identification, conservation, and management of cultural heritage landscapes. As Konrad and Kelly have suggested, a multiscalar approach must be taken to understand the "key processes" in bordering culture (Konrad and Kelly, introduction, this volume). Processes can occur organically as social, cultural, economic, and political elements of the border influence culture production and the creation of identity. Key processes may also be contrived by national, regional, and municipal governments to conserve cultural artifacts that express or maintain identity. Within the boundaries of these political units, land-use planners can direct the conservation of cultural heritage resources (significant artifacts, landscapes, built features, etc.) through the use of policies and guidelines. But cultural heritage resources may cross borders, requiring jurisdictions to work together to achieve conservation. Beatrix Haselberger has argued that land-use planners have a complex relationship with borders, as they have to work within "local, regional, sub-nations, nation, or supra-national territory" while also shaping and reforming boundaries through the act of zoning or designating new planning regions such as secondary plans or heritage conservation districts (Haselberger 2014, 506). The result is an often uneven approach to heritage conservation at the regional level as municipal policies have differing conservation goals within their jurisdiction. This chapter attempts a critical review of municipally driven policies that govern the evaluation and conservation of cultural heritage. In doing so, it will explore the architecture of cross-border heritage policy within the province of Ontario. The border is here understood as a division between political entities. This chapter moves away from questions of national boundaries to explore the implications of borders on the preservation of culture. The Niagara Escarpment will be used as a case study to explore the concept of transboundary biocultural landscapes as it transcends borders, creates a natural geographic boundary through an oft-exposed scarp face and dramatic change in elevation, and functions inpart as an international boundary along the Niagara River Gorge. There is a notable time-depth of cultural use along the Niagara Escarpment, as habitat, refuge, corridor, source of raw material, outlook, landmark, and international attraction.

Central to the chapter is an examination of how cultural production and influence of biocultural landscapes such as the Niagara Escarpment extend beyond conservation district borders, resulting indifferent levels of local, regional, federal, and international protection. A strategy for assessing and evaluating biocultural landscapes will be formulated using a biocultural planning framework with the aim to create a model that might also be applicable to other bioregions in Ontario and beyond. This investigation responds to a lack of regional legislation and policy that effectively integrates the conservation of significant cultural and natural resources, as well as the absence of a methodology that adequately evaluates the cultural significance of features situated at the borderlands or that straddle political borders.

This objective prompts the following question: how can cross-jurisdictional biocultural landscapes be assessed, evaluated, and managed? We propose a bioregional planning approach, through which a system of core, buffer, and transition zones that enable a range of levels of protection and planning controls offers a novel and useful approach for managing biocultural landscapes. (See figure 12.1 for a conceptual illustration of a biocultural planning system.) The objective of biocultural planning is to conserve and manage important cultural and natural resources within their contextual environment so that the contemporary forces of culture, change, and development can coexist to a mutually beneficial end (Brunckhorst 2000). This also makes notions of cultural heritage more relevant and functional by increasing the base of support in a community, beyond the narrowly defined borders of the existing policy framework.

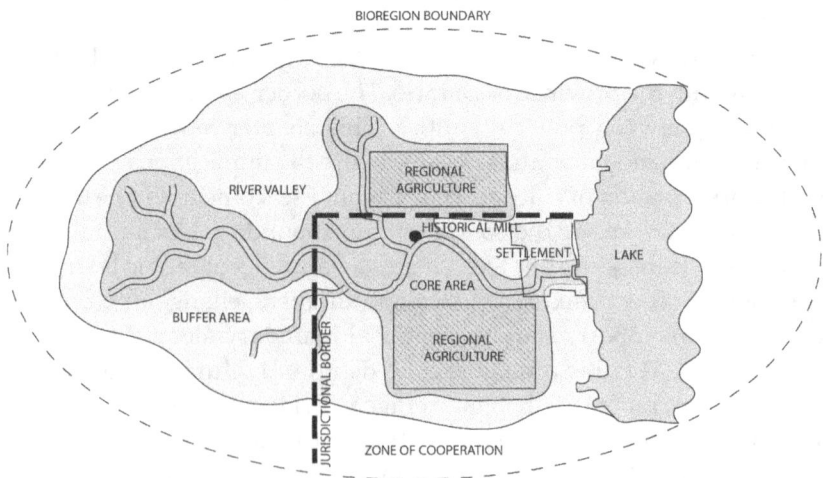

FIGURE 12.1. Conceptual illustration of a biocultural planning system. *Source:* Scott Cafarella, Joel Konrad, and Rebecca Sciarra.

Large-Scale Cultural Heritage Landscape Conservation

The origin of biosphere planning dates to the environmental movement of the 1970s and 1980s, which saw the development of innovative conservation strategies and legal instruments, concurrent with advancements in landscape planning theory (Forman and Godron 1986; Lyle 1985; McHarg 1969; Steiner 1990). UNESCO's Man and the Biosphere Programme (1971) and World Network of Biosphere Reserves (1977) established a new biosphere concept emphasizing conflict-resolution methodologies, the creation of cluster and transboundary reserves, and a greater integration of conservation with development (UNESCO 1995).

Geographer David Brunckhorst defines the bioregion as an area "made up of similar landscape ecosystems with which local human communities identify because of how they see it, use it, and what it produces for them" (2000, 33). Biosphere reserves offer a framework for the management of bioregions that are frequently transdisciplinary and cross-jurisdictional, involve both public and private actors, and democratize decision-making and ownership at the local level (Brunckhorst 2001). The US-Canada border provides many strong examples of cross-border bioregional communities, such as the Cascadia Bioregion or the Great Lakes Bioregion (Alper 1996; Konrad 2012; Riley 2013). Recent scholarship has also drawn attention to the social and cultural impact of modern Great Lakes borders on Indigenous communities (Hele 2008). Research conducted by the Government of Canada concluded that the Great Lakes Bioregion is characterized by mature economic relations and a strong emphasis on single-purpose cross-border organizations such as the International Joint Commission, but no overarching cross-border organization provides leadership in the region (PRI 2008).

UNESCO's Man and the Biosphere Programme and bioregional planning theory were developed in conjunction with each other to further three interconnected goals: the conservation of biodiversity and cultural diversity; the promotion of sustainable and culturally appropriate development; and the facilitation of logistic support for education, training, research, and monitoring (UNESCO 2015). These goals are achieved through the implementation of a consistent zoning scheme, which allows for flexibility in planning and enables the combination of sustainable land use and landscape conservation. The zones consist of core areas, buffer areas, and transition areas (also referred to as the zone of cooperation). Core areas are protected sites designed to preserve biodiversity and ecosystem services. The core requires a strict monitoring and management strategy. Buffer areas usually surround core areas; compatible practices such as education, recreation, ecotourism, and research may exist here. Buffer areas may also preserve cultural diversity through the protection of the traditional cultural use of environmental services. The zone of cooperation is reserved for the sustainable development of resources and may host more intensive land uses such as industrial agriculture and mineral extraction, in addition to traditional land uses (Brunckhorst 2000, 2001; UNESCO 2015).

The Great Lakes Region is understood as an *ecoregion* operating at the sub-continental scale. Smaller bioregions are contained within the Great Lakes Ecoregion. The Niagara Escarpment is one of these bioregions, which in turn is bordered and intersected by three other prominent bioregions: the Carolinian Region, Huron Region, and Georgian Bay Region (Nelson 2012). In its entirety, the Niagara Escarpment is a 1,200-kilometre cuesta that extends in an arc from central New York to Wisconsin. Composed of 450-million-year-old rock, the escarpment edge was once the shore of an ancient shallow sea within Michigan Basin. The rock face observed today was formed by the unequal erosion of bedrock: a dolostone cap protected softer layers of shale underneath. Currently, there exists no international joint commission or agreement between the US and Canada to protect this unique geological and cultural feature and landscape (Nelson and Porter 2002). Conservation of the Niagara Escarpment is most developed in southern Ontario, as described below, although recent research and advocacy by the Western New York Land Conservancy, and the implementation of a Niagara Escarpment protection policy and land planning zoning overlay by the Bay-Lake Regional Planning Commission in Wisconsin, suggests that a more comprehensive, bioregional approach in the US may one day come to fruition (BLRPC 2001, 2010; WNYLC 2014).

Regional and municipal boundaries also pose distinct planning challenges. Although high-level policy is often produced at a national or provincial scale, regions or municipalities are often tasked with the creation of workable conservation strategies and the implementation and monitoring of these frameworks. Despite this, there have been some regional planning successes. In southern Ontario, conservation of the Niagara Escarpment is governed by the Niagara Escarpment

Planning and Development Act. Regulation 235/10 of the act defines the boundaries of the Niagara Escarpment Planning Area. Through the Niagara Escarpment Plan, this planning area is divided into several distinct land-use designations, consisting of natural areas, protection areas, rural areas, mineral resource extraction areas, recreation areas, urban areas, and minor urban centres. Overlaying this framework is the Niagara Escarpment Parks and Open Space System (NEPOSS), which establishes a system of publicly owned and accessible lands along the escarpment. The designation areas roughly conform to Brunckhorst's bioregional planning framework: natural and protection areas form the "core," rural areas are the "buffer," and extraction, recreation, and urban areas form the "zone of cooperation" (UNESCO 2012). Due to the political realities of creating a planning border, buffer areas are occasionally narrow to nonexistent in areas along the escarpment, and the "zone of cooperation" does not extend as far as the literature may suggest (Brunckhorst 2000). Figure 12.2 illustrates the bioregional approach as applied to the Niagara Escarpment in the biosphere self-study (UNESCO 2012).

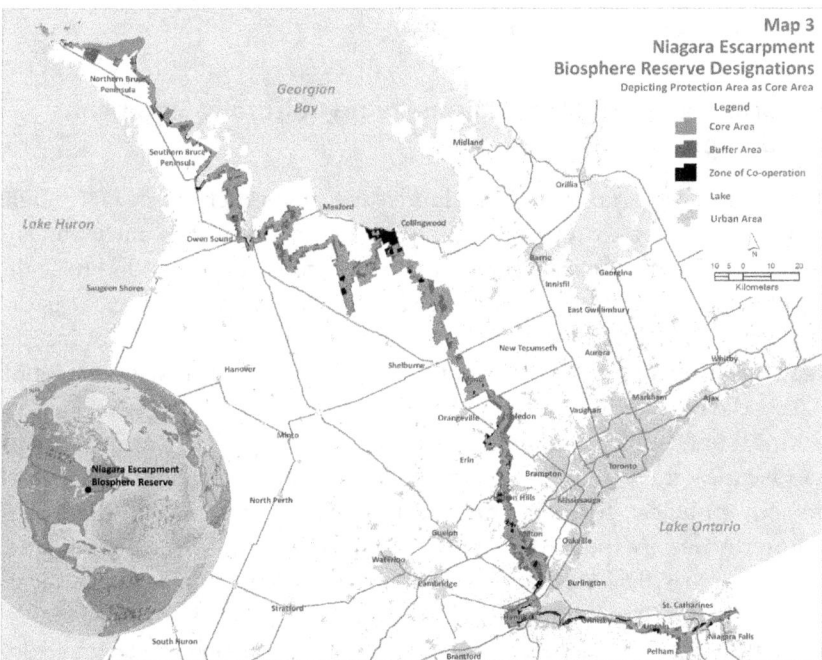

FIGURE 12.2. Niagara Escarpment Biosphere Reserve designations. *Source*: UNESCO 2012.

Typically, landscape management has been segregated by discipline, with cultural landscape management aligned with history, people, and intentional design, and natural landscapes recognized by science-based conservation strategies. In contrast, bioregional planning theory presents a holistic approach to land management that recognizes a culturally inclusive, bottom-up approach is necessary to preserve ecological resources, and that ecologically sustainable practices are required to support cultural traditions and institutions (Antrop 2006). A renewed interest in scaling up land management strategies to the regional scale has been made by the US National Park Service, which had traditionally been concerned with individual parks or sites (National Park Service 2014). To scale up land management means to provide directives for regional landscape plans, to engage multiple stakeholders, and to establish new linkages between various land management systems. The Niagara Escarpment Plan is an early example of a bioregional planning framework in Ontario. This chapter considers an expanded bioregional plan for the escarpment based on a transboundary evaluation methodology of natural and cultural resource management.

Ontario Policy Context for Conserving Culturally Significant Landscapes

In Ontario, regional large-scale landscape plans such as the Greenbelt Plan and the Oak Ridges Moraine Plan (enacted in the early 2000s), and the Niagara Escarpment Plan of the 1970s, were intended to scale up the conservation of ecological resources; however, these plans do not substantially address conservation of specific *cultural* landscape features, areas or zones that contribute to these large-scale regional assets. Additionally, while the province of Ontario introduced strengthened policy statements and definitions for cultural heritage landscapes in recent Provincial Policy Statements and have established policies for engaging Indigenous and non-Indigenous communities in their identification and evaluation, municipal and regional jurisdictions have been slow to specifically manage these assets through recognition and designation in their official plans. Generally, Ontario's current policy context for conserving large-scale, cross-border, culturally significant landscapes is constrained by several factors: use of legal instruments that apply protection to individual property parcels; a restrictive conflation between "culture" and "heritage" as it is defined under the Ontario Heritage Act (Ontario 2019); and an absence of a holistic or bioregional landscape management framework. The following sections describe how this policy trend has been demonstrated over time.

The Ontario Heritage Act

Cultural heritage conservation in Ontario has traditionally been focused on the preservation of old or distinct structures and material culture. Tangible cultural objects are where culture is clearly recognized and more easily conserved: a house or a bridge is a tangible object of culture that can be preserved and repurposed; or an assemblage of archaeological artifacts may be excavated for curation and interpretation or protected in situ. However, this approach can miss the environmental context of heritage, or how culture and landscape interrelate to create meaning and valued places. The more difficult task of cultural resource management comes with managing intangible heritage, heritage with fuzzy borders, and heritage that is not necessarily scenic or even visible. The introduction of the Heritage Conservation District toolkit in 1975 under the Ontario Heritage Act attempted to address the issue of context and regional character. Although this tool can be used at a variety of scales and contexts, it is almost exclusively used in urban or peri-urban areas to preserve built features concentrated within a street block or neighbourhood. Although a regulation under the Ontario Heritage Act in 2005 included criteria for identifying the contextual value of a property, the act remains property-based (Ontario 2006). A more nuanced and landscape-focused instrument is needed to protect the heritage value of the contextual environment.

A significant gap in the Ontario Heritage Act is that it does not address the relationship between natural environments and cultural sustainability. This absence does not align with contemporary policy being developed in the UK and Europe and by UNESCO (Brown, Mitchell, and Beresford 2005; Natural England 2014; UNESCO 2015), and as a result, the unique character of rural areas such as the Niagara Fruit Belt or interjurisdictional and transboundary cultural landscapes such as regional trails, canals, shorelines, or rivers may not be given adequate protection to ensure these resources are conserved for future generations.

Ontario's Provincial Policy Statement

Ontario's Provincial Policy Statement (PPS) gives further direction to municipalities regarding land-use planning policies in the Planning Act (Ontario 2020a; 2020b). The 1997 PPS provided a policy framework for conserving "built heritage" and at that time introduced the idea of conserving "cultural heritage landscapes," defined then as a "geographical area of heritage significance which has been modified by human activity" (Ontario 1997, 13). The 2005 and 2014 PPS further clarified that "cultural heritage landscapes" could be devoid of traditional built or material culture and instead defined by their interrelationships between features such as "spaces, archaeological sites, or natural elements" (Ontario 2005a, 29; 2014, 40), for example. The 2020 PPS continues to give specific policy direction that "significant cultural heritage landscapes shall be conserved" (Ontario 2020a, 31) and recognizes that these areas may be defined by buildings and structures, but also, "spaces, archaeological sites, views or natural elements" (42).

This definition corresponds to the types of landscapes that have been protected as UNESCO World Heritage Sites and that generally align with the following three cultural heritage landscape typologies initially defined by UNESCO and subsequently endorsed by the province of Ontario as providing a useful framework for managing cultural heritage landscapes (see Ontario 2005b; Ontario Heritage Trust 2012): clearly defined landscape designed and created intentionally by man; organically evolved landscapes (relict or continuing landscape); and associative cultural landscapes.

These types of landscapes encapsulate those that are both highly exceptional and typified by significant cultural material (often buildings) linked with landscape components or features, although the "associative cultural landscape" definition does recognize that a site's significance may be rooted in its "powerful religious, artistic or cultural associations of the natural element" (Ontario Heritage Trust 2012, 1). In Ontario, where cultural heritage landscapes have been identified informally or protected through designations under the Ontario Heritage Act or in official plans, they overwhelmingly conform to those that are designed and created intentionally by man or which may be considered organically evolved landscapes.

The 2020 PPS also establishes that Indigenous communities have a distinct interest in cultural heritage and archaeological resources and requires that "planning authorities shall engage with Indigenous communities and consider their interests when identifying, protecting and managing cultural heritage and archaeological resources" (Ontario 2020a, 30, policy 2.6.5). Practicably, engagement with Indigenous communities in this context has tended to focus on understanding their interests in known or potential tangible heritage, notably material culture such as archaeological sites or artifacts. Contemporary writing, planning decisions, academic writing, and community-based initiatives demonstrates that Indigenous communities often recognize important cultural associations with large-scale landscapes such as shorelines, land formations, and watersheds, for example.[1]

A Bioregional Approach to Cultural Heritage Management in Ontario

In response to the challenges of policy to effectively scale up the conservation of transborder biocultural landscapes, this chapter advances a novel method for assessing and evaluating biocultural landscapes in Ontario. In 2015, research was completed through a study that was jointly funded by Archaeological Services Inc. (ASI), an Ontario-based archaeological and cultural heritage consulting firm, and the Borders in Globalization research program. The purpose of this study was to devise a method to assess the relationship between natural and cultural heritage in multi- and cross-jurisdictional landscapes, focusing on the Niagara Escarpment. One outcome of this study was a prototype methodology for cultural heritage landscape analysis and application of this method in the Town of Niagara-on-the-Lake, in Ontario, Canada, a predominantly rural municipality that is bounded by the Niagara River, the US-Canada border, Lake Ontario, and the Niagara Escarpment. The case study included a regional policy analysis, geospatial analysis of primary- and secondary-sourced data of the natural and cultural features of

---

1   See the following examples: Ontario Municipal Board Decision (PL150313; October 6, 2017) on the Burleigh Bay Corporation proposed development on North Shore of Stony Lake (http://www.omb.gov.on.ca/e-decisions/pl150313-Oct-06-2017.pdf); the Great Niagara Escarpment Indigenous Cultural Map (http://www.thegreatniagaraescarpment.ca/destinations); and the Credit Valley Trail (http://cvcfoundation.ca/cvt/).

the region, and a ranking and layering system, resulting in a geospatial data layer illustrating proposed biocultural regions rated based on their importance and cultural sensitivity. Due to limitations in time and resources for the original study, the ranking system employed in this research is illustrative only; in practice, a ranking system would be informed by careful consultation with regional partners and stakeholders to gain a truly representative understanding of community value.

Informed by Ian McHarg's (1969) overlay analysis method popularized by the publication *Design with Nature*, this process was selected for its ease of application, replicability, and customizability. Using a geographic information system (GIS) as an organizing tool, geographical information is collected from existing spatial data and fieldwork investigation. The data is then cleaned and thematically organized. A value is assigned to the features on each map, leading to a final biocultural landscape analysis. The raw product is refined by identifying core and buffer areas based on aggregate value. The zone of cooperation then becomes a unifying matrix for the core and buffer system within the bioregion.

The bioregional approach is highly suited toward cross-jurisdictional landscapes because the zone of cooperation is designed to function at multiple scales and facilitate cooperation across regional and international borders. By its nature subjective, the success of a value-based approach to assessing biocultural landscapes depends on a recognition of the interdependence of natural and cultural processes on the landscape and thorough engagement with stakeholders across political, cultural, and jurisdictional boundaries.

Method

The purpose of this study is to identify, layer, and buffer cultural landscape resources using a GIS to create a bioregional planning framework for the Niagara Escarpment. Through the process of layering multiple resources and summing the values associated with each resource, a system of core areas, buffers, and zones of cooperation will be drawn according to the area's aggregate value. Areas with the highest aggregate value will be designated as core areas. These areas should be given the greatest amount of protection and incompatible development or activity should not occur here. Buffer areas score moderately on the ranking system and are closely related to core areas. Activity in these areas should be closely monitored, and increasingly stricter regulations should be placed on development as it nears the core area. Moderate to low ranking areas that are not close to core areas become the zone of cooperation. Development restrictions are lowest here, and it is expected that industry, government, and private citizens will work toward mutually beneficial solutions regarding the stewardship of cultural resources. Finally, all other areas in the study area become the zone of transition. Most importantly, an overlay analysis method is highly transferable across political boundaries. It is expected that the ultimate policy framework(s) governing the zone of cooperation will reflect the cultural and political diversity within it.

For discussion purposes, a sample typology of cultural features was used in a test case study application of this method. Cultural resources are classified as corridors (road, railways, historic trails, canals), point features (designated heritage buildings, archaeological sites), and cultural areas (Niagara Escarpment, archaeological clusters). The cultural resource inventory and analysis was divided into six map sheets: (1) archaeology; (2) hydrology and landscape ecology; (3) landscape character units and landscape character unit areas; (4) heritage features; (5) community value; and (6) viewsheds.

An additional policy context map is created but will not factor into the overlay analysis. A summary of all feature layers used for this analysis is shown in table 12.1. The typology of each feature is labelled (corridor, point, area), and the process for buffering each feature is described, if applicable. As acknowledged earlier, a limitation of this research was that it did not include consultation with regional partners and stakeholders to create a ranking system that is representative of community values. For the purpose of this case study, an arbitrary ranking system was applied to the landscape layers that was informed by secondary source research.

Following the landscape feature ranking exercise, a system of cores, buffers, and transition zones were created and displayed on the bioregional planning zones map (figure 12.4). Areas that ranked very high, high, or moderately high became the core zones. Areas ranked average, moderately low, or other areas near the core areas became the buffer zones. Low or very low areas, in addition to other areas associated with the core and buffer zones, became the zone of transition. The result is an overlay analysis map that identifies priority management areas within the Niagara Escarpment cultural heritage landscape.

TABLE 12.1.
Feature layers used in GIS bioregional planning analysis of the study area

Map	Layers	Feature Type
Archaeological Sites	Archaeological sites along historic trails	Corridor
	Archaeological sites along the Niagara Escarpment	Cultural area / Corridor
	Archaeological clusters (cultural area)	Cultural area / Corridor
	Archaeological sites along streams and shorelines	Corridor
	Known Hatiwendaronk villages (points)	Point feature
	All archaeological sites (points)	Point feature
Hydrology and Landscape Ecology	Permeable land in an urban area	Cultural area
	Streams, rivers, shorelines and canals	Corridor
	Important ecological connections	Corridor
	Wooded areas	Cultural area
	Conservation areas and Parks Commission lands	Cultural area
Landscape Character Units	Regional agricultural uses	Cultural area
	General agriculture	Cultural area
Heritage Features	Historic roads	Corridor
	Designated structures and heritage conservation districts	Point feature
	Non-designated cultural features based on field work and Niagara open data	Point feature
	Cemeteries	Point feature
	Welland Canal - Abandoned and operational	Corridor
	Rail - Abandoned and operational	Corridor
Community Values	Recreational amenities	Point feature
	Bruce trail	Corridor
	Other trails	Corridor
	Community centres	Corridor
	Wineries	Corridor
	Festivals	Corridor
Viewsheds	Viewpoints: high visibility and accessibility	Point
	Viewpoints: low visibility and accessibility	Point
	Important viewsheds	Cultural area

Source: Scott Cafarella, Joel Konrad, and Rebecca Sciarra.

Case Study

The northeast corner of the Niagara Peninsula, encompassing Niagara-on-the Lake, St. Catharines, Niagara Falls, and Thorold, was chosen as an ideal case study location for its fulfillment of several criteria. This region includes a cross-jurisdictional landscape, and the presence of an international border is closely linked to the economic prosperity, cultural identity, and history of the region. It is a landscape of production, featuring regionally specialized tender-fruit agriculture as well as high-quality agricultural lands. The region contains regionally significant scenic resources and faces competing demands of economic growth and rural-based tourism. The cultural influence of a highly channelized, managed, and exploited watershed is a dominant feature in the landscape, and the influence of the Niagara Escarpment on culture and climate extends far beyond the Niagara Escarpment Planning Area boundary.

Background research on the Niagara region produced a wealth of research and planning documents. A key resource is *Niagara's Changing Landscapes*, edited by Hugh Gayler (1994); this work is a regional study of the Niagara Peninsula, interpreting social, historical, geological, and natural trends. Other informative research has been conducted on the cultural history of the Niagara region (Burghardt 1969; Jackson 1989, 1997; and Jackson and Burtniak 1978). Researchers at Brock University maintain online geographic resources and have conducted research on land management of the Niagara Parks Commission (Brock University Tourism and Environment 2007). An archaeological master plan completed for the Town of Niagara-on-the Lake, and watershed studies of the sub-watershed in Niagara-on-the-Lake are also important precedents for this research (ASI and Cuesta Systems Inc. 2001a, 2001b; Niagara Peninsula Conservation Authority 2008).

Information gathered from these sources, in addition to GIS data available through the Ministry of Natural Resources, Land Information Ontario, ASI Heritage Inc., and the Niagara Escarpment Commission, were compiled into a series of inventory maps. Fieldwork to identify cultural landscape resources, viewpoints, viewsheds, recreational amenities, and ecological services was conducted in July 2015 and integrated into the GIS.

The study area boundaries and policy context map (figure 12.3) illustrates the layers of local, provincial, federal, and international joint management. Key political entities that regulate land management in the region are the Niagara Escarpment Plan, Greenbelt Plan, Niagara Park Commission, Welland Canal, and Niagara River Board of Control.

Known archaeological resources were digitized and mapped. Resources included historic trails, known Hatiwendaronk villages, archaeological sites and clusters, and areas of archaeological potential including waterways, significant soil drainage patterns, and archaeological resources. The value map produced from this inventory shows a high concentration of cultural resource value in Niagara-on-the-Lake, as well as along Four Mile Creek, the Niagara River and Lake Ontario shoreline, and at key sites along the Niagara Escarpment. Ecological and hydrological systems were mapped: the final value analysis indicates the Welland Canal corridor, Four Mile Creek corridor, Niagara River corridor, and Niagara Escarpment as the most valuable resources.

Landscape character units were compiled to represent areas of regionally specific agriculture, including tender fruit, orchards, and vineyards. The mosaic of land tenure and development contributed to the identification of landscape character units. This method approximates the process used for landscape character assessment in the UK (Natural England 2014).

Tangible cultural heritage resources were mapped, including heritage districts, historic sites and structures, cemeteries, historic roads, abandoned and operational railways, and abandoned and operational portions of the Welland Canal. Additionally, the survey grid system illustrates changes in regional governance over time. The community values map employed community-driven data to understand how community values are expressed in the landscape. These included recreational facilities, community centres, festivals, trails, and wineries. The value maps identified a strong cluster along Niagara Stone Road and the Niagara Parkway, as well as a high valuing of the Niagara Escarpment and Welland Canal. Finally, the viewsheds map identified primary and secondary viewpoints and key viewshed. Viewsheds identified include the Niagara cuesta, the Niagara River, and the Lake Ontario shoreline. Secondary viewsheds are also labelled, including central Niagara-on-the-Lake, St. Catharines, and the New York shoreline.

A Biocultural Planning Approach for Managing Transborder Cultural Heritage Landscapes

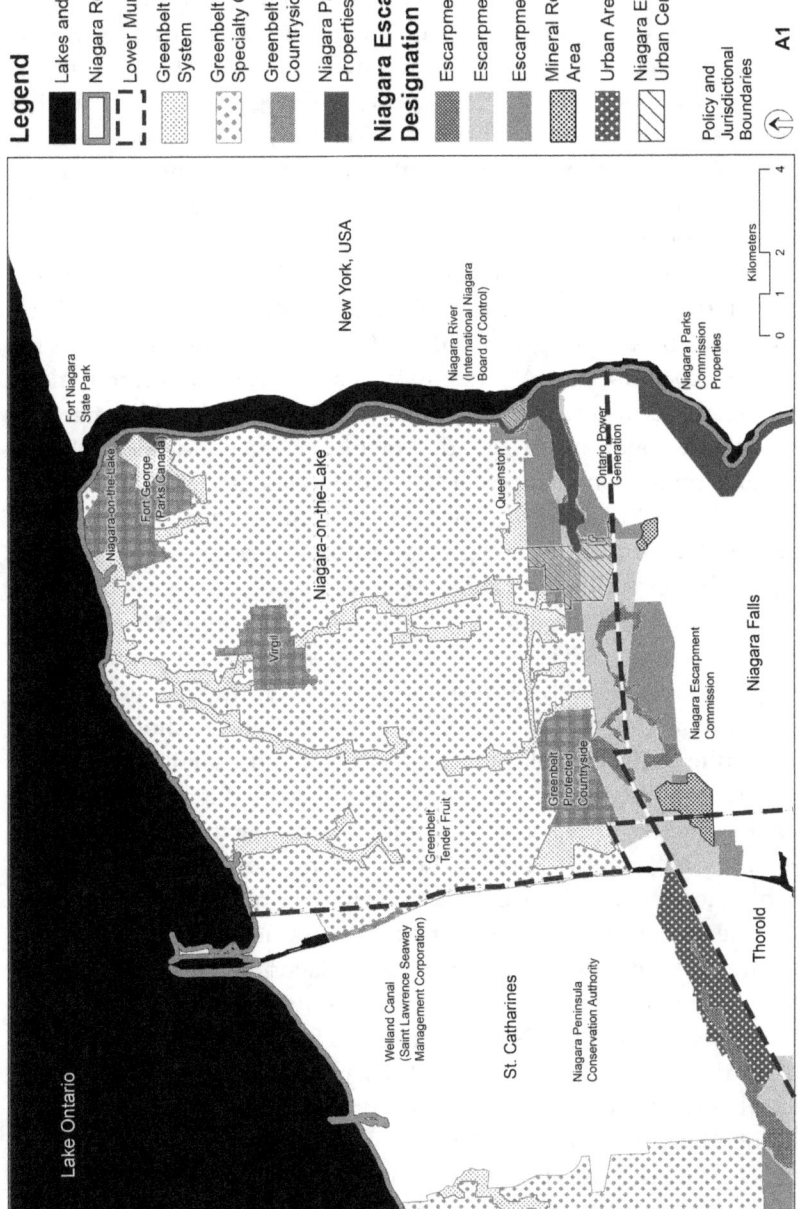

FIGURE 12-3. Study area boundaries and policy context map. *Source:* Scott Cafarella, Joel Konrad, and Rebecca Sciarra.

Results and Discussion

The value maps discussed above were layered to create a final landscape value map. Individual units were assigned values from 0 (the lowest value given) to 28 (highest value given). The numerical rankings were classified into values categories: very low, low, moderately low, average, moderately high, high, and very high. This map represents the raw output of the testing methodology and needs further interpretation to create a functional biocultural landscape planning system. Based on these values, highly ranked areas are core areas, moderately ranked areas are buffers, and low ranked areas are the zone of cooperation.

The final analysis map identifying biocultural planning zones is shown in figure 12.4. The dark green areas are the core areas, which are surrounded by a light green buffer. The yellow-green areas are the zones of cooperation. A system of core areas is formed along the Niagara Escarpment and the Niagara River, with additional core zones. These zones are surrounded by buffer areas. Additional buffer areas give protection to important regional roads such as Niagara Stone Road and Four Mile Creek, as well as the entire length of the Welland Canal. Select rural zones of high agricultural or community value are all given buffer status. The zones of cooperation encompass nearly all of Niagara-on-the-Lake, and much of Niagara Falls and St. Catharines.

The Niagara River and Niagara Escarpment are shown to be highly valuable biocultural resources; however, the inventory places less value on the Welland Canal and Lake Ontario shoreline. This may be due to the singular focus of the Welland Canal, and the relative inaccessibility of the shoreline, respectively. If it is desirable that these resources be conserved, individual site-specific heritage strategies may help identify more detailed connections to local heritage, and how to leverage these connections for community gain.

The map in figure 12.4 is the final product of this sample case study and is intended to be used as a discussion piece for further refinement with cultural and natural heritage stakeholders in the region. Most critically, this output is a tool for lower-tier governments and local organizations to scale up their discussion of cultural and natural resource conservation. This process can help communities visualize how regionally and internationally significant landscapes intersect with the local landscape. For example, the protection of local trails and streams become imperative when viewed from the

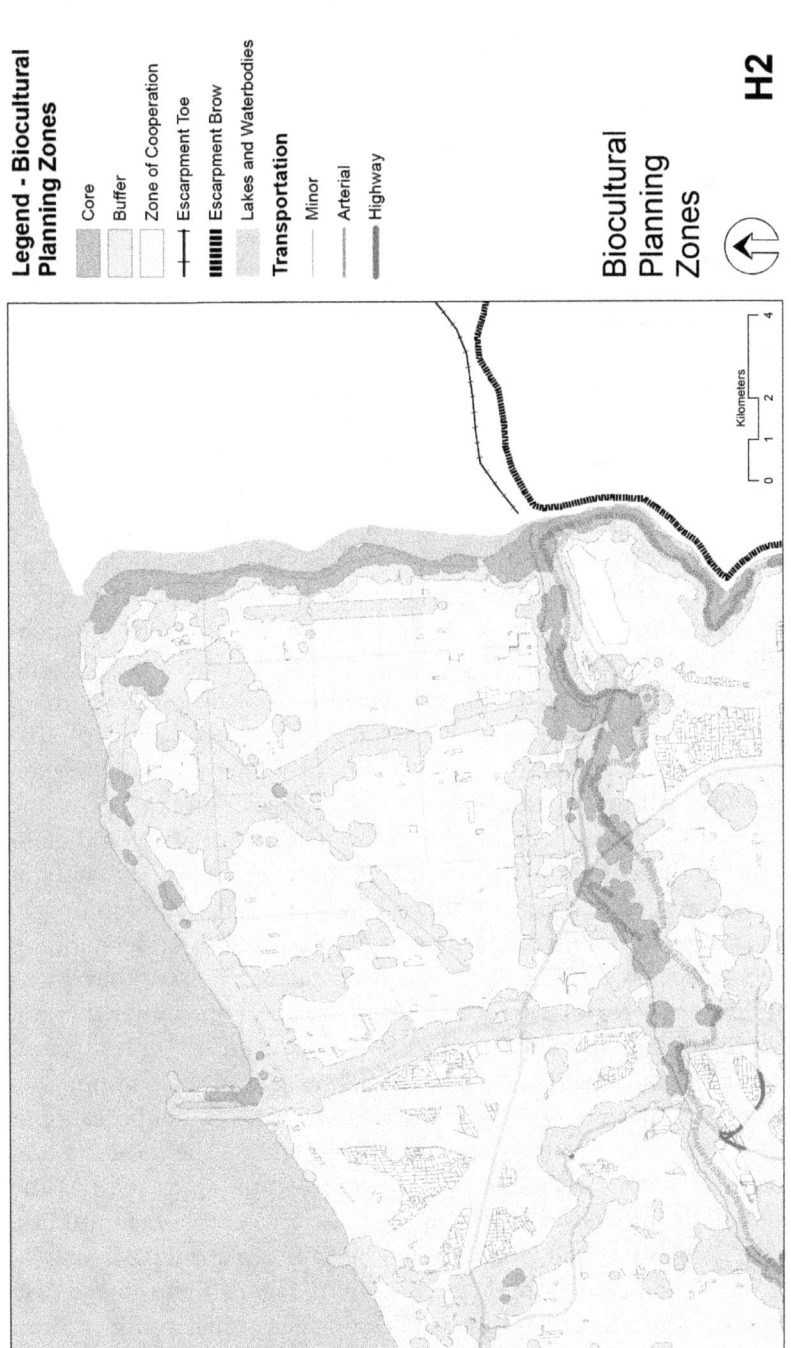

FIGURE 12.4. Biocultural planning zones within the study area. *Source*: Scott Cafarella, Joel Konrad, and Rebecca Sciarra.

perspective of transboundary transportation networks and regional watersheds. This methodology acknowledges that every community across Ontario has a system or network of culturally significant landscapes and provide a means for distinguishing those parts of the network that are the most sensitive to, as well as those most adaptive for, change.

Conclusion

The bioregional planning framework of cores, buffers, and zones of cooperation outlined by Brunckhorst (2000, 2001) is a highly adaptable strategy for the management of biocultural resources. While commonly employed under an ecological agenda, it can also be applied from a cultural landscape perspective, what we have termed a biocultural approach. The strategy addresses many continuing issues in landscape management, specifically how to manage large-scale cultural resources that extend across political borders. The emphasis on holistic planning approaches that study the interaction between nature and culture, rather than studying them independently, is in line with current trends in land management planning that is community driven and values based.

A biocultural approach also offers a management tool that expresses the importance of interaction, affect, and emotion when conserving cultural heritage landscapes. Recent scholarship on the connections between landscape and the concepts of affect and emotion has underscored the importance of applying a sensual paradigm to understanding our surroundings (Waterton 2013). In this approach, *action*, rather than representational *artifact*, is vital to understanding the landscapes we inhabit. The Niagara Escarpment, like other dominant landscape features, is a constant location of encounter that not only provides orientation, cultural artifacts, and an agricultural landscape but also instills a sense of identity and belonging. The management process outlined here demonstrates the importance of accessibility and encounter to further comprehend the meaning and value of cultural landscapes. Thus, a biocultural approach has the potential to integrate current theories in critical heritage studies, human geography, and landscape studies into a planning context.

As a transborder heritage site, the Niagara Escarpment case study also offers a glimpse into the challenges of managing cultural resources that cross national boundaries. A wealth of scholarship exists on the connection between cultural heritage and expressions of the nation, focusing primarily on contested sites of identity, gender, and decolonialization (Silverman 2010; Allen 2012; Munasinghe 2005; Aitchison 1999; Gillis 1996). These studies have emphasized the interplay between heritage and national identities and highlighted the importance of international borders, cultural boundaries, and the concept of the nation in critical heritage studies. Borders are here generally conceived as political constructs that define the nation and retain a degree of cultural impermeability as our increasingly globalized world is resulting in "the shielding of cultures through the politics of difference" and the solidification of "cultural trenches" (Arizpe 2000, 32). Transnational heritage sites complicate national narratives and contend homogeneous national identities predicated on a common political past. Through concepts such as cooperation, buffers, and core areas, a biocultural approach to heritage management could provide a transnational antidote to heritage conservation within national silos.

There are also opportunities for borderlands theory to contribute to a greater understanding of how international and regional borders contribute to the cultural diversity of the Niagara Escarpment bioregion. Viewed through the lens of borderlands theory, international borders are significant cultural and historical resources. The Canada-US border is a site of human migration, shared industrial history, an ecological corridor, and an area of international cooperation and trade. The role of heritage conservation and cultural landscape planning is to illustrate this shared tangible and intangible history, and to create new regional identities (Leibenath, Blum, and Stutzriemer 2010; Soyez 2009).

Opportunities for future research include the refinement of the methodology through additional case studies along the escarpment. The product of the methodology is highly dependent on how the input layers are valued at the outset of the study; therefore, testing different value rankings and consulting with stakeholders is vital to refine the ranking system and to establish a more defensible methodology. The result could provide municipalities with a workable model for the management of large-scale cultural landscapes. Further, the adoption of such a management policy by the provincial government would set a baseline of heritage conservation and reduce the conservation disparity that can occur on different sides of municipal borders.

References

Aitchison, Cara. 1999. "Heritage and Nationalism: Gender and the Performance of Power." In *Leisure/Tourism Geographies: Practices and Geographical Knowledge*, edited by David Crouch, 59–78. London: Psychology Press.

Allen, Richard. 2012. "Heritage and Nationalism." In *Understanding the Politics of Heritage*, edited by Rodney Harrison, 197–233. Manchester, UK: Manchester University Press.

Alper, Donald K. 1996. "The Idea of Cascadia: Emergent Transborder Regionalisms in the Pacific Northwest-Western Canada." *Journal of Borderlands Studies* 11 (2): 1–22.

Antrop, Mark. 2006. "Sustainable Landscapes: Contradiction, Fiction, or Utopia?" *Landscape and Urban Planning* 75 (3): 187–197.

Arzipe, Lourdes. 2000. "Cultural Heritage and Globalization." In *Values and Heritage Conservation*, edited by Erica Avrami, Randall Mason, and Marta de la Torre, 31–37. Los Angeles: The Getty Conservation Institute.

ASI (Archaeological Services Inc.) and Cuesta Systems Inc. 2001a. *The Archaeological Master Plan of the Town of Niagara-on-the-Lake: Technical Report*. Virgil, ON: The Town of Niagara-on-the-Lake.

———. 2001b. *A Master Plan of Archaeological Resources for the Town of Niagara-on-the-Lake: Planning Report*. Virgil, ON: The Town of Niagara-on-the-Lake.

BLRPC (Bay-Lake Regional Planning Commission). 2010. *Niagara Escarpment Overlay Zoning Guide*. http://media.baylakerpc.org/media/47146/ne%20overlay%20zoning%20guide.pdf.

———. 2001. *An Inventory and Assessment of the Resources of the Niagara Escarpment in Wisconsin, Technical Report #77*. http://media.baylakerpc.org/media/47143/niagara%20escarpment%20march%202001.pdf.

Brock University Tourism and Environment. 2007. *Environmental Land Management Plan for the Niagara Parks Commission: Stage 1*. http://www.niagaraknowledgeexchange.com/.

Brown, Jessica, Nora Mitchell, and Michael Beresford, eds. 2005. *The Protected Landscape Approach: Linking Nature, Culture and Community*. IUCN World Commission on Protected Areas. https://www.iucn.org/content/protected-landscape-approach-linking-nature-culture-and-community.

Brunckhorst, David. 2001. "Building Capital Through Bioregional Planning and Biosphere Reserves." *Ethics in Science and Environmental Politics* 1 (1): 19–32.

———. 2000. *Bioregional Planning: Resource Management Beyond the New Millennium*. Amsterdam: Harwood Academic Publishers.

Burghardt, Andrew F. 1969. "The Origin and Development of the Road Network of the Niagara Peninsula, Ontario, 1770–1851." *Annals of the Association of American Geographers* 59 (3): 417–440.

Canada. 2019. *Canada National Parks Act (2000)*. https://www.canlii.org/en/ca/laws/stat/sc-2000-c-32/latest/sc-2000-c-32.html.

Forman, Richard T. T., and Michel Godron. 1986. *Landscape Ecology*. New York: Wiley.

Gayler, Hugh J., ed. 1994. *Niagara's Changing Landscapes*. Ottawa: Carleton University Press.

Gillis, John R. 1996. *Commemorations: The Politics of National Identity*. Princeton, NJ: Princeton University Press.

Haselberger, Beatrix. 2014. "Decoding Borders: Appreciating Border Impacts on Space and People." *Planning Theory and Practice* 15 (4): 505–526.

Hele, Karl S. 2008. *Lines Drawn Upon the Water: First Nations and the Great Lakes Borders and Borderlands*. Waterloo, ON: Wilfred Laurier University Press.

IPBES (Intergovernmental Science-Policy Platform on Biodiversity and Ecosystem Services). 2017. *The Assessment Report of the Intergovernmental Science-Policy Platform on Biodiversity and Ecosystem Services on Pollinators, Pollination and Food Production*. Edited by S. G. Potts, V. L. Imperatriz-Fonseca, and H. T. Ngo. Bonn, Germany: Secretariat of the Intergovernmental Science-Policy Platform on Biodiversity and Ecosystem Services.

Jackson, John N. 1997. *The Welland Canals and Their Communities: Engineering, Industrial and Urban Transformation*. Toronto: University of Toronto Press.

———. 1989. *Names Across Niagara*. St. Catharines, ON: Vanwell Publishing Limited.

Jackson, John N., and John Burtniak. 1978. *Railways in the Niagara Peninsula: Their Development, Progress and Community Significance*. Belleville, ON: Mika Publishing Company.

Konrad, Victor. 2012. "Conflating Imagination, Identity and Affinity in the Social Construction of Borderlands Culture Between Canada and the United States." *American Review of Canadian Studies* 42 (4): 530–548.

Leibenath, Markus, Andreas Blum, and Sylke Stutzriemer. 2010. "Transboundary Cooperation in Establishing Ecological Networks: The Case of Germany's External Borders." *Landscape and Urban Planning* 94:84–93.

Lyle, John Tillman. 1985. *Design for Human Ecosystems: Landscape, Land Use, and Natural Resources*. New York: Van Nostrand Reinhold.

McHarg, Ian L. 1969. *Design with Nature*. Garden City, NY: Natural History Press.

Munasinghe, Harsha. 2005. "The Politics of the Past: Constructing a National Identity Through Heritage Conservation." *International Journal of Heritage Studies* 2 (3): 251–260.

National Park Service. 2014. *Scaling Up: Collaborative Approaches to Large Landscape Conservation*. https://www.nps.gov/orgs/1412/upload/Scaling-Up-2014-508.pdf.

Natural England. 2014. *An Approach to Landscape Character Assessment.* https://www.gov.uk/government/uploads/system/uploads/attachment_data/file/396192/landscape-character-assessment.pdf.

Nelson, Gordon. 2012. *Beyond the Global City: Understanding and Planning for the Diversity of Ontario.* Montréal and Kingston: McGill-Queen's University Press.

Nelson, Gordon, and James Porter. 2002. *Building the Great Arc: An International Heritage Corridor in the Great Lakes Region.* Waterloo, ON: Heritage Resources Centre, University of Waterloo.

Niagara Peninsula Conservation Authority. 2008. *Niagara-on-the-Lake Watershed Study.* Prepared by Aquafor Beech Limited. https://npca.ca/watershed-plans.

Ontario. 2020a. *2020 Provincial Policy Statement Under the Planning Act.* https://files.ontario.ca/mmah-provincial-policy-statement-2020-accessible-final-en-2020-02-14.pdf.

———. 2020b. *Planning Act, R.S.O. 1990, c. P.13.* https://www.ontario.ca/laws/statute/90p13.

———. 2019. *Ontario Heritage Act, R.S.O. 1990, c.O.18.* https://www.ontario.ca/laws/statute/90o18.

———. 2014. *2014 Provincial Policy Statement Under the Planning Act.* https://www.ontario.ca/document/provincial-policy-statement-2014.

———. 2006. *Ontario Heritage Act, Ontario Regulation 9/06: Criteria for Determining Cultural Heritage Value or Interest.* http://www.ontario.ca/laws/regulation/060009.

———. 2005a. *2005 Provincial Policy Statement.* http://www.mah.gov.on.ca/AssetFactory.aspx?did=11112.

———. 2005b. *Ontario Heritage Tool Kit: Heritage Conservation Districts: A Guide to District Designation Under the Ontario Heritage Act.* Queen's Printer for Ontario. http://www.mtc.gov.on.ca/en/publications/Heritage_Tool_Kit_HCD_English.pdf.

———. 1997. *Provincial Policy Statement (1996, amended in 1997).* https://web.archive.org/web/20140410161221/http://www.mah.gov.on.ca/Page1491.aspx.

Ontario Heritage Trust. 2012. *Cultural Heritage Landscapes – An Introduction.* https://www.heritagetrust.on.ca/user_assets/documents/HIS-020-Cultural-heritage-landscapes-An-introduction-ENG.pdf.

(PRI) Government of Canada, Policy Research Initiative. 2008. *The Emergence of Cross-Border Regions Between Canada and the United States: Reaping the promise and public value of cross-border regional relationships, Final Report.* https://www.aims.ca/site/media/aims/CrossBorder.pdf.

Riley, John. 2013. *The Once and Future Great Lakes Country: An Ecological History.* Montréal and Kingston: McGill-Queen's University Press.

Schama, Simon. 1996. *Landscape and Memory.* New York: Vintage Books.

Silverman, Helaine. 2010. *Contested Cultural Heritage: Religion, Nationalism, Erasure, and Exclusion in a Global World*. New York: Springer.

Sohn, Christophe. 2014a. "The Border as a Resource in the Global Urban Space: A Contribution to the Cross-Border Metropolis Hypothesis." *International Journal of Urban and Regional Research* 38 (5): 1697–1711.

———. 2014b. "Modelling Cross-Border Integration: The Role of Borders as a Resource." *Geopolitics* 9 (3): 587–608.

Soyez, Dietrich. 2009. "Europeanizing Industrial Heritage in Europe: Addressing its Transboundary and Dark Sides." *Geographische Zeitschrift* 97 (1): 43–55.

Steiner, Frederick R. 1990. *The Living Landscape: An Ecological Approach to Landscape Planning*. New York: McGraw-Hill.

UNESCO (United Nations Educational, Scientific and Cultural Organization). 2015. *Main Characteristics of Biosphere Reserves*. http://www.unesco.org/new/en/natural-sciences/environment/ecological-sciences/biosphere-reserves/main-characteristics/.

———. 2012. *Niagara Escarpment Biosphere Reserve: Periodic Review*. https://www.escarpment.org/NiagaraEscarpment/UnescoWorldBiosphereReserve/PeriodicReview.

———. 1995. *The Seville Strategy for Biosphere Reserves*. www.unesco.org/mab/doc/brs/Strategy.pdf.

———. 1973. *Records of the General Conference, 17th session, Paris, 17 October to 21 November 1972, v. 1: Resolutions, recommendations*. https://unesdoc.unesco.org/ark:/48223/pf0000114044.page=147.

Waterton, Emma. 2013. "Landscape and Non-Representational Theories." In *The Routledge Companion to Landscape Studies*, edited by Peter Howard, Ian Thompson, and Emma Waterton, 66–74. London: Routledge.

WNYLC (Western New York Land Conservancy). 2014. *Niagara Escarpment Legacy Project*. http://wnylc.org/site/wp-content/uploads/2014/05/Report-Niagara-Escarpment-Legacy-Project-May-2014.pdf.

CONCLUSION

Borders, Culture, and Globalization

Some Conclusions, More Uncertainties, and Many Challenges

Melissa Kelly and Victor Konrad

A poster for the EU region Sønderjylland-Schleswig states that "kultur ist einfach" (culture is easy). The sense of this statement, arising from the "kulturfokus" initiative coming out of Denmark and Germany, is that the shared culture of the cross-border region is a "no-brainer," a given in the borderlands context (Kulturfokus.dk 2016). Border culture, then, while it is acknowledged, acceptable, apparent, even natural, is not actually easy in the sense of simplicity. In fact, as we have learned from this volume, border culture is exceptionally complex and multifaceted, and, in globalization, this complexity and multiscalar representation of culture grows and has impacts in various, and often unpredictable ways (Laine 2016; Casaglia and Laine 2017; Popescu 2011; Parker and Vaughan-Williams 2014; De Genova 2012; Diener and Hagen 2009).

Border culture is in motion and in process, with anchors uprooted from territorial legacies and traditional spaces and places, familiar coordinates blurred or lost, many more cultural entities and affiliations intertwined, and novel associations and alignments apparent in spaces of integration and contestation (Konrad and Brunet-Jailly 2019; Konrad 2015; Rodney 2017; Amilhat Szary and Giraut 2015; Konrad and Nicol 2011). Border culture is shifting in and out of focus, resulting in more uncertainties in multiscalar bordering of our worlds, offering numerous challenges for the consideration and study of border culture, yet providing some conclusions to advance our understanding of border culture.

These conclusions, as well as the uncertainties and challenges to understanding border culture are discussed in the context of Canada's borders, bordering, and borderlands. In Canada's borderlands shared with the United States, and in Canada's virtual and imagined borders, where we increasingly engage varying parts of the world, border culture is produced or altered to perform, document, and establish our identities (Roberts 2018). Yet these conceptions of who we are, how we build the spaces around us, where we share or divide these real or imagined spaces, are loosened and adrift from traditional notions defined in territorial containers and well-rehearsed scripts of nationalism and identity.

Canadians in all regions of the country continue to wrestle with bounded conceptions of Indigeneity and multiculturalism. Racism, sexism, exceptionalism, and more, all are revealed by borders and bordering within Canada and at its edges. These faces of border culture need more examination and acknowledgement in our considerations of how border culture is formed and reformed in globalization. We have chosen to address these issues in all of the sections of this volume—viewing the border, borders and culture in motion, and, particularly, placing and replacing border culture—but, more needs to be done to reveal the insidious components of border culture aligned with corruption and hate and fuelled by power, status, wealth, and entitlement. Canadians use the border with the United States to differentiate Canadian virtue from American excess, as if a border can create a barrier, or a filter at least, to stem the flow of unwanted and even reviled characteristics of American culture. Yet border culture is also the conduit to enable the flow and Canadians, linked yet differentiated from Americans, need to recognize and understand how border culture is constituted, articulated, controlled, and even subverted in order to benefit from its potential for ameliorating interaction, and to identify and address its capacity to enable harm.

As a contribution to the wider Borders in Globalization project, this volume, and the extensive research efforts that it is derived from, set out to better understand the transformations taking place in and around Canada's borders. In addressing the relationship between culture and borders, the volume began with a double-barrelled question:

how does culture alter borders and how do borders alter culture? Our efforts to address these questions, and many other queries emerging from them, have engaged a multidisciplinary team of scholars and practitioners with a primary goal to advance our understanding of border culture. The various chapters presented in this volume are reflective of the diverse backgrounds of their authors; many different theoretical and substantive issues were raised across the chapters. Despite coming from different academic disciplines and applied fields, however, the contributors speak to common themes and issues concerning how borders and culture are related in an increasingly globalized world.

This final chapter will synthesize the volume's broader contributions and discuss the implications of the work undertaken. It will begin by considering how the volume contributes to a new paradigm for understanding the relationship between borders and culture. This will be followed by a discussion of how this new paradigm helps us to understand the relationship between borders, culture, and power. Finally, the chapter will conclude by considering the policy implications stemming from this work.

Toward a New Paradigm for Understanding Borders and Culture

Culture flows, through interactions between people, through deterritorialized mediums such as the Internet, and through the consumption of cultural goods and commodities. As it moves, it gives new meaning to borders and vice versa. Globalization has transformed human culture, bringing diverse people into closer contact more than ever before (Huntington 1993; Said 1978). Ideas, people, goods, and capital now flow between places both physically and through cyberspace at new intensities and in new ways, having profound implications for how people experience and make sense of the world (Popescu 2011; Bhabha 1994; Appadurai 1996; Ghemawat 2011). In this context, borders, as human artefacts, are being transformed and imbued with new meaning, and this meaning extends everywhere and infuses everyday life (van Houtum, Kramsch, and Zierhofer 2005; Jones and Johnson 2014). In an increasingly complex and dynamic world, what borders represent, how they are managed, and how they are crossed have all changed to reflect evolving relationships between people and places at different levels of scale

(Brambilla 2015; Laine 2016). Borders can no longer be understood simply as demarcations between political territories representing homogeneous cultural containers (Agnew 1994). Instead, they are multidimensional, implicating different types of boundaries between people. Culture sometimes aligns with borders, but sometimes it transcends them, creating new boundaries and giving new meaning to the physical lines that divide countries, regions, and even communities.

In order to explain these transformations taking place, a much more sophisticated approach to understanding the relationship between borders and culture is needed (Brambilla 2015). This approach needs to accommodate recent understandings of emerging borders in globalization, and the major revelations about culture derived from social and cultural theory. As argued in the introduction to this compilation, this involves integrating formative thinking about borders and culture culminating in Fredrik Barth's insights into the social organization of cultural difference (Barth 1969) with the more politically charged views of culture offered by social theorists. Among these views are Antonio Gramsci's (2012) perspective on the hegemony of culture and how this grows the political dimension in culture, and how culture becomes politics (Mitchell 2000), and also evokes a culture of political unconsciousness (O Tuathail and Dalby 1998). Yet within this pervasive atmosphere of the border politic, border culture is framed in human agency (Latour 2005) and body politics (Mignolo and Tlostanova 2006), and fraught with competing universalities (Butler 2004), the burden of perpetual difference (Derrida 1991), and the prevalence of dissensus (Rancière 2015).

Our goal, as the editors of this volume, was to explore the relationship between borders and culture from a broad range of perspectives. Rather than rooting the work in one school of thought, as is often done in scholarly works that consider the relationship between borders and culture, we focused instead on common themes observed across different theoretical and disciplinary frameworks. As a result of this effort, we believe we have made considerable progress toward the development of a new approach for understanding border culture and how border culture is placed and replaced in globalization. Collectively, the contributions in this volume considered culture in the diverse forms that it takes, giving due attention to the embodied aspects of culture, the culture that people produce (including art and literature), and also cultural politics.

While we divided the volume into three sections for the purpose of analytical clarity, there were many common themes across all of the chapters. Together, the authors have contributed to the development of a non-binary, multidimensional and multiscalar understanding of borders (Brambilla 2015; Laine 2016). They have shown how local, regional, and global levels of scale often intersect (in variable ways) to influence the relationship between borders and culture, giving way to cultural production and new spatial forms at and beyond the borderline itself. Together, the chapters in this volume showed that while physical borders remain important in the lives of those who live near them (or attempt to cross them), borders are increasingly difficult to precisely locate. Borders, and border culture, are linked in motion (Konrad 2015), and, perhaps, even more specifically in relational motion (Ptak et al. 2020).

A new approach for understanding borders and culture needs to remain mindful of nation-state borders and national cultures while viewing these as only one dimension of border culture in an increasingly multidimensional display and interaction of border culture. The contributions in this volume showed how various types of boundaries, such as those based on language, religion, and identity, intersect with and sometimes challenge geographical borders in a variety of ways. These are all components not only of "deterritorialization" and "reterritorialization" but also "aterritorialization" as illustrated in extensive and substantial social construction of borders away from and beyond national boundaries (Konrad and Brunet-Jailly 2019).

The emphasis of many of the chapters has clearly been on the meaning attributed to borders through embodied experiences, symbols, interpretations, and imaginings of borders (Shweder and LeVine 1984; Mignolo and Tlostanova 2006; Schimanski and Wolfe 2017). These contributions, while policy-relevant, have frequently illuminated the perspectives of individuals and groups rather than states. It is hoped that this has helped to challenge the dominant imaginings of borders cultivated by state-centric perspectives and that it has advanced a more nuanced understanding of borders and bordering processes. Adopting this approach has also drawn attention to the subjectivity and agency of borderlanders and border crossers.

While popular conceptions of borders typically portray them as lines dividing distinct territorial units, this volume has emphasized the need to think past this simplistic representation to instead consider the multifaceted ways borders are imagined and manifested and how they are influenced by culture and vice versa. We hope that, collectively, the chapters in this volume have provided readers with new ways of viewing borders and understanding their multidimensionality and multiscalar characteristics.

Borders, Culture, and Power

Borders wield considerable power over cultural flows, and yet culture itself is a pervasive force that plays a role in shaping borders. One can therefore not understand the relationship between borders and culture without giving due attention to the issue of power (Newman 2003). Several of the contributions in this volume have illustrated how power plays out at the border and have raised questions about how borders can and should be reconstructed to be more inclusive and just.

Growing international interconnectedness has, in many ways, made it easier for culture to transcend borders than was previously the case. At the same time, barriers have also been erected to slow, limit, or prevent the free mobility of people, ideas, and goods across boundary lines. Culture in its various forms, therefore, crosses borders selectively. Despite the cultural forces that have usurped aspects of the nation-state's dominance, geopolitical borders remain very important in determining cross-border flows. Under globalization, most national governments have opened their borders to some degree, allowing for the flow of capital, cultural commodities, and people, but only if and when deemed beneficial. The continued tendency to view national governments as rightful gatekeepers of borders and filters for "good" and "bad" culture reflects the way boundaries between people (in the form of culture, identity, and belonging) are typically imagined and understood. The fact that borders may be seen as natural rather than as social constructions may help to justify stringent border controls and restrictions on who and what can cross the dividing lines between states.

Perhaps the domain in which power struggles over borders and culture have been debated the most in recent years concerns human migration. Where people are from and the kind of culture they are associated with may make them more or less eligible to cross borders. This issue was taken up in this volume by Melissa Kelly (chapter 5), who pointed out how the snowbirds, Canadian retirees who go to the United States for long-term stays each winter, face few barriers to seasonal migration. The Canadian snowbirds' cultural similarity to American snowbirds, and the lifestyles they lead during their time in the US, have led them to be viewed as unthreatening and even beneficial to American society. This is in stark contrast to the cases touched on in some of the other chapters in the volume. Anelynda Mielke and Nadya Pohran (chapter 3), for example, drew attention to the unwelcoming environment some asylum seekers face when claiming refugee status in Canada, leading them to hide and live without even basic human rights. A narrative has emerged whereby the openness of borders is seen as both an opportunity and a threat depending on who and what is crossing borders, with ideas about "culture" increasingly used as a filter to decide who is and is not welcome to cross.

The extent to which a country is open to other cultures can itself become a part of its national and cultural identity, and something that distinguishes it from neighbouring countries. The Canadian government's efforts to quickly settle Syrian refugees, as discussed by Renata Grudzien (chapter 8), was a testament to the state's openness to newcomers and consistent with its long-standing policy of multiculturalism as well as its humanitarian commitments. This is in stark contrast to the United States' recent approach, which increasingly restricted immigration in favour of greater insularity. Such statements about culture and the nation, however, are unduly homogenizing, and overlook cultural and political differences within national containers framed by borders. It is therefore important to understand the significance and impact of the nation-state's hegemony (in both symbolic and practical terms), without oversimplifying the diversity that exists within state borders.

As has been emphasized throughout the volume, culture does not always fit within the contained boundaries of nation-states. Instead, the power of culture may be wielded by way of other divisions that cut across national borders such as ethnicity, race, and language. It is perhaps because of this that the borderline itself is another place where power is clearly asserted and contested. In the borderlands, communities divided by borders may become spaces where the key concepts of confluence, differentiation, the transcendence of binaries, and shifting interfaces (all of which were discussed in the introduction to this compilation) visibly play out. International borders are sometimes placed without due attention to the histories, identities, and daily practices of the people living in proximity to them. The presence of a highly securitized international border in such spaces is reflective of the nation-state's determination to keep national culture tightly in place. Many of the chapters in this volume touched on this noting, as Sandra Vandervalk (chapter 6) does, for example, how the experiences of those living in borderland areas are often misunderstood, and how other markers of identity such as ethnicity and language may be overlooked in a world of enduring nation-state dominance. This is very problematic insofar as it divides what might be otherwise united communities. In Indigenous contexts, the legacy of colonial bordering processes may interfere with borderland communities' sense of self-identification and way of life. This point was elaborated on by Evelyn P. Mayer (chapter 9) and Laetitia Rouvière (chapter 10).

In light of this growing complexity, the imperative of belonging has become accentuated in globalization. While global forces have in many ways made the world a smaller, more integrated place, borders and boundaries have also taken on new meaning for people's sense of belonging, as illustrated in different ways by Lee Rodney (chapter 1) and Alexander Rudolph (chapter 7). Belonging may be found at the intersections of different types of boundaries and scales. Moreover, borders and boundaries play a dual role. They may, in some cases, help people to belong, while in other cases they pose a challenge to belonging. They are therefore a social construct that can be used as a resource, one with considerable power as portrayed in the application of border culture knowledge and understanding in associative natural and heritage planning (Cafarella, Konrad, and Sciarra, this volume, chapter 12). Borders can be used to defend hegemonic conceptions of belonging, but they can also be used to change existing narratives and create new notions of belonging and inclusivity.

The framework for understanding borders that we have advanced in this volume is one that challenges the notion that borders are static and unchanging. Instead, they are viewed as dynamic and processual social constructions, constantly evolving in response to complex economic, social, and cultural factors. This conception of borders opens the possibility that the functions and meanings of borders may change, as they are resisted, reimagined, and renegotiated by different actors. Several of the chapters have demonstrated this possibility by showing how there is a growing space for questioning, contestation, and even activism at and beyond the borderlands. As the chapters illustrate, the starting point for challenging hegemonic border constructs may be changing the way borders are viewed.

While seeing the border in new ways was a theme explored across the volume, the first section, "Viewing Border Culture," spoke to it most directly. The contributions by Rodney, Michael Darroch, Mielke and Pohran, and Victor Konrad and Srimoyee Mitra all reflected on how borders are viewed and proposed alternative ways of seeing them.

Art and literature can be a particularly effective way to challenge dominant conceptions of borders, particularly at the borderlands itself. This was recognized in Rodney's chapter, for example, which depicted borderlands as "sites for a number of activists, artists, and writers to question the ways that contemporary bordering practices condition our thinking about territory, power, and belonging." Mayer's analysis of Thomas King's work similarly highlighted the power of literature to challenge preconceptions and to show alternatives to the status quo. The visual and literary arts have the potential to be very closely aligned with political context and are capable of creating new narratives that may have political salience and bring about cultural change. It is for this reason that King is called an "activist," an activist by artistic means. While ways of seeing the border inspire artistic and symbolic representation, the same is also true the other way around, with representations of borders having implications for the way borders are viewed and understood.

Like the arts, technology also has the capacity to wield considerable cultural change in a cross-border context. The widespread accessibility of television, Internet, and other communication technologies has made it possible for culture to more easily transcend state boundaries. This is discussed in Rudolph's chapter, which considered Canada's inability to dominate the Internet in the face of American competition. Canadians' consequent exposure to American culture by way of the Internet may lead to cultural homogenization between Canada and the US; at the same time, the Internet has created new opportunities for minority cultures to assert themselves and promote their identities digitally. Heidi Weigand and Colin Howell similarly showed how strategic use of the Internet may be used to assert Indigenous identities, and how the media may be used to gain sympathy for Indigenous rights.

Changing borderscapes, as well as an emergent, conscious understanding of borders as dynamic and negotiable have created new challenges and new opportunities for furthering social and cultural change and for challenging the dominance of certain actors, most notably the state, in the definition of border constructs. While the de-bordering and re-bordering brought by globalization have in some cases limited the flow of culture, new spaces have also opened up for the creative negotiation of identities, belonging, and rights. In a context of heightened change due to globalization, it is important to reflect on the power dimensions of border-culture relationships and to think about what kind of social and cultural changes are possible and desirable. This is best done by adopting a cultural lens that gives due attention to the subjectivity, history, and daily practices of borderlanders.

Implications for Cross-Border Policy

While culture may be a central topic of focus in some policy fields, such as migration and integration, as stated at the outset of this volume, less explicitly, border culture touches on a number of wide-ranging cross-border issues. Border culture is intimately linked with concerns as diverse as national security, environmental management, and trade. Culture, therefore, must be given due consideration when considering how to develop effective policy on a number of cross-border issues.

In a world where the relationship between borders and culture is increasingly being shaped by complex, globalizing forces, what is the role of policy? In recent years, transnationalism and cross-border flows have led new policy issues to come to the fore, while many existing policy issues have become recognized as increasingly complex. While the volume included contributions from practitioners directly working to improve border policy, even the more theoretically informed chapters had strong policy implications, drawing attention to the need to rethink how policy is understood and what its role could be.

Collectively, the contributions of this volume have identified a number of key considerations for policy. The first is the importance of viewing policy issues from the perspectives of multiple stakeholders. In an increasingly complex world, it has become more important than ever to consider how the transformations that are occurring are impacting different groups of people in a variety of ways. The diverse subjects taken up by this volume, and the variety of perspectives from which they have been explored, have shown the value of considering these new issues from a range of perspectives. Relevant stakeholders may include various levels of government, people who want or need to cross borders, residents in places affected by cross-border flows, and consumers of cultural commodities. They may also include different segments of the population such as Indigenous peoples, refugees, and people with different genders, sexualities, and ethnic backgrounds.

Secondly, it is hoped that the volume's focus on the more subjective dimensions of bordering, such as identity and meaning making, have given policymakers a new understanding of the importance of putting cultural concerns at the centre of policy analysis. As the various contributions have shown, it is not only economic and political factors that implicate bordering processes, but also people's sense of belonging and the way they view, imagine and experience borders in their day-to-day lives. As chapters such as Vandervalk's have shown, certain groups of people, such as borderland dwellers, may have a relationship to borders that non-border dwellers find difficult to understand. If these cultural modes of being in the world are not taken into account, it is possible that they may be overlooked in policy, leaving people alienated, misunderstood, and frustrated.

Finally, the chapters of the volume have shown how the border-culture relationship is not only about the political spaces created by physical borderlines and that due attention must therefore be given to various types of boundaries, including ethnic and linguistic boundaries, which may intersect with political borders in a variety of ways. Developing an understanding of the various boundaries that intersect with political borders is essential for developing policies that are sensitive to the needs of individuals and communities. This was evident across the three sections of the volume, but most explicitly in those chapters addressing Indigeneity as it is experienced in the context of the Canada-US border.

The contributors have also done well, however, to raise additional questions about the emerging role of policy, especially in an increasingly globalized world. These questions will require further thought and reflection. The first question concerns what role policy should play in regulating the flow of culture across borders. Should national cultures be protected? And if so, how? Rudolph's chapter posed this question by illustrating how as Canadians consume increasing amounts of American-produced media and entertainment through the Internet, there are implications for Canadian culture, especially for minority groups. Rudolph cited opportunities for encouraging Canadian content through, for example, public-private partnerships and the use of content-sharing platforms such as YouTube. He noted, however, that to date, the federal government has done little to address this issue. While the outcomes of this approach are still to be seen, he anticipates more cultural integration between Canada and the United States over time. The extent to which Canada should provide funding or adopt other measures to protect Canadian culture is perhaps a matter for debate.

A second, and related question, concerns the responsibility for policy when culture transcends borders. As already discussed, complex spatial relations are leading to the production of new social spaces, creating vagueness around who is and is not responsible for managing the flow of people and cultural commodities across borders. Policy may need to adapt to these changing spatial formations and to devise innovative approaches that take account of the new multiscalar realities that are emerging. As the chapters have shown, one way to do this is to develop policy, sometimes from the bottom-up, through engagement with stakeholders. Hence, it may be necessary, for example, to enact different levels of government than has been traditionally done, including less commonly acknowledged political actors, such as Indigenous communities and advocacy groups. This was the subject of Rouvière's chapter, which showed how border security policies are being developed in Akwesasne, as the local Mohawk community collaborates with both the Canadian and American governments on border security issues. The new forms of cooperation that occur signify shared identities and objectives, and, somewhat ironically, transform the border into a resource for the community as it asserts its sovereignty and identity.

Finally, it may be necessary to look for new opportunities to scale up or better coordinate existing policies to make them more effective in an increasingly interconnected world. This was one of the messages conveyed in Scott Cafarella, Joel Konrad, and Rebecca Sciarra's chapter, which showed the value of transferring cultural practices and knowledge across borders by way of a case study focusing on the Niagara Escarpment area. They argued that tools used by lower-level governments and local governments could be scaled up to improve the management of transboundary cultural and natural resources. Weigand and Howell's chapter similarly showed how the Jay Treaty has made it possible for Haudenosaunee people to cross the Canada-US border with a Haudenosaunee rather than an American or Canadian passport. However, these passports cannot be used to cross other borders, thereby limiting the recognition that Haudenosaunee people receive as an independent sovereign nation. Policymakers may wish to think about how successful interventions could be expanded or altered to reflect the changing international reality and how policies could be better coordinated, even across varying levels of geographical scale. If traditional policy frameworks and power structures cannot garner change, new approaches will be needed to meet the changing needs.

Understanding border culture is a key component in comprehending borders in an increasingly globalized world. It is hoped that the chapters in this volume have drawn attention to important challenges for policymakers and others concerned with the management of borders in a range of capacities, and given new ideas and inspiration for how to approach these challenges. The contributions in this volume have provided a number of ideas for how borders can be reimagined, studied, and understood. We hope that this has provided relevant stakeholders with new tools to engage with these concepts and explore how they can be applied.

Moving Forward:
Borders and Culture in the Twenty-First Century

Media coverage of borders, as well as reality television shows that show border security guards at work, tend to normalize borders as zones of high security, where the flow of goods is monitored, where mobility is controlled, and where "insiders" and "outsiders" are unproblematically defined. This has influenced how borders are conceptualized in the popular imagination, causing a tendency for them to be seen and represented as fixed lines and sometimes even walls that divide geopolitical space; in these representations, culture is seldom taken into account. But, as has been emphasized throughout the chapters of this volume, a more nuanced understanding of borders, and the relationship between borders and culture, is needed in order to understand how they function and what they mean to people under conditions of globalization.

We are clearly faced with an increasingly complex and contradictory world. On the one hand, ideas, people, commodities, and capital are flowing across borders like never before, creating new possibilities for cultural change. Political borders are, in this process, being moved and even transcended, their meaning redefined. These are cultural and political acts. On the other hand, these processes have been challenged by the construction of new boundaries and barriers, as people try to defend existing conceptions of border culture, identity, and belonging. This volume has highlighted some of the emergent opportunities and challenges for border theory, social change, and policy making. The empirical cases discussed in this volume have, in our view, provided a new way of looking at borders, and their relationship with culture. This collective work, while extensive and broad has considered only some of the many topics relevant to the study of borders and culture; there is much more conceptual, empirical, and comparative work to be done in this emergent field.

The importance of understanding the relationship between borders and culture has taken on new salience in the current political context. As we prepare the components of this volume for publication, it is impossible not to reflect on the numerous instances where culture and border collide along the Canada-US border alone. Although this border remains ostensibly "between friends," and it receives substantially less attention than its southern counterpart, it has become a site of cultural collision. While Canada and the United States have much in common in terms of language, culture, and history, there are significant political differences that divide them. President Trump and Prime Minister Trudeau frequently expressed different views on migration, security, gun laws, and the Black Lives Matter movement. At the moment, the border is closed to non-essential travellers due to the very different responses taken to control the COVID-19 pandemic in the two countries. Just prior to the pandemic, migrants from Central America, the Caribbean, Africa, and Asia, no longer safe in Trump's America, waited at checkpoints to enter Canada. Yet the multicultural embrace of Canada is measured and slow at best, and, increasingly, refugee claimants are sent back to the US. This has only become worse due to the border closures imposed in response to COVID-19. Border culture is aligned between the US and Canada to expedite the snowbird migrations, but this border culture may not accommodate "others."

References

Agnew, John. 1994. "The Territorial Trap: The Geographical Assumptions of International Relations Theory." *Review of International Political Economy* 1 (1): 53–80.

Amilhat Szary, Anne-Laure, and Frédéric Giraut. 2015. *Borderities: The Politics of Contemporary Mobile Borders*. New York: Springer.

Appadurai, Arjun. 1996. *Modernity at Large: Cultural Dimensions of Globalization*. Minneapolis: University of Minnesota Press.

Barth, Fredrik. 1969. *Ethnic Groups and Boundaries: The Social Organization of Cultural Difference*. Boston: Little, Brown.

Bhabha, Homi K. 1994. *The Location of Culture*. London: Routledge.

Brambilla, Chiara. 2015. "Exploring the Critical Potential of the Borderscapes Concept." *Geopolitics* 20 (1): 14–34.

Butler, Judith. 2004. "Competing Universalities." In *The Judith Butler Reader*, edited by Sara Salih and Judith Butler, 258–277. London: Blackwell.

Casaglia, Anna, and Jussi Laine. 2017. "Towards a Re-articulation of the Relationship Between State, Territory, and Identity Through a Situated Understanding of Borders: Conclusion." *Europa Regional* 24 (1/2): 93–96.

De Genova, Nicholas. 2012. "Border, Scene and Obscene." In *A Companion to Border Studies*, edited by Thomas M. Wilson and Hastings Donnan, 492–504. New York: Wiley.

Derrida, Jacques. 1991. *A Derrida Reader: Between the Blinds*. New York: Columbia University Press.

Diener, Alexander C., and Joshua Hagen. 2009. "Theorizing Borders in a 'Borderless World': Globalization, Territory and Identity." *Geography Compass* 3 (3): 1196–1216.

Ghemawat, Pankaj. 2011. *World 3.0: Global Prosperity and How to Achieve it*. Boston: Harvard Business Press Books.

Gramsci, Antonio. 2012. Selections from *Cultural Writings*. Edited by David Forgacs and Geoffrey Newell-Smith. Translated by William Boelhower. London: Lawrence and Wishart.

Huntington, Samuel P. 1993. "The Clash of Civilizations?" *Foreign Affairs* 72 (3): 22–49.

Jones, Reece, and Corey Johnson. 2014. *Making the Border in Everyday Life*. London: Ashgate.

Konrad, Victor. 2015. "Toward a Theory of Borders in Motion." *Journal of Borderlands Studies* 30 (1): 1–17.

Konrad, Victor, and Emmanuel Brunet-Jailly. 2019. "Approaching Borders, Creating Borderland Spaces, and Exploring the Evolving Borders Between Canada and the United States." *The Canadian Geographer/Le Géographe canadien* 63 (1): 4–11.

Konrad, Victor, and Heather N. Nicol. 2011. "Border Culture, the Boundary Between Canada and the United States of America, and the Advancement of Border Theory." *Geopolitics* 16 (1): 70–90.

Kulturfokus.dk. 2016. *Kulturportal for Sonderjylland-Schleswig*. http://www.kulturfokus.dk.

Laine, Jussi. 2016. "The Multiscalar Production of Borders." *Geopolitics* 21 (3): 465–482.
Latour, Bruno. 2005. *Reassembling the Social: An Introduction to Actor-network Theory*. New York: Oxford University Press.
Mignolo, Walter D., and Madina V. Tlostanova. 2006. "Theorizing from the Borders: Shifting to Geo- and Body-Politics of Knowledge." *European Journal of Social Theory* 9 (2): 205–221.
Mitchell, Don. 2000. *Cultural Geography*. Oxford: Blackwell.
Newman, David. 2003. "On Borders and Power: A Theoretical Framework." *Journal of Borderlands Studies* 18 (1): 13–25.
O Tuathail, Gearoid, and Simon Dalby. 1998. *Rethinking Geopolitics*. New York: Routledge.
Parker, Noel, and Nick Vaughan-Williams. 2014. *Critical Border Studies: Broadening and Deepening the "Lines in the Sand" Agenda*. New York: Routledge.
Popescu, Gabriel. 2011. *Bordering and Ordering the Twenty-First Century: Understanding Borders*. Lanham, MD: Rowman and Littlefield.
Ptak, Thomas, Jussi P. Laine, Zhiding Hu, Yuli Liu, Victor Konrad, and Martin van der Velde. 2020. "Understanding Borders as Dynamic Processes: Capturing Relational Motion from Southwestern China's Radiation Center." *Territory, Politics, Governance*. https://doi.org/10.1080/21622671.2020.1764861.
Rancière, Jacques. 2015. *Dissensus: On Politics and Aesthetics*. London: Bloomsbury.
Roberts, Gillian. 2018. *Reading Between the Borderlines: Cultural Production and Consumption Across the 49th Parallel*. Montréal and Kingston: McGill-Queen's University Press.
Rodney, Lee. 2017. *Looking Beyond Borderlines: North America's Frontier Imagination*. New York: Routledge.
Said, Edward. 1978. *Orientalism*. New York: Vintage.
Schimanski, Johan, and Stephen F. Wolfe. 2017. *Border Aesthetics: Concepts and Intersections*. Oxford: Berghahn.
Shweder, Richard A., and Robert A. Le Vine. 1984. *Culture Theory: Essays on Mind, Self and Emotion*. Cambridge: Cambridge University Press.
van Houtum, Henk, Olivier Kramsch, and Wolfgang Zierhofer. 2005. *B/Ordering Space*. Aldershot, UK: Ashgate.

Contributors

Scott Cafarella, MLA, OALA, is a landscape architect practicing in public land management and park development in Ontario. Scott's work includes public realm design, ecological restoration, and development of low-impact recreational trails and facilities in environmentally sensitive areas. Scott holds a Master of Landscape Architecture from the University of Guelph, and a Bachelor of Arts from Queen's University in Kingston, Ontario.

Dr. **Michael Darroch** is Associate Dean, Academic and Associate Professor of Cinema & Media Arts, York University. He previously served as Associate Dean, Partnership Development & Interdisciplinary Studies in the Faculty of Arts, Humanities & Social Sciences at the University of Windsor where he taught Media Arts and Culture in the School of Creative Arts. He is co-director of the research-creation hub IN/TERMINUS focused on participatory urban art interventions and exhibition curation in the Windsor-Detroit urban borderlands. His research is focused on the interdisciplinary influence of urban planning, architecture, anthropology, and borderlands cultures on the history of media studies and arts pedagogy.

Renata Grudzien's passion for peoples' freedom of mobility and movement has carried her throughout her studies. She wrote her Borders in Globalization chapter during her Territory and Territoriality course while completing her Master's at Carleton University's Norman Paterson School of International Affairs. She holds a Bachelor of Arts (Honours) in Political and Health Studies from Queen's University where she focused on political theory and border concepts. Her desire to innovate and reconceptualize global political theories was a significant inspiration for her chapter. Currently, Renata works for the federal public service and also has a variety of interests that link her passion for movement and her love of cooking.

Dr. **Colin Howell**, BA and MA, Dalhousie; PhD, Cincinnati, is Professor Emeritus in History, recently retired Academic Director of the Centre for the Study of Sport and Health at Saint Mary's University, and a former co-editor of the *Canadian Historical Review*. He has published widely in the field of sport and health studies and is the author of *Northern Sandlots* (1995), *Blood, Sweat and Cheers: Sport and the Making of Modern Canada* (2021) and a number of edited collections.

Melissa Kelly holds a PhD in Social and Economic Geography from Uppsala University. Her doctoral dissertation investigated the economic, social, and cultural factors influencing the onward migration of refugees from Sweden to third countries. She focused specifically on Iranian-born individuals who spent several years in Sweden before subsequently moving on to other parts of the Iranian diaspora. Following the completion of her PhD, Melissa was awarded a Freestanding Postdoctoral Fellowship by the National Research Foundation of South Africa. She carried out a study on the everyday experiences and multiscalar belonging of cross-border migrants living and working in the city of Bloemfontein, South Africa. Following this, she became a postdoctoral fellow with the Borders in Globalization Project at Carleton University. Her research focused on seasonal retirement migration in the North American context and its implications for regional integration. Melissa is currently a research fellow with the Canada Excellence Research Chair in Migration and Integration at Ryerson University. Her research interests include diversity, inclusion and community building in rural and remote areas, and regional approaches to migration governance. In addition to her academic pursuits, Melissa has contributed extensively to the development of immigration and labour market programs for the Government of Canada.

Joel Konrad, PhD, CAHP, is a Senior Cultural Heritage Specialist and Cultural Heritage Lead, Ontario with WSP. Dr. Konrad's work has focused on directing cultural heritage projects that identify and evaluate heritage resources, assess potential impacts, and provide mitigative strategies to best conserve heritage resources. His areas of expertise include cultural heritage landscapes, participatory GIS, heritage conservation, heritage impact assessment, and heritage policy. He actively participates in the fields of critical heritage studies and impact assessment, presenting his findings at the Ontario Association for Impact Assessment Conference, Ontario Heritage Conference, and the Association of Critical Heritage Studies Conference.

Victor Konrad teaches Geography at Carleton University, in Ottawa. Recently, Professor Konrad was Visiting Professor at Eastern China Normal and Yunnan Normal Universities in Shanghai and Kunming; Radboud University, Nijmegen, Netherlands; and the Karelian Institute of the University of Eastern Finland. In 2009, he was visiting fellow at the Border Policy Research Institute, Western Washington University. From 1990 to 2001, he established the Canada-U.S. Fulbright Program and the Foundation for Educational Exchange between Canada and the United States. During the 1970s and the 1980s, he was a professor of geography and anthropology at the University of Maine and Director of the Canadian-American Center. Professor Konrad is author and editor of more than a hundred books, articles, and book chapters in cultural geography, border studies, and Canadian studies. The most recent book, *North American Borders in Comparative Perspective*, was co-edited with Guadalupe Correa-Cabrera and published by the University of Arizona Press. Dr. Konrad is past president of both the Association of Borderlands Studies and the Association for Canadian Studies in the United States, and recipient of the Donner Medal. He serves on the editorial boards of the *Journal of Borderlands Studies* and the *Borders in Globalization Review*. Victor Konrad is the culture lead for the Borders in Globalization Project.

Evelyn P. Mayer holds an MA degree in Conference Interpreting for German, English, and French, and a PhD in American Studies (Johannes Gutenberg University Mainz, Germany). During her PhD work, she spent a year in Ottawa and Bellingham, Washington, conducting border research. Her book *Narrating North American Borderlands: Thomas King, Howard F. Mosher, and Jim Lynch* was published in 2014. Evelyn has worked as an English coach and a lecturer in university, teaching on borders, literature, and mobility. She currently works as an interpreter and translator in Munich, Germany.

Anelynda Mielke-Gupta is a PhD candidate in Sociology at Carleton University. Her ethnographic fieldwork focused on slum activism around water and sanitation in Mumbai, India. Using her training in ethnography, Anelynda founded and currently runs a venture called

Boomerang at RBC Ventures, which is focused on creating meaningful social connections among ageing Canadians through the sharing of useful skills.

Srimoyee Mitra is Director of Stamps Gallery, Stamps School of Art and Design, University of Michigan. Srimoyee is a curator and writer whose work is invested in building empathy and mutual respect by bringing together meaningful and diverse works of art and design. She develops ambitious and socially relevant projects that mobilize the agency within creative practices and public audiences. Her research interests lie at the intersection of exhibition making and participation, migration, globalization, and decolonial aesthetics. During her time as Curator of Contemporary Art at the Art Gallery of Windsor (AGW), she developed an award-winning curatorial and publications program. *Border Cultures* was exhibited at the AGW from 2013 to 2015, and the book *Border Cultures* was co-published by AGW and Black Dog Publishing in 2015.

Nadya Pohran is a cultural anthropologist whose research explores the boundaries and borderlines of interdisciplinary fields of scholarship—particularly within the fields of Anthropology of Christianity and Hindu-Christian Studies. Her PhD research at the University of Cambridge was based on an ethnographic study of a Christian ashram in the north of India, for which she explored questions pertaining to cross-cultural and interreligious relations as well as existential belonging. Presently, she is pursuing research in the area of multiple religious belonging and transnational religion with a focus on Hindu-Christian contexts.

Lee Rodney is Associate Professor in Media Arts and Cultures at the University of Windsor. An interdisciplinary writer/curator/media artist, she has written on contemporary art and media culture in a range of publications. Her interest in borders began over a decade ago and has resulted in several projects and publications including *Looking Beyond Borderlines: North America's Frontier Imagination* (Routledge, 2017), which addresses the mediated and shifting representation of borders in North America since their formation in the mid-nineteenth century. Media projects include The Border Bookmobile Project (2010-2013), frontierfiles.org and Buoyant Cartographies (2018). With Dr. Michael Darroch, she co-directs the IN/TERMINUS Research Group, which recently began the four-year SSHRC-funded project Mapping, Media and Migration. She and Dr. Karen Engle co-edited "Sensing (Borders)/ Ressentir (les frontières)" (Issue 34, 2019) of the online journal *Intermedialites*.

Dr. **Laetitia Rouvière** is currently a Professor of Economics and Social Sciences in Avignon, France. Her postdoctoral research at Carleton University, in Ottawa, focused on cross-border cooperation and Indigenous identity across the border between the United States and Canada. This work continued her doctoral research in political science focused on Latin American borderlands of Chile, Peru, and Bolivia. The themes of her research deal with the articulation and complementarity between national state building and Indigenous borderlands.

Alexander Rudolph is a PhD candidate in the Department of Political Science at Carleton University, in Ottawa. His research primarily explores structural explanations for state-society relations in cyberspace, with a focus on cyber conflict and strategic thought of cyberspace. His dissertation work explores explanations of cyber conflict through structuration theory influenced by information security and hacker methodology. Outside of his academic work, Alex is also a consultant and policy analyst.

Rebecca Sciarra, MA, CAHP, is a Partner and Director with Archaeological Resources Inc., one of Ontario's largest specialized heritage consulting firms. She has evaluated and assessed hundreds of cultural heritage resources in accordance with the Ontario Heritage Act, Ontario and Canada Environmental Assessment Acts, the Green Energy Act, the Planning Act, the Provincial Policy Statement, and as required by municipal official plans across Ontario. Over the last ten years, she has been a major contributor to cultural landscape components of Heritage Conservation District Studies and Plans, Planning Act applications, and Municipal Official Plans across the Province of Ontario.

Sandra Vandervalk is a PhD candidate in Cultural Anthropology at Carleton University, in Ottawa. Her research focuses on the social construction of borders: what it means to live alongside one, and how borders are enacted in everyday life. Theoretically, she works at the intersection of phenomenology and performance theory. Recently, she has completed fieldwork for her dissertation in Northern Ireland. Specifically, her current research explores identity issues in a place defined by borders and boundaries, in light of the vote by people of the United Kingdom to exit the European Union.

Dr. **Heidi Weigand** is a member of the Safe Assured research team in Dalhousie University's Rowe School of Business. Her work focuses on leadership development, systemic discrimination, and resiliency. Examples of her work include the study of a leader's ability to manage the balance of positive and negative emotions, and the extent to which this practice vicariously affects the development of an innovative mindset in followers. Her work also includes the study of motivating factors that influence Generation Z leaders to drive responsible change and choose communication technologies to mobilize their message, and the study of health-care leaders and the extent to which they inform patient safety health-care policy.

Index

A
abjected sites in the cultural imagination, 43
Aboriginal flag, 288
Aboriginal liaison officer, 267, 271
Aboriginal national identity, 285
Aboriginal peoples, 288
Aboriginal sovereignty, 27, 255–272
Aboriginal territory, 255
Abrams, Percy, 284, 287
Acland, Charles, 190, 192, 196, 204–205, 208, 212
acquired experiences, 174
active viewers, 191, 193
activism, 27, 49, 57, 97–100, 102, 104–105, 115, 126, 233–234, 236, 243, 250, 256–257, 260, 326, 339
acts of transformation, 236
advocations, 102
aesthetics, 16, 21–22, 43, 48–49, 57, 116, 340
aesthetics of politics, 43
affect, 21, 23, 47, 110, 183, 202, 256, 312
affective economies, 39, 41, 63
affirming cultural specificities, 256
Africa, 12, 42, 96, 332, 338
African Americans, 240
African Borderlands Research Network (ABORNE), 12
agency, 2, 18, 28, 78, 111, 114, 116, 123–124, 141, 165, 192, 206–207, 211, 269, 278–279, 288, 322–323, 340
Agnew, John, 17, 30, 134–135, 156, 217–218, 227, 322, 332
Aguilar, Gaelyn and Gustavo, 50–51, 58
Ahrens, Jill, 133, 156

Akwesasne, 27–28, 35, 240, 255–256, 258–271, 274–275, 280, 330
Akwesasne Mohawk Police, 268–269
Akwesasne Partnership Initiative, 268, 274
Alfred, Taiaiake, 272
alien, 181
Allen, Richard, 313–314
Allison, Janet B., 257, 274
Alonso, Andoni, 134, 156
Alper, Donald, 8, 31, 297, 314
alterity, 39
alternative mapping practices, 52
alternative spatial imaginary, 54
Alvarez Perez, Marcela, 217, 227
Amazon, 193
ambiguously bordered spaces, 85
ambiguous state of being, 170
American mass culture, 188–189, 191, 193, 203, 206, 211–212
Amilhat Szary, Anne-Laure, 4, 20, 24, 31, 42, 57–59, 109–110, 127, 258, 272, 319, 333
Anaulataq, 278
Anderson, Benedict, 217, 227
Anderson, Malcolm, 257, 272
Andrews, Jennifer, 235, 253
Angus Reid Institute, 190, 193–194, 208, 212
Anthropocene, 246
Antrop, Mark, 300, 314
Anzaldúa, Gloria, 19, 31, 40, 42, 58
Appadurai, Arjun, 321, 333
Arapi, Enkeleda, 165, 185
archaeological clusters, 305

Archaeological Services Inc. (ASI), 36, 303
archival formations, 40
Arctic, 109, 278
Arizona, 31–33, 51, 59, 82, 132, 137, 185, 264, 339
artefacts, 321
Art Gallery of Windsor, 23, 44, 78, 107, 112, 115, 340
art geopolitics, 110
artistic activism, 27, 233–234, 236, 243, 250
artivism, 49
ascription, 178
Asia, 332
associative cultural landscape, 302
asylum, 23, 64, 85–86, 97, 100, 221–222, 325
asymmetries, 20
aterritorialization, 323
attachments, 133, 144, 150, 155–156, 214
Audience Lab, 205, 212
Australia, 96, 131, 205, 284–285, 289

B

Balibar, Étienne, 20, 31
Banff National Park, 294
Barkhuus, Louise, 191–192, 206, 211–212
Barney, Robert, 278, 291
Barr, Nancy B., 71, 82
Barry, Andrew, 89–90, 103
Barth, Fredrik, 12, 16, 31, 178, 184, 322, 333
Basch, Linda, 133, 156
Bates, Catharine, 244, 253
Bates-Eamer, Nicole, 4, 9, 32–33
Battiste, Jaime, 285–286, 289
Bay-Lake Regional Planning Commission, 298, 314
Bedford, David, 261, 272
Beers, George, 280
Beezley, William, 278, 289
being in the world, 25, 163–164, 172–173, 175–176, 180–183, 329
Belaouni, Abdelkader, 86, 88, 91, 94, 96–103

Bellfy, Phil, 54–55, 58
Belmore, Rebecca, 116, 123–124, 128
belonging, belongers, 2, 14, 21, 25, 27, 33, 39, 41, 48, 114, 117, 127, 132–136, 144, 148, 151, 154, 156–157, 177–178, 190, 234–235, 238, 245, 249, 251, 264, 312, 324, 326–329, 332, 338, 340
benchmarks for refugee resettlement, 215
Benson, Michaela, 136, 157
Beresford, Michael, 301, 314
Berger, Mark T., 217, 227
Berkowitz, Irene S., 205–206, 210–212
Between Friends/Entre amis, 109
Beylier, Pierre-Alexandre, 266, 274
beyond binaries, 18–19
Bhabha, Homi, 321, 333
Bhandar, Davina, 165, 184
binary opposition, 183
biocultural, 29, 293, 295–296, 303–304, 310, 312–313
biocultural planning approach, 28, 293–313
biocultural planning zones, 29, 310
bioregion, 296–298, 304, 313
biosphere, 297, 299, 317
Blackfoot, 236–242
Black Lives Matter, 122, 332
Blanc, Christina S., 133, 156
bloodthirsty savage, 241
Blum, Alan, 63, 66, 82
Blum, Andreas, 313, 315
Boas, Franz, 16, 31
bodily metaphors, 22, 42
body politics, 322
Boltanski, Luc, 86, 88, 95–96, 103
border art, 108
border as a process, 219
border as mobile organism, 26
border authorities, 51, 88
Border Bookmobile, 44–48, 60, 340
border community, 21, 31, 163
border construct, 26, 215–221, 223–226
border controls, 324
border crossers, 93, 95, 99, 123, 125, 167, 237, 240–241, 323

border crossing, 2, 7, 21, 26, 28, 44, 51, 109, 166, 170, 217, 222–224, 234, 238–239, 241, 259
border culture(s), 3–4, 8–24, 27, 30, 34, 42–44, 57, 59, 61, 63, 65, 78, 102, 107–127, 255, 272, 319–323, 326, 328, 331–332, 340
Border Enforcement Security Task Force (BEST), 268
border fluidity, 244, 247
border guards, 123, 167, 236–239
border imaginaries: life securing, life sustaining, life enriching, 21
bordering excesses, 30
bordering Mohawk identity, 263
bordering process, 2, 28, 277–288
bordering, re-bordering, de-bordering, 1–3, 9, 11–12, 21, 26–28, 30, 41, 43, 57, 86–88, 90–91, 94, 97, 101–102, 108–111, 114, 258, 277, 295, 320, 323, 326–329
bordering things, 85–102
border in one direction, 217
border in process, 26
Border Integrity Technology Enhancement Project (BITEP), 270
borderities, 20, 31, 58, 272, 333
borderland(s), 1, 3, 8–11, 13–24, 39–44, 48–50, 52, 54, 57–58, 61, 64, 75, 109–110, 116–117, 134, 163–165, 168, 172, 177, 180, 183, 187, 190–191, 193, 197–205, 207, 211–212, 216, 219–220, 233–237, 239–240, 242, 244, 246, 250, 255–258, 260, 262–263, 266, 271–272, 278–280, 296, 313, 319–320, 325–327, 329, 336–337, 339, 341
borderland communities, 28, 257, 266, 278, 280, 326
borderland dwellers, 164, 329
borderlanders, 21, 25, 164, 172–173, 177–180, 182–183, 323, 328
borderlands of cyberspace, 191, 205
borderlands theory, 33, 59, 313
borderline, 22, 40–41, 44, 48, 50, 57–58, 62–63, 85, 88, 90, 176, 238, 323, 325
borderline condition, 63

border markers, 259
Border Policy Research Institute (BPRI), 7, 31, 33, 339
border representation, 27, 233
border rhythms, 23
borders as colonial artifacts, 41
borderscape, 17, 20, 42, 57–58, 327
border security, 28, 41, 108, 123, 134, 138, 255–272, 275, 330–331
Border Security Summits, 263
Borders in Globalization (BIG), 1, 4
borders in motion, 17, 21, 24, 32, 165, 185, 218, 228, 273, 333
border struggle, 23, 85, 91, 99, 102
border studies, 12–13, 17–18, 32, 34, 42, 59, 86, 107–108, 110, 133, 165, 184, 218, 229, 246, 333–334, 339
Boucher, Nancy, 277, 289
boundary(ies), boundary studies, 1–2, 8, 10, 15–17, 19, 22–24, 27, 29, 40–41, 46, 48, 52, 54–55, 75–76, 87, 91, 109–110, 114, 116, 124, 126, 148, 166–169, 171–172, 177–178, 182, 190, 234, 237–241, 244, 258–260, 271, 288, 293–295, 298–299, 304–305, 307, 309, 312–313, 322–327, 329, 332, 340, 342
Brambilla, Chiara, 15, 17, 20, 31, 153, 156, 322–323, 333
Brexit, 135
Brighenti, Andrea, 94–95, 100, 103
Bright Water, 233, 242–253
Britain, 109, 135, 280, 282–283, 290
Brković, Čarna, 85, 93, 102–103
broadband Internet, 187
Broken City Lab, 79–80, 82, 118
Brown, Barry, 191–192, 206, 211–212
Brown, Jessica, 301, 314
Brubaker, Rogers, 257, 272
Brunckhorst, David, 296–299, 312, 314
Brunet-Jailly, Emmanuel, 1, 4, 12, 31, 257, 272, 319, 323, 333
Bucktooth, Brett, 281, 286–287
buffers, 304–305, 310, 312–313
built heritage, 302
Bunge, William, 76, 82
Buoyant Cartographies, 52–54, 56, 58, 340

Burghardt, Andrew, 307, 314
Burridge, Andrew, 202, 213
Burtniak, John, 307, 315
Butler, Judith, 95–96, 103, 322, 333
Byrd, Jodi A., 257, 272

C

Cafarella, Scott, 28, 293, 296, 306, 309, 311, 326, 330, 337
Caglar, Ayse, 133, 156
Calder, Jim, 281, 289
California, 132, 137, 206
Cameron, James, 287
Canada National Parks Act (2000), 294, 315
Canadian adaptation, 194
Canadian Border Services Agency (CBSA), 259
Canadian content, 188, 191–196, 201, 203–206, 208–210, 329
Canadian context, 279
Canadian culture, 14, 26, 187, 189–191, 193–196, 199, 204, 206–208, 211, 329, 330
Canadian identity, 13, 132, 155, 188, 196, 211, 237
Canadian Immigration and Refugee Protection Act 2001, 221
Canadian Internet Registration Authority (CIRA), 196
Canadian mass culture consumption, 188
Canadianness, 32, 151, 177–178, 184, 196
Canadian productions, 188, 194, 205
Canadian Radio-television and Telecommunications Commission (CRTC), 191
Canadians, 30–31, 78, 109–110, 131–133, 137–138, 140–142, 145–146, 151–152, 154–158, 161, 166–167, 178–179, 182, 187–191, 193–197, 199–201, 203, 205–208, 210–213, 264, 280–281, 320, 327, 329, 340
Canadian self-definition, 187, 191
Canadian Snowbird Association (CSA), 140
cannabis culture, 8
Carens, Joseph, 135, 156

Caribbean, 332
Carlier, Melissa, 138, 156
Carolinian Region, 298
Casaglia, Anna, 319, 333
Cascadia, 8–9, 31, 36, 297, 314
Castles, Stephen, 134–136, 156
Cayuga, 261, 281
Central America, 145, 332
centrality of objects, 85–86, 100–101
Certificate of Indian Status, 263–264
chain migration, 141
Chakrabarty, Dipesh, 89–90, 93, 103
Charon, Joel M., 190–191, 193, 213
Chibber, Vivek, 89–90, 103
Chicoine, Hugues, 141, 158
Chidley-Hill, John, 286, 289
Chouliaraki, Lilie, 86, 95–96, 103
citizenship, 25, 96, 104, 111, 114, 119–120, 132, 135–136, 151, 153–155, 161, 166, 168, 171–172, 177–179, 182, 228, 238–239, 264, 286
Clairmont, Don, 268, 273
classification, 25, 144, 178, 205
Clinton, Hillary, 284, 287
Coates, Ken, 132, 137, 142, 157
codes of behaviour, 258
coexistence of culture and conservation, 294
Cohen, Anthony P., 12, 31
collapsed dichotomies, 234
collective identity, 280
colonial borders, 280
colonial, colonialism, 28, 41, 48, 52–55, 57, 64, 89, 116, 118–119, 124–217, 235, 238, 240, 242–243, 247, 261, 278–280, 283, 285, 326
colonization, 51, 247, 256, 285, 294
Colorado, 280
common culture, 187
common discursive space, 133, 197
communication technologies, 134, 327, 342
communities, 7, 14, 25, 28, 39, 41, 52, 57, 76, 78, 108, 112, 114, 120, 122–123, 132, 136, 141–154, 156, 163–164, 166–168, 172, 203, 209, 224, 238, 255, 257, 259, 271, 277–280, 285,

Index   347

294, 297, 300, 302–303, 310, 322, 325–326, 329–330
communities of sense, 39, 57
complexity, 11, 20, 27, 57, 121, 126, 221, 234, 239, 259, 279, 319, 326
Conference Board of Canada, 131, 137, 157
confluence, 18–19, 116, 325
consciousness, 16, 23, 25, 40–41, 43, 85, 90, 132, 173, 175–176
consensus, 10, 20, 22, 44
conservation, 29, 293–298, 300–301, 303, 306, 310, 313, 338
conservation of cultural heritage, 295
content creator, 194–195, 206, 209
content curators, 205, 209
contest, 51, 58, 93
contested borderland communities, 28, 280
continental integration, 25, 132, 154–155
control visibility, 94–95, 99–100, 102
Convention and Protocol Relating to the Status of Refugees, 221, 229
Convergence Research Group Ltd., 196–197, 204, 211, 213
Conway, Kyle, 58, 165, 184
core areas, 297–298, 304–305, 310, 313
Cornell, Stephen E., 32, 156, 285, 289
Cornwall Island, 259
Coronavirus pandemic, COVID-19 pandemic, 7, 13, 30, 332
Correa-Cabrera, Guadalupe, 13, 31–32, 40, 59, 339
corridor, 266, 295, 305, 308, 313
counter-cartography, 57
Craig, David, 206, 210, 213
creative edge, 108
creolized, 18
critical geography and anthropology, 17
critical heritage studies, 312–313, 338
cross-border bioregional communities, 297
cross-border city, 71
cross-border community, 21, 163
cross-border context, 327
cross-border flows, 324, 328–329
cross-border heritage policy, 295

cross-border region, 8, 134, 319
cross-border settings, 278
cross-border territoriality, 256–257
cross-jurisdictional, 29, 296–297, 307
cross-jurisdictional landscape, 29, 307
crowded cultural marketplace, 210
Cuesta Systems Inc., 307, 314
cultural and political acts, 332
cultural appropriation, 278
cultural areas, 305
cultural assets, 295
cultural borders/boundaries, 236, 245, 313
cultural change, 27, 327, 331
cultural collision, 332
cultural commodities, 324, 329–330
cultural continuity and discontinuity, 14, 19
cultural diversity, 11, 293, 297–298, 313
cultural empowerment, 28
cultural energy, 76
cultural exchange, 126, 279
cultural flows, 324
cultural hegemony, 16
cultural heritage, 10, 22, 26–27, 29, 285, 293–296, 300, 302–303, 305, 308, 312–313, 338, 341
cultural heritage landscape, 27, 295, 297, 300, 302–303, 305, 312, 338
cultural homogenization, 327
cultural identity, 15, 19, 207–208, 268, 285–286, 307, 325
cultural integration, 9, 188, 201–203, 330
cultural islands, 14
cultural landscape, 11, 29, 293, 300–302, 304, 307, 312–313, 341
cultural lens, 328
cultural meaning, 16–17, 21–22, 40
cultural movement(s), 10, 24–25, 131, 135–156
cultural politics, 322
cultural practice(s), 29, 201, 246, 252, 257, 265–266, 293, 330
cultural-semantic modelling, 26
cultural sensitivity training for border officers, 263
cultural shells, 18

cultural shift(s), 135, 188, 192, 200
cultural value(s), 191, 195, 198
Culture and the Canada-US Border (CCUSB), 4
culture at the margins, 17
culture/cultural production, 10, 13, 21–22, 110–111, 246, 295, 323
culture of suspicion, 123
cumulative discourse, 19
Cunningham, Stuart, 206, 210, 213
curator(s), 24, 107–114, 340
Curtis, James, 190, 214
cyber new regionalism, 26
cyberspace, 26, 188–189, 191, 194, 197–200, 202–203, 205–206, 321, 341

D

Dalby, Simon, 322, 334
darkness, 23, 62, 66, 71, 73, 75–76, 79, 81
Darroch, Michael, 22–24, 46, 52, 58, 61, 63, 71, 81–83, 108, 111, 113, 327, 337, 340
Daudelin, Jean, 256, 273
Davidson, Arnold E., 235, 253
Davis, Charles H., 205–206, 210–212
Dead Indians, 241–242
Dear, Michael, 202, 213
decolonial aesthetics, 49, 340
decolonialization, 313
De Eyre, Steve, 157
De Genova, Nicholas, 319, 333
Deleuzian cartography, 50
Dell'Agnese, Elena, 57, 59, 110, 127
Demetriou, Olga, 86–87, 90, 102–104
Demos, T. J., 117, 126–127
Derby Line, Vermont, 21, 25, 85, 163, 165–166, 184
Derrida, Jacques, 322, 333
Design with Nature, 304, 315
Desrosiers-Lauzon, Godefroy, 141, 150–151, 157
deterritorialized/deterritorialization, 201, 321, 323
Detroit, 22–23, 44–47, 52–57, 59–82, 108, 113–114, 116–118, 120–122, 337
Detroit After Dark, 71, 78, 82

Detroit Institute of Arts, 71, 78, 82
Dewing, Michael, 192, 213
dialectic, 19, 199
Diener, Alexander C., 319, 333
differential cultures, 42
differentiation, 3, 10, 16, 18–19, 173, 179, 325
diffusion, 202, 272, 279, 288
Dimmel, Brandon, 279, 289
Dimova, Rosita, 86–87, 103–104
discursive normative space, 198
disenfranchised communities, 203
disputed places, 110
dissensus, 20, 22, 43–44, 322
diversification, 133
diversity, 11, 142, 151, 195–196, 259, 293, 297–298, 305, 313, 325, 338
DLECTRICITY, 66
Domidion, 250–251
domination-resistance binary, 262
Dominion Forest Reserves and Park Act (1911), 294
Donnan, Hastings, 12, 16, 31–32, 165, 184, 186, 333
Downey, 278, 279, 289
draft dodgers, 240
dual citizenship, 166, 168, 172, 178–179, 182
dying savage, 241
Dyreson, Mark, 277–278, 289
dystopian realm, 252

E

ecocide, 248, 252
ecoregion, 298
Edensor, Tim, 63, 71, 75, 82
edge places, 17
Elden, Stuart, 218, 227
Electronic Disturbance Theatre, 49, 59
embedded symbolic power, 101
embodied experiences, 40, 42, 63, 323
embodied self, 163
embodiment, 24, 172
emotion, 98, 312
empire, 278
endosymbiotic reality, 91

Engle, Karen, 63, 81–82, 341
Enhanced Tribal Card Program, 264
environmental management, 328
essentialism, 165
ethnic and linguistic boundaries, 329
ethnicity, 134, 240, 325–326
EUBORDERSCAPES, 12
Euro-Canadian communities, 294
Europe, 12, 42, 114, 135, 229, 277, 301, 317
European Union (EU), 1, 229, 273, 342
everyday life, 107, 109, 118, 171, 259, 321, 341
everyday politics, 90
everyday resistance, 89
exceptionalism, 11, 320
exclusion, 120, 225, 294
experiential regions, 181
extraterritorial borders, 40

F

FaceTime, 148–149
Fakhrashrafi, Mitra, 111, 127
Federation of International Lacrosse (FIL), 281
feel of the border experience, 226
Fein, Seth, 18, 31
Fenton, William N., 261, 273
Ferguson, James, 19, 32
figurative borderlands, 27, 233
First Nation(s), 64, 117, 235, 241, 253, 255, 271, 273, 275, 279, 284, 294, 315
First Nations' participation, 255
Fiske, John, 191, 213
Fletcher, Chris, 290
Fletcher, Ron, 281, 289
Florida, 25, 132, 137–138, 141–145, 148–155, 157–161
fluid borders, 285
Forest, Patrick, 165, 185, 294
Forman, Richard, 297, 315
Forsyth, Janice, 279, 289
Foucault, Michel, 19, 32, 91, 103
Four Mile Creek, 308, 310
Fraisse, Paul, 220, 228
Francophone minorities, 237
French Canadian(s), 166, 203, 280

Frisch, Jack A., 261, 273

G

Galasinska, Aleksandra, 220, 228
Gallagher, John, 64, 82
Games and Empires, 278, 289
gated community, 147
gatekeeper(s), 199, 324
Gayler, Hugh, 307, 315
gender, 13, 313
genetic makeup of the border, 220
geographical affiliation, 134
geopolitical border(s)/boundary(ies), 27, 236–242, 244, 324
geopolitical space, 53, 331
George-Kanetiio, Douglas M., 256, 273
Georgian Bay Region, 298
Ghemawat, 321, 333
Ghemawat, Pankaj, 279, 289
Gilbert, Emily, 111, 127
Gillibrand, Kirsten, 287
Gillis, John, 313, 315
Gill, Warren, 9, 32
Giraut, Frédéric, 20, 24, 31, 42, 58, 258, 272, 319, 333
Glick-Schiller, Nina, 133, 156
globalization, 2–3, 8–12, 16, 19–22, 24–25, 30, 40–41, 43, 47, 111, 117, 126, 133–136, 153–154, 218, 227, 248, 277, 279, 319–320, 322, 324, 326, 328, 331, 340, 367
globalized world, 277, 288, 313, 321, 329, 331
Globe and Mail, 283, 291
glocalization, 278
Godron, Michel, 297, 315
Government of Canada, 188, 209–211, 213, 228, 235, 297, 316, 338
Grabb, Edward, 190, 214
Gramsci, Antonio, 16–17, 30–32, 322, 333
Gray, Charlotte, 235, 248, 250, 253
Great Lakes Bioregion, 297
Great Law of Peace, 261, 272
Greenbelt Plan (Ontario), 300, 308
Green, Sarah, 87, 103
GreenSweep, 244, 251

Gregory, Derek, 95–96, 103
Grimson, Alejandro, 164–165, 184
Grinde, Donald A., 264, 273
Grudzien, Renata, 26, 96, 153, 215, 325, 337
Grundy-Warr, Carl, 17, 20, 34
Gruszczak, Artur, 258, 273
Guha, Ranajit, 23, 32, 86, 88–90, 92–93, 97, 101, 104
Gupta, Akhil, 19, 32, 339
Gustafson, Per, 133, 157
Guswhenta, 285
Guttmann, Allen, 278, 289

H

Hagen, Joshua, 319, 333
Haitian migrants, 138
Hallgrímsdóttir, Helga, 9, 32–33
Hamill, Kristen, 284, 287, 289
Handsome Lake Code, 261
Hardwick, Susan, 137, 157–158
Harper, Stephen, 235, 253
Harris, Laura, 285, 289
Haselberger, Beatrix, 295, 315
Haskell Library and Opera House, 166
Hataley, Todd, 165, 184
Haudenosaunee, 28, 241, 253, 260–261, 263, 265, 279–281, 286–291, 330–331
Haudenosaunee Confederacy, 241, 260, 265, 280–281, 290
Haudenosaunee passport, 241, 253, 263, 286, 288
Hayes, Matthew, 136, 157
Hay, Roy, 278, 290
healthcare, 25, 121, 136, 139, 151, 153, 155, 224
Healy, Robert, 132, 137, 142, 157
Hele, Karl, 253, 297, 315
Helleiner, Jane, 21, 32, 165, 184
Hemlock, Kanen'tokon (Tyler), 285–286
heritage, 3, 10, 22, 26–29, 203, 213, 236, 281, 285, 293–296, 300–303, 305–306, 308, 310, 312–313, 316, 326, 338, 341
Heritage Canada, 204–205, 208
heritage conservation district, 295, 306

heterogeneity, 19
Hettne, Bjorn, 200–201, 206–207, 214
Heyman, Josiah, 20, 32
highlighting, 101, 108, 180, 219, 283
historical resources, 313
Hobsbawm, Eric J., 89, 104
Hollywood, 206, 213
Holman, Andrew C., 279, 290
home(s), 55, 92, 98, 116–117, 119, 125, 132, 139, 142, 144–146, 148–152, 154, 160, 166, 171, 177, 180, 182, 205, 243, 245, 248–249, 251, 259, 282–284
homes, land, 107, 116–120
homogeneity, 15, 19, 126, 164, 170, 203
Hopper, Damien, 288
horizon metaphor, 174
Houkamau, Carla, 285, 290
House, Mark, 138, 158
Howell, Colin, 28, 241, 263, 277–280, 290, 327, 330, 338
human geography, 198, 312
humanitarian commitments, 325
humanizing the border, 108
human migration, 122, 133, 313, 324
human rights, 30, 114, 117, 270, 287, 325
Huntington, Samuel P., 321, 333
Huron Region, 298
Huysmans, Jef, 258, 273
Hu, Zhiding, 34, 334
hybridity(ies), 19, 22, 40–41, 128, 165, 199
hybridization, 18–19, 202
hypervigilance, 94

I

ice bridge, 259
iconographic, 109
identification measures for Indigenous people, 263
identity formation, 189, 193, 207, 278
identity(ies), 2, 8, 10–22, 25, 27–29, 50, 71, 88, 95, 100, 109, 116–117, 121, 123, 126, 132, 134–135, 151, 154–155, 164, 171, 177–180, 182–183, 188–189, 193, 196, 199–203, 207–208, 211–212, 223, 233–240, 242–243, 249, 251–252, 256–257, 264–265,

268, 278–280, 282, 284–288, 293, 295, 307, 312–313, 320, 323–330, 332, 341–342, 367
identity negotiation, 27, 233
illumination, 23, 62–63, 65–67, 75–77, 79, 81
image capture, 86
image(s) of the border, 9, 88, 108, 238
imaginary(ies) of the border, 24, 109
imaginary, 17, 22, 24, 53–54, 58, 65, 246
imagination, 8, 15–16, 22, 40, 42–43, 51, 63, 76, 78, 115, 119, 126, 181, 234, 236, 240, 246, 251, 293, 331
imagined communities, 277
imagined places, 40–42, 63
imaging, 108
immersive installation, 117
immigration, 41, 52, 78, 94, 98, 101, 123, 215, 218, 222, 227–228, 325, 338
Immigration, Refugees and Citizenship Canada (IRCC), 215, 221–224
in-betweenness, 164
in-between place, 25, 163–164, 168, 171–172, 180
in-between way of being, 25, 180, 183
inclusion, 120, 189, 200, 225, 243, 255, 262, 268, 338
inclusivity, 326
incomprehensible, 181
indeterminacy, 173, 176, 238
Index of the Disappeared, 124
Indigeneity, 9, 14, 40, 55, 237, 254, 272, 320, 329
Indigenous communities, 123, 238, 271, 279, 285, 297, 300, 302–303, 330
Indigenous (cross)border culture, 272
Indigenous cultural affirmation, 256
Indigenous mobility, 118, 240
Indigenous nationality, 282, 288
Indigenous people(s), 8, 28–29, 41, 52, 55, 110, 117–118, 209, 235–238, 241–242, 248, 252, 257–258, 263, 278–279, 285–286, 288, 294, 329
Indigenous Rights and Treaties, 284
Indigenous territoriality(ies), 256–257
Indigenous traditions, 252, 278

inhabit different worlds simultaneously, 172, 182
innate ambiguity, 87
Inner City Voice, 116, 121
insufficiently patriotic, 164
Integrated Border Enforcement Team (IBET), 268
integrated border spaces, 25, 145–148
integration, 3, 9, 14, 16, 19, 25–26, 30, 76, 109, 132–134, 137, 140, 142, 148, 154–155, 188, 200–203, 207, 224, 271, 297, 319, 328, 330, 338
intercultural space, 181
intermedial, 53
international boundary, 1–2, 8, 48, 52, 54, 172, 237, 239–241, 259–260, 271, 295
international cooperation, 313
international interconnectedness, 324
International Joint Commission, 297
International Olympic Committee (IOC), 288
international policy and governance, 294
Internet service providers (ISPs), 192
intersectional dimensions of national identity, 28, 280
intersubjective space, 164, 178
intersubjectivity, 176–180
intimate onlooker, 23, 81
Inuit, 235, 241, 252, 278
Ipsos, 194–195, 214
Iroquois, 28, 241, 260–263, 265, 273, 275, 277, 279–292
Iroquois Confederacy, 260–261, 265, 273, 280, 282
Iroquois National Lacrosse Team, 28

J

Jackson, John, 307, 315
Jacobs, Ben, 224, 228
Jarvis, Eric, 137, 150, 157
Jay, Paul, 12, 32
Jay Treaty, 241, 263, 273, 330
Jeffery, Laura, 133, 157
Jensen, Stef, 16, 32
Johnson, Corey, 321, 333
Johnson, David E., 12, 20, 32–34

Jones, Reece, 19, 35, 262, 273, 321, 333
Journal of Borderlands Studies, 9, 31–33, 59, 127–128, 184–185, 228, 254, 273, 314, 333–334, 339
jurisdictional boundaries, 304

K

Kalman, Ian, 259, 273
Kaplan, Thomas, 282–284, 287, 290
Karibo, Holly, 64, 78, 83
Kaswentha Wampum Belt, 261
Kearney, Michael, 12, 32
Keenan, Thomas, 86, 95, 104
Kelly, Melissa, 1, 5, 7, 25, 63, 131, 133, 143, 156, 164–165, 168–169, 171–172, 177, 180–181, 295, 319, 324, 338
Kidd, Bruce, 277, 290
King, Thomas, 27, 33, 233–254, 327, 339
Kirk, Jessica, 111, 127
Kolossov, Vladimir, 12, 32
Konrad, Joel, 28, 293, 296, 330, 338
Konrad, Victor, 1, 5, 7–8, 11, 13–16, 19–20, 24, 31–34, 40, 59, 63, 107–108, 111, 134, 138, 157, 165, 167, 185, 216, 218, 228, 234, 240–241, 253, 257, 273–274, 295, 297, 306, 309, 311, 315, 319, 323, 326–327, 333–334, 338–339
Kramsch, Olivier, 321, 334
"kulturfokus" initiative, 319
Kurasawa, Fuyuki, 95, 104
Kurdi, Alan, 215

L

Laine, Jussi, 16, 18, 33–34, 133, 153, 156–157, 319, 322–323, 333–334
Lake Ontario, 303, 308, 310
Land Information Ontario, 307
land management, 294, 300, 307–308, 312, 337
landscape(s), 11–12, 17, 21, 27, 29, 56, 71, 78–79, 121, 189, 211, 243, 251, 293–313, 337–338, 341
Landscape and Memory, 293, 316

landscape character assessment in the UK, 308
landscapes of domination, 17
landscape value map, 310
land-use planners, 295
language(s), 8, 16, 125, 137, 145–146, 154, 166, 172, 175, 178, 182, 199, 202–205, 207–209, 215, 220, 224, 226, 234, 245, 247, 261, 285, 323, 325–326, 332
Lasserre, Frédéric, 165, 185
Latour, Bruno, 23, 33, 86, 92, 100–101, 104, 322, 334
law enforcement cooperation, 263, 270
Lecker, Robert, 12, 14, 33
LeDuff, Charlie, 64, 83
Leech Lake, 249
Leeworthy, Daryl, 278–280, 290
Legal Indians, 241
legislation, 29, 188, 190, 210, 221, 282, 294, 296
Leibenath, Markus, 313, 315
Leistle, Bernhard, 181, 185
leitmotif, 242, 248
LeVine, Robert, 323
Levitz, Stephanie, 226, 228
liberal political culture, 89, 90
Libicki, Martin, 197, 214
lifestyle community(ies), 132, 142, 144, 150
light tower(s), 67–69
liminal, 25, 164, 168–171, 177, 180–183, 236–237, 239–240, 245, 247, 252
liminality, 25, 27, 164, 169–176, 182, 234, 238–239, 246
liminal zone, 25, 164, 168, 177, 181
line dancing, 21, 36
Lipset, Seymour Martin, 11, 33, 138, 155, 157, 189, 203, 214
Lischke, Ute, 246, 248, 253
Liu, Yuli, 34, 334
Live Indians, 241–242
local community(ies), 113, 136, 147, 149, 250–251, 278–279
location of encounter, 312
locations for resistance, 17
Loyalists, 240

Luckmann, Thomas, 176, 185
Lu, Flora, 217–218, 229
Lyle, John Tillman, 297, 315
Lynch, Jim, 8, 33, 253, 339

M

Machine Readable Zone, 264
Mackinac National Park, 294
Maffei, Dan, 284
magnetism of the border, 65
Maguire, Joseph A., 278, 290
make sense, 46, 155, 181–183, 321
Man and the Biosphere Programme (1971), 297
Martinez, Oscar J., 12, 33, 172, 185
Martyn, Scott G., 278, 291
Mason, Philip P., 75, 83
Mason, Scott J., 165, 184
mass culture, 187–198, 200–201, 203, 205–206, 211–212
materialization, 15–16
Mayer, Evelyn P., 19, 22, 27, 33, 233, 242–244, 247, 253, 326–327, 339
McDonald, Matt, 258, 274
McGreevy, Patrick, 109, 128
McHarg, Ian L., 297, 304, 315
McMahon, Marian, 120–122, 128
meaning making, 200, 329
media coverage, 331
media platforms, 195, 204, 209
mediated space, 95
Memento, 120
memory space of the border, 238
Merleau-Ponty, Maurice, 25, 34, 164, 173–176, 180–181, 185
Metcalfe, Alan, 277, 291
methodology(ies), 132, 141–144, 294, 296–297, 300, 303, 310, 312–313, 341
Métis, 55, 113, 235, 241
metropolitan fallacy, 278
metropolitan perspective, 278
MeTube, 206
Mezzadra, Sandro, 120, 128
Michaelsen, Scott, 12, 20, 32–34
Michigan Basin, 298

Mielke, Anelynda, 23, 85, 88–89, 93, 100–101, 104, 176, 325, 327, 339
Mignolo, Walter D., 322–323, 334
migrant invasions, 43
migration, 2, 10, 21, 25, 41, 44, 48, 50, 52–55, 64, 111, 114, 120, 122–123, 132–133, 135–141, 145, 154–155, 233, 313, 324–325, 328, 332, 338, 340
migratory aesthetics, 49
Miles, Tiya, 55, 57, 59
Miner, Dylan, 40, 55, 59, 113, 116–118, 123, 125
Minghi, Julian V., 12, 34–35
Ministry of Natural Resources, 307
Minneapolis, 249
minority cultures, 327
minority groups, 329
missing and murdered Indigenous women, 235, 248
Mitchell, Don, 16–17, 34, 322, 334
Mitchell, Nora, 301, 314
Mitra, Srimoyee, 24, 34, 44, 59, 78, 108, 110, 112–116, 118, 120–121, 123, 126–128, 327, 340
mobile borders, 20
modernity, 218, 279
modernization, 279
Mohanty, Chandra, 117, 128
Mohawk, 28, 35, 255–256, 258–269, 271, 273–275, 281, 285, 330
Mohawk identity, 28, 263, 265
Montréal, 103, 280, 291
morality, 78, 277
Morrison, William, 132, 137, 142, 157
Movement festival, 66
Muller, Pierre, 267, 274
Multicultural Centre, 114
multiculturalism, 11, 126, 320, 325
multidimensional, 22, 24, 26, 322–323
multifocal habits of vision, 61
multiple jurisdictions, 261
multiplicity, 2, 27, 126, 234, 278, 288
multiscalar, 16, 18, 20, 26–28, 133, 153–154, 295, 319–320, 323–324, 330, 338
Munasinghe, Harsha, 313, 315
municipal context, 293

354 BORDERS, CULTURE, AND GLOBALIZATION

municipal government(s), 224, 295
municipal policies, 295
Murison, Jude, 133, 157

N

Nakoda (Stoney) First Nation, 294
narrative(s), 41, 44, 46–47, 55–56, 58, 76, 92, 95–96, 117, 121, 123–124, 141, 153, 220, 233–234, 238–239, 246, 279, 313, 325–327
national culture(s), 43, 172, 323, 326, 329
national identity(ies), 25, 28–29, 155, 164, 178–179, 183, 188–189, 200, 203, 280, 282, 284–288, 313
nationalism, 134, 155, 320
nationalist discourses, 155
nationality, 16, 146, 154, 221, 236, 240, 282, 288
national narratives, 44, 46, 56, 313
national security, 27–28, 255–272, 279, 283, 288, 328
national settler cultures, 39
national sport, 280
national tropes, 155
nation-building, 279
nationhood, 119, 239, 256, 262, 277, 284–287
nation-state dominance, 326
Natives and Newcomers, 279, 292
natural and cultural heritage, 293–294, 303
Natural England, 301, 308, 316
natural environment, 29, 245, 294
natural resources, 29, 294, 296, 330
negotiated border, 242
Neilson, Brett, 120, 128
Nelson, Gordon, 81–82, 298, 316
Netflix, 41, 133, 192–193, 204–206, 208
Newman, David, 12, 16, 34, 217, 219–220, 229, 257, 274, 324, 334
new meanings of being Canadian, 25, 150
new media, 26, 28, 187–189, 192, 195–197, 199–211, 280
new spatial forms, 323
New York, 28, 43, 59, 60, 83, 103, 105, 122, 124, 127–128, 145, 157–158, 185, 213, 229, 253–254, 256, 259, 268, 273–275, 280, 282, 287, 289–291, 298, 308, 315–317, 333, 334
New Zealand, 278, 285, 289
Ngugi, Kamau, 221, 223, 225, 229
Niagara, 21, 29, 109, 128, 184–185, 294–295, 298–301, 303–310, 312–317, 330
Niagara cuesta, 308
Niagara Escarpment, 294–295, 298–299, 303–308, 310, 312–313, 330
Niagara Escarpment Commission, 307
Niagara Escarpment Parks and Open Space System (NEPOSS), 299
Niagara Escarpment Plan, 299–300, 308
Niagara Escarpment Planning and Development Act, 298
Niagara Escarpment Planning Area boundary, 307
Niagara Falls, 109, 128, 307, 310
Niagara-on-the-Lake, 303, 307–308, 310, 314, 316
Niagara Parks Commission, 307, 314
Niagara Peninsula Conservation Authority, 307, 316
Niagara River, 295, 303, 308, 310
Niagara's Changing Landscapes, 307
Nicol, Heather N., 14–16, 19–20, 33, 40, 59, 109, 128, 138, 157, 165, 167, 185, 240–241, 253, 257, 274, 319, 333
nighttime cultural life, 23, 61
Nine-Eleven 9/11, 7, 10, 20, 30, 44, 47, 65, 108–109, 115, 118, 123, 125, 138, 167, 184–185, 268, 283, 287
Nischik, Reingard M., 238–240, 254
noble savage, 241
non-binary, 323
non-Indigenous communities, 300
non-mediated space, 95
North America, 22, 26, 35, 39–44, 46–49, 55, 58, 60, 70, 81–83, 114, 123, 184, 200–201, 203, 207, 211, 239, 242, 246, 248, 253, 256, 274, 277, 282, 285, 294, 334, 340
North American culture, 190, 200
North American Free Trade Agreement (NAFTA), 201
northeastern borderlands, 279

Northern Tribal Border Summit, 263
Northwest Sound, 8, 32
Novak, Paolo, 257, 274
Nunavut, 139, 248, 252
NVIVO, 144
Nye, David, 67, 83
Nyman, Jopi, 12, 15, 35

O

Oak Ridges Moraine Plan, 300
obscurity, 67
oeuvre, 235–236, 242
Oiarzabal, Pedro J., 134, 156
Olympic Games, 277, 281
on edge, 163
Oneida, 261, 281
O'Neill, Jamie, 137, 158
oneiric state, 71
online borderland(s), 190, 197–198, 207, 212
online cultural borderland(s), 187–212
Onondaga, 261, 281, 287
Ontario, 5, 28–29, 45, 52, 54–56, 58–59, 61–63, 72, 74, 79, 112, 139, 141–143, 145, 148, 150–153, 160, 184, 256, 259, 270, 275, 280, 289, 294–296, 298, 300–303, 307–308, 310, 312, 314, 316, 337–339, 341
Ontario Heritage Act (2019), 301–302, 316, 341
Ontario Heritage Trust, 302, 316
O'Reilly, Karen, 136, 157
organically evolved landscape, 302
Orrom, Michael, 78, 84
Ostrand, Nicole, 221, 229
othering, 15
O Tuathail, Gearoid, 322, 334
outsider(s), 169–172, 178, 180, 250, 331
over spilling of borders, 87

P

Paasi, Anssi, 12, 16, 34, 133, 157–158, 257–258, 274
Paglen, Trevor, 125, 128
Papastergiadis, Nikos, 120, 126, 128
Parallel Encounters, 13, 35, 60, 253–254

Parker, Noel, 12, 34, 258, 274, 319, 334
Pasch, Timothy, 58, 165, 184
passport(s), 45–46, 65, 99–100, 167–168, 171, 177, 217, 241, 263, 282–288, 330
patriotism, 25, 277–278
patriots, 164
Penobscot Building, 23, 71–72
perform difference, 179
performing the border, 265
perimeter, 271
periodic contestation, 258
personal video recording devices, 192
Pertusati, Linda, 256, 274
Phase 1: Identifying Syrian refugees to come to Canada, 222
Phase 2: Processing Syrian refugees overseas, 222
Phase 3: Transportation of Syrian refugees to Canada, 223
Phase 4: Welcoming Syrian refugees to Canada, 223
Phase 5: Settlement and community integration, 224
"phases" of #WelcomeRefugees, 215
phenomenology, 25, 164, 173, 342
Pisani, Michael J., 20, 34
place-image, 62, 66
placing and replacing border culture, 3, 10, 15, 27, 320
planes of border culture, 18
Planning Act (Ontario), 302
Pohran, Nadya, 23, 85, 91, 104, 176, 325, 327, 340
Poiret, Guillaume, 266, 274
policymakers, 141, 156, 172, 180, 225, 258, 293, 329, 331
political borders/boundaries, 29, 293, 296, 305, 312, 329, 331
political unconsciousness, 322
politics of aesthetics, 43
politics of difference, 17, 29, 313
politics of materiality, 23, 86
Poole, Chris, 199, 214
Popescu, Gabriel, 319, 321, 334
Pope, S. W., 277, 290–291
Popsicle sticks on pavement, 99–100
porosity and selectivity of borders, 234

Porter, James, 298, 316
port of entry (POE), 51, 166, 168–169, 171, 178, 259, 267, 271
Postcommodity, 51–52, 59
postmodern era of art and politics, 115
Poulter, Gillian, 278, 291
power, 11, 16–17, 19, 21, 28, 40–41, 56–57, 70, 81, 88, 90–94, 97, 99–101, 109, 120, 126, 134, 180, 196, 202, 217–218, 234, 238–240, 242, 248, 251, 256, 258, 261, 266, 279, 283, 286, 320–321, 324–328, 331
Pratt, Martin, 10, 34, 257, 274
precarity, 120, 123, 177
Prescott, J. R. Victor, 12, 34
presubjective world, 164
processes of bordering, 30, 108
Provincial Policy Statement (PPS) (Ontario), 300, 302, 316, 341
Ptak, Thomas, 9, 20, 24, 34, 323, 334
public-private partnerships, 208, 329

Q

Quebec, 9, 21, 25, 28, 43, 50–51, 58, 85, 137, 139, 141, 151, 163, 165–166, 179, 184–185, 190, 206–208, 237, 256, 259, 270, 280, 368
Québécois, 50, 141–142, 151, 199, 208, 237
Quinn, Gabriel, 245, 247–248, 251–252

R

race, 46, 76–77, 81, 121, 221, 286, 325
racialized space, 76
racialized women artists, 111
Racing Home, 59, 121, 128
racism, 46, 65, 121–122, 235
Rajaram, Prem Kumar, 17, 20, 34, 42, 57, 60
Ramsden, Peter G., 280, 291
Rancière, Jacques, 20, 22–23, 34, 43–44, 60, 86, 92–93, 101, 104, 322, 334
rave culture, 66
Ray, Arthur J., 235, 254
real-izing, 91
refugees, 26, 96, 117–119, 126, 215–216, 221–228, 325, 329, 338

regional assets, 300
regional governance, 308
regional identity(ies), 29, 151, 203, 293, 313
regionalization of mass culture, 204
regionness, 201, 207
region(s), 1, 8–10, 17, 29, 39, 41, 43, 44, 46–48, 51, 54–55, 61, 63, 81, 97, 108, 110, 118, 127, 133–134, 143, 154, 163, 165, 168, 172, 181–183, 188, 200–202, 207, 216, 218–220, 238, 265, 278–279, 293, 295, 297–298, 304, 307–308, 310, 319–320, 322
Reid, John, 279, 291
Reid, Mara, 250
reimagining borders, 116
reinvented forms of belonging and encounter, 127
relational aesthetics, 49
relational motion, 20, 24, 323
religion, 8, 28, 146, 221, 247, 261, 323, 340
Repellent Fence, 51–52, 59
representation(s) of borders, 327, 340
reserve(s), 27–28, 242–252, 256–259, 261–263, 266, 270, 285, 297
resistance, 14, 17, 21, 27, 30, 39, 50, 89–91, 93, 101, 125, 188, 233–234, 243, 246, 256, 259, 262, 270, 278
restrictive function, 233
resuscitating borderlands, 22, 39–44
reterritorialization, 323
Re/Thinking Paul Bunyan, 50–51, 58
retirement community(ies), 136, 144–145
Richardson, Bill, 287
Richardson, Chad, 20, 34
Ricou, Laurie, 8, 35
Riley, John, 297, 316
rite(s) of passage, 169–170
ritualized culture at the border, 17
ritual performance, 170
Robbins, Joel, 165, 185
Roberts, Gillian, 4, 12–16, 18, 27, 35–36, 40, 60, 237–239, 241, 253–254, 320, 334
Robertson, Roland, 278, 291
Rocky Mountains Park Act (1887), 294

Rodney, Lee, 15, 20, 22, 24, 35, 39–40, 43, 45–46, 49, 53, 60, 63–64, 71, 74, 82–83, 88, 108, 110–111, 113, 314, 319, 326–327, 334, 340
Rosaldo, Renato, 19–20, 35
Rosière, Stéphane, 19, 35
Ross, Greggory MacIntosh, 279, 291
rounders, 147
Rouvière, Laetitia, 27, 35, 240, 255, 257, 260, 275, 326, 330, 341
Royal Canadian Mounted Police (RCMP), 167, 268, 270
Rudolph, Alexander, 26, 133, 153, 187, 326–327, 329, 341
ruin porn, 64, 77
Rumford, Chris, 20, 35
Rutherford, Paul, 188–189, 193, 197, 203, 211, 214

S
Sack, Robert, 257, 275
sacred items, 266
Sadowski-Smith, Claudia, 12, 35, 235, 241, 249, 254, 273
Sahlins, Peter, 12, 35, 257, 275
Said, Edward, 321, 334
Salish Sea, 8, 36
Salt and Cedar, 114
Salter, Mark B., 217, 229, 262, 275
Samaritan Bay, 247–250, 252
Sami, 288
sanctuary, 23, 85, 91–92, 101, 104
Sanctuary Inter/rupted, 111, 127
scale(s), 1, 25–26, 28–29, 50–51, 61, 71, 80, 118, 125, 133, 148, 150, 155, 170, 219, 272, 298, 300–301, 304, 321, 323, 326, 331
scaling, 20, 300
Schama, Simon, 293–294, 316
Schiffman, Howard, 285, 291
Schimanski, Johan, 12, 15, 18, 35, 57, 60, 110, 128, 246, 254, 323, 334
Schindler, Gewas, 282
Schivelbusch, Wolfgang, 66, 83
School of Exile, 119
Schütz, Alfred, 176, 185

Sciarra, Rebecca, 28, 293, 296, 306, 309, 311, 326, 330, 341
Scotland, 280
Scott, James C., 89–91, 104
seasonal migration, 155, 325
secession, 217
Secure Certificate of Indian Status (SCIS), 264
securitized, 41–42, 52, 255, 325
security, surveillance, 107, 116, 123
seen crossers, 94
self-determination, 117, 285, 288
self-directed police services, 268
self-government, 284
self-identification, 178, 326
self-sufficiency, 284–285
semantic layer, 197–198, 203, 211
Seneca, 261, 281
sense of belonging, 14, 25, 133–134, 144, 148, 151, 154, 156, 177, 245, 326, 329
sense of place, 8, 29
settler colonies, 279
sexism, 320
Sheller, Mimi, 25, 35, 133, 135, 158
Shield River, 244
shifting atmospheres of illumination, 62
shifting interfaces, 18, 20, 325
shifting modes of belonging to community, 148
Shweder, Richard A., 17, 35, 323, 334
Sibley, Chris G., 285, 290
Silicon Valley, 206, 213
Silverman, Helaine, 313, 317
Simpson, Audra, 262, 275
Simpson, Penny, 137, 145, 158
singularity of the borderline, 58
site of invasion, 41
Six Nations, 260–261, 291
skyline, 23, 62–65, 71, 74–75, 80–81
Skype, 112, 134, 148–149
Sliwinski, Sharon, 86, 96, 104
Smith, Hanako, 205–206, 210–212
Smith, Heather, 137, 157
Smith, Joanna, 285–286, 291
Smith, Stanley K., 138, 158
Smith, Timothy W., 281, 291
Smoke River, 244, 247, 249, 252

snowball sample method, 143
snowbird lifestyle, 140, 142, 146, 153
snowbird(s), 25, 131–156, 159–161, 164, 324–325, 332
snowbird trips, 131
social change(s), 134, 332
social construction(s), 323–324, 326, 341
social media, 41, 189, 287
Social Sciences and Humanities Research Council of Canada (SSHRC), 1, 4, 10, 29, 58
social trails, 22, 51, 57
sociocultural integration, 142
sociopolitical margins, 256, 258
Söderbaum, Fredrik, 200–201, 206–207, 214
soft operational culture of the border, 42
"soft" side of border studies, 110
Sohn, Christophe, 29, 36, 293, 317
Soiffer, Stephanie, 256, 273
Solanki, Gopika, 89, 105
Sontag, Susan, 86, 105
sovereign nation, 331
sovereignty, 20, 27–28, 211, 241, 255–272, 287, 330
Soyez, Dietrich, 313, 317
space of exception, 262
space of experimentation, 262
space of refusal, 262
spaces of prominence, 17
space-time compression, 133
Spanglish, 202
Sparke, Matthew, 8, 36, 256, 275
spatial formations, 136, 330
spatial horizon, 174
spatial identities, 134
spectacle(s), 23, 41, 80, 86–88, 94–97, 99–102, 104, 127, 157
Spencer, Bree, 256, 275
Spiekermann, Klaus, 219, 229
sporting culture, 278–279, 288
sportive nation building, 278
stakeholder, 244, 257, 272, 300, 304–305, 310, 313, 328, 330–331
Stanstead, Quebec, 21, 25, 85, 110, 163–184
state-centric perspectives, 323

state of exception, 262
Statistics Canada, 131, 137, 158, 166
Staudt, Kathleen, 59
St. Catharines, 307–308, 310, 315
Steger, Manfred B., 25, 36, 132, 158
Steiner, Frederick R., 297, 317
Stenning, Philip C., 268, 275
St. Gabriel's Church, 98–99
Stirrup, David, 4, 12–15, 18, 35–36, 40, 60, 237–238, 241, 253–254
Strahl, Chuck, 283, 291
strands of narrative art, 234
Straw, Will, 66, 82, 83
St. Regis, 273
stressful crossings, 152
structure of feeling, 78
Stutzriemer, Sylke, 313, 315
"Stygian" space, 247
subaltern(s), 90, 92–93
subjective dimensions of bordering, 329
subjective language, 220
subjectivity(ies), 115–116, 119, 121, 124, 126–127, 176–180, 323, 328
subjugation, 92–93, 97, 101, 294
sub-nations, 295
sudden rupture, 258
Sugars, Cynthia, 238, 254
Sugrue, Thomas J., 76, 83
Sun Belt, 138
superimposition of the international boundary, 240
supra-national territory, 295
survivance, 27, 233–234, 242–252
sustainable development, 298
suture, 52, 217
Swimmer, Monroe, 242–244, 246, 251
Switzerland, 206, 286
symbolic object(s), 23, 85, 88, 93, 101
symbolic representation, 327
symbol(s), 92–94, 99–101, 124, 170–171, 176, 217, 24, 264, 268, 323
syntactic layer(s), 197–199
Syrian migrants, 138

T

Talbot, Deborah, 76, 83

Taylor, Peter J., 257, 275
technology(ies), 77, 79, 81, 108, 133–135, 149, 153, 167, 191, 204, 258, 264–265, 327, 342
Tecumseh, 250
teichopolitics, 19
temporal dimension of Canada's border construct, 216, 225
temporal horizon, 174
terrain of border studies, 17, 18
territorial containers, 320
territorial identity, 285–286
territorial legacies, 319
territorial margins, 258
territorial trap, 1, 17, 217
Texas, 34–36, 137, 140, 145, 158
The Back of the Turtle, 27, 233–234, 236, 242–253
The Creator's Game, 279, 289
The Inconvenient Indian, 27, 233–236, 239, 241–243, 247, 252–253
The Named and the Unnamed, 116, 123, 128
The Truth About Stories: A Native Narrative, 233, 246, 253
thickening border, 65
Thorold, 307
threshold place, 25, 164, 172
time-space map, 219, 225
Tlostanova, Madina V., 322–323, 334
Together Forever/Never Apart, 116, 118
Tolazzi, Sandrine, 263, 275
top-up medical insurance, 152
Torchin, Leshu, 96, 105
Torkington, Kate, 136, 158
Toronto Star, 285, 291
tourism, 7, 137, 140, 158, 307
tower lights, 69
trade, 2, 7, 10, 52, 54–55, 109, 111, 313, 328
traditionalism, 124, 261, 279
traditional knowledge, 284
traditional media, 188, 190, 192, 194–196, 204–206, 208–211
traditional producers, 195
tradition(s), 8, 124–125, 199, 207, 251–252, 262, 278, 285, 300
transborder heritage, 312
Transborder Immigrant Tool, 49

transboundary biocultural landscapes, 295
transition zones, 296, 305
translocal resistance, 39
transnational, 9, 12–13, 17–18, 21, 43, 61, 95, 120, 133–134, 136, 141, 148, 154, 238, 241, 278, 288, 313, 340
transnational configurations, 278
transnational identities, 134
transnationalism, 22, 117, 328
transnational lifestyles, 136, 141
transnational sporting culture, 278
transnational theory, 133
Trautman, Laurie, 7
treaty rights of Indigenous peoples, 294
Tremblay, Rémy, 137, 141, 158
tribal homelands, 240
Tribal Homeland Security Grant Program, 271
tribal identification documents, 287
tricycle-print labs, 118
Trigger, Bruce G., 279, 292
Trudeau, Justin, 235, 332
Trump, Donald, 138, 146, 155, 217, 332
Truth & Bright Water, 233, 242–253
Turner, Victor, 25, 36, 125, 164, 169–170, 185, 234, 238, 254
Turtle Island Education Centre, 113
Tuscarora, 261, 281
Two Row Wampum Belt treaty, 285

U

UN Universal Declaration of Human Rights, 287
UNHCR, 221–222, 229
unicultural border, 11, 63
United Kingdom, 28, 229, 279–282, 284, 342
United Nations Educational, Scientific and Cultural Organization (UNESCO), 294
United States, 3, 7–11, 13, 25, 28, 30, 32–34, 39, 52–53, 59, 63–64, 94, 108–109, 122, 131, 133–134, 137–141, 144–145, 151–152, 154–155, 157–158, 160, 169, 185, 189–190,

193–194, 196–197, 200–207, 210–211, 213–214, 216, 224–225, 229, 236–237, 239–240, 246, 253–255, 259–260, 264, 271, 274–275, 279, 281–285, 287, 289, 294, 315–316, 320, 324–325, 330, 332–333, 339, 341
United States Immigration and Customs Enforcement (ICE), 94
unity along the line, 109
universalities, 322
urban border environments, 61
urban electrification, 67, 69
Urry, John, 20, 25, 35–36, 133, 135, 158
US Border Patrol, 8, 123, 167–168
US Customs and Border Protection (CBP), 268
US Department of Homeland Security (DHS), 271, 273, 287
US Director of National Intelligence, 224
US Director of the Federal Bureau of Investigation (FBI), 224
US Federal Emergency Management Agency, 264
US hegemony, 11, 237
US House of Representatives, 224
US Library of Congress, 14, 68, 70
US National Park Service, 300
US State Department, 283, 287

V

Valdivia, Gabriela, 217–218, 229
Van Bottenburg, Maarten, 279, 292
Vandervalk, Sandra, 21, 25, 36, 85, 163, 239, 326, 329, 341
van der Velde, Martin, 34, 222, 229, 334
van Gennep, Arnold, 169, 185
van Houtum, Henk, 321, 334
van Liempt, Ilse, 133, 156
van Naerssen, Ton, 222, 229
Vaughan-Williams, Nick, 12, 34, 319, 334
Venables, Robert W., 261, 275
Vermont, 21, 25, 85, 163, 165–166, 179, 184
vernacular aesthetics, 116
vessel of engagement, 30
victimization, 242, 250

video-sharing platform(s), 26, 193n, 205, 208–209
Vietnam War resisters, 240
viewing the border, 320
virtual and imagined borders, 320
virtual places, 40–42, 63, 125
visibility of the common, 44
visual culture, 61, 70, 75
Vizenor, Gerald, 233–234, 242, 248, 250–252, 254
Vowel, Chelsea, 235, 254
vulnerability, 77, 171

W

Wagman, Ira, 190, 192, 196, 204–205, 208, 212
Waldenfels, Bernhard, 181–182, 185
Wales, 280
Walters, William, 12, 36, 96, 105
Wasilewski, Jacqueline, 285, 289
Wastl-Walter, Doris, 59, 198, 214
Waterman, Denise, 282–283
Waterton, Emma, 312, 317
Way Past Kennedy Road Collective, 111
Web 2.0, 189, 214, 285
Weber, Max, 217, 229
Wegener, Michael, 219, 225, 229
Weigand, Heidi, 28, 241, 263, 277, 327, 330, 342
#WelcomeRefugees, 26, 215–216, 218, 220–221, 223–228
Welland Canal, 306, 308, 310
Wenn, Stephen R., 278, 291
Western avant-garde, 110
Western Hemisphere Travel Initiative (WHTI), 263, 285
Western New York Land Conservancy, 298, 317
Whipple, Fred H., 67, 68, 84
Williams, Raymond, 43, 60, 78, 84
Willows, Jeff, 256, 273
Wilson, Thomas M., 12, 16, 31–32, 165, 184, 186, 333
Windsor, 22–23, 44–47, 52–56, 59, 61–66, 70–84, 107–108, 112–115, 117–118, 120–122, 337, 340

Windsor Women Working with
    Immigrant Women, 113–114, 122
Wisconsin, 298, 314
witnessing fever, 95
Wolfe, Stephen F., 12, 15, 18, 35, 110, 128,
    246, 254, 323, 334
Wolford, Wendy, 217–218, 229
working of the border, 28
work, labour, 107, 116, 120–123
Workman, Thom, 261, 272
World Heritage Convention (1972), 294
World Lacrosse Championship, 28, 277,
    279, 280–284, 287
World Network of Biosphere Reserves
    (1977), 297
Wyile, Herb, 239

Y
Yellowstone, 294
YouTube, 82, 193, 204–206, 208–209, 212,
    214, 330

Z
Zierhofer, Wolfgang, 321, 334
zone(s) of cooperation, 298–299, 304–305,
    310, 312
zone of transition, 305
zoning, 295, 297–298
Zyfi, Jona, 226–227, 229

Politics and Public Policy

Series Editor: Geneviève Tellier

There has been a resurgence of the study of politics, inspired by debates on globalization, renewed citizen engagement and demands, and transformations of the welfare state. In this context, the study of political regimes, ideas, and processes, as well as that of public policy, contributes to refreshing our understanding of the evolution of contemporary societies. Public policy is at the heart of political and state actions. It defines the course and the objectives adopted by governments and steering citizen initiatives and collective actions. Political analysis is increasingly complex and dynamic, embracing more diverse political, social, economic, cultural, and identity-related phenomena. The *Politics and Public Policy* series is an ideal forum in which to present titles that promote an exploration of these questions in Canada and around the world.

Recent Titles in the *Politics and Public Policy* Series

Diane Saint-Pierre and Monica Gattinger, eds., *Cultural Policy: Origins, Evolution, and Implementation in Canada's Provinces and Territories*, 2021.

Julien Landry, *Les* think tanks *et le discours expert sur les politiques publiques au Canada (1890–2015)*, 2020.

Sarah Todd and Sébastien Savard, eds., *Canadian Perspectives on Community Development*, 2020.

Frances Widdowson, *Separate but Unequal: How Parallelist Ideology Conceals Indigenous Dependency*, 2019.

Helaina Gaspard, *Canada's Official Languages: Policy Versus Work Practice in the Federal Public Service*, 2019.

Marie Drolet, Pier Bouchard, and Jacinthe Savard, eds., *Accessibility and Active Offer: Health Care and Social Services in Linguistic Minority Communities*, 2017.

John Hilliker, *Le ministère des Affaires extérieures du Canada Volume I : les années de formation, 1909-1946*, 2017.

Monika Jezak, ed., *Language is the Key: The Canadian Language Benchmarks Model*, 2017.

Linda Cardinal and Sébastien Grammond, *Une tradition et un droit : le Sénat et la représentation de la francophonie canadienne*, 2017.

Hélène Knoerr, Aline Gohard-Radenkovic, and Alysse Weinberg, eds., *L'immersion française à l'université : politiques et pédagogie*, 2016.

For a complete list of University of Ottawa Press titles, visit:
www.press.uOttawa.ca

www.ingramcontent.com/pod-product-compliance
Lightning Source LLC
Chambersburg PA
CBHW061343300426
44116CB00011B/1963